"As a former talk show host, I can't really help but imagine how awesome someone would be as a guest. I play that game all the time when I have conversations with people.

And when I get the opportunity to chat with Gunnar Rohrbacher, I'm constantly reminded of how deeply he cares about the craft of comedy. He would be the kind of guest that would make my job almost too easy.

Example: "So, Gunnar... multi-camera sitcoms?"

I would then sit back for 5 to 10 minutes of the most riveting, exacting and revealing insights on how to make multi-cam sitcoms world-class: He'd talk about actors, writers, directors, casting people, camera crew – anyone involved – and give the back story of how they all contribute to the success of the show. He'd probably break down a current hit as an example, and tell you why it wouldn't work as a single-cam, what audience it serves, why it's important to the history of comedy and how it will be remembered.

All I'd have to do is nod my head and smile. People would think I was a genius for booking him.

See, Gunnar is the genius, one that just can't help himself. He insists on discovering (and luckily for all of us, then teaching) every aspect of our craft. He has to know how all the moving parts of comedy work, and how to make them work on a best-of-breed level. And he knows how to share what he knows and has perfected in a way that engages and inspires his acting and writing students on a very deep level.

I've watched him direct actors in scenes, lead writers through the development of their stories and help an auditioner nail a character.

Every time, I find myself nodding in agreement. He GETS it.

And when he surprised me one day and said, "Hey... I've written a book about comedy..." I thought just one word: "Finally!"

Now, we all have a reference guide on what this all means, how to get started, what skills we need, how to present ourselves in the production centers of the world, how to audition, how to work with crew, how to do our jobs, how to move forward in our journey, what to call things we've always been curious about, even do research to help us explore our comedy characters.

All in one, awesome book: *The Comedy Code*.

Thank your lucky stars you've picked up this book, and that you've now got a million-dollar roadmap for your comedy journey. Enjoy."

David H. Lawrence XVII

David's accomplishments are many. He is an acclaimed on-camera actor, assiduous voice actor, storytelling coach, instructor, innovator and entrepreneur. He is the creator of the VOHeroes voiceover curriculum and also created the wildly popular, industry standard Rehearsal Pro app that helps actors organize and work with their audition scripts in one place.

"One of the great joys of my life is making Gunnar laugh. I make a lot of folks laugh... a lot. But when you "get" Gunnar, you've done something fine. This is because he is unflinchingly honest with a keen eye, fierce intellect and a broad base of knowledge both of the industry and the world. This book channels all of this and more of Gunnar's many gifts. It's possibly the most intelligent book ever written on a craft that is almost purely instinctual.

Script analysis, breakdown of characters, revealing archetypes; it's all here. And this book, unlike any other I've read, does something heretofore thought impossible: it teaches that which cannot be taught and, almost, cannot be named. It gives you the tools to create and make manifest your own genius. You can take every book that's been written or will be written on the craft and chuck them in the dustbin; this is all you will need. Treat it lightly at your own peril."

Carolyn Hennesy

Carolyn is an award-winning actor who trained at American Conservatory Theatre and The Royal Academy of Dramatic Art, London. She created the *Pandora* children's book series and penned the New York Times Best Seller, *The Secret Life of Damian Spinelli*.

"I love this book. I've been begging Gunnar for it for over a year and he did not disappoint. He's created a cheat sheet for actors working in comedy! Auditions are a race against the clock. We are given a twelve hour window to prepare for an opportunity that can change our lives. This book gives actors valuable short-cuts to streamline their process and be the most competitive in the room. I can't wait to re-read it and squeeze as much juice out of it as possible!"

Audrey Moore

Audrey is an actor best known for her roles in the Netflix series *Godless* as well as *Better Call Saul* and *Manhattan*. She is also the creator and host of the extremely popular podcast, Audrey Helps Actors.

"*The Comedy Code* is magical and spellbinding."

Julia Butters

Julia portrays Anna-Kat Otto on the ABC comedy series *American Housewife* and appears in Quentin Tarantino's *Once Upon a Time... in Hollywood*.

"Thank you, Gunnar! *The Comedy Code* is my acting bible and will never leave my side. It has everything you need to know about show business, all in one place. I'll be taking it everywhere; on auditions, on set, to the gym... I just hope it's not too heavy!"

Kate Linder

Kate has portrayed Esther Valentine on *The Young and the Restless* since 1982.

"What an adventure it's been creating Actors Comedy Studio. Gunnar and I have worked together for nearly two decades. Our relationship has grown from acting teacher, to mentor, to business partner. Before saying an enthusiastic "Yes!" to becoming a part of ACS, I was on the path to becoming a studio teacher. Specifically, a studio teacher is an educator and welfare worker for minors who are employed in the entertainment industry. The road to becoming a studio teacher seemed impossible at times. Gunnar, my biggest cheerleader, taught me that a little persistence goes a long way. I am now, more than 10 years later, an IATSE Local #884 studio teacher. There are approximately 140 of us. No small feat. I work on shows like *Lucifer, American Housewife* on ABC, *The Big Show Show* on Netflix and *Sydney to the Max* on the Disney Channel. If there's a kid on the set, myself or another studio teacher will be present.

ACS is our baby. Gunnar and I are 'work married' in every sense of the term and he is an exceptional work husband. He's encouraging, a good listener and patient. He has supported my ambitions with all of his heart. He is extremely supportive of me as a young business owner and woman working in Hollywood. Gunnar also tells me that I should brag more about myself as an educator. He's right. I hold two California teaching credentials; a Single-subject in English and a Multiple-subject, along with a Masters Degree from Loyola Marymount University in Reading Literacy Instruction. I am a reading specialist and a welfare worker in the state of California. I am also an individual member of The National Association of Schools of Theater and an Academic Member of the Television Academy. Thank you, Gunnar.

Admittedly, as Gunnar's work wife, my review is destined to be biased. However, I can assure you that this book will change your life and the way you think about training as a professional actor. I believe with every part of my being that what is written in *The Comedy Code* has never been explained so clearly to actors. While I'm at work on set as a studio teacher, I have conversations daily with writers, directors, actors and executive producers all of whom, in one way or another, praise and ultimately validate *The Comedy Code*. Everyone in the entertainment industry is constantly on the lookout for a way to make things more efficient. The appreciation this book has received from people in all facets of this business has been astonishing. All I have to do is casually leave a copy lying around on set and by the end of the day, it's the topic of major conversations. "What is this? Who wrote it? Where do I get a copy?"

"It's the ultimate guide to acting and writing for TV comedy. My business partner, Gunnar. Amazon or wherever else you buy books," I reply. *The Comedy Code* is a comprehensive reference guide that should always be in your arsenal. Get a copy for yourself and never leave home without it!

Lauren Bertoni
Co-founder, Actors Comedy Studio

THE
COMEDY
CODE

THE COMEDY CODE

Your COMPLETE GUIDE
to Acting & Writing for Television
in the Digital Age of Hollywood

ACTORS COMEDY STUDIO

Gunnar Rohrbacher

WARFOX PUBLICATIONS

Copy edit credit: Dexter Collins, Jaxy Boyd, Tiffany Berube
Photo credit: Laura Burke
Design Credit: Maria Liana Moisescu

ISBN# 978-0-9982884-4-4

Dedication

This book is dedicated to my three mothers:

Sharon Rohrbacher, the mother who guarded my life
Cynthia Szigeti, the mother who guided my life
Sandra Canada, the mother who gave me life

And my grandmother, Evelyn Warren, who graced my life

Thank you, ladies.

I live to make you proud.

A Foreward by Elaine Hendrix

DEAR HEROES,

You will soon discover from this magnificent goldmine of a book, *The Comedy Code*, there are multiple aspects within us, and we are never only one but a unique combination of them all. So, in honor of this concept, there are three distinct messages I'd like to share for this foreword.

THE PERSONAL

When Gunnar asked me to write the foreword for *The Comedy Code*, I cried. I cried because I knew his journey to and through this book. The endless hours and boundless energy he's poured into it. The decades of performing, studying and teaching from which he's drawn every ounce of his information and inspiration. The unwavering dedication to trying, failing and ultimately succeeding not only for himself but for the benefit of those around him. This book is the culmination of all of this in addition to the infinite, untold mechanics of day-to-day existence that involves putting one foot in front of the other for a life's purpose. It's ultimately a love letter to what Gunnar champions more than anything in life: creativity. And he's sharing it with the world. We are so lucky.

I also cried because he and I have been through so much life together. I was there when he opened Actors Comedy Studio,

Code brings with it a giant breath of relief. This is because it shares details that are so deeply familiar. You will instantly recognize yourself and others within each page. It is an invaluable roadmap for your journey along this wonderfully wacky path of creativity. Don't leave your imagination without it.

INSPIRINGLY YOURS,

Elaine Hendrix

Elaine is an award-winning actor best known for portraying Meredith Blake in Disney's *The Parent Trap*, Lisa Luder in *Romy and Michele's High School Reunion* and Alexis Carrington on the CW's *Dynasty*. She is also a writer, producer and acting coach as well as a fierce animal advocate and activist.

Contents

Acknowledgements

Lauren Marie Bertoni is my business partner. She worked tirelessly to make Actors Comedy Studio a reality. Our school is now a welcoming, world-class training facility where actors and writers acquire all the skills they need to succeed in one place.

Together, we designed the school we wished we had for ourselves. Every day it generates magic. We added The Self Tape Place as we grew, and practically every day we help actors book work. I'm sure there are more adventures on the horizon. I would not have done any of this differently. Thank you, Lauren. You grew up well.

Special thanks to our guest faculty. Your insights and loving guidance on career and craft are embedded in these words:

Phyllis Katz, I love you to the end of the earth and back. Thank you for everything you've taught me. We should get together and talk about dogs more often.

Dorian Frankel, our standing date every six weeks is something I look forward to with reverberating joy. What a dear pal you are.

Sarabeth Schedeen, your wisdom continually astonishes me. Your wit is only outdone by your compassion and kindness to all artists.

Elaine Hendrix, I love your gorgeous heart. So did Baron. Your generosity toward other actors is rare. Your reach for purity through creativity is majestic.

Carolyn Hennesy, every writer needs a muse. You're my one and only. I learned much of what I know about great acting by acting with you. We're funny together.

Jason Murphy, thank you for being my brother then and my wisest guardian angel now. I miss you every damned day.

To all my students, I offer my deepest gratitude. I never knew when I started teaching how much I'd learn from you. I didn't know some of the finest people I'd ever meet would be the ones who came through my classroom door. My intention has always been to simply help and encourage you the way my teachers championed me. If I have, I'm a much better man for it. I never imagined how much I'd learn about real life by exploring fictional lives with you.

Some of the best times I've had have been spent inside of a classroom. During the worst times of my life, the classroom became my safe haven. In the swirling chaos of existence, learning has always been a constant. In the moments I didn't know where else to turn, I taught. Things always got better. I like having students. You inspire me and make me happy. Teaching all of you has brought the world to me, so I thank you for that with all of my goofy heart.

How to Use This Book

To a large extent, I think of *The Comedy Code* as the answer to the question: "What should I ask that I don't even know I should ask?"

Whenever I want to master something, I find an expert and ask them that. Typically, the questions I already had get answered along with valuable insights I didn't even know I needed. I'm ever grateful when I know how to build my dreams a home without wasted effort.

The Comedy Code is a reference guide for actors and improvisers, TV and sketch writers, and all comedy creatives. Fans of television comedy love it because it explores dozens of great series and their characters throughout history in depth.

Agents, managers, casting directors, and producers find this book helpful because it includes a holistic review of the collaborative nature of the industry. Specifically, I'm enlightening talent on how to incorporate the nuances of show business into their daily lives. Further, I'm teaching them how they can be proactive within the process so they can compete like polished professionals. In turn, we all work together in greater synchronicity.

With a fundamental understanding of how the entertainment industry actually works, creatives can form better relationships with their representation, casting, and production. Show business is intimidating until it is demystified. We all win when common misconceptions are eliminated and replaced with easily applied, standard expectations.

I like efficiency. *The Comedy Code* will save you valuable time on many fronts. You now possess a modern reference guide that will aid you in better acting, auditioning, and writing within the current marketplace starting right now.

The Comedy Code seamlessly weaves creative and business tenets together. Acting and writing professionally is entrepreneurial. My hunch is that everyone entering the industry knows that but are not certain what it means for them personally. I will demystify show business and make it accessible for you.

This book is an excellent resource for beginners. There's nothing to *unteach* you. You'll be on the right path from the beginning. It's great for actors and writers with moderate experience who have collected training from various sources. Many have not been able to weave their collective and sometimes contradictory knowledge together into a comprehensive system that maximizes success. *The Comedy Code* will help you do that.

It's a perfect guide for actors who have obtained a theater degree and want to transition to on-camera work as smoothly as possible. Lastly, it's invaluable for experienced and professional creatives who simply need the finishing touches on their process. *The Comedy Code* contains an archive of terminology working actors and writers need to streamline workflow.

Comedy in general has literal elements we will explore; jokes, surprise, exaggeration, etc. Scripted comedy also deals with basic human psychology and how contrasting personalities impact close, interpersonal relationships. I refer to the great characters of television history as The Heroes of Comedy. A large part of this book presents case studies of many of our most beloved ones.

We gain understanding of why things are funny by considering why we are the way we are. Getting to know The Heroes of Comedy assures we all imagine funny, substantial characterizations in both writing and acting. *The Comedy Code* will teach you things about yourself that will manifest in better, deeper work. Our reflection on the sharpest characters ever constructed in television history will make you a better you.

Actors and writers always need good, better, and superlative words. We need these words to express ourselves as do our characters when we are creating them. A broad vocabulary of feelings, actions, and character traits is essential in order to break down scenes well. *The Comedy Code* will help you harness the power of expression. You will master the art of articulating your thoughts quickly and easily.

HEART is a thesaurus of emotional words categorized in a way that helps you label how a character feels based on what's happening in the scene. SPARK is a thesaurus of verbs (also known as intentions or actions) that helps you label how a character wants their dialogue to affect the person to whom they are speaking based on what's happening in the scene. With these comprehensive resources, your ability to articulate choices will expand exponentially. The industry hires creatives who can get to the point quickly and say what they're thinking succinctly.

Each of The Heroes of Comedy includes a list of adjectives (character traits) that writers can write to and actors can advantageously incorporate into their performances. I've also included a list of words and phrases for each that are often used in actor breakdowns but are *not* particularly helpful descriptions. I've done the work of translating those conceptual and sometimes derogatory words into human descriptors that lead to great performances. Your character development is about to explode!

iCAMERA is a bulletproof system of breaking down scripts quickly. When actors see what's in a script the way writers do, everything changes for the better. I will help you learn how to establish the facts of the scene that are not subjective and distinguish them from your acting choices that are.

The Audition Code will give you definitive answers about what goes into great auditions. You will never doubt whether or not what you're doing on the mark is right or wrong again. With all fear eliminated, you're free to do your best work anytime, anywhere, for anyone.

The Comedy Code is an encompassing resource consisting of organized knowledge that will help you effortlessly execute your ideas. You can think of this book as an actual collaborator. We all need reliable parameters and trustworthy guidance bolstering our creativity. Whether you're in class or on a studio lot, acting, writing, or auditioning, the clearly labeled sections of this guidebook will always support your best efforts.

Comedy is simply a conduit for joy, by the way. That's what I found once I cracked the Code.

THE PATH

PART 1

UNPACKING WHAT YOU'VE WATCHED

1

Are They Still Called Sitcoms? An Introduction

Question: What is a sitcom? Answer: A television series in which the same set of characters is involved in various amusing situations. **Sitcom** is a compound word formed from the term **situation comedy**. Simple.

Over the years, a number of synonyms have emerged; **multi-camera comedy**, **single-camera comedy**, **half-hour comedy**, **comedy series**, **dramedy**, and **hybrid**. At their core, all these terms mean essentially the same thing. In the next section, I elaborate on the differences between multi-cam and single-cam sitcoms in detail.

Both actors and writers should understand the core differences between those two sitcom styles. For now, we'll note that a series is a sitcom whether it's shot live in front of a studio audience or not, and whether you hear their laughter while watching it or not.

Half-hour, comedy series, dramedy, and hybrid are terms that surfaced as sitcoms became more diverse in tone. Some television comedies are bittersweet and it may be hard to tell by watching any given episode if a series is a comedy or drama. There is no rule that dictates how they're labeled. There is no right or wrong regarding how funny or dramatic a show should be.

In fact, when it comes to labels, producers and networks don't always know whether to submit their own show as a comedy or drama for award consideration. In 2014, Uzo Aduba won a Primetime Emmy for Outstanding Guest Actress in a *Comedy* Series portraying Suzanne "Crazy Eyes" Warren on *Orange Is the New Black*. The next year she won a Primetime Emmy for Outstanding Supporting Actress in a *Drama* Series for playing the same character on the same show. *Shameless* is another series that has had Emmy nominations as both a comedy and drama.

Although there are a few rare exceptions, shows generally pick a lane and stay in it. Comedy-dramas are now as common as series that are either entirely comedic or dramatic. Despite the variety of tones we encounter, half-hour shows tend to still be largely comedic and hour-long shows are mostly dramatic.

Most sitcoms we've watched throughout television history are episodic. Episodic comedies consist of stand-alone episodes; the audience can watch them in any order without confusion. The main story or plot of any given episode resolves by the end of that episode. Episodic series do feature broad storylines that arc over multiple episodes, especially when it comes to developing romantic relationships. However, the architecture of episodic shows is different from serialized shows.

The main ("A" story) and supporting ("B" and "C" stories) all wrap up with each episode. *The Mary Tyler Moore Show*, *Cheers*, *Seinfeld*, *Friends*, *The Office*, *Will & Grace*, *30 Rock*, *Frasier*, *The Big Bang Theory*, etc., are all episodic comedies. Relationships between main characters may evolve over an extended time frame, but each individual episode has its own plotline.

If a show is not episodic, it's considered serialized. The difference is just a matter of whether the show features a *continuous* main storyline maintained throughout seasons. Serialized comedies play out more like a soap opera or film that's been edited into episodes. The audience needs to watch them in order to appreciate the series fully. While there are subplots within a serialized comedy, there is ultimately one, clear main storyline that connects all the episodes.

The HBO series *Barry* is designed that way; a comedy-crime series that follows a war veteran turned hired assassin who becomes an actor. If you jump into episode two of season two, you'll be missing a lot of context. You may enjoy what you're watching, but it won't make much sense. *Ugly Betty*, *Glee*, *Desperate Housewives*, *Russian Doll*, *Fleabag*, and *Atlanta* are also serialized comedies. All these examples incorporate mystery, betrayal, intrigue, and even death into their main storylines.

These dark undertones are very much a part of what warrants the decision to design a serialized show as opposed to writing it with stand-alone episodes. Scripted comedy generally trades on openness, while secrets and lies are the force behind drama. It takes time and multiple circumstances for a main character's deeply held secret to surface. Since the main characters of both *Barry* and *Fleabag* are hiding facts and feelings from their respective tribes, for example, it makes sense that they are designed as serialized shows.

The term "hybrid" can mean either comedy-drama like *Weeds*, *Ballers*, and *Nurse Jackie*, or comedy plus another genre. *Stan Against Evil*, *iZombie*, *Ash vs Evil Dead*, *Scream Queens*, and *The Santa Clarita Diet* mash up comedy and horror. *A Series of Unfortunate Events* is a comedy-fantasy hybrid, as are *Pushing Daisies* and *The Good Place*. *The Orville*, *Rick and Morty*, *Alf*, *Mork & Mindy*, and *3rd Rock from the Sun* all combine comedy and science fiction. *Get Smart*, *Archer*, and *Chuck* are all comedy-action-spy series.

What does all that tell us? Comedy is flexible and anything is funny viewed through the right lens with a smart sensibility. The rest of this book explores more widely known shows. The afore-mentioned series serve as examples of current terminology, as well as television's diverse programming. Although a few other terms have surfaced as TV has evolved, "sitcom" simply means comedic television show. Like the entertainment industry itself, I use the terms interchangeably throughout the book.

Okay, so how do sitcoms, or comedy series, work?

As different as each show may feel to watch, their DNA is basically the same. TV comedies are ongoing stories about a tribe of people banded together by the bonds of love. The tribe can be a traditional family, nontraditional family, a group of friends who function as a family, or a group of coworkers who function as a family. Every sitcom you've ever seen meets this basic narrative criterion.

In order to tell a story, there needs to be conflict. An over-arching difference between comedy and drama is the *result* of conflict. As bad as circumstances might get, The Heroes of Comedy stay together in the end. Stretching familial bonds all the way to their limits is funny. Breaking the bonds of family is drama.

Sitcoms work best when there is unconditional love, ad-miration, or both between characters. In this sense, fictional characters don't operate any differently than we do in real life. If we love someone, or at least admire them, we can forgive, try to understand, and commit to finding solutions when problems arise. They can offer us the same.

We can fight with and criticize people who truly love us and ultimately feel safe even though there is risk in speaking our inner truth. We can be ourselves with our worst faults exposed in the presence of those who love us. True, we may fear the naked vulnerability we feel when our lesser selves are exposed, yet as long as we know that we won't be rejected for who we are at our core, we can act out, lash out, and flame out in full view of our tribe. We can be furious with someone and still love them **unconditionally**. This is the bedrock of scripted comedy.

Sitcoms are the humorous examination of how and why people care for each other despite obvious faults. When a series feels more dramatic than comedic, it's not usually because something deeply sorrowful like illness or death has occurred. Although those realities may arise, it's more often the case that lack of humor stems from relationships that are coming undone. When characters betray each other and run out of forgiveness, the comedy stops.

Who is the Hero, What is Their Journey?

I've observed that sitcom titles tell you a lot, if not everything about what (or really *who*) the series is about. A core tenet of writing fiction is sending a hero on a journey. Most people know that even if they haven't taken a writing course. However, for the sake of storytelling, a hero can be more than one person. It's a mistake to think a show can gain traction just because of its concept. People might tune in because of an interesting idea, but they only stay if they like the characters and their relationships. An audience only continues to watch when it can get behind the show's hero.

Sitcoms can feature a single hero, a pair acting as the show's hero or a group functioning as the show's hero equally. This is reflected consistently throughout television history in show titles. All shows will have an ensemble cast and multiple lead actors. The focus of the show, however, stays on the hero throughout its lifespan. The main storylines relate to the hero (singular or plural) and the other characters' storylines inevitably circle back to the hero.

Here are some examples of sitcoms following a single hero's journey: *I Love Lucy*, *The Mary Tyler Moore Show*, *Roseanne*,

Seinfeld, *The Fresh Prince of Bel-Air*, *Murphy Brown*, *Newhart*, *Frasier*, *King of the Hill*, *The Bernie Mac Show*, *Everybody Loves Raymond*, and *Veep*. All these shows feature amazing casts. The focus of the show, however, stays squarely on the title character throughout the entire series.

Sitcoms that follow a pair or couple as the show's hero: *The Odd Couple*, *Sanford and Son*, *Perfect Strangers*, *Bosom Buddies*, *Laverne & Shirley*, *Mork & Mindy*, *Kate & Allie*, *Dharma & Greg*, *Mike & Molly*, *Will & Grace*, *2 Broke Girls*, *Rick and Morty*, *Broad City*, *Baskets*, *Grace and Frankie*, etc. The focus of the show stays squarely on the main pair, who are the series' hero together.

Sitcoms that follow a group equally as the show's hero: *All in the Family*, *Arrested Development*, *A Different World*, *Scrubs*, *The Golden Girls*, *Friends*, *The Simpsons*, *Community*, *The Office*, *Modern Family*, *Happy Endings*, *The Good Place*, *Schitt's Creek*, *Superstore*, *The Goldbergs*, *Brooklyn Nine-Nine*, *Parks and Recreation*, etc. The focus of the show is divided evenly among all characters.

Of course there are exceptions, but you can see how show titles often act as a thesis statement for a series. The shows with one character's name in the title always give the main storyline to that character. Ensemble characters will also have strong storylines, but they will invariably need something from the main character, even if it's just advice or comfort. The show takes us on the title character's journey. Roughly speaking, it's their world and the other characters are living in it.

This follows through with pairs. Audiences love a buddy comedy, and that's basically what's happening when your show's hero is a duo. While Karen (Megan Mullally) and Jack (Sean Hayes) are essential to the success of *Will & Grace* as a series, their storylines always lead back to either Will or Grace or both. As the show's hero pair, Will and Grace have storylines that don't ultimately impact Karen and Jack. While they always know what's going on with Will and Grace, Karen and Jack are not always included in the conflict and resolution of their storylines. The same dynamic occurs on *Laverne & Shirley* with ensemble characters Lenny (Michael McKean) and Squiggy (David L. Lander).

There is no better example of a series with a group as its hero than *Friends*. The show is beloved and watched over and over again by fans all over the world. One reason for its success that most people don't consider is that it features a tribe as the show's hero. A family of choice is something a lot of us can relate to. There are times in many of our lives when our chosen group of friends comprise our most important day-to-day relationships.

Brilliant in its simplicity, *Friends* takes us on the journey of a tribe of friends finding their way into adult relationships, careers, and parenthood together. If you think *Friends* is a typical sitcom like others that came before it, you couldn't be more wrong. The architecture of *Friends* is quite rare. It's one of the only shows in television history to feature **six** equally billed, adult lead actors that isn't set in a workplace.

Friends generated 236 episodes over 10 seasons. Most of the show took place on just three sets: Monica and Rachel's apartment, Joey and Chandler's apartment and Central Perk. It's no easy feat of writing to keep a show alive for a decade with your characters anchored in the same locations throughout. The show's shared hero journey set *Friends* up for near infinite storylines. Since any one of the character's lives could move the show forward at any given time, *Friends* has a freedom within the writing that series with a single lead or a pair of leads lack.

Living Single is another example of a hit sitcom that features a group of friends on a journey as a collective hero. It premiered the year before *Friends* in 1993 and deserves credit for first establishing the template of a tribe of six career-minded friends living in New York.

You can see how other group hero show titles infer that the tribe will be working as a unit to overcome the obstacles that lie before them. *Community* is synonymous with the word group. *The Good Place*, *Brooklyn Nine-Nine* and *Superstore* are all locations where we know a tribe will exist. When a show title is a place, that's a strong indicator the series will move forward with a group hero.

Once the hero is established, the adventures begin. Details of a show can vary wildly. The tone can be quite different from series to series even within a broad genre like drama or comedy. Shows certainly evoke different responses from us; we love some, we hate some, we're indifferent to others. Yet it's worth noting that all shows tell stories about the same universal themes. The characters you love in television and film (and literature) are contained within stories about the acquisition or loss of love, status, and money.

When you consider the specifics of any show, it may seem there's much more to it, but ultimately there is not. *The Mary Tyler Moore Show* deals with the status of Mary Richards and women in the workplace in the 1970s. *Roseanne* deals with the socioeconomic status of the Conner family in the 1980s. *Mad About You* explores romantic love via married urban adults without kids in the 1990s. *Scrubs* examines the employment status of interns becoming doctors in the 2000s. *2 Broke Girls* explores the financial aspirations of its lead characters in the 2010s.

Sure, these are broad examples that summarize the entire span of these series. However, the storylines for individual episodes address the same concerns because these three themes permeate our thoughts in real life. Are we finding romance or ending one? Are we respected by our peers or dismissed by them? Are we on track for a promotion? Succeeding in our career choice? Do we have money in the bank or are we broke?

I may have never met you, but I know what you care about the most: your heart, your ego, and your bank account. Think of any scene from any show you love, and you'll see that this is the case for The Heroes of Comedy as well. The actions of the characters are driven by the need to fulfill one or more of these core human concerns. Just like us.

Relationships are the Key to Success

So, in order to make a comedy series, we create a tribe held together by the bonds of love. One of them is the hero, perhaps a pair, or life's load is distributed evenly amongst a group. Each of the characters spends most of their waking life thinking and talking about their romantic prospects, their overall place in life and how much money they have or don't have.

How is that funny?

It's not. That's just the infrastructure we need to build an authentic, relatable world.

It's funny when enlivened comedically through the lens of codependency and dysfunction within our core group. Our point of view on the world and our means of communication inform our transactional tribal dynamics. Expressing ourselves poorly is funny and so is reacting childishly to incoming communication from our group. Our imperfect procedures for handling life are, in fact, quite hilarious.

What are Transactional Tribal Dynamics?

Transactional Tribal Dynamics are the ways in which tribe members influence and regard one another in day-to-day exchanges. Present moments are informed by history and upbringing. Transactional tribal dynamics stimulate responses between tribe members both consciously and subconsciously. Parent-child and sibling relationships are typically the most influential regarding our outlook on life and response to conflict, followed by grandparent-grandchild, cousin, aunt/uncle-niece/nephew, etc.

An example is when a person or character has a big emotional response to the news that their parents are coming to town, particularly a negative one. Transactional tribal dynamics are how we respond to smaller moments within our tribe because of how we've conditioned ourselves and each other. Knowingly or not, we all teach others in our orbit how to treat us. A large part of our evolution as adults is learning how to respond more maturely in daily interpersonal exchanges than we responded to our moms, dads, brothers, and sisters as kids.

These concepts are serious, but we can also consider that they're just clinical ways of saying we're all flawed. The Heroes of Comedy respond to the world like their much younger selves. If everyone was fully evolved and handled every one of life's conflicts with a steady hand and clear head, there would be nothing to laugh at. There would be no fools or folly. In reality, we often don't know we're being immature, clingy, rash, foolhardy, or flat-out absurd until we're given feedback from our tribe or society at large.

So, we talk about getting laid (love), whether people like us (status), and how broke or rich we are (money) like poorly parented teenagers in adult bodies. We have those conversations with the family we are born into, the family of friends we choose, or the family we create from our coworkers. We speak of our lives with our tribe.

None of whom are any more evolved than we are. We were all given incomplete and often incompatible instructions on how to be humans. We laugh at each other because of and despite our hearts being in exactly the right place. We're living our own sitcoms every day. Our situation is that we're alive. The comedy is that we don't quite know why.

What is Codependency?

Generally, codependency is a behavioral condition within relationships where a person tries to get all their emotional needs met from another person or tribe. Their self-esteem and sense of personal worth is reliant on others and can't be obtained from within.

The complex is compounded when the other tribe members are indifferent, unsupportive, or adolescent in response. Codependency is how our *personal* immaturity shows up within relationships. When the people closest to us in daily life don't challenge us to be our best selves or worse, they actively interfere with us becoming our best selves, those relationships likely have layers of codependency.

What is Dysfunction?

Dysfunction as it pertains to family dynamics is when conflict, misbehavior and emotional neglect occur continuously and unchecked amongst the tribe. Children sometimes grow up in dysfunctional families with the understanding that such an arrangement is normal.

When they encounter interpersonal conflict as adults, they lack the tools to handle it well, if at all. For example, it shouldn't be hard at all to break off a romantic relationship that isn't healthy, but it often is. It shouldn't be hard for an adult to set clear, consistent boundaries with an overbearing parent, but it often is. When we don't address unhealthy elements that surface in our relationships quickly and directly, it's due to dysfunction.

Here are seven characteristics of a dysfunctional family:

1. Addiction
2. Perfectionism
3. Unpredictability
4. Conditional love
5. Lack of boundaries
6. Lack of intimacy
7. Poor communication

These are not the only indicators of dysfunction, but they are common ones. All of them can be treated comedically, dramatically, or a mix of both. Sam Malone (Ted Danson) is an alcoholic on *Cheers*, widely regarded as one of the great sitcoms of all time. Samantha Jones (Kim Cattrall) is a sex addict on *Sex and the City*.

All the Neurotic Heroes of Comedy suffer from perfectionism, like Monica Geller-Bing (Courteney Cox) for example. Cosmo Kramer (Michael Richards) is defined by unpredictability on *Seinfeld*. Marie Barone (Doris Roberts) conducts a master class in conditional love on every episode of *Everybody Loves Raymond*. She offers and withholds approval to keep her family beholden to her.

All The Heroes of Comedy suffer from lack of boundaries. They're all codependent with one another.

Lack of intimacy and poor communication may be full-time traits for certain characters, or they may be issues that bubble up to the surface depending on storylines.

Of course sitcoms need jokes, humorous situations, and outrageous, funny characters. But all stories; comedy, drama, action, crime, horror, fantasy, etc., are constructed from heroes overcoming conflict. It's easy to create melancholy out of tension and discord, but what about laughter?

In order to fight funny, The Heroes of Comedy need to be uniquely but equally flawed. Codependency and tribal dysfunction are the common ground where all great sitcom characters meet. To varying degrees, and in their own way, they all suffer from arrested development; it was a psychological affliction long before it was a sitcom.

As you read on, we will spend time reflecting on the greatest comedies in television history. We'll break down why they work, unpack why they're beloved, and credit hundreds of actors for their contribution to the genre and the characters they portrayed. Before we do that, we should take a moment to applaud the writers who created The Heroes of Comedy and the worlds in which they live.

Even if a sitcom has a great premise, its real value lies in its reflection of the human condition. The audience needs to relate to the individual characters and even more importantly, the reasons they spend all their time together. Even when it seems like they're at odds. Threading jokes through the spindly needle of fractured egos is like playing hopscotch in a minefield. It takes a deft hand to trigger a character's neuroses without going too far. Challenging society's conventions without crossing the line of good taste is tricky.

In order to manipulate laughter from chaos and crisis, we must understand our own psychology. The lighthearted examination of how distinct personalities interact with the world and each other makes sitcoms culturally significant. They give us much more than humor; they mirror our humanity. We need them to get to know ourselves better. But what we love the most about our favorite shows must show up on what begins as a blank page first. In the words of the penultimate television actor, Ms. Betty White, "The writers are the stars of every really successful sitcom."

"I just love doing sitcoms. I'd be in them 'til I was grey if they'd have me."

2

Single-cam Sitcoms vs.
Multi-cam Sitcoms

To begin, let's make sure everyone is clear that single-camera sitcoms and multi-camera sitcoms are two entirely different television comedy formats. Multi-cams are shot live in front of a studio audience and single-cams are shot more like films. Single-cam sitcoms employ more than one camera during production, despite their name.

"Single-cam" and "multi-cam" are simply the common terms universally used to describe each. Examples of single-camera sitcoms are: *30 Rock, Arrested Development, Parks and Recreation, The Office, Glee, Schitt's Creek, Barry,* and *The Good Place.* Examples of multi-camera sitcoms: *Seinfeld, The Big Bang Theory, I Love Lucy, The Golden Girls, Roseanne, Will & Grace, Friends,* and *2 Broke Girls.*

The differences between single-camera sitcoms and a multi-camera sitcoms are significant. Some of those differences are quite subtle and others are more profound. There is also an intersection where they are very much the same. It's worth understanding that single-cams and multi-cams are distinct styles of shows that are designed, written, and shot differently.

If you're a writer, you should decide clearly what format you want to write in *before* you start developing your show. There are vital differences in the DNA of each genre that many creatives don't consider while they're honing their concept. I often have to send writers back to the drawing board because they unintentionally fuse the two styles together and create unnecessary problems within the draft of their shows.

Here's a quick illustration: A writer decides to create a show in a multi-cam sitcom format and writes an action line that directs the camera. For example, the writer may want the camera to zoom in on a character's phone so the audience can see a text message. Writers cannot direct the camera within the multi-camera format. A character can still get a surprising or funny text message, but the message has to be read out loud. Think of a character in a play getting texted on a stage. The audience can't *see* it. They'd have to *hear* it.

This is one of many critical distinctions I make when teaching how to write television comedy. This example might *seem* obvious, but it definitely is *not* to many new writers. In fact, many experienced writers alike incorrectly think the only major distinction between the two kinds of shows is hearing laughter during the performance or not. Nothing could be further from reality. Most of the differences between writing a play and writing a movie exist equally between writing the two different types of sitcoms. Actors should take these differences to heart as well.

There are also a lot of myths and misconceptions about these two subgenres of television comedy that I will dispel. Within this chapter we'll thoroughly review their similarities and distinctions. As an actor, once you are certain of what is being asked of you when offered sides, you will be able to easily and quickly craft a bookable, accurate performance that will blow casting directors and producers away. If you're interested in writing comedy, this review will help prevent you from making critical errors that can occur when you're unsure of the important differences that exist within the architecture. Let's make sure your pilot idea meets industry standards in the marketplace!

Differences in Format

Single-camera sitcoms are shot more like feature films on sets that are actual real locations or designed and constructed to look as three-dimensional and authentic as possible. The shot composition is therefore largely tighter and closer up on the actors. This gives single-camera sitcoms a certain intimacy with the viewing audience. We might also say that single-camera sitcoms are more cinematic or that they resemble movies more than live theater.

Writing single-cams means you can direct the camera. You can write how it moves and how the audience will see visual elements unfold. *The Good Place* is a great example of imaginative writing for a single-cam sitcom. The writers of that show can have animals rain down from the sky and the characters can teleport from place to place. There is no way to execute those ideas on a multi-cam. Single-camera shows can have tracking shots so the actors can "walk and talk"; multi-cams cannot. Single-cam shows can easily execute fantasy sequences as they often did on *Scrubs*. Multi-cams can but they have a much harder time.

Whatever you can imagine the camera capturing in a movie, you can imagine for a single-cam sitcom. Shot composition is taught in film schools, but you don't need a degree in filmmaking to embrace these distinctions. It just takes awareness and a little common sense. Whether you're acting or writing, a deeper understanding of how each genre of comedy is assembled will help your work.

Multi-camera shows are shot on soundstages, mostly (but not always) live in front of a studio audience. While the sets are realistic to an extent, they are built on flats, much the same way theater sets are designed and constructed. Multi-camera sets don't have the same depth and dimension as single-camera sitcom sets because they are stretched out sequentially in a line, facing the audience.

That's why living rooms, kitchens, and bullpens (open work areas), in particular, are so large on multi-camera sitcoms. They are the primary sets on which most of the series takes place. They rest inside an even larger soundstage and have a very open feel because there is no ceiling and only three solid walls. The audience and cameras watch through the open **fourth wall**. The fourth wall is the imaginary wall or conceptual barrier created between a performer and audience. In the same vein, theater has a fourth wall between the stage and audience.

The shot composition of multi-cams is therefore generally wider than single-camera shows. Directly opposite the sets are bleacher seats for 150 or so audience members. In between them is the pit where the cameras are stationed along with the director, writers, and crew. Multi-cams feature fewer close-up shots and two-shots of the actors. If you imagine your favorite multi-cam sitcoms, the image in your mind is likely of a wide view where you can see a whole group. How often were all six lead actors assembled in Rachel and Monica's apartment on *Friends*? Quite often. They may have all been in the living room or spread out into the kitchen. Either way, it requires a wide shot to capture them. With bigger groups, the actors are often blocked further apart than they are on single-cams.

When actors perform in front of an audience, theater is created. Whether you watch a multi-cam sitcom being recorded live or through a screen after it's been edited for broadcast is irrelevant. You are experiencing theater nonetheless. For this reason, some people love multi-cams and others find that they feel artificial. To that I say everything on TV is artificial, so whether

I hear laughter or not isn't a distinguishing factor for believability or authenticity. More on that later.

Differences in Writing

Multi-cam sitcoms generally have a more traditional joke structure with setups and punchlines embedded within dialogue. They are also likely to feature turnaround jokes (reversals) comprising two lines quickly contradicting each other. Multi-cams also incorporate triplets (words or ideas in threes) and a more prominent musical composition of dialogue than single-cam sitcoms. The same word or phrase can be used multiple times for comedic effect. Likewise, different words can be used in a list of threes to create a patter. While there is some crossover between formats, multi-cams are more dependent on classic joke construction integrated into character dialogue. Strong jokes are more likely to get an entire audience to laugh in sync.

Here are some quick examples.

Setup/Punch Line from *The Golden Girls*

BLANCHE: Oh, you don't have to worry about me, honey. I never get sick. I take very good care of myself. I treat my body like a temple.

SOPHIA: Yeah, open to everyone, day or night.

Turnaround/Reversal from *The Big Bang Theory:*

LEONARD: (to Sheldon) People get things they don't deserve all the time. Like me, with you.

Triplet from *Everybody Loves Raymond:*

FRANK: Maybe that's why I like animals. Woof. Moo. Quack. They tell it like it is.

Lastly, operative, or key, words have heightened importance in multi-camera shows. Operative words are the words within the dialogue that merit emphasis within each sentence. Identifying and executing operative words can definitely enhance a joke or humor in general. Conversely, placing emphasis on wrong words can destroy a joke entirely. (I elaborate on operative words and joke identification in greater detail further on.) For now, here's an example from the Operative Word Master himself, Chandler Bing of *Friends*:

> **CHANDLER:** I say more dumb things *before* nine a.m. than most people say *all day*.

Operative word usage applies to single-cam sitcoms, too. However, understanding and emphasizing operative words matters much more in regard to multi-cams because of the shared timing, rhythm (musicality), and pacing between actors and audience. Craftsmanship with language as a comedic tool ideally begins in the writing and is carried through by the actors.

Performing on a multi-camera sitcom is inherently more difficult than performing on a single-camera sitcom for this very reason. Actors not only need to hit the jokes the writers wrote; they need to speak *certain* words a *specific* way in order to elicit laughter from the audience. Some jokes only work with a particular inflection. Some lines are only funny when emphasis is placed on one word but not another.

Great multi-cam actors are attuned to the audience and prepared to hold for their laughter when it occurs. Multi-cam sitcom writers need to strive for jokes that will prompt universal laughter from a studio audience. Single-camera comedies need to have humor, but the writers do not necessarily need to craft jokes that elicit group laughter.

The stylized way of speaking that is incorporated within multi-cams harkens all the way back to vaudeville, America's original variety/comedy performance medium — The *X Factor* of the late 1800s, so to speak. Vaudeville was wildly popular before radio, television and film existed, spawning influential comedians still recognized today like Abbott and Costello, George Burns and Gracie Allen, Jack Benny, Moms Mabley, and W.C. Fields, et al.

Because of sitcom's theatrical roots, episodes of multi-cams were originally referred to as **teleplays**. This term first surfaced during the 1950s in order to distinguish television scripts from stage plays written for theater and screenplays written for films. All three have different formats, conventions, and constraints. In the scheme of time, television is not that old. Invented in the 1920s, televisions were not common in American households until the 1950s.

The term "teleplay" was broadly used throughout the 1970s and began to vanish from the lexicon in the 1980s. By that time, it was no longer necessary to point out that a television script is different than a theater script. However, if you look closely at the closing credits of some current sitcoms, you'll see the word tele-play has made a recent comeback. Nostalgia for great sitcoms is ever present and the affection people still have for this special mix of theater and studio recording even includes terminology!

Single-camera shows generally have fewer traditional jokes per page. The dialogue is more representative of real-life conver-sations with a heightened sense of urgency, mania, or absurdity *in regard to the situation*. There are several reasons for this.

First, there is no audience laughter on single-cam sitcoms. Laughter breaks tension. This is true in everyday life, as well as in regard to a performance and its audience. Without a laugh break, tension has a greater opportunity to build and grow. Second, single-cam sitcoms utilize the camera differently. As we reviewed, the shots are closer up, which can heighten the stakes with a feeling of claustrophobia.

Zooming in on a character's reaction can give the scene an extra jolt of urgency. The audience might even feel a dizzying effect from the camera following a character, which it cannot do on a multi-cam sitcom. Further, writers of single-camera sitcoms can direct the camera to take actions. Zooming is one potential action, but you can also ask the camera to track, widen to reveal, pan, intercut, angle on a particular character's point of view, and many other options within the single-camera format.

In lieu of a greater number of jokes per page, single-cam characters tend to rant more than multi-cam characters. Likewise, they are more likely to narrate their emotional standing and mental condition out loud. They live in a near constant state of exposing their id. With no need to include an audience or pause for their laughter, single-cam characters are free to talk on and on about how they feel and what they are like.

There is often low-level anxiety running through single-cam sitcoms that creates a palpable tension as we watch them. Think of when a character glances furtively at the camera or speaks directly to it on shows like *The Office*, *Parks and Recreation*, or *Modern Family*.

The emotions, intentions, and characterizations are every bit the same on both kinds of shows. The tenets of good acting are the same. The Heroes of Comedy are the same on both kinds of shows. However, emotions are more likely to be internalized on single-camera sitcoms and scaled or projected in regard to a more intimate shot composition. Since there is no audience, there is likewise no theater being captured by the cameras.

Further, single-cam sitcoms tend to rely on absurd situations with rapidly escalating circumstances, much more than multi-cams. It's really single-cam sitcoms that emphasize the "situation" of the phrase "situation comedy" (sitcom). There is certainly an intersection of what can happen in either format. However, with fewer traditional jokes and no audience laughter, a circumstance (situation) tends to spiral much further downward and more wildly out of control within single-cam comedies versus multi-cams.

If you watch carefully and through an unbiased lens, you'll begin to notice that, by and large, the things that happen to the characters on multi-cam shows probably could happen to you in the way they are depicted. What happens to characters on single-cam sitcoms are often less likely to happen to you the way in which they are depicted.

I'm not addressing characterization or the scale of performances. I'm making an observation derived from watching thousands of episodes of both types of sitcoms. Simply put, without stand-up-style jokes and an audience to laugh at them, single-camera sitcoms rely on preposterous depictions of common events much more so than multi-cams.

For example, if you're a fan of *Arrested Development*, think of the stair car (a car you might drive up to an airplane door) the family regularly uses for casual transportation. If you enjoy *Schitt's Creek*, think of the wigs in Moira's collection that each have names. *The Marvelous Mrs. Maisel* begins her stand-up career when she drunkenly wanders onto a stage in a negligee and flashes her breast to an audience, which sparks her success. All funny, but quite preposterous. The chances of any of you experiencing those events or taking those actions are close to nil.

Arrested Development's ongoing stair car joke is hilarious and a great running gag. It's *only* a single-camera sitcom joke. There is no way to employ it on a multi-camera show. Multi-camera sitcoms exist almost entirely on the interior. Outdoor shots occur only on extremely rare occasions.

For the most part, the confines of a multi-cam set limit absurd depictions of a particular circumstance. On multi-cams, things don't often happen seemingly by magic or via a trail of complicated logic. Multi-cams are more straightforward in how they depict daily life. In other words, you can't see a barbeque explode and hurl rotisserie chickens on a multi-cam show or whisk a character away in a helicopter. Those things can and do happen easily on a single-cam sitcom.

Many people generalize multi-cam sitcoms as the broader of the two formats; either can be broad or not. But generally, single-cams have broader (less realistic) premises just like many well-regarded comedic feature films. Consider *The Hangover*. It's a hilarious movie and fun to watch. A *very* brief summary of the film if you don't know it: A group of friends travel to Vegas for a bachelor party weekend. One friend accidentally roofies the rest and they wake up the following morning with no memory of what they did the night before. The next day they encounter Mike Tyson, a tiger in a hotel bathroom, and a gang of dangerous drug dealers.

Plus a whole lot more. There is no way all the things that happen to the group of friends in that movie could really happen to a group of friends over the course of a weekend in Las Vegas. It's fantasy because the events are unbelievable and go further than is realistically probable. This isn't a criticism of the film, just an explanation of how it's broad.

A sitcom example in a similar vein is *Schitt's Creek*, a hilarious single-cam series that grows funnier and deeper with every season. The premise centers on a wealthy family relocating after they lose their fortune. They rebuild their lives with their sole remaining asset — a small town named Schitt's Creek, which they bought their son as a joke birthday gift years earlier.

I am a big fan of *Schitt's Creek* and have watched and re-watched every episode. The concept is, by definition, broad. I'm positive that none of you reading this book will ever move to a town that was bought for you... by your dad... as a joke. Moreover, the show relies on a totally blown-out premise, and the characters undertake a sequence of highly unlikely and unrelatable actions to produce humor. Much more so than a show like *Friends*, which simply features a group of people spending time together throughout their 20s. The premise of *Friends* is not inherently broad. Historically, most multi-cam sitcoms throughout history are not driven by broad concepts. Quality multi-cams do not feature broad acting.

These are some examples to illustrate how written **circumstances** and **actions** are often further afield from day-to-day life on single-camera sitcoms. Whether it's the overall series premise or an individual episode, single-camera sitcoms rely on unusual, heightened, or fantastical situations and circumstances more than multi-cams.

Differences in Acting

Characterizations can range from mundane to outrageous, from literal to theatrical, from real to entirely fabricated on both types of show. Any notion that single-camera sitcoms feature acting that is more "real" than multi-cam performances is easily debunked.

Unbreakable Kimmy Schmidt is a single-cam sitcom with extremely heightened, theatrical performances across the board. *Two and a Half Men* is a successful and extraordinarily profitable multi-cam sitcom that features very true-to-life, down-to-earth performances from the main cast. Charlie Sheen is cool as a cucumber as Charlie Harper, Jon Cryer is neurotic, but believably so as his brother Alan, and Conchata Ferrell underplays low-key housekeeper Berta as dry as the Sahara.

On multi-cam hit *Will & Grace*, Eric McCormack and Debra Messing portray Will and Grace quite naturalistically. Megan Mullally and Sean Hayes portray Karen and Jack with sustained, heightened theatricality. More and less straightforward performances occur within the same show, however, they are *all* authentic because the actors are well-trained and entirely committed to their choices. Their words are spoken truthfully from a distinct point of view.

Conversely, we can observe the same within the cast of *Modern Family*, a single-cam smash. Julie Bowen, Jesse Tyler Ferguson, and Ed O'Neill portray Claire, Mitchell, and Jay in a grounded, direct manner. Ty Burrell, Sofia Vergara, and Eric Stonestreet embody Phil, Gloria, and Cam with theatricality and heightened flair. There is no universal rule that dictates the scale, projection, theatricality, or magnification of a character on any kind of sitcom.

While a character begins with the writer, the casting process sheds light on many possibilities and the actor who is ultimately cast rounds the character out. That actor can be great because they're outstanding at playing a version of themselves, or because they can create a theatrical character from scratch that they're nothing like, but understand deeply and can sustain indefinitely.

It all depends on where actors are trained and what personal strengths they've decided to cultivate. Varying abilities between actors aren't just random deviations based on genetic talent. It has everything to do with DNA, *plus* teachers, mentors, directors, practice, experience, and overall quality of training.

Part of becoming a booking actor includes cultivating interesting personas and characterizations *ahead* of the breakdowns, not *after* you've received an audition notice. In Hollywood, you're behind if you are reacting to a breakdown for a lead role like you're starting from zero. For example, if the breakdown describes an Eccentric, the actor who ultimately books the role has more than likely cultivated and practiced that aspect of themselves and refined it to professional standards. Even further, there's a great chance they suggested to casting directors and producers that they play that type of character well via their headshots and reel footage. Working actors know how to cast themselves. They have at least some sense of their brand.

To that end, actors who book work regularly already have a good, if not totally solid, understanding of what their particular version of a character described in a breakdown is. They know who they are, what they look/sound like, and what their individual outcome will be for most types of characters they go out for. By and large, they are not guessing or hoping they are getting it right. If they are not certain, they work with a coach. Nearly all working actors have a relationship with a teacher or coach to guide them when necessary.

More often than not, actors who are performing in a more heightened, theatrical manner in television have had the training and experience to warrant the effort. It's unlikely they crafted their audition in a few hours after being emailed sides.

With a background in improv and sketch, plus on-camera acting, writing, and casting, I developed a unique skill set as a comedy coach. I'm working on multiple tracks; I train actors and writers for television comedy with a deep and rich understanding of the intersection between theater, stage comedy, and technical on-camera work.

We play and grow in front of audiences, but the financial payoff for comedy actors and writers comes when we book work on sets and soundstages. That work is only obtained through auditioning for it, so I fortify actors with script analysis training and professional-level audition technique. Together, we blend each person's unique, creative voice with career-advancing skills that theater and improv schools don't address. My goal is to make acting fun and fearless in *every* step of the career building process. We have way more fun on our journey when we're ahead of the curve, not behind it.

PART 2

LADIES AND GENTLEMEN, THE HEROES OF COMEDY

"If you know your archetypes - and not just yours, if you know how to perceive the world in archetypes, through archetypes - everything changes. Everything. Because you have two things: you can see through one eye which is impersonal, and through the other, which is personal. That's the way the game is written down here."

- Caroline Myss

3

Archetypes Are Essential

efore we dive into The Heroes of Comedy, it is essential that we first dispel any misconceptions or prejudices that may exist regarding archetypes. It's equally important that we distinguish between *archetype* and *stereotype*, so that we begin with a clear palate regarding the tremendous value of learning about the characters that writers incorporate into their scripts 100% of the time.

The definition of an archetype is as follows:

Archetype *(n)*: a very typical example of a certain person or thing; types that fit fundamental human motifs.

The use of archetypical characters and situations gives fictional work a universal acceptance. The audience can readily identify the characters in their social and cultural context. By using common archetypes, the writers attempt to impart realism to their works, as the situations in which the characters find themselves are drawn from the experiences of the world.

Most of the television shows and films we have watched our whole lives incorporate archetypical characters. Not at all to be confused with stereotypes, archetypes simply help establish a baseline familiarity and structure between the writer and audience. There are absolutely fundamental human themes that run through our lives and it makes perfect sense stories would be created that reflect them. It further makes sense that the stories are populated by characters with personalities, jobs, and levels of status we *already* recognize *before* we've even met them.

Stereotypes, on the other hand, are oversimplified depictions of people or groups that are reductive in nature. Stereotypes diminish humanity and often contain negative biases. Especially for the purposes of artists, the difference can be summarized thusly: Archetypes are a broad *starting point* for creating a specific character by adding further definition to suit a role. A stereotype is a dismissive conclusion already drawn about a character.

Archetypes offer a universally recognized foundation that can be built upon with layers of traits and idiosyncrasies, offering a relatable, but ultimately unique, depiction of a fictional person that feels real. Stereotypes limit individuality and shrink the potential for a character to be well-rounded and substantial. A stereotypical character may still be recognizable, but there's a great chance they'll also be needlessly offensive.

Actors often have a negative reaction to the words typical, standard, average, etc., however, they shouldn't. Those words are used all the time by casting professionals in breakdowns for good reason. The stories written for television and film are about a Hero's Journey — a person, pair of people, or group of people moving forward in life while overcoming obstacles. If the story is dramatic, then the journey is perilous and filled with intrigue, betrayal, and fear. If the story is comedic, the journey is filled with tribal tension, absurdity, and love.

Either way, the character types in most of what we watch are not unique. That's not to say they are overused, tired or worn out, either. They're not. They are identifiable reflections of the societal structure that we are all born into. The details of our lives may vary wildly, but the basic structure does not — we are born into this world from our parents; we attend school, then work; we explore relationships via family, friends, and romance; we traverse basic rituals like learning to walk, drive, and develop complex emotional relationships. We graduate, marry, perhaps divorce, and retire.

The nature of our evolution as humans demands that this basic outline of life holds true for almost everyone. Our cognitive abilities at different eras of our lives combined with the acceptable norms of society at large create parameters to which nearly all of us adhere as we travel through life. We can do anything we want, but typical consequences act like guardrails that keep us in clearly marked lanes most of the time.

There are infinite ways to achieve success, goals, or aspirations. Most of us, however, choose known and previously trod routes in our endeavors most of the time. Our souls, spirits, and personal stories make us unique. A dispassionate observation of many cultures reveals that most people who exist within modern society lead extremely similar lives. We belong to tribes, ones we're born into and ones we choose. The stories we tell most often are tales of how well we are faring or not within those tribes. We want to talk about our acquisition or loss of love, money, and status; so do the characters you will be portraying.

Our entertainment and literature reflect that truth. Sitcoms reflect that truth. Understanding and embracing that overarching tenet makes your job as an actor easier because you already know what you're heading into when you're given sides or a part for the first time. More than a likelihood, it's almost a *guarantee* that the part you'll be playing and the characterization you'll be creating falls within a common archetype that has been called into play countless times. Further, it's almost assuredly an archetype that you are personally already familiar with, to some degree, whether you're aware of it or not. I hope to make you aware of how much you already know about the scripts you haven't read or written yet.

The Heroes of Comedy will save you valuable time when fleshing out a character breakdown and creating an appropriate characterization and audition performance for yourself. You will literally present as a smarter and better actor for offering production your fully realized version of what they were looking for. The alternative is a shot-in-the-dark, half-baked version with uncertain, weak choices, or even worse, a performance that is deliberately skewed because you think the obvious choice is not interesting enough.

All scripted, episodic shows you have seen on television, comedy and drama alike, involve characters that are part of a family, or they are friends or coworkers who function as a family. That's it. You've seen this dynamic played out over and over again. So it makes great sense that there are archetypical characters — or traditionally understood roles — that need to be fulfilled within the narrative.

Writers are generally not reinventing the wheel when they create a show. If their product is destined to reach a broad audience, it's almost certain that the characters and circumstances are like those that have been seen before. Even when the circumstances are unique, the characters are not.

This universal truth is consistent even on a high-concept show like *The Good Place*, which occurs in the afterlife. The characters are all deceased and the action takes place within depictions of heaven and hell; The Good Place and The Bad Place. Firstly, the locations the audience sees most often are houses, offices, and interior sets that look like most other shows. There are exceptions because the show is born of fantasy, but by and large the sets used on *The Good Place* could exist elsewhere on television.

Secondly, the characters are clearly and easily identifiable archetypes. Each lead character is squarely one of The Heroes of Comedy. In fact, it's worth noting that *The Good Place* has become a multi-season smash hit *because* the character types are instantly recognizable. We have seen characters just like these characters on other shows before.

That's neither a statement of judgement nor conjecture. It is inarguable. If the premise featured an entirely imagined plane, not known to mankind and the characters were additionally un-recognizable, *The Good Place* would be a chaotic mess. Instead it's a thought-provoking, philosophical, laugh-out-loud funny success because we can quickly and easily see ourselves re-flected in these characters. We know them already despite the fact that they exist in a state we have yet to experience — death.

So even when a show takes place in another realm featuring characters who are no longer alive (plus a Janet; a program-mable guide who lives in a void), it's not only wise, but *essential* that the audience be able to identify individual personalities, as well as relationships, quickly.

Acting is telling the story of our lives through the prism of a character. It is pointedly *not* about playing the concept, outline, or the idea of a person. We act from the inside out, not the outside in. You cannot embody a character and observe a character at the same time. This should be obvious, but when it comes to acting comedy with depth, that immutable truth is sometimes forgotten or not properly understood.

I often ask my students, "What is your character like?" When they answer with the circumstance of the character (what's happening in the scene, who they are with, their occupation, etc.), only a one-word answer, "She's a Buffoon," or a review of the character's actions (what they're doing in the scene or what they want to gain), I know they don't have a handle on the characterization. They are revealing that they are undertrained in developing characters with distinct, outwardly observable personality traits and the psychological underpinnings to complement them.

The answer should be something like, "She's an overbearing blowhard who thinks she's the smartest girl in the room, but *never* is. She *always* takes the easy way out and shirks responsibility, assuming other people can just as easily do her work for her. She's defiantly lazy. She has tremendous self-assuredness for someone who *consistently* falls flat on her face. For someone so socially dimwitted, she has a lot of unearned confidence. So much so, she makes other people uncomfortable. It appears that unsettling other people with her awkward energy is her only discernable skill."

The reason this is an example of a much superior answer is twofold: One, it's more specific and detailed, but **much more importantly**, it addresses who the character is all the time and who she has always been up until this point in her life, **not** simply examining what she's like within one scene. I italicized the words *always*, *never*, and *consistently* because when it comes to creating sturdy and believable characters, those are the kinds of words that should be used the most by actors but are in practice most avoided!

Your character's personality should be made of cement with rebar running through it for additional support. Emotions should be fluid, channeled through the unbreakable vessel of a carefully crafted characterization.

Who someone is shouldn't be a guess, or a narrow, shallow depiction of a human being based on something they have chosen to do or has happened to him or her in a scene. We are not who we are because of the whims of fate. What someone is doing may be an *indication* of who they are, but an action in a scene certainly does not define them. During a typical day, I answer a ton of emails, walk my dog, cook, eat, shop, socialize with my friends, teach classes, drive, and often end the day with a glass of wine. What am I like? It's hard to tell based on mundane daily actions in which most of us engage.

Maybe I'm arguing with someone close to me. That I'm arguing tells you nothing. It's not noteworthy. Everyone argues. *How* I'm arguing tells you what I'm like. If you're developing *character* and not merely *circumstance*, you expand your analysis from my point of view in the argument and extend it to my whole life. Then you begin to understand me as a complete person, not just a person who argues because he didn't like the action or behavior of the other person.

Let's go a little bit deeper. Say, for example, I'm supposed to meet a friend for lunch, and they don't show up. Let's assume I do the obvious first and call or text them but get no response. I've effectively been stood up.

Here is a list of possible reactions from that point:

1. I become worried whether my friend is safe or not and call some mutual friends to see if I can find out. (Anchor)

2. I become irate that anyone would dare to keep someone as important as me waiting. (Narcissist)

3. I become embarrassed to sit alone in public and make jokes with strangers to hide it. (Dreamer)

4. I order for two, figuring if they show up, we've saved time and if they don't, I get a bonus lunch. (Innocent)

5. Relieved, I dine alone because that's my preference anyway, not particularly interested in why my friend didn't show. (Rebel)

6. I become distracted by the gorgeous waiter and refocus my energy on getting his number. (Player)

7. I notice the restaurant has art on the walls and treat myself to a museum opportunity, ignoring the other diners as I browse. (Eccentric)

8. I frantically scour my calendar and email chain to see who exactly messed up what, knowing I'll feel much better once I understand how this happened. (Neurotic)

9. I roll my eyes, get up after 10 minutes and leave because who cares anyway? (Cynic)

10. I wait in silence, growing ever suspicious that I've been set up to look foolish then make a pretend phone call, speaking loudly enough that the other patrons can hear about my friends' "emergency cancellation." (Buffoon)

I present you with 10 different reactions to the same stimulus. Each one is from the point of view of one of The Heroes of Comedy. Once you decide on an archetype, either correct or incorrect, your work is not finished; it's just getting started. If you determine, based on my reaction to being stood up, that I am a Rebel, for example, your next step is to review the characteristics of the Rebel from those listed in this book.

Take a breath, then gauge the characteristics you identify with the most and that apply to this *particular* Rebel. Every single characteristic does not necessarily apply to every version of an archetype. Next, locate and specify those qualities within yourself so that the work will feel authentic and personal.

Finally, review and summarize the entire personality of this character and conclude with certainty what they have always been like based on a *reaction* to a circumstance. You meet your characters in moments. Those moments contain clues. It takes training and discipline to extract those clues from the dialogue, separate the character from the circumstance, define their daily identity, then put them *back* into the scene and into action.

The persona precedes the event. The event does not dictate the personality.

What may happen to someone has no bearing on what they're like. Your instructions for character development are contained within the character's reactions. We all get sick. What are you like when you catch a cold? Are you a baby? A trooper? A drama queen? That a character caught a cold tells you nothing. How they react to being under the weather tells you a lot. People respond the way they do to events and predicaments because of their core personality, which is elastic, but ultimately consistent. In addition, we all have an enveloping point of view regarding life and its meaning or lack thereof.

A human being is the culmination of a soul, genetics, upbringing, and experience. The deduction actors need to make is not what the character is *doing* in the scene. That is simple reading comprehension. What actors need to assess is *why* someone would behave the way they are behaving given a particular stimulus. We work backward from the moment we meet characters in scenes or sides, review their history through a lens crafted of primary characteristics then bring them back to the present with an understanding of their psychology in the NOW.

Describing how someone is handling one situation in one moment of their life is not character development. Extrapolating how they grew up, how they see the world around them, how they respond to conflict and what they *certainly* must be like all the time is character development. It takes strong critical thinking skills and personalization of several characteristics along with layered emotional reactions to play a character with integrity as opposed to playing "at it."

You will always meet your characters living a life already in motion. It's your duty as an actor to enliven them with depth. Your job is to deeply understand their motivation for speaking all the words they say. When you don't have a handle on why a character is saying what they're saying, it shows. Further, it is to provide your characters with a rich, well-defined personality and clearly detailed process of handling life, which organically drives them through moments on an instinctive, subconscious level.

This is when the "acting" disappears and the actor and character merge seamlessly and authentically. This is when actors begin to think in character as opposed to stating memorized lines. People are identifiable and categorizable. Every time we meet a new person, we unconsciously assign them roles and put them in a place in our minds. It is an actual survival mechanism inherent in our DNA. Our acquaintanceships may start out very basic; you look at someone and think "safe" or "not safe," "kind" or "mean," "smokin' hot" or "no thanks." With time, (and not even a lot of time — mere minutes) we then move on to more specific assessments of personality: chatty, intelligent, self-absorbed, funny, needy, boring, etc.

We all make these assessments and we all come to similarly limited conclusions. Our vocabulary and, therefore, our means of expression are limited. We do not have infinite words. There are not infinite ways to describe people. Anyone who is truly indescribable is probably threatening, malformed, or both. However, even with no understanding of this kind of person or why they are the way they are... I've still described them.

You are all casting directors.

You have been deciding what people you meet are like as fast as possible your whole life and you're probably not often wrong. Unless someone is deliberately deceitful, they *are* like what they *seem* like. If you don't accept that easily as a person or actor, the doubt and uncertainty stems from you. If this applies to you, it would be worthwhile to examine why you question the authenticity of others without cause.

People in life and characters on the page aren't all that difficult to identify. As everyday people, we broadcast what we're like without even realizing it. Characters often self-describe. They literally announce their primary traits all the time, often as justification for their behavior. While that may result as a joke for the audience, the character is never joking. They're speaking their truth. We all long to be understood and to that end we're all pretty forthcoming about what we're like. It helps me when you understand me. Who has time to be coy?

So don't overthink or overanalyze or second-guess. Grab the most obvious clues characters offer about themselves and look for how they are described by other characters. The goal is to play an obvious character description well enough to book the part and exclude other actors from the conversation. The challenge is heightened because you're additionally tasked with showing your mettle in an audition setting. Perhaps you're asked to self-tape and submit, which means you also get no verbal or even visual clues as to whether you're on the right track. No adjustments. No direction. The New Age of Digital Television is here; it's online and moves at breakneck speed.

4

Who Are You in the Breakdowns?

Knowing more about the kinds of characters writers are writing will also help you identify your strengths and castability as an actor. We aren't destined to play any and every role that is created, at least not for on-camera work. Stage acting is different. There is latitude for people portraying characters of different ages. Theater has an allowance for imaginative casting that may involve costumes, wigs, and makeup that changes an actor's appearance.

Not so for television and film. Exceptions occur, but mostly for shows based in a fantasy genre. Even then, only actors who play monsters, freaks, and aliens have their appearance radically altered; think *Walking Dead*, *Star Trek*, *Game of Thrones*, etc. For the most part, actors are cast in their roles looking exactly how they look in real life.

Which of The Heroes of Comedy suits you best? The ones who *most* sync up with your personal nature on most days of your life. It's great if you can imagine being like anyone. It's true for most of us that we have a persona that is easily defined or identified by those who know us. Most people are not hard to describe in a few words. Those words are your best casting.

Most commonly, any given actor has an average of three archetypes that best suit their strengths. On one end of the spectrum, a few actors have a look and essence that leaves them castable as only one type of character. At the other end of the telescope, a handful of actors have a look and essence that enables them to play any character believably. Casting doesn't have rules, but it does present actors with certain realities. It's up to each of us to simply know what our personal look plus essence equals. Generally speaking, almost everyone has a definable range or wheelhouse and casting outside of that range has limited payoff.

Rather than trying to play *anything*, actors have a much greater chance for success if they offer themselves to casting directors and producers with a vision. Actors who cultivate alter egos or personas that are refined and authentic are ahead of the game. Actors who know themselves and play to their strengths win. Those who don't tend to get lost in the shuffle. If you're good but general, you're worth less than you could be. If you're refined and specialized, you're worth more. Simple.

One of the difficulties of casting is that the vast majority of actors deliver auditions that are good, but not noteworthy. In other words, unmemorable. Sadly, most actors lead with fear and restraint when auditioning. I can't tell you how many times I've seen this while working in casting myself or while coaching actors. They're afraid of coming off as "too big" and don't want to overact.

5

Go Bold or Go Home

Understandable, but in order to carve out a career as an actor, there has to be something bold and/or unique in what you're offering. There has to be a confidence and joy that radiates from within you as you're performing under scrutiny. That confidence derives not only from training and practice, but innate knowledge that the performance you're offering is great, authentic to you as a person and absolutely *right* in a way you can support from the dialogue.

The goal of a working actor should not be to play anything, it should be to define and heighten *yourself;* to be so intriguing and certain in who you are, that when the right role comes along, it cannot be easily taken away from you. Your goal should be to stake the strongest possible claim to the fictional life on the page.

It's hard to deny you a role when what you've instilled into the character is so vital, that it becomes hard to imagine someone else playing it with your personal essence removed. And that will only happen if you develop yourself as a person, then as an actor, in that order, before you receive a breakdown that may become the role of your lifetime.

For the record, I don't use vague or judgmental terminology when I teach. Even when an actor does overshoot when I'm working with them, I guide them toward the strongest choices possible that are still true. The analysis is *not* "too big" versus "right."

Performances are either honest and believable or they are not. Scaling is a separate factor. You don't have to be an actor, comedian, or teacher to know a performance is off; an audience member can tell you that. A comedy teacher who can't help you maximize your potential within a scene is not worth your time.

More often than not, actors who are able to carve out a career and continue working most or all of their lives are trading on a small set of core characteristics that are highlighted in their true personality at most times on most days of their lives. They are emphasizing their assets and shamelessly showing them off.

Compared to the rest of the pack, the choices made by *working* actors in comedy will *always seem bigger in comparison to actors who work less.*

Actors who book will often risk being seen as "too big" by someone in the room.

Actors book work *because* of big, bold choices, not *in spite of them.* I think actors instinctively know that, but don't always know where to find a teacher, mentor, or artistic director who is experienced enough to guide them toward their ultimate comedic worth. The industry needs categorization to function efficiently. It also needs comedic performers who are fearless about making adventurous choices.

The Heroes of Comedy will help you do just that without guessing or wondering if you've gotten it right. They aren't an acting gimmick or writing trick. They are a summary of what real people are like, with elaboration on why. They are a thorough review of human nature and psychology that explain impulses, reactions, motivation, interpersonal communication abilities, and behavior. They are an aid for actors and writers to build sturdy, distinct characters that feel like they could be alive in the real world, even when experienced through a screen. Understanding The Heroes of Comedy is simply understanding humans.

6

Grab Your Cape, It's Time to Save the World

Whether you're discovering who you are or getting to know yourself better, I hope you have fun with the following chapters. I've detailed how writers craft these distinct personalities and how actors can find their personal way into portraying them.

Each one ends with three in-depth reviews of that archetype from well-known sitcoms. I have distilled thousands of hours of research into an analysis of each archetype as it exists on a family-based sitcom, a friend-based sitcom, and a work-based sitcom. Aside from dissecting their identities, I aspired to expose how each Hero is steadfast in their nature, no matter where they turn up. Archetypes are necessarily consistent and recognizable.

I've also included a section that reflects how each of The Heroes of Comedy is described in the breakdowns that are sent out to actors by casting directors. Sometimes the words used to describe a character within the industry are not helpful. The description can be vague, include contradictory words, overly general words, or words that need further interpretation to be helpful to a solid performance. Like, "bohemian," for example. Most people know what is meant by that, but you can't play bohemian without interpretation because it is conceptual.

Bohemian is an abstraction comprising several other words that an actor can play, but we have to unpack it first. You can personalize and play: fluid, shameless, opinionated, imaginative, open, tolerant, and effervescent. You can play a fully humanized bohemian character when you incorporate specific traits that provide definition and depth. I have done the work of gathering and categorizing the most commonly used conceptual descriptors of each Hero for you. If you know how to translate them in advance, you'll further eliminate guessing how you should approach playing a character.

I have been teaching with these archetypes for more than 25 years, so I can tell you from personal experience they are powerful and empowering. I have played these characters both onstage and on camera myself. I have written them into scripts. I have directed actors, utilizing the distinct attributes contained within each. I have taught thousands of actors the deeper meaning of our collective nature, and comedy itself, through the hearts and minds of The Heroes of Comedy. May you find your truest self and greatest strengths in the words that lie ahead.

Who Are They?

Anchors are most in touch with teaching. Whether gladly or reluctantly, they are the voice of reason to those around them. They know how the world works and offer comfort and guidance to their friends and family who don't. They have a reasonable amount of book smarts, but their superpower is plain old common sense. Anchors enjoy the attention and respect they receive from being known as the most stalwart member of their tribe. They are smart, straightforward, sensible, and loving. The Anchor gives great advice.

They are not only intelligent, but seemingly omnipresent. Anchors are always in the know when it comes to what is going on with their circle of friends and family. They move through the world with a balanced understanding of structured group dynamics and measured tough love.

Everything they say and do makes complete sense to themselves and most people. Unfortunately, Anchors are surrounded by others who are foolhardy, selfish and uptight or a combination thereof. The other members of the tribe need to be parented or managed. The resolute Anchor is never off the clock.

Since it's exhausting to always be the most sensible one in the room, Anchors often have an aura of martyrdom surrounding them. As loving as they are, they do carry the weight of the world on their shoulders. Either someone is asking the Anchor for help or, out of an innate sense of duty, they feel obligated to correct, train, or enlighten those around them, oftentimes without being asked.

Because of their inherent need to teach and support, the Anchor experiences a tremendous amount of frustration, which they internalize and suppress for the greater good. Simply stated, it's hard telling everyone what to do all the time. In their view, they don't get nearly enough gratitude! The job of the Anchor within a group is critically important but, more often than not, thankless.

Nine of the 10 Heroes of Comedy use sarcasm to produce humor. The Innocent is the only one who doesn't, and I'll elaborate more on that within their chapter. The Anchor, on the other hand, *thrives* on sarcasm. I'd even go as far as proffering that an actor needs a strong, personal relationship with playful sarcasm in order to fully realize the potential of this archetype.

Sarcasm is the Anchor's primary comedic tool and nearly the *only* way in which they produce humor. They do not have quirks or inherently comical personality traits on which to rely for laughs. They're not wacky and they lack neuroses, selfishness, or immaturity that make other archetypal characters intrinsically comical.

When Anchors, in particular, are sarcastic to those around them, which they often are, they are accomplishing two very important things; they are blowing off steam a little bit at a time so they don't explode. Additionally, they are adhering to their life agenda, which is to nudge those around them in the right direction. If the Anchor didn't joke, tease, and cajole with sarcasm, all they would ever do is lecture.

The Anchor's sarcasm might veer toward sharp and pointed on occasion, but it usually has an undercurrent of loving humor and education. When the Anchor ignites sarcasm, they're usually saying something in the subtext akin to, "Do you *really* think that was a good idea?"

It doesn't always feel good to be pierced by a sarcasm-dipped dart, but self-reflection sometimes stings. Even when sarcasm is mean or causes embarrassment, it's also a cue for the recipient to review their behavior or thought process.

Debra Barone (Patricia Heaton) of *Everybody Loves Raymond* fame is one of the best examples of an Anchor ever depicted on television. Patricia Heaton won two Primetime Emmy Awards for Outstanding Lead Actress in a Comedy Series for playing the long-suffering wife and mother who gave up a professional public relations career for family life.

Debra is smart, college-educated, dedicated to her family, and a giant martyr. She is married to a great, big man-baby, Raymond (Ray Romano), whom she practically has to care for as a fourth child. Debra and Raymond live across the street from Raymond's disapproving and overbearing parents.

Philip Rosenthal, the creator of *Everybody Loves Raymond*, used Ray Romano's stand-up as source material for the iconic series, and set up the perfect environment for the Anchor's inherent abilities to be simultaneously maximized and challenged. Debra is smart, loving, and right. She is also perennially frustrated, martyred, and sarcastic.

Debra clearly loves Raymond, but she often calls him an idiot literally, as well as in subtler ways:

RAYMOND: I know how your mind works.

DEBRA: You don't even know how *your* mind works.

It's established in the series that before Raymond, Debra dated better educated and wealthier men. It begs the question, then, why did she marry someone to whom she feels superior? In theory, smart people (evolved people) want an equal partner. Perhaps her ego gets validation from the inequity she perceives between her and her husband's overall intelligence.

Debra seems exhausted by Raymond most of the time, but he's the exact same man she chose to marry. Ideally, we'd all celebrate the primary qualities of our partner, not spend our marriage chastising them for being the person they've always been and expecting they'll change. When we consider this paradigm, we start to see the cracks in the steel-forged Anchor.

Another way in which *Everybody Loves Raymond* is masterful in examining the psychology of an Anchor centered in the eye of a family hurricane, is Debra's series-long quest for approval from her mother-in-law, Marie Barone (Doris Roberts). Debra is reasonable, stable, and rational as are all Anchors.

Marie is a disapproving, smothering Narcissist who is critical of Debra in every way, with no signs that she'll ever change her opinion. Yet, as smart as she is, Debra wants Marie to not only like her, but also validate her as a great wife, mother, and daughter-in-law. That's exactly what Marie does *not* want to do because it would only serve to loosen her stranglehold on her family. Marie is the matriarch of *two* households and only sees Debra as a potential threat, especially if she were to thrive as a stay-at-home mother like she has.

Debra would be a lot less frustrated if she managed her expectations, let go of caring about what Marie thinks of her, and set better boundaries. She tries throughout the series, but almost like an addict, she relapses back to her investment in Marie's opinion of her.

The disapproving mother-in-law is an often-mined trope; we've seen it time and time again in stories both comedic and dramatic. It's an example of why the simple exploration of family life will always be interesting to watch. We all go through trials of this nature in our lives; it helps to examine and process our own family challenges when they are reflected on TV.

Debra thinks of herself as the most clear-headed and logical of the bunch. I'd agree that she's smart, but her self-awareness and evolution as a truly enlightened being are in question. It's definitely a challenge if someone in your family causes you to feel badly or insecure about yourself. However, it's always your option to change how you react and/or distance yourself from anything or anyone that discourages you.

Fortunately, Debra's lack of introspection leads her to one of my personal favorite television meltdowns. After their son Michael (Sullivan Sweeten) writes a story about a "mean family," his teacher calls Raymond and Debra in to school to discuss Michael's emotional well-being. The conversation veers precariously toward the implication that Debra, out of everyone, is the instigator of strife in the family. Debra is gobsmacked and instinctively defends herself, revealing her true feelings about her in-laws, which lurk just beneath the surface of her put together facade.

 DEBRA: Eileen... you have no idea what I have to put up with. When I got married, I didn't just get a husband; I got a whole freak show that set up their tent right across the street. And that would be fine...if they stayed there! But every day – *every day* – they dump a truckload of their insane family dreck into my lap! How would you like to sit through two people in their 60s, fighting over who invented the lawn? The *lawn!* And then the brother! "I live in an apartment. I don't even have a lawn; Raymond has a lawn!" But you can't *blame* them when you see who the mother is! She has this kind of sick hold on the both of them, and the father's about as disgusting a creature as God has ever dropped on this planet! So no wonder the kid writes stories! I should be writing stories! My life is a Gothic novel... and until you have lived in that house, with all of them in there with you day after day, week after week, year after friggin' year, *you are in no position to judge me!*

What a perfect example of the Anchor at her breaking point. It would seem someone forced this life on Debra, yet it's the life she chose. If she thinks Raymond's mother is deranged and his father is the living definition of disgusting, why does she care what they think of her?

It seems she has genuine pity for Raymond and his brother for having been raised by these people, but she desperately wants their approval. She depicts her life as a daily test of patience and tolerance, while viewing herself as the central figure in the group who is normal, sane, and right. That's martyrdom plus codependence; the dysfunctional motor that powers the Anchor as they willingly tow everyone's baggage through life.

What Is Their Strength?

The Anchor's greatest strength is their ability to ground others, calm them, and keep them attached to the earth. Everyone needs a lifeguard and the Anchor is it. Got arrested? Call an Anchor for bail. Bad breakup? The Anchor will dry your tears. Guilty conscience? The Anchor will guide you toward the right choice, even if it's painful. Practical as the day is long, the Anchor has cash stashed away in the cookie jar for a rainy day.

Anchors have a strong sense of family, given or chosen, and will put their own needs selflessly aside in order to take care of other people. They can be an actual parent or easily fulfill that role as a friend, coworker, lover, or spouse. They know how to listen and aren't afraid of other people's problems.

In the pilot of *Parks and Recreation*, we meet Ann Perkins (Rashida Jones) a nurse, living with her boyfriend, Andy Dwyer (Chris Pratt). Andy is a simple, sweet, unemployed guy who plays in a band and has two broken legs because he drunkenly fell into a large, open pit. Ann meets the woman who is destined to become her best, albeit needy, friend, Leslie Knope (Amy Poehler), because she's trying to get the city to fill in the dangerous, open pit that rests right in the middle of her neighborhood. Just what any practical, conscientious community member would do.

Ann is happy to care for Andy, making him pancakes on demand as he recovers. He's oblivious to Ann's sacrifice and she doesn't mention it, choosing to swallow her resentment instead. Couch-bound, Andy strums his guitar and plays video games, asking more and more of Ann as he grows increasingly accustomed to being pampered. Unaware that she's compromising her own happiness for another's, Ann works hard to heal Andy physically and manage their relationship alone. At one point, Leslie even calls her out on it: "He's got three crutches, and one of them is you. And the other two are crutches!"

As with all Anchors, Ann's strength morphs directly into her weakness when taken too far. It's like when a superhero uses their power past its fullest extent, and they're left drained and debilitated until they recharge. Ann breaks up with Andy at the end of the first season when she discovers that Andy could have had his leg casts removed two weeks earlier than he did. He lied to Ann because he enjoyed her devoted caretaking so much that he delayed their removal as long as possible. Like a demanding child, Andy unwittingly pushed his superhero past her breaking point.

Although Ann ended her romantic relationship with Andy, her nurturing tendencies and codependent nature relocated themselves to her relationship with Leslie for the remainder of the series. It's nearly impossible to review the Anchor — even their strengths and virtues — without discussing their weaknesses alongside them. On the surface, giving all of yourself to those in need all the time is considered good by most people. However, most therapists make their living by helping patients resolve this one issue alone: codependency. When the plane is going down, you need to put your oxygen mask on first.

What Is Their Weakness?

All The Heroes of Comedy suffer from arrested development, codependency, and the inability to set clear boundaries. The Anchor, however, is the worst of all of them in this regard.

Because of their practically perfect facade, they start buying into their own hype that they alone are the one within their tribe who is ever dependable and always right. It's not entirely their fault — *most of the time they are*. However, they almost always take that meme too far and can easily acquire a reputation as a downer, bossy know-it-all.

The Anchor's nurturing and caring nature drives them to become too involved in other people's business. Their investment stems from love, but it often overwhelms others who want *some* help, but are ill-prepared for the avalanche of advice-bordering-commands headed their way. Anchors are so busy correcting everyone else's behavior they can't see the codependent forest for the dysfunctional trees.

More often than not, they cause their own strife by taking on other people's worries and problems too much and not caring for themselves enough. We should all be willing to help the people in our inner circle, whatever our essential core traits. However, the Anchor is the only archetype or personality who will become more invested in the solution to someone else's problem than the person they're committed to helping.

The other characters around the Anchor may indeed be less together, but they are also more likely to acknowledge, own and even embrace their flaws and idiosyncrasies. The Anchor is so busy shoring up everyone else's weaknesses, they forget to take care of themselves, which ironically weakens them. In an effort to keep everything on track, they also fail to recognize any problem with their own behavior whatsoever.

Sometimes, a really powerful Anchor will go as far as to try to solve the problems of an entire nation; a noble aspiration, but probably too much responsibility for a single human to bear. Julia Sugarbaker (Dixie Carter), grande dame of the series *Designing Women*, would often try, however. In a televised debate with a pandering city councilman, Julia makes one of her iconic social justice speeches.

"I do not think everyone in America is ignorant! Far from it! But we are today, probably, the most uneducated, underread, and illiterate nation in the western hemisphere. Which makes it all the more puzzling to me why the biggest question on your small mind is whether little Johnny is going to recite the Pledge of Allegiance every morning!

I'll tell you something else, Mr. Brickett. I have had it up to here with you and your phony issues and your Yankee Doodle yakking! If you like reciting the Pledge of Allegiance every day, then I think you should do it! In the car! In the shower! Wherever the mood strikes you! But don't try to tell me when or where I have to say or do or salute anything, because I am an American too, and that is what being an American is all about!

And another thing, I am sick and tired of being made to feel that if I am not a member of a little family with 2.4 children who goes *just* to Jerry Falwell's church and puts their hands over their hearts every morning that I am unreligious, unpatriotic, and un-American! Because I have news for you, Mr. Brickett: all liberals are not kooks, any more than all conservatives are fascists! And the last time I checked, God was neither a Democrat nor a Republican! And just for your information, yes, I am a liberal, but I am also a Christian. And I get down on my knees and pray every day — on my own turf — on my own time.

One of the things that I pray for, Mr. Brickett, is that people with power will get good sense, and that people with good sense will get power and that the rest of us will be blessed with the patience and the strength to survive the people like you in the meantime!"

When sitcoms are written and performed at the top of their game, they can do several things at once; uplift, broaden, entertain, educate, and inspire. The particular episode in which Julia made this speech first aired in 1988. The substance of it is still relevant today. It will be interesting to see how far into the future it remains relevant.

As she often did, in order to cut through the white noise and make a point, Julia used her superpowers to their fullest extent. She exhausted herself for the good of the many but lost to her less capable and notably unkind opponent by a landslide. Rest, recover, and regroup, intrepid Anchor. Your work is never done. I mentioned it in the preface, but I'll remind you again here and throughout these chapters: archetypes are not a literary contrivance; they are a representative summary of the kinds of people we know and witness as we move through life.

How Do Others See Them?

The Anchor thinks they're the designated safeguard against chaos and utter foolishness within their personal universe. Everyone around them thinks they're all work and no play and wonder why they don't shirk some responsibility, lighten up, and just have some fun. The other, less responsible Heroes of Comedy think the Anchor is an oppressive stick in the mud. As a result, they respond to the Anchor like children testing boundaries against an authority figure. Like kids trying to provoke a reaction from mommy and daddy.

The ever-dutiful Anchor gets picked on a lot. Though they would never admit it, all the other archetypes are jealous of the Anchor. That envy might live way down in our emotional cellar, but somewhere inside, we all wish we were straightforward, practical, and worthy of universal respect. Most of the Anchor's qualities are admirable.

All their hard work and tenacity provides stability and structure, which is requisite for fun and freedom to flourish. We all sense that deep in our core, even if we're reluctant to acknowledge it openly. Someone has to pay the bills on time; somebody has to keep the lights on.

The way her housemates dissed Dorothy (Bea Arthur) on *The Golden Girls*, you would have thought she was a one-eyed troll. As the show's dedicated Anchor, Dorothy Zbornak is a teacher, mother, daughter, and friend. She has the most day-to-day responsibility of anyone in her tribe and does her level best to be the perpetual voice of reason.

As a result, all the Girls tease her relentlessly and unprovoked, including her own mother, Sofia (Estelle Getty). "Jealousy is a very ugly thing, Dorothy. And so are you in anything backless," she offers for no particular reason. Not everyone wants the responsibility that comes with being an Anchor, but they ultimately envy the Anchor's ability to manage life's daily tasks and crises. A jab here and there keeps them from becoming too superior.

How Do Writers Use Them?

Writers use Anchors as pack mules. They put great burdens on them so the audience can watch them struggle to get uphill with a heavy load. It's been that way since the beginning. *I Love Lucy*'s Ricky Ricardo (Desi Arnaz) had his hands full with his wife, Lucy (Lucille Ball), constantly scheming to break into show business.

He got so frustrated with her shenanigans, it sometimes seemed like steam was coming out his ears. Lucy is flighty, irreverent, and unpredictable. It is therefore Ricky's job as the Anchor to keep her grounded and rein in her endless desire. Too big a job for one man alone, Ricky often enlists the aid of their friends, Fred (William Frawley) and Ethel (Vivian Vance), to help keep Lucy tethered to the real world. A bandleader by trade, managing his wife's misplaced ambition is his second career.

On *The Golden Girls*, Sophia lived at the Shady Pines retirement home until it caught fire and burned. Displaced, she moves in with Dorothy, Rose (Betty White), and Blanche (Rue McClanahan), putting Dorothy in the onerous position of parenting her elderly mother while struggling to make a living. In addition, Dorothy has a freeloading ex-husband, Stan (Herb Edelman), who cheated on her, but still hovers around post-divorce looking for an occasional handout. Dorothy has a full plate with a second helping already heaped on.

As the Anchor on *Glee*, Will Schuester (Matthew Morrison) takes over the beat-up glee club, which consists of a ragtag group of misfits. A man on an admirable mission, he works to restore the performance group to its former glory, while simultaneously defending it from villainous cheerleading coach Sue Sylvester (Jane Lynch), who seemingly lives only to see the glee club destroyed.

A teacher with an archrival is the perfect dynamic with which to exploit all the Anchor's core characteristics. Part of the fun of watching *Glee* is the music, but what is essential for its successful six-season run is the universally relatable tenet of a mature and grounded adult caring for a diverse and vulnerable troop. Will has to nurture, support, parent, protect, and stabilize an entire tribe of artistically gifted kids who are needy, often ungrateful, and mock him constantly.

You can see a clear throughline in Anchors of both genders and how writers use them to create conflict and drive narrative over many years of a series. The Anchor chooses their life, but simultaneously feels trapped and occasionally suffocated by it. They have the greatest obligations of all The Heroes of Comedy and their practicality can be a bore. In the end, however, we'd be lost without their intelligence, clarity, and sound judgment.

What Is Your Way In?

As with all The Heroes of Comedy, the closer you are to the Anchor's core characteristics and daily world point of view, the more organic the fit and easier it is for producers to cast you in the role.

All of us can be caring, but not all of us identify as care*takers*. Not everyone is dutiful and aware of what's going on with everyone in their stratosphere. For example, I've found coaching and casting thousands of actors over the years that actors who are married and have children in real life have a very real advantage in being cast as spouses and parents. Don't get me wrong, anything can happen. Everyone has a shot at playing a character successfully.

But if your reality is that you work, manage your personal ambitions, and take care of your own household every day of your life, you automatically bring a deeper understanding of core family dynamics with you to a role that's defined by those circumstances. There's no way around it — maintaining a marriage and/or parenting is a very different experience of life than remaining free and single through your 30s and beyond, even if you have other responsibilities. This axiom applies to all characters. Imagination lets us pretend anything. In reality, a day-to-day understanding of a character's *primary* qualities and life circumstances makes casting an actor in a role easier and more seamless.

Your way into this archetype is to personalize the work with your understanding of management, leadership, duty, teaching, and responsibility. Personalizing your work as an actor *need not be literal*. Perhaps you're called upon to play a spouse and you've never been married. Have you been in any committed relationships? Do you have children in your life who look up to you? Nieces, nephews, or cousins who model themselves after you? Maybe you've been a camp counselor or a lifeguard for a summer. Do you take care of a pet or have you had to care for a parent?

This could be who you are on most days of your life within this stage of your life. If so, then the Anchor is a comfortable fit. If not, think of any time in your life when you've had to step up to the plate for a person, a group, or a team and really be there for someone else.

Most of us have tended to the well-being of someone or something other than ourselves at some point. Consider when that might have been the case for you and that's where you start designing your version of this sturdy human being who keeps the train on the track against formidable, sometimes ridiculous odds.

The Anchor in a Family-Based Series: *Roseanne*

Roseanne Conner (Roseanne Barr) is the quintessential television wife and mother. There are plenty of other great moms throughout television history, but there's no question their day-to-day lives were idealized. When *Roseanne* came along, audiences across America and eventually the world finally got to see a highly relatable working-class family struggling with typical problems that ranged from a broken sink to teenage pregnancy to trying to pay the rent with an Anchor mom at the helm.

From the second *Roseanne* aired, it was just so remarkably easy to watch. There is no high concept to buy into. There's not even much of a story in the first episode. The Conners were simply living their Midwestern, blue-collar lives and one day America started watching them and rooting for them.

We've met all those people before, we've had those conversations, and it felt like home. For my money, the pilot and the bulk of the series is an exercise in the sublime. There is no hook with *Roseanne*. It begins quietly and explores typical family life with astounding depth and intelligence.

Roseanne was truly revolutionary and in its own, simple way more subversive, feminist, and dangerous than any other sitcom featuring a nuclear family with young children. I can summarize the reason why in one word: Roseanne. Based on her stand-up act in which she proclaimed herself a Domestic Goddess, Roseanne singlehandedly unleashed the full power and authority of the word, "Mom."

It wasn't until *Roseanne* arrived, that we were *finally* treated to a series driven by a previously overlooked, very basic, globally universal truth: smart moms are nearly always in charge of the household, and it's a woman's perspective that defines the day-to-day life of the family as a whole. Period. Full stop.

Are there exceptions? Sure. There are exceptions to everything. But *Roseanne* the show and Roseanne the character finally gave the world a series about *keeping a loving family together*, viewed through the lens of a smart, capable woman who could stare down a grizzly bear and get dinner on the table nightly. Are all moms like that? No. Does everyone want a mom like that? Yes.

Roseanne Barr won a Primetime Emmy Award for Outstanding Lead Actress in a Comedy Series portraying Roseanne Conner. While her acting career is otherwise unnoteworthy, Roseanne Barr grew into the role of Roseanne Conner incredibly well. She held her own against two powerhouse, award-winning actors — John Goodman and Laurie Metcalf.

Roseanne is invested in her family and frighteningly omni-present. Her husband and her children fear her, but they would be utterly lost without her. Throughout the series, Roseanne expresses her personal ambition, which is to write, but she's so attuned to caring for her kids that she never follows through.

The woman it seems who could do anything, fix anything, and defend her family against any threat could never make time and keep time for herself. Like all Anchors, Roseanne's weakness is codependency. She hides her fears and insecurities about losing her identity as a mom behind her aura of authority.

As the series progresses and the children get older and less dependent, we see Roseanne moved off her center. She holds on too tightly, particularly when her two teenage daughters become young women and develop romantic relationships with brothers.

At different points, Roseanne invites both of her daughter's boyfriends to live in her house so she can keep everyone close and stay involved. Smothering is only one letter away from mothering and her kids call Roseanne out on that quite often.

Throughout this book, I quote characters' dialogue to illustrate their point of view, but in this one instance, I will quote Rosanne Barr, the Domestic Goddess herself. "There's a lot more to being a woman than being a mother, but there's a hell of a lot more to being a mother than most people suspect." Roseanne Conner couldn't have stated it better herself.

The Anchor in a Friend-Based Series: *Will & Grace*

The next best thing to having a stable, grounded parent is having a great friend who will fill the void in the absence of one. Will Truman, played with unnerving efficiency by Emmy Award winner Eric McCormack on *Will & Grace*, seems to have it all. He is handsome. He is witty. He is a successful lawyer with a great apartment in New York City. He is also the figurative foster father of three.

As the Anchor on *Will & Grace*, Will supports his friend Jack (Sean Hayes) financially to a large degree, and Jack very much treats Will's home like his parents' house. He walks in unannounced, eats what he wants, takes what he needs, and stays as long as he pleases. Will serves as Grace's (Debra Messing) human emotional support blanket, and although she's never not insulting him, whenever Karen (Megan Mullally) needs a lawyer, which she often does, she goes straight to Will. He manages all their disparate, daily needs and is paid back with ridicule.

Even as adults we're apt to lean on our parents from time to time. So it's worth asking why Grace, Jack, and Karen didn't seek support from theirs. Well, let's review...

Grace's mother is a hypercritical theater actress who upstages Grace whenever she's around and sucks up all the oxygen in the room. Her father is a withholding, distant curmudgeon, who Grace says, "Hasn't noticed anything I've done since I was 12 years old, left the door open, and let the cat get out. Tells the story over and over... it's not even funny."

Jack was conceived at a pool party for swingers in the 60s and treated horribly by his stepfather, who he thought was his real father for most of his life.

Karen was used by her con artist mother to help cheat people out of their money. She'd make Karen pretend she was sick or blind to manipulate people into making charitable donations.

There's sufficient evidence that, however the rest of the group feels about their parents, they don't seem to be people who are equipped to help them with their lives as they are at this point. So they use Will as a surrogate parent whom they can come home to whenever the going gets tough.

Karen and Jack aside, Will's relationship with Grace alone provides enough material to write a psychological case study on codependency. Will and Grace met in college and began dating before Will became fully accepting of his sexual attraction to men.

Will initially proposed marriage to Grace in order to avoid having sex with her or telling her that he thought he might be gay. Forced to either come out or start planning a wedding, Will ultimately told Grace the truth. They fought, didn't speak for a year, then reunited and became best lifelong friends. With that history, their friendship has more layers than most.

They became roommates after Grace broke up with her fiancé Danny. A year later Grace moved out, but right across the hall from Will's place. Will and Grace later decide to have a baby together through in vitro fertilization and make a pact to raise it together.

However, Grace takes pause when she meets a handsome man on a horse, Leo (Harry Connick, Jr.). Will feels hurt and betrayed when Grace changes her mind about having a baby with him and they tear into each other with an epic and not at all humorous argument, which nearly annihilates their friendship.

WILL: Oh, I can't believe this! This is only the most important thing we've ever done together, and you flake out on me? I don't know why that's surprising; you're a flake!

GRACE: All I asked for was one month. One month! To see where this is going.

WILL: Oh, let me tell you where this is going. You'll end up hating him in three weeks because – I don't know – he has a weird chest hair pattern. Or he doesn't like watching E! Or he'll end up hating you because you're too needy. Then you'll fall apart, I'll pick you up and then *magically*, you'll be ready to have a baby.

GRACE: Look, I'm sorry I met someone because I know how much you hate it when I'm happy.

WILL: Oh, that is such a load!

GRACE: Admit it! You're happiest when I'm miserable. I mean, c'mon… isn't that our thing? Because then you don't have to look at how miserable you are.

WILL: Shut up, Grace!

GRACE: But I am not gonna be miserable for you! I am gonna try to be happy. And if you can't deal with that, then you are even more pathetic than I thought!

WILL: Get outta here.

GRACE: Go to hell!

WILL: No, I mean it! I want you outta here in two weeks. You don't live here anymore.

Even though he's gay, she's straight, and she's trying to move forward with a healthy romantic relationship of her own, Will is the one who holds on tightest to the image of he and Grace as a couple; platonic but eternally committed. Good money would have been on Grace being the intractable one in their convoluted bond. After all, Grace was in love with Will and Will was never in love with her.

But Will *needs* Grace. He turns out to be the one who's come down with a severe case of codependency, which is defined by a one-sided relationship where one person relies on the other for meeting nearly all their emotional and personal needs. (I want a baby and if you don't give me one, I hate you and want you out of my life. Ouch.)

It also describes a relationship that enables another person to maintain their irresponsible, addictive, or underachieving behavior. (I want you to sacrifice a chance at a real husband for me because creating a pretend family with you feels safer than creating one with another man.)

As bad as that fight is, and as complicated as their lives together are, Will and Grace reconcile. Things stay good between them but not for long. The original series finale is bittersweet.

Grace ends up marrying Leo, who later cheats on her. She divorces him and heads straight back to Will. After becoming roommates again, Grace coincidentally runs into Leo on an airplane and hooks up with him in the sky. Shortly thereafter, she finds out she is pregnant with Leo's child, but at the time, he's engaged to another woman and lives in Rome, so Grace doesn't tell him.

Instead, she and Will revisit the idea of raising a child together, even though this time, the baby's father is Leo. As *Will & Grace*'s original run comes to a close, Grace decides to reunite with Leo, and Will comes undone once again.

This time the stakes are higher since unbeknownst to Grace, Will breaks up with his boyfriend, Bobby, in order to keep his commitment to Grace and her unborn child. In the end, Will and Grace drift apart. It seems that if they can't be friends who exist as a married couple, they can't be friends at all.

In Will Truman, we again have an Anchor who is exhausted by the endless work of helping his tribe cope with life. From his point of view, he extends himself further than most would because of a vague notion that he *has* to. But no one *has* to do anything they don't want to do. Even if there is a certain expectation of participation in his closest friends' lives, he doesn't have to extend himself *as much as he does*.

People behave in ways that work for them. They only change when that behavior stops working. That's as true a statement for you and me as it is for Will. In truth, Will likes feeling superior and spending time with less competent friends feeds that hunger. Will would not likely describe himself as someone with adolescent tendencies and arrested development. But we are all defined by our actions, not our perceptions. Upon review, Will Truman's behavior does not sync up with his own self-image.

The Anchor in a Work-Based Series: *Arrested Development*
Speaking of "arrested development"… Michael Bluth (Jason Bateman), you could have moved away from that shallow, vain, and constantly troubled family of yours at any time, you know! You've even talked about it once, twice, or a thousand times. When we meet you in the pilot, you say you're leaving town with your son, George-Michael (Michael Cera), but you don't go. You

keep on staying, claiming they can't live without you. Or is it really the other way around and you just can't see it?

Most people see multiple Emmy Award-winning and critical darling *Arrested Development* as a family-based show. I certainly don't disagree. The resilient series that rebounded onto Netflix with new episodes seven years after its cancellation on the Fox network features arguably the overall most dysfunctional family in television sitcom history.

But that family owns a business, The Bluth Company. The storylines of *Arrested Development*, especially in the beginning, are very much driven by the events that occur within their multi-pronged corporation. The opening scene of the pilot of *Arrested Development* features a shot of Michael Bluth on a boat where his father's retirement party is taking place.

There is a title card in the first moment of the show, which reads, "Michael Bluth, Manager/The Bluth Company." Ron Howard's voice narrates as we meet Michael for the first time, "This is Michael Bluth. For 10 years, he's worked for his father's company, waiting to be made a partner. And right now… he's happy."

In order to prove his loyalty to the family business, Michael and his son George-Michael live in a model home of his father's latest housing tract, which consists of just that one generically decorated house surrounded by barren, undeveloped land. For his part, George-Michael works at the Bluth's Original Frozen Banana stand on the pier.

When George Bluth, Sr. (Jeffrey Tambor) makes his big announcement back on the boat, he appoints wife Lucille (Jessica Walter) as his successor, not Michael. The very next moment the police arrive along with the Securities and Exchange Commission, who board the boat and arrest George for "defrauding investors and using the company as his personal piggy bank."

Once it becomes clear that George will be in jail for a while, Lucille punts her responsibility for running the company to her most malleable of three sons, Buster (Tony Hale). Fearing ever-responsible Michael will cut off the endless flow of money she siphons off the publicly traded Bluth Company, Lucille makes the rash decision, which she quickly comes to regret.

When high-strung Buster has a panic attack and collapses his first day on the job, the family stages an intervention to keep Michael from leaving town and stay to run the company. Because his family is unaware of what an intervention actually is, Michael has to ask his mother, his brother Gob (Will Arnett), and his sister Lindsay (Portia de Rossi) for an explanation as to why they are all gathered.

> MICHAEL: I'm sorry, I'm sorry... what *exactly* is this intervention for?

> LUCILLE: We need you to come back and run the business.

> MICHAEL: Ah! Okay. So technically, it's not really an intervention. It's a little bit more of an imposition? If you think about it...

> LINDSAY: Oh, whatever you call it.

> MICHAEL: I'd love to call it an imposition. (THEN) Well, I'm sorry. It's just... It's too late. I'm moving to Phoenix. I got a job.

They all stare blankly.

> MICHAEL: It's something you apply for and then they pay you to, uh... never mind! I don't want to ruin the

surprise. So, no hard feelings, adios. Sayonara. I'll see you when the first parent dies.

Lindsay suggests Michael at least visit their father in prison before he leaves town. Michael considers this and decides to give his father "the courtesy of a formal resignation." Once Michael actually says the words, "I quit," his father explains that he didn't hand over the company to him because he knew it would make Michael an accomplice and he'd wind up in jail too. Cold comfort to Michael, who is still resigned to head to Phoenix with his son, until he stumbles on George-Michael saying an emotional goodbye to his Aunt Lindsay, expressing his desire to spend more time with his family.

A widower, Michael is moved. As dysfunctional as his family is, it's the only one he's got. The fact that his son has no mother is an important factor in Michael sticking around. He starts to reconsider and ultimately changes his mind to stay after talking it over with Lindsay, who hasn't been in town for over a year and came only for their father's retirement party.

When Michael asks her where she's been, Lindsay admits she and her husband Tobias (David Cross) are broke and in a lot of debt. She didn't want Michael to know because he's so judgmental, which he adamantly denies. She adds that she also knew he would be disappointed in her. Michael is genuinely confused for a moment.

MICHAEL: I'm not disappointed in you!

LINDSAY: You are.

MICHAEL: So, I'm disappointed in you. But, c'mon, what is not disappointing about my life? I mean Dad

GUNNAR ROHRBACHER: THE COMEDY CODE

didn't give me the promotion... Dad's in jail. How disappointing is that?

LINDSAY: So, we're a disappointing family.

MICHAEL: We're an incredibly disappointing family. But we are a family. And I want my son to be happy. So maybe we should be in each other's lives.

With that, Michael decides to stay in California and try to save the family business. He moves his down-on-their-luck sister and brother-in-law into the Bluth model home, along with his niece Maeby (Alia Shawkat). He doesn't get a single bit of gratitude in return.

Interestingly, all the other Anchors mentioned in this chapter are reviewed over many seasons. Their strengths, weaknesses, core characteristics, neuroses, and personalities revealed themselves over time. In the case of *Arrested Development*, Michael Bluth's caring, martyred, codependent feathers are on full display from the beginning, like a pushy peacock in need of therapy but without any time for it.

Characteristics of the Anchor

- Bossy
- Caring
- Competent
- Confrontational
- Cooperative
- Direct
- Efficient
- Far-sighted
- Frugal
- Grounded
- Hardworking
- Homey
- Insightful
- Intelligent
- Intuitive
- Judicious
- Maternal/Paternal
- Motivational
- Nurturing
- Patient
- Pragmatic
- Present
- Protective
- Rational
- Reasonable
- Reliable
- Responsible
- Sarcastic (Particularly)
- Shrewd
- Smart-ass
- Solid
- Stable
- Stoic
- Supportive
- Sympathetic
- Tolerant
- Trustworthy
- Understanding
- Vigilant
- Weary

Anchors Throughout the History of Television

CHARACTER	ACTOR	SERIES
Penelope Alvarez	Justina Machado	One Day at a Time (2017)
Debra Barone	Patricia Heaton	Everybody Loves Raymond
Vanessa Baxter	Nancy Travis	Last Man Standing
Pam Beesly	Jenna Fischer	The Office
Mark Berman	Damian Young	The Comeback
Mike Biggs	Billy Gardell	Mike & Molly
Michael Bluth	Jason Bateman	Arrested Development
Carol Brady	Florence Henderson	The Brady Bunch
Mike Brady	Robert Reed	The Brady Bunch
Kyle Broflovski	Matt Stone	South Park
Joelle Brooks	Ashley Featherson	Dear White People
Jamie Buchman	Helen Hunt	Mad About You
Andi Burns	Liza Snyder	Man with a Plan
George Burns	George Burns	The Burns and Allen Show
Cheryl	Courtney Thorne-Smith	According to Jim
June Cleaver	Barbara Billingsley	Leave It to Beaver
Wally Cleaver	Tony Dow	Leave It to Beaver
Ward Cleaver	Hugh Beaumont	Leave It to Beaver
Travis Cobb	Dan Byrd	Cougar Town
Mary Cooper	Zoe Perry	Young Sheldon

Roseanne Conner	Roseanne Barr	Roseanne
Philip Drummond	Conrad Bain	Diff'rent Strokes
Debbie Eagan	Betty Gilpin	GLOW
Florida Evans	Esther Rolle	Good Times
Fiona Gallagher	Emmy Rossum	Shameless
Nell Harper	Nell Carter	Gimme a Break!
Emily Hartley	Suzanne Pleshette	The Bob Newhart Show
Carrie Heffernan	Leah Remini	The King of Queens
Cate Hennessy	Katey Sagal	8 Simple Rules
Georgina Hobart	Gwyneth Paltrow	The Politician
Leonard Hofstadter	Johnny Galecki	The Big Bang Theory
Finn Hudson	Cory Monteith	Glee
Clair Huxtable	Phylicia Rashad	The Cosby Show
Alice Hyatt	Linda Lavin	Alice
Khajidah James	Queen Latifah	Living Single
Cathy Jamison	Laura Linney	The Big C
Louise Jefferson	Isabel Sanford	The Jeffersons
Lana Kane	Aisha Tyler	Archer
Elyse Keaton	Meredith Baxter	Family Ties
Steven Keaton	Michael Gross	Family Ties
Mindy Kominsky	Sarah Baker	The Kominsky Method
Alice Kramden	Audrey Meadows	The Honeymooners
Joanna Loudon	Mary Frann	Newhart

Wanda Mc-Cullough	Kellita Smith	The Bernie Mac Show
Barney Miller	Hal Linden	Barney Miller
Sharon Morris	Sharon Horgan	Catastrophe
Nanny	Juliet Mills	Nanny and the Professor
Didi Ortley	Niecy Nash	Getting On
Greg Otto	Diedrich Bader	American Housewife
Shirley Partridge	Shirley Jones	The Partridge Family
Ann Perkins	Rashida Jones	Parks and Recreation
Hawkeye Pierce	Alan Alda	M*A*S*H
Donna Pinciotti	Laura Prepon	That '70s Show
Charlotte Rae	Mrs. Garrett	The Facts of Life
Alex Reiger	Judd Hirsch	Taxi
Ricky Ricardo	Desi Arnaz	I Love Lucy
Rochelle	Tichina Arnold	Everybody Hates Chris
Ann Romano	Bonnie Franklin	One Day at a Time
Johnny Rose	Eugene Levy	Schitt's Creek
Lynette Scavo	Felicity Huffman	Desperate Housewives
Will Schuester	Matthew Morrison	Glee
Jerry Seinfeld	Jerry Seinfeld	Seinfeld
Tommy Solomon	Joseph Gordon-Levitt	3rd Rock from the Sun
Samantha Stephens	Elizabeth Montgomery	Bewitched

Julia Sugarbaker	Dixie Carter	Designing Women
Arthur Tack	James Urbaniak	Difficult People
Jill Taylor	Patricia Richardson	Home Improvement
Andy Taylor	Andy Griffith	The Andy Griffith Show
Will Truman	Eric McCormack	Will & Grace
Abe Weissman	Tony Shalhoub	The Marvelous Mrs. Maisel
Malcolm Wilkerson	Frankie Muniz	Malcolm in the Middle
Gloria Windsor	Bernadette Peters	Mozart in the Jungle
Dorothy Zbornak	Bea Arthur	The Golden Girls

How Anchors are Described in the Breakdowns

Appealing, caretaker, competent, decent, earth mother, fatherly, feminist, full of an easy kind of love, matriarch, motherly, natural leader, nice, normal, nurturing, only sane one in the bunch, patriarch, pillar of the family, poised, pragmatic, principled, sharp, solid, straight arrow, upstanding, voice of reason in a sea of chaos.

Lead Body Part: Feet

The Anchor has a balanced, athletic stance. Their feet rest directly underneath their shoulders and knees bent slightly. They are ready to pivot at any given moment. They oversee, teach, and manage others around them, so they must be ready to move in any direction at any given time. Stable as an ancient redwood, the Anchor is rooted to the ground and not easily thrown off center. With the wisdom of trees, Anchors draw energy upward from the earth to provide for their tribe in myriad ways.

DREAMER

"Happy Valentine's Day, no one!"

—*Liz Lemon*/*30 Rock*

Mantra: "I hope"

Strength: Resilient

Weakness: Immature

Typical jobs: Artistic, Survival Gig, In Search of Purpose, Lower Level in Career, Blue Collar

Who Are They?

Dreamers are open hearts on two legs. They live in a world of endless hope and aching desire. Everyone has dreams, but the Dreamer is defined by their ambitions in a way the other Heroes of Comedy are not. Sometimes they march toward their goals with boundless energy and enthusiasm, and sometimes we see them slog through the muddy swamp of self-doubt and self-loathing. Whatever the emotional temperature is that day, however, they *keep on going*.

All Dreamers vacillate between radiating optimism at the mere thought of a chance for success and wallowing in despair when the universe serves them yet another cosmic smackdown. You can spot them in stories as the person whose goal always seems to be just out of reach.

The goal can be as simple and universal as the desire for a rewarding career and happy romantic relationship. That's all Grace (Debra Messing) wants on *Will & Grace*, the same as Chandler Bing (Matthew Perry) on *Friends*, Molly Flynn (Melissa McCarthy) on *Mike & Molly,* and a long list of others.

Conversely, the Dreamer can strive for a goal that lies beyond fulfillment of common, daily life. Their dream can be grand, illusory, outside of their skill set, ill-conceived, nearly impossible to obtain, or a combination thereof.

Leslie Knope (Amy Poehler) on *Parks and Recreation* wants to create a better world through a well-functioning government bureaucracy. Maura Pfefferman (Jeffrey Tambor) wants a drama-free, broadly accepted transition from living as a man to a woman on *Transparent*. Hailey Rutledge (Lola Kirke) on *Mozart in the Jungle* wants to join the New York Symphony as one of its youngest members. Those are all worthy objectives that have small odds of success. The resilient and tenacious Dreamers acknowledge the mountainous obstacles and soldier forward nonetheless.

On *The Big Bang Theory*, Penny is the resident Dreamer. Of course, she is. She's a young woman who moves from Omaha to Los Angeles to become an actor. The writers of *The Big Bang Theory* did an excellent job of humanizing Penny's journey and depicting the life of an aspiring actor realistically. In the beginning of the series, Penny waits tables and books occasional acting jobs (of note, a hemorrhoid commercial), but never scores a big win.

As the series progresses, she quits her money-making gig at The Cheesecake Factory and transitions to working in pharmaceutical sales with the aid of her friend, Bernadette (Melissa Rauch). She soon earns significantly more money than her physicist husband Leonard (Johnny Galecki).

However, she ultimately reveals that she hates her new career, but also does not want to return to waitressing or acting. Penny has occasional triumphs, but she's never satisfied with her place in the world the way her friends are. Maybe that's why she drinks so much. Sometimes a yearning for something undefined sets the course for the Dreamer as much as a desire for a specific ambition. Remember this valiant Dreamers, "All that is gold does not glitter, not all those who wander are lost." J.R.R. Tolkien.

On *I Love Lucy*, Lucy (Lucille Ball) is also laser-targeted on breaking into show business. Her husband, Ricky, is a famous singer and bandleader. They live in New York and during the series, travel to Hollywood for an extended stay. She lives agonizingly close to the limelight, but is constantly thwarted by both her lack of talent and encouragement by her friends and family. When she nevertheless forces her way in, things usually proceed poorly, fall apart entirely or she is literally dragged off the stage. Back in the days of vaudeville, theater managers kept a long hook in the wings to drag off incompetent but stubbornly persistent performers. Lucy got the hook a lot.

Dreamers are substantial human beings. They roll up their sleeves and try. They get knocked down all the time and get back up again, somehow managing never to lose their enthusiasm and zest for life. They are not to be confused with people you would consider passengers in life — daydreamers who sit at home and idly imagine a different life as the world spins around.

Dreamers do not stare into clouds and ponder. Just the opposite. The Dreamer archetype is probably the most often used hero in storytelling because more than any other, the Dreamer embarks on their journey with all their might. We see our own aspirations reflected in the Dreamer not because they are *wishing*, but because they are *doing*. Their whole existence is a verb.

Dreamers are hope in action.

They try. The Dreamer also fails a lot. Their stumbles are always out in the open for everyone to see. That's tough. Although their egos are frequently bruised and battered, they endure and find their way back toward optimism even when their hopes are trammeled.

They're acutely aware of the humor within the horror. They will be picked on, teased, and laughed at and it will sting their open hearts. If they can take themselves down a peg first, then they've beaten the world to the punch. There is some cold comfort and a tiny bit of power in saying, "I know I'm a loser" to the world before the world has a chance to say it to you.

What Is Their Strength?

The Dreamer's strength is their ability to remain hopeful even when there are no visible signs they should. Dreamers are resilient. They have to be because they rarely, if ever, get what they want. When they do achieve a goal, it's not easily or immediately. The internal support mechanism for their ability to try, try, and *try again* is hope. Dreamers rebound after a setback like no other because of boundless optimism.

Their attachment to their deeply felt personal desires keeps them afloat even when sailing on rocky seas. Some would assess the Dreamer as delusional; others would admire their persistence. Perhaps there is a fine line. Many great human achievements took a long time to culminate with critics assailing all chances for victory along the way. Are mistakes and obstacles fatal to any given endeavor? Or are they perhaps opportunities to learn and refine a plan that may result in delayed victory? It's all a matter of perspective, really.

Each of us is the only one who truly knows what our heart wants and what we're willing to sacrifice to acquire it. A dream is only as worthy as the person enabling it. In that regard, Dreamers are vessels for possibility.

Artists are inherently dreamers. We have to be. Actors, writers, singers, dancers, and visual artists display their creativity for the world to see knowing it will be judged. Whatever the reviews, it takes great resolve to live an extraordinary life and share your perspective, talents, and gifts. Hopefully all of you reading this can relate to this archetype to some degree.

The Dreamer is ultimately the universal archetype for storytelling because it can be pared down to a single word that includes every person who ever lived or ever will. It's their mantra; hope. Everyone experiences hopefulness, and no one is immune to it. There are dozens of characteristics to describe someone that are not *at all* universal. Is *everyone* in the world... bold? No. Empathetic? No. Hypersexual? No. Trusting? No. Paranoid? No. Generous? No. Vapid? No. Intimidating? No.

But everyone hopes for something. Even if their circumstances are miserable, there is always hope they won't be forever. The case for hope is founded in an inexorable truth — life is metamorphosis. Nothing is static. It's not cliché to say, "There is always hope." There actually *is* always hope because change is constant and indifferent.

Whether the change is good or bad is a matter of individual perception. The Dreamer knows this instinctively in their heart whether or not they ever come to a complete understanding of why hope *really does* spring eternal in their head.

In order for this concept to fully coalesce, it's important to note that hope is not exactly the same as desire and other words that may seem synonymous. Desire is a yearning for a specific thing or outcome. Desire can disappoint.

Hope is the feeling that what is wanted can be had or that events will turn out for the best. Hope is desire plus trust. It's connectivity to our collective consciousness and the belief that we are cared for by something greater than the sum total of our experiences. Hope is a philosophy unto itself.

Kimmy Schmidt (Ellie Kemper) is the embodiment of resiliency nourished by hopefulness on *Unbreakable Kimmy Schmidt.* "Be you. Be what you want. And then become unbreakable," she declares.

The premise of the show is outlandish; Kimmy is rescued from a doomsday cult where she was held captive in an underground bunker for 15 years. Upon being rescued, she starts life anew in New York City. While unrelatable to most in the literal sense, the series is a metaphor for freedom from male oppression and traditional societal norms. The psyche of *Unbreakable Kimmy Schmidt* is similar to *The Mary Tyler Moore Show*, although the tone of each show is significantly different.

Kimmy Schmidt refuses to be viewed or portrayed as a victim even though she's a young woman moving forward from a recent setback, embarking upon a fresh start in a new city. Although she's overwhelmed by new circumstances, she treats her new lease on life as a spectacular adventure. If you replace Kimmy's name with Mary Richard's (Mary Tyler Moore), the similarities to both shows' throughlines become instantly apparent.

Kimmy, in particular, could easily make a case for hopelessness. She was forced to marry a creepy reverend who kidnapped her and held her hostage for half of her life. Instead, she focuses on the infinite opportunities that lie ahead of her now that she's past that unfortunate reality. Hope is a feeling that permeates all her experiences. It's not an emotion singularly dedicated to one particular ambition.

Kimmy is resilient in ways that astonish those around her. She instinctively understands what can be done or overcome with hope as both shield and wings. "I have hope! Hope that got me through 15 years in the bunker. I don't quit." We withstand and overcome misery with hope.

If it weren't for Dreamers, life would be uninspiring and lack adventure. Tenacious, generous, and charming, a good Dreamer is always prepared to include their friends and family in their exploits. If anyone ever criticizes your dream, just know they are lacking hope. Offer them some of yours because there is an infinite supply.

What Is Their Weakness?

At their best, Dreamers are dazzling. At their worst, they are totally immature. They are teenagers (or younger) in adult bodies, stricken with Peter Pan syndrome. Why would a Dreamer ever want to grow up? I'll circle back to Lucy as a case in point. When she doesn't get her way, she famously, epically, cries. She is a grown, intelligent woman but her default response to disappointment is to pout, throw tantrums, retaliate out of sheer spite, and weep openly for everyone to witness. She may get an ounce of sympathy for her outbursts, but not a ton of respect.

The definition of Peter Pan syndrome is an adult male or female who is socially inept or immature. Meet Nick Miller (Jake Johnson) from *New Girl*. Nick is great at assessing other people's emotions but terrible at expressing his own. He's just plain bad at adulting on all fronts. He can't cook. He's a slob. He likes his privacy but can't function living alone. He's an awkward dater and manages his finances poorly. He rashly dropped out of law school with no other plan for his life. For much of the series he tends bar and merely drifts along. "Drinking to forget?" he reflects. "That's my sweet spot." Sarcastic, self-loathing, and vulnerable all at once.

Nick might sound like the exact opposite of Kimmy Schmidt, but that's not the case. He's merely on the other end of the same spectrum. We simply meet Nick while he's wandering and aimless, which Dreamers sometimes *need to be*. He's actually quite passionate, but he lacks direction. He knows what he doesn't want to do with his life but is slow to figure out what he does want to do with it. That happens to a lot of us, but not all of us, depending on our core personality traits.

Tellingly, when he finally lands on an ambition, it's of an artistic nature. Nick becomes a writer at the back end of the series. So even though it was latent, Nick has a deep reservoir of hope. He just needed more time to mature than his friends. He is reluctant to grow up and step into adult responsibilities longer than most, which is quite typically part of the Dreamer's overall profile.

Dreamer Molly Flynn (Melissa McCarthy) on *Mike & Molly* follows a similar trajectory.

Molly is an elementary school teacher when we meet her. A few seasons into the show's run, she quits, or you might say escapes, by exiting the classroom through the window during a rainstorm while having a meltdown about the state of her life in front of her dismayed students. Her final words of wisdom to the kids: "Okay, listen up because this might be the best lesson I ever teach you. Don't settle. Follow your dreams. Wherever they may take you."

Thud. She slips, swinging her way out of the windowpane, crashes hard and soaking wet to the ground. Is there a less mature way to quit your day job? Survey says, "No."

To be sure, there is a very real self-effacing, even self-loathing aspect to the overall nature of the Dreamer. It's difficult to have the highest self-esteem in the world when you're constantly trying to achieve a goal or find a goal that interests you and success remains elusive. The flip side of all the best qualities of the Dreamer is that they are, by definition, not accomplished. They rarely know the feeling of having the highest status in the room, if ever.

There is, therefore, always a part of the Dreamer that does not like themselves. It's often very challenging for actors to incorporate the element of self-loathing honestly and in a personalized way into a comedic character. It either feels too dramatic or serious, or the actor is under the false perception that the genre of comedy itself excludes real negative emotions or ugly characteristics. But that's far from the truth. We laugh at suffering among other things. We laugh both at what we love *and* despise about ourselves.

The Heroes of Comedy are not shiny, happy people or outlines of people. They are personality types that are best depicted with a full array of human traits, particularly the negative ones because they are essential for producing conflict and authentic characterizations.

Although self-loathing can certainly be detrimental, Dreamers (if you envision them as action-oriented, which I urge you to) are never deterred by it. It's remarkably easy to become comfortable living your life without fully loving yourself. Millions of people do it every day. To really get into the psyche of the Dreamer and play this character comedically for all it's worth, it's important to incorporate at least some percentage of real inward-directed enmity.

It can be sobering to acknowledge that we're less loving to ourselves than we could be. In order to create characters with dimension and impact, we must press ourselves to do so. One of comedy's greatest challenges is to find the levity within our tempestuous humanity. The Dreamer is the most common and accessible archetype to captain that mission.

How Do Others See Them?

Everybody loves a Dreamer; just ask Raymond (Ray Romano) from *Everybody Loves Raymond* or Lucy (Lucille Ball) from *I Love Lucy*. Interesting that there are two iconic sitcoms that feature the word "love" in reference to the character the show revolves around, and that character happens to be a Dreamer.

Cheers has many patrons and employees, but it's resident Dreamer Norm (George Wendt) alone who gets a chorus greeting from the group when he bounds through the door. It makes sense because Dreamers wear their hearts on their sleeves. With a winning combination of vulnerability, optimism, charm, and self-effacing, sarcastic humor, Dreamers simply feel good to be around. How seriously everyone takes them is a different matter.

Everyone makes plans and sets goals, but you know you're in the presence of a Dreamer when someone embarks on a quest that seems doomed from the outset, but they go all in anyway. Or the plan may be simple, but the poor Dreamer can never seem to pull it off as easily as those around them. Basic life goals like romantic relationships, career achievements, or a peaceful day-to-day existence seem to be harder won for the Dreamer than the other Heroes of Comedy.

Therefore, their friends and family respond to them with a range of pity to scorn, depending on what they're up to. Oftentimes, the rest of their tribe will simply find the Dreamer utterly ridiculous. In contrast to the Anchor, Dreamers don't get teased quite as much by their peers. Their self-deprecating humor means they'll take the first shot at themselves, thank you very much.

Besides, it's not all that swell to kick someone when they're down, and the Dreamer is down a lot. As an additional layer of protection against the unpleasantries of life, the Dreamer is also prone to stubbornly ignore reality until it's become unavoidable. Their defense mechanisms are many and sophisticated.

Leslie Knope (Amy Poehler) on *Parks and Recreation* is a great example. Leslie's lifelong dream is to run for public office. She is asked by party leadership to run for a seat on the city council in season four. But because she's already working in city government along with her boyfriend, Ben (Adam Scott), she has to choose one or the other.

The city has a fraternization policy that prohibits coworkers from dating and Ben is the Assistant City Manager of Pawnee, which also makes him Leslie's boss. Running for office and continuing a relationship with Ben would cause a scandal and threaten her candidacy. Additionally, if she were to win, there would always be a question of whether Leslie won on her own merits or because of inside help from her male supervisor and lover.

It's great writing and a great example of how even though a character's circumstances change, their core qualities do not. If Leslie is to have her greatest desire fulfilled and remain a Dreamer, she has to be given something else to wish for. It's the fate of the Dreamer to gain one thing only by losing another. So she and Ben stop seeing each other romantically.

Ever-hopeful Leslie is disappointed but deeply grateful that Ben understands why their budding romance has to pause. He supports her unconditionally and it seems all is well. Leslie manages her expectations and steps back into "crush" mode with Ben, finding comfort in still being able to see him at work. Ben, on the other hand, is not able to find the same peace in being Leslie's pal and coworker. To Leslie's dismay, Ben ultimately decides to pull out of the Parks and Recreation Department and stop working with Leslie altogether. Devastated, but in denial, Leslie processes the news with her bestie, Ann (Rashida Jones).

LESLIE: He's not even attending the ribbon-cutting ceremony of a park we made together.

ANN: Sorry, Leslie.

LESLIE:	I'm just freaking out. The only thing we have left is work and now he doesn't want to work together anymore. What does that all mean?
ANN:	I think you know what it means.
LESLIE:	Yeah. I should just drag out that tiny park project for as long as possible so Ben and I can keep working together.
ANN:	That's almost exactly the opposite of what I meant.
LESLIE:	No, what I'll do is I'll get the neighborhood all riled up and then maybe they'll ask for an environmental impact report, and then Ben and I will work together for at least another year. Good idea, Ann.
ANN:	Leslie, for God's sake...
LESLIE:	No, Ann, please I beg of you, will you just shut your beautiful pie hole? Just sit there and let me stare are at you while you silently support me on this game plan.
ANN:	Leslie...
LESLIE:	Shh... Ann...
ANN:	Leslie...
LESLIE:	Your quiet support means the world to me, as does your tacit endorsement of all my behaviors.

GUNNAR ROHRBACHER: THE COMEDY CODE

Hopeful, desperate, optimistic, vulnerable, tenacious, and willfully disavowing reality, Leslie avoids the negative feelings that come with accepting the truth like a grown up.

How Do Writers Use Them?

Everyone has ambition of some kind. All personalities and archetypes do. That is not unique to the Dreamer. Of note, different kinds of people traverse similar ambitions differently. Some people set goals, meticulously work toward them, and achieve them in a linear, timely fashion. Some people get lucky and get to where they want to be quicker than expected. Some people are born with direct connections and access to their desires. Some people give up after a time and just stop trying.

None of those aforementioned circumstances set up the Dreamer as an archetype in storytelling. So, while everyone can dream (and they do), not everyone is a Dreamer. Here is a clearer setup for the life of a Dreamer: The Dreamer is every woman and man who wants something they can imagine but does not know how to get it when they begin their journey toward it. Driven by desperation, they are likely to make rash, impulsive decisions that make them appear less intelligent than they are.

Any of The Heroes of Comedy can be the hero of a story, if theirs is the story being told. However, the Dreamer is the hero of the broader "Hero's Journey," as is commonly referred to in storytelling and writers' vernacular. Universal in their indulgence of hope, writers use this archetype to represent the joyful reward of overcoming adversity.

Dreamers cannot have an easy time getting what they want, or they become something else. While winning the war may be a long way off, they need to win an occasional battle, or they become pathetic. It is in this regard that the Dreamer is the common denominator of all narrative and instinctively understood by everyone in some capacity. Writers use the Dreamer to show us who we are as long as we are willing to try with a glad and open heart.

What Is Your Way In?

I've already made reference to writers, actors, and artists as Dreamers, but it's really the best answer, so I'll elaborate. If you're reading this book, there is almost a 100% chance you're in the arts and/or entertainment industry. That means you're in touch with a desire to arrive somewhere in life that did not have a clear path laid out and you set out upon that path anyway. Do you realize how brave you are for doing that? What a Dreamer you are!

After a few of decades of teaching, however, I've learned that sometimes we're too close to our careers as artists because they're so deeply personal and let's be honest — they can be filled with turmoil and disappointment.

So, just to explore other options, look inward and ask yourself some questions. Do you frequently make fun of yourself or crack jokes at your own expense? Do you make plans that seem really smart at first but upon execution were never strong enough to work out? Are you trying to like yourself more than you do right now? Do you use humor to defend yourself against how much the world can suck sometimes? Do you study and train to become better at anything than you were before?

If you answered yes to any or all those questions, you have a way into playing the Dreamer that involves action as much as dreaming.

The Dreamer in a Family-Based Series: *Modern Family*

"I'm sort of like Costco. I'm big, I'm not fancy and I dare you to not like me." Dreamers know they can win you over.

Modern Family's resident Dreamer, Cameron Tucker (Eric Stonestreet), is a classically trained clown who wants that aspect of his life to not only be taken seriously, but also revered by his husband, Mitchell. That's not going to happen. But Cameron hopes for it anyway. He has a chip on his shoulder about it (which is immature) and becomes easily defensive on the topic, "It's hard to have a relationship and a clown career. That's the reason there are so many single clowns."

Yet he hopes that Fizbo, his jester alter ego, can be taken as seriously as, for example, Mitchell's law degree, despite mountains of evidence that he will *never get what he wants*. Cameron is continually offended and disappointed that the only reaction Fizbo ever seems to elicit from those he loves is an eye roll and a sigh.

So, what's the deal? Is Mitchell the source of Cameron's misery in this regard, or is it Cameron himself? I'd say after the first time or two of being mocked and disrespected for his clowning, Cameron is now 100% responsible for his own disappointment, although he doesn't see it that way. Why? He's in denial about the odds of other people changing their opinion about clowns. We can't control other people's thoughts or actions, only our reactions to them. So, why doesn't Cameron just do that, then? Easy. He doesn't want to.

We all have desires. But it's the Dreamer that has a particularly difficult time managing their expectations. We all want something, but it's the Dreamer who, more often than not, wants what is improbable or impossible despite being highly intelligent. When our desire, no matter how trivial, cannot be abated, we are a Dreamer.

Eric Stonestreet won two Primetime Emmy Awards for Outstanding Supporting Actor in a Comedy Series playing tenderhearted Cameron Tucker. Raised on a farm in Tonganoxie,

Missouri, Cameron has traditional small-town American values and a heart as big as the great outdoors. "Missouri is more cosmopolitan than you give it credit for. It's got a very vibrant cowboy poetry scene," he says of his home state.

Cameron has a definitive artistic nature, like most Dreamers. He's an accomplished vocalist. An avid doer, he formed the a cappella group, The Greensleevers, although he was ultimately ousted from it. He's a brilliant drummer and also plays the ukulele and piano. If that weren't enough, he's also an adept visual artist and a fantastic, award-winning cook.

As a gay man from America's heartland, Cameron symbolizes life for many other LGBTQ folks. Since Cameron and his partner, Mitchell (Jesse Tyler Ferguson), were in a committed relationship at the beginning of the series debut in 2009, the writers of *Modern Family* were able to officially marry the couple at the end of the fifth season in 2014, when same-sex marriage became the norm.

Unfortunately, Cameron's long-awaited, historically relevant wedding was a complete disaster. The trouble begins when Cam realizes that the dry cleaners gave him the wrong tuxedo. Cam, Mitchell, and their daughter, Lily (Aubrey Anderson-Emmons), head back to the dry cleaners to rectify the mistake. By the time they arrive, the dry cleaners is closed. Cameron panics, which escalates rapidly when he receives news that there is a wildfire raging near the wedding venue and the nuptials need to start four hours earlier.

Cameron half-heartedly suggests Mitchell break into the dry cleaners through an express garment bag drop box, out of desperation. Since he's too big, the dads opt to send Lily through instead, who quickly gets caught in the revolving, mechanical clothes rack. She's rescued when the alarm is triggered, and the store owner arrives. Lily is safe, and Cameron gets the right tux. Mitch and Cam arrive at their wedding early/on time only to find it is being shut down by firefighters who inform everyone the wildfires are spreading faster than expected and it is no longer safe to proceed.

To summarize, the Dreamer's wedding day starts off badly, degenerates quickly, and involves a harebrained scheme that is destined to make things worse. If only it ended there...

The couple's wedding planner finds another available venue that arises due to a last-minute cancellation, and the guests are shuttled off on a school bus. It seems the problem is solved, but the wedding is again interrupted, this time by the couple that had originally booked the venue for the day. Pathetically, the wedding is finally shuffled to Mitch and Cam's apartment. Ever-hopeful Cameron tries his best to remain excited as his dream wedding spirals into a chaotic mess. Yes, it's Mitchell's wedding, too, but Dreamer Cameron needs the public validation a wedding provides much more.

With their small home woefully overcrowded and more than half the guests on the lawn, the husbands-to-be admit defeat and call "time of death" on their own wedding. Although generally tenacious, Cameron thinks there are too many ominous signs to ignore and the wedding just isn't meant to be.

With one last twist in their march to the altar, Jay (Ed O'Neill) reveals that throughout the day's tumult, he has managed to book his country club and the wedding is still on. Jay and Gloria (Sofia Vergara) escort Mitchell down the aisle and Cameron's mom and dad follow suit. The constantly bickering but perfectly suited pair get married in grand fashion by Phil. Mitchell's best person, Claire (Julie Bowen), toasts their union.

"I remember it like it was yesterday. The day that Mitchell came home from the hospital in a very unfashionable white diaper with three strands of scraggly, Raggedy Andy hair... We were inseparable. I was his big sister, his big brother, his nemesis, his protector, his best friend. I was his first partner. And I loved every minute of it. So, naturally, I was a little picky when it came to who was going to be replacing me, and then I met this Cam... and sure he was warm and funny and loving. I wondered... was he really everything I wanted for my brother? Was he really the best person? No. I'm the best person. And now I'm very pleased to raise a glass and introduce for the first time ever, on our fourth try, great husbands, Mitch and Cam!"

The downside to being a Dreamer is that the road they travel toward their desires, even the most commonplace, is invariably filled with detours, speed bumps, and potholes. The upside is that their open hearts bring warmth and affection back to them tenfold when they need it the most. Claire's toast veers away from sappy sentiment, but in passing the torch as Mitchell's protector, she makes one thing clear: her charming and friendly Dreamer brother-in-law is both an acceptable replacement and beloved.

The Dreamer in a Friend-Based Series: *Friends*

Matthew Perry did a masterful job playing Dreamer Chandler Bing on *Friends*. His self-effacing sarcasm was so pronounced, Chandler practically self-flagellated through inflection. "Could she *be* any more out of my league?" he'd query. Chandler's speech pattern is recognized globally and by his tribe. He asks Phoebe, "They *do* me?" She clues him in, "Yeah, you know, like, okay...um, 'Could that report **be** any later?'"

Neither a comedic crutch nor a vocal gimmick, Perry helps the audience feel what it's like to live in the skin of the Dreamer by feeling it intensely himself. So much so, his words are literally imbued with emotion and his core characteristics. There is a strong vein of self-loathing in Chandler. That's not an inherently fun quality to spend time with. However, when you combine it with tenacity, hope, and active desire that keeps a man motivated to reach for his goals against the odds, a hero is born.

An unlikely, everyday hero. An underdog banking to beat the odds. Chandler Bing is a regular guy with aspirations for a typical American life; a fair measure of success in romance, career, and family. Easy, right? Um, not so fast.

Who he is at his core and the challenges that neverendingly fall from the sky make Chandler's existence seem at a glance anything but heroic. "Hi, I'm Chandler. I make jokes when I'm uncomfortable." He's perennially frustrated, stymied, and blindsided by new and increasingly difficult obstacles as he approaches life's milestones.

That's an aggravating reality for an overall good person and it would be sad if Chandler let the problems get the better of him and gave up. But he doesn't. So, yes, at first glimpse, his lack of fulfillment doesn't point to an exceptional man. But heroes are carved from the stone of adversity. We are not defined by what happens to us, we are shaped by how we respond to it. We are everyday heroes when we overcome.

Throughout 10 seasons of *Friends*, Chandler has two loves; Janice Litman (Maggie Wheeler) and Monica Geller (Courteney Cox). Mostly remembered for her obnoxious laugh, Janice and Chandler were in a tumultuous on-again, off-again romance for the first three seasons. People often forget that she and Chandler were together when the series began and went through considerable turmoil together.

Perhaps that's because Chandler spent a considerable amount of time trying to get rid of her; a throughline that spans the series. He breaks up with her several times, two of them on New Year's Eve and Valentine's Day. He chickens out on breaking up with her once by telling her his job is transferring him to

Yemen, which she believes for quite a while. Despite all that, they reunite another time and Chandler professes his real love for her.

This time things are complicated when Janice's feelings re-ignite for her estranged husband. During the previous lapse in their sporadic romance, Janice got married and had a child. She loves Chandler, but she also loves her husband. They come to a crossroads and Chandler does exactly what every good Dreamer should do. He does the right thing like grown ass man. Then changes his mind and throws a tantrum at Central Perk.

CHANDLER: Janice, I have something I need to tell you and I want you to let me get through it, because it's, it's... it's not gonna be easy.

JANICE: Okay.

CHANDLER: I think you should go back with Gary. I don't want to be the guy that breaks up a family. You know, my parents split up, it was *because* of that guy. And whenever I would see him, I would always think, you know, you're the reason. You are why they are not together. And I... I hated that guy. And it didn't matter how nice he was or, you know, how happy he made my dad.

JANICE: Wow.

CHANDLER: Yeah. Well... it's the right thing to do.

JANICE: Ah, you're right. Oh, God... But before I can say goodbye, there's something I really need you to know, Chandler. The way I feel about you? It's like I finally understand what Lionel Richie's been singing about. You know? I mean, what we have, it's like movie love. You're my soul-mate. And I can't believe we're not going to be spending the rest of our lives together.

BEAT

CHANDLER: *Then don't leave me!*

JANICE: What?

CHANDLER: Forget what I said! I was babbling! Pick me!

JANICE: No, you were right. You were right. I mean, I've gotta give my marriage another chance.

CHANDLER: No, you don't! No, no, no... I say you've got to give your *divorce* another chance.

JANICE: I'm sorry.

CHANDLER: Oh, don't go.

JANICE: I've gotta go.

They embrace. Janice kisses him and tries to exit. He clings to her pathetically.

CHANDLER: No. No, *no!*

JANICE: Honey, people are looking.

CHANDLER: I don't care. (To the patrons) I DON'T CARE!

JANICE: Yeah, um... okay. I'm leaving now.

CHANDLER: You can't leave! I have your shoe!

JANICE: Goodbye, Chandler Bing.

Let the record stand that within their relationship, Janice was the mature one of the two. Chandler exhibited nearly every positive and negative trait of the Dreamer in this one scene — tenacious, resilient, charming, hopeful, persuasive, optimistic, lovable, child-like, passionate, desperate, immature, needy, vulnerable, defensive, irresponsible, and so on. It's a perfect example of presenting an archetype with a universal circumstance that could happen to anyone and watching them react in their unique, highly specific way. It would make no sense for any of the other five friends to respond this way to the end of a wishy-washy romance.

Fortunately, that was not the end of Chandler's love life. While he dated a few other women, by season four he finds his *actual* soulmate in Monica. While they settle into a great partnership for the remainder of the series, Monica marries a Dreamer and all his requisite stumbling blocks to success.

In the beginning of their romance, they feel they have to keep it a secret since becoming a couple will change the dynamic of the group, and they want to be sure it's more than a fling. Chandler goes from a choppy love life to a secret one. While it's fun at first, the secrecy soon becomes a burden. Generally, when people fall in love, they want their closest friends to know. The opposite was true for Chandler.

The dominoes start to fall when Joey (Matt LeBlanc) connects the dots. Next, Rachel (Jennifer Aniston) discovers the truth. Then Phoebe (Lisa Kudrow) finds out on her own, leaving Ross (David Schwimmer), Monica's brother, the last to know and he's not at all happy about it. Ultimately everyone is glad and supportive, but only after tremendous upheaval over a basic life milestone.

It's worth noting that Dreamer Chandler did not announce his relationship with Monica to anyone. His closest friends all found out incidentally.

Things go smoothly for a bit, but as Chandler is about to propose, Monica's ex, Richard, surfaces, throwing off Chandler's game. He recovers. When they are about to marry, Phoebe spills the beans that Monica really wanted to hook up with Joey the night she slept with Chandler in London. He's thrown another curveball, but he recovers. Janice wants to attend their wedding. He panics, then recovers. Minor obstacles, but consistent.

A greater disturbance occurs when Chandler is transferred to Tulsa, Oklahoma for his work. Newly married, he finds himself in a long-distance relationship with his wife. He quits at Christmastime and returns home because he can't stand being away from his friends and his love. Although he's happy to be back home, he's unemployed.

Without many options, he takes an internship at an ad agency. Now at 30 years old, he has to start building his career anew. When the internship ends, Chandler is offered a job as a copywriter. Like so many other Dreamers, he finds fulfillment in a creative position.

With his romance and career pitfalls behind him, there is only one avenue left to challenge Chandler: parenthood. Unsurprisingly, he and Monica are not able to conceive due to his sperm's "low motility," coupled with Monica's uterus deemed an "inhospitable environment" by their fertility doctor.

They are selected for adoption by a single mother as the series begins to wrap. She delivers them a healthy baby boy and it seems something finally goes right for Chandler, for once. The doctor announces the arrival of the *next* baby momentarily. To everyone's surprise but the doctor's, the birth mother was carrying twins without realizing it.

CHANDLER: What do we do?

MONICA: What do you mean, what do we do?

CHANDLER:	Twins! Twins!
MONICA:	Chandler, you're panicking.
CHANDLER:	Uh-huh! Join me, won't you?! (THEN) Okay, what do you say we keep one and then just like… have an option on the other one.
MONICA:	We can't split them up!
CHANDLER:	Why not? We could give each of them half a medallion. And then *years* later, they'll find each other… and be reunited. I mean, that's a great day for everybody.
MONICA:	Okay, what if the person who adopts the other one is horrible?
CHANDLER:	What if they're not? What if it's adopted by a king?

Shaken only for a moment, Chandler quickly comes around and is glad to become a father of two, albeit abruptly and with no warning. Although this circumstance is quite different from his final breakup with Janice, his reaction is not. Immaturity is the Dreamer's comfort zone. Desperate, needy, and rash, Chandler becomes overwhelmed by responsibility and looks for a way out. Though he recovers fast, Chandler is inescapably the product of his point of view and impulses, which are consistent from the very beginning to the back end of the show.

The great writing team of *Friends* gave Chandler countless trials and surprises over the course of a decade. Matthew Perry played the parameters of the Dreamer with energy, depth, and consistency. Such is the recipe for iconic television.

The Dreamer in a Work-Based Series: *30 Rock*

There is something in Liz Lemon's name. Colloquially, when someone says, "It's a lemon!" that's not a good thing. In fact, it means "this is something that *should* be great but isn't." *30 Rock's* Liz Lemon (Tina Fey) is lovable, enthusiastic, and eternally hopeful, but flawed as the day is long. She is terrible at romance, binges on junk food, has no fashion sense whatsoever, makes analogies through Star Wars references, and her mouth turns to mush when she tries to express herself emotionally.

Liz Lemon is basically a teenage boy in a 30-something woman's body. Although she is a successful writer and showrunner, the rest of her life is in shambles, as is her self-esteem. Lemon is the embodiment of untapped potential. If only she had a role model or coach... a mentor! Enter Jack Donaghy.

After a mere glance at her in the pilot, her new boss, Jack (Alec Baldwin), peers into her soul when Liz mentions she doesn't cook very much: "Sure. I gotcha. New York, third-wave feminist, college-educated, single and pretending to be happy about it, over-scheduled, undersexed. You buy any magazine that says, 'healthy body image' on the cover, and every two years you take up knitting for... a week". His review is unnervingly accurate. As the meeting wraps, he concludes, "I like you. You have the boldness of a much younger woman." Liz is confused and repulsed. An iconic television work friendship is born.

A highly complicated, wordy, boundaryless friendship that is hard for even them to fully define.

LIZ: Work-husband, slash uncle.

JACK: Coworker, slash little brother.

He elaborates, "It's a symbiotic relationship. I'm a mighty, great white shark, Lemon, and you are a remora, clinging to me with your suction cup head. I give you a free ride and in exchange you, uh… eat my parasites."

Jack offers to formally mentor Liz on the day he meets her. She refuses initially, but it doesn't take her long to become enamored by Jack's power and persuasiveness. Although he judges her harshly, Jack takes a liking to Liz immediately. They bond effortlessly, and it isn't long before they begin interacting like a married couple.

At one point, they actually become accidentally married. Although it was a fluke and temporary, NBC's human resources manager nonetheless calls them into a meeting, as per the corporations' fraternization policy. He's required to ensure that Liz isn't receiving preferential treatment from Jack since he's her supervisor and, at that moment, husband.

Jack and Liz had already been arguing over employee benefits and budget cuts, so when they enter the interview, things are already tense.

> WEINERSLAV: Alright, let's just dive on in. Does the employee spend an inordinate amount of time in the employer's office, compared to other employees?

> JACK: Well, yes, but I suppose that's because Miss Lemon is incapable of doing anything on her own.

> LIZ: Ah, please! Half the time when I go up there, it's to help you choose a tie and they're all red or blue.

> JACK: Where I come from, if you have more than two colors on a tie, it means you're looking for a certain kind of bar.

WEINERSLAV: Are all workday conversations business related or do personal issues often dominate
discussion? Including, but not limited to: mothers, diarrhea, having babies, problems in the
bedroom, neckties, food issues, foot disorders,
'having it all'?

JACK: Okay! Yes, in the past we have advised each
other.

LIZ: For instance, Jack taught me not to wear tan
slacks with a tan turtleneck. I thought it looked
nice, but he — rightly — pointed out that it
made me look like a giant condom.

JACK: And Lemon is the only of my subordinates
who's not afraid to warn me when I'm being
too authoritative or... handsome.

LIZ: Or when you have eye boogers.

WEINERSLAV: Have you spent time with each other's families?
Have you attended special events together?
Such as class reunions, birthday or holiday
celebrations, weddings, or extended car trips?
Are you each other's emergency contacts?
Do you ever drink together at work? Perhaps
while summarizing what you've learned over
the day or week? Have you shared intimate
details of your fears, hopes, and dreams? Both
personal and professional? Is this the longest
and perhaps most meaningful relationship in
your life? Do you often find yourselves thinking

JACK:	I apologize, Lemon.
LIZ:	I'm sorry, Jack.
LIZ:	I never should have tried to blackmail you. I'll sign the papers.
JACK:	And I shouldn't have threatened your show. I'll leave that to the parental decency groups.

Although Weinerslav's questions are absurdly on point, they highlight the intensity and depth of Liz and Jack's relationship. In reviewing what they've been through together and what they mean to each other, it's difficult for them to stay cross with each other.

A lot of us can relate to having a work-wife or work-husband. Busy career people often spend more of their waking hours at work than they do at home. Rebel Jack loves the idea of creating someone in his own image. Dreamer Liz is titillated by the thought of becoming a more polished version of herself with his guidance. She does. But their convoluted attachment to each other almost breaks their bond entirely in the final episode.

With Liz's show canceled, she asks Jack to help her find work again. She finds him in his office distant and lost as he realizes he's literally achieved all his goals yet can't find true happiness. His perspective has changed, and it seems as if the floor drops out from underneath Liz when she takes her final problem to him and he declines to help.

LIZ:	What am I gonna do now?
JACK:	I could try and help you. Make some calls, see what bridges I haven't burned. But I'm not

going to. For your own good. Work is never going to make you happy, Lemon. And anyone who tells you differently is a fool.

LIZ: Are you kidding me? What have we been talking about for the last seven years?

JACK: I don't know anymore. For the first time in my life, I don't know what I need. Maybe I'll buy a boat.

LIZ: Oh, my God. This whole time you've been telling me how to run my life, you didn't know what you were talking about! You're just an alcoholic with a great voice.

JACK: Careful, Lemon. You're playing with fire.

LIZ: You made me buy into this whole life. When I met you, I was perfectly happy with what I had; eating night cheese and transitioning my pajamas into day wear. You're the one who told me to want more. And now, when I need you most, you are bailing on me?

JACK: You're an adult, Lemon. You didn't have to listen to me.

LIZ: Really?! When was that an option?

JACK: Look, if you want someone to blame, blame yourself. You're the one who wormed your way into my brain with your endless hand-wringing and feelings. I used to be a shark and then you unsharkulated me. I called you up here for one meeting seven years ago and you *kept coming up!*

LIZ: So, we ruined each other. Good to know. You know, it's for the best that my show is over. And you've quit and we're all going our separate ways. I guess you and I were just a boss and his employee and now we're not anymore.

JACK: Yes, that pretty much sums it up.

Of course, it doesn't. Liz and Jack make up tenderly before the end of the episode. In a twist, Jack makes a prolonged speech that implies he loves Liz, but before he can say the actual words, if he ever will, Liz interjects, "I love you too, Jack." For the once-awkward Lemon, who was nearly debilitated by expressing emotion, it's a huge level up. It took her a bit to realize it, but Jack had not betrayed her in any way. Simply, the last thing he taught her was that she no longer needed him as her mentor.

Characteristics of the Dreamer

- Amiable
- Bright
- Charming
- Creative
- Desperate
- Determined
- Emotional
- Flighty
- Foiled
- Friendly
- Frustrated
- Headstrong
- Hopeful
- Idealistic
- Immature
- Impulsive
- Infantile
- Irresponsible
- Lovable
- Needy
- Openhearted
- Optimistic
- Passionate
- Persistent
- Persuasive
- Pushy
- Resilient
- Self-loathing
- Self-deprecating
- Sensitive
- Spontaneous
- Steadfast
- Stubborn
- Tenacious
- Transparent
- Trusting
- Unpredictable
- Unsettled
- Vulnerable
- Whimsical

Dreamers Throughout the History of Television

Artie Abrams	Kevin McHale	Glee
Grace Adler	Debra Messing	Will & Grace
Kevin Arnold	Fred Savage	The Wonder Years
Raymond Barone	Ray Romano	Everybody Loves Raymond
Chip Baskets	Zach Galifianakis	Baskets
Chandler Bing	Matthew Perry	Friends
Jan Brady	Eve Plumb	The Brady Bunch
Rebecca Bunch	Rachel Bloom	Crazy Ex-Girlfriend
Adam Burns	Matt LeBlanc	Man with a Plan
Drew Carey	Drew Carey	The Drew Carey Show
Jimmy Chance	Lucas Neff	Raising Hope
Chris	Tyler James Williams	Everybody Hates Chris
Beaver Cleaver	Jerry Mathers	Leave It to Beaver
Barbara Cooper	Valerie Bertinelli	One Day at a Time
George Cooper Sr.	Lance Barber	Young Sheldon
Richie Cunningham	Ron Howard	Happy Days
Laverne DeFazio	Penny Marshall	Laverne & Shirley
John Dorian	Zach Braff	Scrubs
Amy Dubanowski	America Ferrera	Superstore
Grayson Ellis	Josh Hopkins	Cougar Town
Cyril Figgis	Chris Parnell	Archer

Fran Fine	Fran Drescher	The Nanny
Molly Flynn	Melissa McCarthy	Mike & Molly
Eric Forman	Topher Grace	That '70s Show
Tobias Fünke	David Cross	Arrested Development
Barry Goldberg	Troy Gentile	The Goldbergs
Jim Halpert	John Krasinski	The Office
Dr. Bob Hartley	Bob Newhart	The Bob Newhart Show
Frankie Heck	Patricia Heaton	The Middle
Doug Heffernan	Kevin James	The King of Queens
Payton Hobart	Ben Platt	The Politician
Kurt Hummel	Chris Colfer	Glee
Dr. Cliff Huxtable	Bill Cosby	The Cosby Show
Arnold Jackson	Gary Coleman	Diff'rent Strokes
Paul Jamison	Oliver Platt	The Big C
Jim	Jim Belushi	According to Jim
Charlie Kelly	Charlie Day	It's Always Sunny in Philadelphia
Leslie Knope	Amy Poehler	Parks and Recreation
Sandy Kominsky	Michael Douglas	The Kominsky Method
Liz Lemon	Tina Fey	30 Rock
Sean Lincoln	Stephen Mangan	Episodes
George Lopez	George Lopez	George Lopez
Dick Loudon	Bob Newhart	Newhart
Fran Lovett	Fran Drescher	Happily Divorced

Oscar Madison	Jack Klugman	**The Odd Couple**
Stan Marsh	Trey Parker	**South Park**
Ann Marie	Marlo Thomas	**That Girl**
Earnest "Earn" Marks	Donald Glover	**Atlanta**
Susan Mayer	Teri Hatcher	**Desperate Housewives**
Mike McLintock	Matt Walsh	**Veep**
Bernie "Mac" McCullough	Bernie Mac	**The Bernie Mac Show**
Marnie Michaels	Allison Williams	**Girls**
Nick Miller	Jake Johnson	**New Girl**
Andy Millman	Ricky Gervais	**Extras**
Gabe Mitchell	John Patrick Amedori	**Dear White People**
Melanie Moretti	Valerie Bertinelli	**Hot in Cleveland**
Rhoda Morgenstern	Valerie Harper	**The Mary Tyler Moore Show/Rhoda**
Elaine Nardo	Marilu Henner	**Taxi**
Dave Nelson	Dave Foley	**NewsRadio**
Rob Norris	Rob Delaney	**Catastrophe**
Katie Otto	Katy Mixon	**American Housewife**
Danny Partridge	Danny Bonaduce	**The Partridge Family**
Penny	Kaley Cuoco	**The Big Bang Theory**
Norm Peterson	George Wendt	**Cheers**
Maura Pfefferman	Jeffrey Tambor	**Transparent**

Christy Plunkett	Anna Faris	Mom
Peter Prentice	Adam Pally	The Mindy Project
Stuart Pritchard	Stephen Merchant	Hello Ladies
Edgar Quintero	Desmin Borges	You're the Worst
Tootie Ramsey	Kim Fields	The Facts of Life
Sally Reed	Sarah Goldberg	Barry
Dee Reynolds	Kaitlin Olson	It's Always Sunny in Philadelphia
Lucy Ricardo	Lucille Ball	I Love Lucy
Hailey Rutledge	Lola Kirk	Mozart in the Jungle
Kimmy Schmidt	Ellie Kemper	Unbreakable Kimmy Schmidt
Mary Jo Shively	Annie Potts	Designing Women
Sister Bertrille	Sally Field	The Flying Nun
Will Smith	Will Smith	The Fresh Prince of Bel-Air
Buddy Sorrell	Morey Amsterdam	The Dick Van Dyke Show
Tim Taylor	Tim Allen	Home Improvement
Jack Tripper	John Ritter	Three's Company
Cameron Tucker	Eric Stonestreet	Modern Family
Jane Villanueva	Gina Rodriguez	Jane the Virgin
Ruth Wilder	Alison Brie	GLOW
Hal Wilkerson	Bryan Cranston	Malcolm in the Middle

How Dreamers are Described in the Breakdowns

Always draws the short straw, artistic, beneath a timid exterior beats the heart of a warrior, carefree, disheveled, doesn't worry about details, down on their luck, hopelessly in love with..., irresponsible with money, likes to see where the day takes her, lives in the moment, lovable loser, more sensitive than they care to admit, pothead, put together in a chardonnay and Target kind of way, scrappy, sidekick-type, snarky but lacking confidence, stoner, third man.

Lead Body Part: Spine

The Dreamer stands tall in the face of unrelenting adversity. Hope and optimism challenge us to take action toward our desires. Dreamers are not daydreamers. They are warriors of innovation, creation, and invention. They fail. Dreamers have a relationship with disappointment. When they're down, they might ball up with their back curved, their chin tucked, and their head bowed. When they recover, they straighten their spine and lengthen it anew.

NEUROTIC

"When I'm really upset, concentrating on a table of contents helps me calm down. It's like a menu, but the food is words."

— *Chidi Anagonye/*The Good Place

Mantra: "I worry"
Strength: Organized
Weakness: Insecure
Typical jobs: Science/Technology, Physician/Psychiatry, Academia, Upper Management, Degree-Oriented Position

Who Are They?

Neurotics possess powerful minds and have a tendency to rely on evidence, patterns, and structure to feel secure within a chaotic world. They think a lot. Then they think some more. Then they *overthink*. All of that thinking often leads to anxiety, stress, and worry. They are the most cerebral of The Heroes of Comedy. Their high-wattage brains are capable of serious multitasking, quite often at the cost of severe panic disorders.

Neurotics have many great qualities that are clear assets, like above-average intelligence and sophisticated analytical abilities. The downside to this type of personality is that they are prone to burnout and overload. It's difficult to quiet a rapidly moving mind, and for any given circumstance, the Neurotic is capable of processing a multitude of outcomes. Foreseeing every possible eventuality from given data is fine for a computer, but it can be quite stressful for a human being. This is how the Neurotic experiences life's myriad transactions.

Quite often Neurotics are not thought of as particularly emotional, but just the opposite is actually true. Their complicated thought process causes them to suppress their emotions in favor of reason. In turn, their emotions become internalized while they think things through. Unresolved or unexpressed (internalized) emotions are what lead to classic Neurotic behaviors like obsessive-compulsive disorder (OCD), germophobia, and hypochondria.

Emotions will always have their due in the mechanism of a human body. There is no way around it. The analytical Neurotic, although highly intelligent, isn't the best at getting in touch with their emotions and expressing them freely. The tendency to bottle them up creates an austere facade, a detached nature, and habitual patterns of behavior that are unconsciously used to self-soothe.

Many types of people have neuroses of some sort, but the Neurotic is defined by their intellect and the need to filter the moments of life through evidentiary experience. They curb imagination, actively dislike the unknown, and rely on what they can prove in order to feel safe.

Because they're so smart, they have been right often throughout life, about a lot of different things. This can make them seem arrogant, and they may be, but that's not their driving characteristic. They have lived their lives in a feedback loop that validates their assumptions about everything; what they *thought* was correct ended up *being* correct. It's therefore very difficult to shake a Neurotic off their mental flowchart.

Modern Family is one of two well-known sitcoms that feature Neurotic adult siblings, the other is *Friends*. Both series employ two different Neurotics as lead characters in order to utilize the full spectrum of this archetype's attributes and comedic possibilities. The Neurotic is complicated and, on occasion, more than one per show is not only acceptable, it's necessary to fully reflect the fast-paced world in which we live.

Mitchell (Jesse Tyler Ferguson) and Claire (Julie Bowen) are Neurotics. However, Mitchell exemplifies the intellectual, internalized aspects of this archetype. In the beginning of the series, for example, Mitchell is uncomfortable with public displays of affection. Although he's an out gay man with a boyfriend (he and Cameron marry later on), Mitchell doesn't want anyone seeing him kiss Cameron in a store.

Cameron complains into camera: "Mitchell has a problem with public displays of affection. I remember once at a New Year's Eve party, stroke of midnight, he high-fived me. Two problems with that: One, gays don't high-five. Two, gays don't high-five."

Mitchell experienced a lack of control that made him extremely uncomfortable, so he defaulted to an awkward behavior and locked his emotions in an interior vault. He has rules about expressing affection that Cameron does not and additionally cannot understand. Although he is an out gay man and brave in many ways, his deep-seated insecurity surfaces when he cannot control other people's narrative of him.

Claire is a perfectionist and has a heightened sense of urgency for control in any given moment. Whether it's creating the scariest house on the block for Halloween or basic parenting, she knows she's right. Her experiences have reinforced that her way of doings things produces the best outcome for the greatest number of people.

As a mother, Claire is a great example of why the Neurotic is not motivated by arrogance, but rather an odd mix of insecurity and certainty. When you're sure there is a right way to accomplish something, it doesn't leave room to consider alternate opinions.

In her dream world, Claire would do everything herself so it would be done correctly.

Since that's not possible, she has to settle for relying on other people like her husband, Phil, to move forward in life. It leaves her constantly on edge and fearful of either an unknown outcome or an unsatisfactory outcome that she predicted and tried to prevent. "Oh, honey, don't take this the wrong way, but I have almost no faith in you," says Claire to her husband.

Neurotics are extremely judgmental, but their judgement doesn't stem from a shallow place, as is the case with the Narcissist. It's born of lightning-paced, binary cerebral analysis that leads to only one correct conclusion and a lifelong, comforting relationship to making adroit calculations that produce winning results. The Neurotic's consistent mental acuity knits a warm blanket to keep away the chill of chaos.

What Is Their Strength?

They say if you want something done, you should ask a busy person. An old adage that could be easily switched to, "...ask a Neurotic." Since their minds are always whirring, Neurotics are always busy. They are great organizers, multitaskers, and project managers. Their careers often reflect their meticulousness. Here are a few examples.

Ross Geller anxiously executed by David Schwimmer (*Friends*) is a paleontologist. Niles Crane portrayed with manic vigor by David Hyde Pierce (*Frasier*) is a psychiatrist. Infinitely insecure Amy Brookheimer played by Anna Chlumsky (*Veep*) doubled up as Chief of Staff to Vice President Selina Meyer and presidential campaign manager. Simon Helberg's Howard Wolowitz (*The Big Bang Theory*) is an aerospace engineer *and* astronaut. And although it took her a while to achieve notoriety, Monica Geller-Bing characterized with frenzied lunacy by Courteney Cox (*Friends*) is a chef. All these vocations require intelligence, mental stamina, and attention to detail. To say most Neurotics accomplish a lot with their particular genius is an understatement.

What Is Their Weakness?

When it comes to the Neurotic, you have to wonder what all that anxiety is about. Worry and fret seem to run counter to intelligence and structure. Actually, they are flip sides of the same coin. Underneath their neatly compartmentalized lives, Neurotics are highly insecure. When everything is as it should be, Neurotics are content and satisfied, maybe even a little smug. When the organizational flowchart in their mind is disrupted, however, it feels to them like a train crashing in slow motion.

Chaos is the enemy of the Neurotic. They know it and try valiantly to avoid it at all costs. They do not want the Jenga blocks to come tumbling down! That's what all the planning and preparation is for. The pulsating need for order and the compulsive behaviors are symptoms of a congenital fear of being imperfect. A true Neurotic would say, "Of course. Everyone's like that." No, Neurotic, they're not.

While high standards are a good thing, perfection is eminently subjective and ultimately unattainable, if not entirely poisonous to a healthy outlook on life. The perfectionist tendencies exhibited by Neurotics further reveal their free-floating anxiety. If Neurotics are so intelligent and put together in so many ways, why is fear such a driving force for them?

In American culture, being smarter than average is great once you're an adult. Growing up, not so much. Nobody gets it all. The insecurity starts in school once a Neurotic realizes they're intellectually gifted. Chances are, if you were scholarly and got above-average grades in school, you weren't a top athlete or as popular as the class clown. Being above average, by definition, means you're part of a smaller group and that can be isolating, especially for a kid. Excelling in any other measurable area as a child is far easier than being intellectually remarkable.

The "perfect" grades are a way of attaining validation from teachers and parents (adults), whom Neurotics tend to relate to more anyway. This pattern carries on throughout high school and college. Suddenly, the Neurotic kid has passed through their teen years and becomes a young adult.

Now in a position to put their apt mind to use in a suitable career, they still experience the world through the prism of feeling validated only when they are correct or outdoing someone else. This may instill a defensive, hypercompetitive nature in the Neurotic. Here's how Ben Wyatt (Adam Scott) of *Parks and Recreation* would put it, "Nerd culture is mainstream now! So when you use the word 'nerd' derogatorily, that means that you're the one that's out of the zeitgeist!" Defensive? Check. Competitive? Absolutely.

In real life, Neurotics can get therapy, work through their hang-ups and learn to relax. On television, they remain eternally uptight and awkward, feverishly seeking approval from their immediate core group, as well as society at large.

How Do Others See Them?

To some degree, Neurotics do get the validation they seek from their friends and family. Once we're out of school, it becomes abundantly clear that we need smart people with orderly thoughts to manage this world. They are ultimately appreciated for their organizational abilities.

Otherwise, Neurotics are thought of as high-strung, prickly, or even downright terrifying. Bree Van De Kamp (Marcia Cross) of *Desperate Housewives* was often casually alarming, "Good friends offer to help in a crisis; great friends don't take no for an answer." Others with more casual personalities do not relate to the Neurotic in the slightest. All work and no play, Neurotics have a difficult time unwinding and enjoying life. They have a lot of rules, which make them a bore for the rest of the crowd and an easy target for mockery.

There is no better example than Felix Unger (Tony Randall) of *The Odd Couple*. *The Odd Couple* originated as a play written by Neil Simon that premiered on Broadway in 1965. A few years later, it was adapted into a film starring two legendary American actors, Jack Lemmon and Walter Matthau. Its first adaptation as a television series came in 1970, starring Tony Randall and Jack Klugman. In 2015, *The Odd Couple* was revived once more into a short-lived series starring Thomas Lennon and Matthew Perry. The premise is timeless, as it hinges on a single, basic premise: an uptight Neurotic, Felix Unger, living with and being mocked by slovenly Oscar Madison.

Felix is persnickety (note his name, writers!) and Oscar likes to have fun. The vast majority of the audience relates to Oscar's point of view; live life and have a good time without having to analyze every experience. Only another Neurotic can truly appreciate Felix's fastidiousness.

OSCAR: That's fun fat. Everybody has that.

FELIX: I don't.

OSCAR: You don't have any fun either.

In theory you could put any two personalities together and generate story with conflict. However, the Neurotic is far and away the best choice as one of the pair, because whether we realize it (or admit it) or not, we're still laughing at, not with, the kid who was smarter than us in school.

How Do Writers Use Them?

Stories need conflict. Some archetypes are more useful than others when it comes to walking conflict directly into a scene. With their heightened sense of anxiety, the Neurotic can easily exacerbate a situation with a calculable overreaction. When you observe a pair or group of characters dealing with an issue, uncomfortable situation, or difficult news, the Neurotic is likely to blow things out of proportion and not let misfortune roll off their back. The Neurotic's stress-based reaction to unfolding events is therefore bound to heighten tension and produce fodder for humor.

Additionally, the Neurotic's hyperactive thought process manifests through words. So, they talk a lot. The Neurotic is a great character to use for laying out exposition. It's in their nature to word vomit, so writers often take advantage of their frenetic energy to get large chunks of story out on the table. Whenever you see larger blocks of dialogue within a script, there is a good chance that character is Neurotic. There are, of course, exceptions but, by and large, the other archetypes simply don't monologue as much or frequently as the Neurotic.

Since Neurotics are smart and have a lot of knowledge, it also makes sense that writers would use their intelligence to solve problems after the initial hysteria has died down. Neurotics are like walking encyclopedias, so they are great for inserting facts and esoteric information that wouldn't make sense for other characters to have at their fingertips.

Neurotics have so much to say that they sometimes even become the narrator of their own thoughts, the show itself or both. Carrie Bradshaw (Sarah Jessica Parker) provides narration for *Sex and the City*, Adam Goldberg (Sean Giambrone) voices his thoughts on *The Goldbergs*, and Ally McBeal (Calista Flockhart) comments on her own life through voiceover in the character-titled series, *Ally McBeal*. Other archetypes can easily provide narration, but the Neurotic is the most winning choice for a lead character to analyze and discuss the events of their world with the audience.

What Is Your Way In?

It's hard for a real-life Neurotic to believe, but some people are not prone to worrying at all. Imagine! If you've read about the Neurotic and thought I was describing you, personally, then you know your way in. Just be your ever-analytical self.

Here is some guidance for those who are not chronically nervous. We have all worried about something at some point in our lives. Ever had insomnia? Couldn't fall asleep at night because of thoughts racing through your head? Shocked by a panic attack that came out of nowhere? While not hilarious, those reactions are the result of stress and are honest ways to personalize anxiety. If you're *not* a Neurotic, you probably think of those as unfortunate, isolated incidents you'd rather not recall. If you *are* a Neurotic, you're more likely to think of those as typical demons you fight every day.

Have you ever had obsessive thoughts? While most people don't have a serious problem in that regard, there are times when we can't let go of something we should. Breakups aren't always easy, for example. Have you ever continued to think about an ex long past the point of the end of the relationship?

Maybe you even did a little social media stalking to see if they were with someone else yet. Not anyone's proudest moment, but that's what we're like. People are insecure, and we sometimes do odd things. The angst that drives you to want to know what's going on with someone who is no longer part of your life is a super real way of generating sense memory in your body to activate the palpable energy that drives the Neurotic through life.

Should you happen to possess above-average intelligence, that can also be a way for you to successfully get into the skin of the Neurotic. Not all smart people are worrywarts. Those qualities often go together, but not always. If you consider yourself a scholar, an academic, a person with refined tastes who enjoys cultural leisure activities, then perhaps that is how you might embody a Neurotic.

As with all the archetypes, there is no singular way or right way to play them. Acting is always about telling the truth on all fronts, the best way in which you are able.

There are many ways you can twist the prism in order to honestly reflect the point of view of this complicated and energetic archetypical character. Remember to communicate quickly and articulate artfully. Neurotics are experts at expressing their wise words expeditiously.

The Neurotic in a Family-Based Series: *Frasier*

Frasier's little brother, Niles Crane (David Hyde Pierce), is very likely the best-developed Neurotic in television history. One of the most celebrated sitcoms ever with a total of 37 Primetime Emmy Awards, *Frasier* ran for 11 seasons and garnered Pierce four Emmy wins for Best Supporting Actor in a Comedic Role.

There have been some amazing Neurotics before and there will be great ones to come, but if there was a Neurotic Olympics, Niles Crane would have to be the clear winner because he was given *every single* trait and characteristic with which a Neurotic could be afflicted, blessed, or cursed. A fan of the opera, theater, and classical music, he is prone to panic attacks and hyperventilating. He chews anxiety like bubble gum. "I've always liked the notion of meeting the great figures of history. But then I think: What if it's like high school and all the really cool dead people don't want to hang out with me? Mozart'll tell me he's busy, but then later I'll see him out with Shakespeare and Lincoln!" he frets.

Niles is shockingly insecure, considering he's an incredibly successful psychiatrist. He's hypercompetitive, has low self-esteem, Mensa-level intelligence, gourmet tastes, a long list of phobias, rare allergies and medical conditions, many of which are clearly psychosomatic.

> FRASIER: Frankly, I wish you'd start seeing someone about this bug phobia of yours.

> NILES: It is not a phobia! I have a healthy fear of our natural predators. It's us versus them, and frankly, I'm starting to wonder just whose side you're on!

His nose bleeds whenever he tells a lie or acts against his code of ethics, and then he faints at the sight of his own blood. When divorcing his never-seen wife, Maris, he starts suffering from stress-induced narcolepsy. He's obsessive-compulsive, perennially persnickety, a leading authority in the field of psychiatry, physically weak, and woefully uncoordinated. "The only things we Crane boys are skilled at catching are sarcastic nuances and the occasional virus," he admits.

If that weren't enough, he's a complete hypochondriac who constantly obsesses over his health, "Have you seen how stale these pistachios are? It's like swallowing gravel. It's a wonder I escaped permanent injury." Everything about the way Niles Crane was constructed by the brilliant writers of *Frasier* and then portrayed by David Hyde Pierce is a masterclass in the comedic composition of the Neurotic psyche.

When *Frasier* begins, Niles is enduring a marriage that has seemingly no positive attributes. He famously has a Freudian slip while advising Frasier, "It is possible to move a relationship along too fast and ultimately marry too hastily. You could find a few years down the line that the person isn't really right for you. And then what happens, if you meet the right person, someone who *really* excites you and makes you feel alive, but you can't act upon it because you're trapped in a stale, albeit comfortable Maris... Marriage. I have to go now."

Niles suppresses his feelings about the state of his relationship with Maris for many years. When the reality of his loveless marriage surfaces and becomes too real and apparent, he has to excuse himself. A classic case of a Neurotic's internalized safety mechanism against pain, loss, and rejection. However, this uncomfortable situation sets him up to pine for his father's caregiver, Daphne Moon (Jane Leeves). As the series progresses, Niles and Maris divorce, his feelings for Daphne are revealed, and they eventually marry. Along the way, they have to work through a particular issue unique to their relationship.

Daphne sees a therapist who tells her she may have gained a significant amount of weight to subconsciously create a barrier between herself and Niles, since he idolized her from afar for seven years. In a misguided attempt to assure Daphne, he sees the "real" her, his literal nature causes a massive faux pas.

DAPHNE: I'm going to make myself some dinner. Would you like to join me?

NILES: I would love that! (THEN) Actually, wait, Daphne... I'm going to pass on dinner.

DAPHNE: Oh, it's no trouble.

NILES: No, I know. It's just that... I don't really care for your cooking.

DAPHNE:	What?
NILES:	Well, you're not the best cook in the world. In fact, you're not very good at cooking. At all. Bad, bad cook! (THEN) You okay?
DAPHNE:	How could I be after that horrible thing you just said to me?
NILES:	Well, I'm sorry, darling, I was just trying to show you that I see you the way you really are.
DAPHNE:	And who I am is a bad cook, is that what you're saying?
NILES:	No, no, no, no... No, that's not fair. I thought that this is what you wanted.
DAPHNE:	Well, it still hurts. I have feelings, you know? I thought you loved my cooking. Well, you certainly could have handled this better!
NILES:	Then I don't know what you want! I can't read minds, you know. And by the way, neither can you!
DAPHNE:	Are you saying you don't think I'm psychic?
NILES:	Not if you thought I loved your cooking.
DAPHNE:	Well, I'm sorry it's not that hoity-toity crap you eat!
NILES:	What does that mean? You think I'm pretentious?
DAPHNE	You'd eat a worm if I gave it a French name.

NILES:	Well, fine, if that's the way you feel, maybe I'll just have dinner by myself.
DAPHNE:	Well, good! It'll spare you the hell that's my cooking!

Niles exits slamming the door, then immediately returns.

NILES:	I am so sorry! I love you so much! I didn't mean any of those things.
DAPHNE:	Yes, you did! And I did too. You're a pretentious snob with your wine and your opera...
NILES:	Well... YOU NEVER GIVE OPERA A CHANCE! You're too judgmental.
DAPHNE:	And you're a clean freak.
NILES:	Well, I hate your unicorn collection.
DAPHNE:	And I hate that your closet is bigger than mine!
NILES:	Well... you're too tall!
DAPHNE:	You're too short.

Their passions overtake them, and they melt into each other, kissing frantically.

Neurotics have a tendency to get into trouble by taking words said by others too literally. Their internal programming is linear, like computer code. They can forget other personality types are more outwardly emotional and less adherent to rules. Such is the case with Niles when he tries to take Daphne off the pedestal he's placed her upon and see her as a multidimensional human being.

This passage is also a great example of how to create humor by simply having characters tell each other what they're like. It's funny, it's specific, and it narrows the margins from infinity. When characters are well-crafted and live consistently within the parameters of their archetype, they can create humor just by showing up with their recognizable traits intact.

Sure, I can come to my own conclusions about what a character is like, but here Daphne is making it all the easier. She reads Niles as a pretentious, clean freak, hoity-toity, snob who has a really large closet for a guy. She's got Niles tagged and bagged. Notice he's irritated in return by the qualities that define her as an Eccentric. Much funnier and sophisticated than if they were throwing each other shade about not putting the toilet seat down or nagging, etc. Their words cut right to the heart of who they each are as individuals. And while he's unique in his own way, Niles is undoubtedly and by every measure a complete and total Neurotic.

The Neurotic in a Friend-Based Series: *Friends*

Honorable mention here goes to the aforementioned Tony Randall for his portrayal of Felix Unger in the original *The Odd Couple* television series. Also an Emmy winner, Randall was nominated five out of the six years the show ran. Although the series, a product of the 1970's, is now dated, his performance is not. Any actor, male or female, who strives to elevate their portrayal of a Neurotic should study Tony Randall's intricate work as one of history's most notable comedic characters.

Ross Geller (David Schwimmer) and Monica Geller-Bing (Courteney Cox) are more contemporary examples of fully realized TV Neurotics. There are six lead ensemble characters on *Friends*. It's notable that only one archetype is duplicated and, of course, it's the Neurotic. Similar to Mitchell and Claire on *Modern*

Family, Ross and Monica are siblings who inhabit the opposite ends of the Neurotic spectrum.

Like Mitchell (a lawyer), Ross has a degree-oriented job suited for an intellectual. He is a paleontologist with a PhD from Columbia University. Ross has a very cerebral nature and David Schwimmer does an extraordinary job of conveying the character's overactive internal monologue. Heady and sophisticated in relation to his peers, Ross is clearly academic in his approach to life.

"We were on a break!" Ross cries out in defense, like, *all the time!* When he and Rachel take a break from their romantic relationship, Ross sleeps with another woman. The pair attempts to reconcile the next day, but when Rachel learns Ross slept with someone the one night they were apart, she can't make it work. Although they do end up together in the end, this puts their romantic feelings for each other on ice for quite a while.

Volumes were written about Ross and Rachel's romance. The fate of the two "Friends" captivated audiences worldwide. "We were on a break!" is a line that is brought back many times thereafter during the series' 10-year run. It's also a sturdy defense for having sex with another person in an entirely clinical, intellectual way. Emotionally and from a woman's point of view, however, it's got serious problems.

Ross and Rachel did not define the terms of the break and Rachel even confesses to Monica the next day that they "broke up." In every way, both Ross and Rachel interpreted the break as a breakup. The vagueness of that specific point was a brilliant way to create conflict and carve the couple up for a while.

There must have been something very relatable about this conundrum because to this day, *Friends* is rewatched by millions in syndication and streamed over and over again. Ross and Rachel's love affair is an enormous part of *Friends'* popularity.

The audience is invested in the characters and the writing, but I think they are also invested in the minutiae of this particular argument. People are titillated by the idea of being broken up for just one night and what might happen, if it happened to any of us. How soon is too soon? At what point do you know a love affair is *truly* over? It spurred water cooler conversations. Did Ross do something wrong or not? Is Rachel overreacting or isn't she?

It only matters to the people in the relationship. The take-away, however, is this — Ross is a Neurotic and his actions made sense to him and his way of thinking. He is not a cheater; he hadn't cheated on Rachel or anyone else before, and this wasn't cheating in his framework of understanding since he and Rachel were on a break.

There is a flowchart in his brain that leads to a logical con-clusion, and only *one* conclusion. From his point of view, he and Rachel should be able to move forward. Plus, they love each other, he apologized, and genuinely meant it. Staying together makes a lot of intellectual sense.

If Rachel was also a Neurotic, she might see his perspective. But not only do women generally have different emotional ba-rometers regarding intimate relationships than men, Rachel is also a Narcissist. She is the *least* likely archetype to tolerate any-thing that feels like being cheated on or discounted in any way.

Pairing a Neurotic with a Narcissist turned out be an incredibly potent combination. It left Ross forever trying to figure out how to please someone who can never be fully satisfied. His busy brain never stopped ruminating on Rachel. In fact, he thought about her (obsessed over her) so much that when he attempted to marry someone else, he said Rachel's name instead of hers while giving vows at the altar. Poor Emily!

Monica, on the other hand, is cursed with the compulsive behavioral traits. She's far more down to earth than her brother, much like Claire Dunphy. "Now, I need you to be careful and efficient. And remember: If I am harsh with you, it's only because you're doing it wrong," Monica instructs. In many instances, her dialogue is interchangeable with Claire's.

She's very well-known within her tribe as a clean freak. Monica's entire identity is wrapped up in her need to control her environment. She is obsessive to the point that she cleans her cleaning supplies, using a dustbuster to remove dirt from a vacuum cleaner, and wishing there was yet another vacuum to clean the dustbuster. "If only there were a smaller one to clean this one!"

After her very own birthday party, Rachel offers to help her clean up. Monica replies, "Are you kidding? You had your party. Now I'll have mine!" As the series progresses, it is eventually revealed that Monica has a hallway closet jam-packed with junk that doesn't fit into any of her categories. She therefore shoves the extra stuff into the closet of shame so she doesn't have to see a mess and feel like a failure. It's a great detail to add to Monica's behavioral profile. Only a Neurotic would have a failsafe for their already perfect organizational plan.

Much like Mitchell and Claire from *Modern Family*, Ross and Monica perfectly complement opposite ends of the Neurotic spectrum.

The Neurotic in a Work-Based Series: *Scrubs*

Like so many other Neurotics both real and fictional, Dr. Elliot Reid (Sarah Chalke) on *Scrubs* finds herself in the unenviable position of having both a mother and father as adversaries. It makes sense that issues of inferiority in an otherwise accomplished and intelligent person arise as a byproduct of not-so-great parenting. In countless instances, we learn that a series-regular Neurotic has issues with mom or dad or both.

Elliot is a prime example of this circumstance. She has multiple neuroses and crippling insecurity. For example, even as a doctor, she has an extremely difficult time pronouncing certain parts of human anatomy. When fellow doctor Turk (David Faison) needs relationship advice, Elliot offers assistance, but to no avail:

TURK: Elliot, I can't talk to you about sex. I don't understand any of that crazy gibberish you use. Penis is schwing - something...

ELLIOT: Schwing-schwong, peepers or peep.

TURK: Right. And vagina is...?

ELLIOT: Disgusting, but also, bajingo or hoo-hoo.

A doctor who uses euphemisms for private body parts suffers from some serious control issues. So, where do they come from? Elliot grew up privileged but love-starved. She once attributed her many neuroses to the way she was treated by her parents. Elliot's mother is a cold, self-absorbed alcoholic, and her über controlling father did his best to micromanage her career. He wanted Elliot to specialize in gynecology, and when she refused, preferring to become a doctor of internal medicine, he cut her off financially. Harsh.

He also wanted her to be a boy. Although she wasn't, he gave her a boy's name anyway. This isn't the first or only time we've seen gender resentment included in a character's backstory between parent and child. However, it's an excellent example of nature vs. nurture in our upbringing. Elliot's life began with her father bestowing a permanent reminder that he wished she were something else. That's bound to set the stage for a maladjusted psyche later on.

In terms of driving narrative, it's a great platform though. Writers can now use this element to create lifelong tension and conflict within these relationships. This conflict can be literal and direct as is exemplified between Elliot and her father, Simon, as adults or indirect. The indirect tension she endures throughout her life would be her numerous neuroses.

Even if she's aware that her parents' attitudes toward her affected her negatively throughout her childhood, she's not necessarily aware of the compulsions, phobias, or psychopathy that sprang forth from her upbringing.

The lack of parental approval is a big factor in a person's, or character's, neurotic tendencies that stem from their environment and circumstance as opposed to their nature. In one stunning moment, Elliot admits to attempting suicide when she was 16 in order to comfort a patient who's just tried to take his own life; quite a serious bit of backstory for a sitcom character.

"I once tried to kill myself." She confesses to everyone's complete surprise.

> ELLIOT: I'm not even sure why I did it. I guess things just catch up with you, you know? You get lonely, you're not happy with what's happening in your life, and...

> J.D.: An amazing guy breaks up with you −

> ELLIOT: J.D., this is not about you! I was sixteen. I was all into poetry back then, you know, Sylvia Plath and Virginia Woolf, I know, shocker. Well, they both killed themselves. Plath stuck her head in the oven, but that was not an option for me because every time my head gets hot, I need to pee and I was not about to be found lying

in a puddle of my own urine. Not again. Not after the prom fiasco. So... I decided to do it like Virginia Woolf. I walked into a lake and tried to drown myself. Got up early on a Saturday, put on my bikini...

PATIENT: Whoa, why would you wear a bikini?

ELLIOT: Oh, my one-piece was in the back of Coach Pongetti's car. That story informs this one, but I'm not going to tell it. Anyhow, I swam out to the middle of the lake and I couldn't bring myself to go under, so I just started, you know, floatin' around, waiting to get tired and then, bam, bam, bam, bam... I got hit in the head by four oars as our school's rowing team passed by and then they just picked me out of the lake and took me home.

We're examining the life of a fictional character, so ostensibly anything the writers imagine could have happened. However, most of the main cast of *Scrubs* is gathered around the patient's bedside in this particular scene; in other words, a collection of several different archetypes. The confession of a teenage suicide attempt could have come from anyone but makes the most sense from the point of view of a Neurotic. In this case, Elliot.

She had the currently observable traits and established back-story to believably support a half-hearted attempt to end her life. Even for a fictional television character, information of that nature can't come completely out of nowhere. There has to be some logical basis for it. With her monstrous parents and dismal childhood, Elliot is by far and away the most likely candidate to know something about wanting to not exist.

Characteristics of the Neurotic

- Ambitious
- Analytical
- Anxious
- Apprehensive
- Awkward
- Capable
- Cautious
- Clever
- Competitive
- Cultured
- Engaged
- Fastidious
- Fussy
- Have Their Own Rule Book
- High-Strung
- Inflexible
- Inhibited
- Insecure
- Internal
- Intrusive
- Invested
- Isolated
- Literal-Minded
- Meticulous
- Obsessive-Compulsive
- Overwrought
- Perfectionist
- Persnickety
- Precise
- Proficient
- Refined
- Restless
- Rigid
- Superior
- Tasteful
- Tense
- Uptight
- Verbose
- Well-Educated
- Wired

Neurotics Throughout the History of Television

Chidi Anagonye	William Jackson Harper	The Good Place
Buster Bluth	Tony Hale	Arrested Development
George-Michael Bluth	Michael Cera	Arrested Development
Carrie Bradshaw	Sarah Jessica Parker	Sex and the City
Amy Brookheimer	Anna Chlumsky	Veep
Danny Castellano	Chris Messina	The Mindy Project
Diane Chambers	Shelley Long	Cheers
Alice Charles	Julia Schlaepfer	The Politician
Jules Cobb	Courteney Cox	Cougar Town
Niles Crane	David Hyde Pierce	Frasier
Alex Dunphy	Ariel Winter	Modern Family
Claire Dunphy	Julie Bowen	Modern Family
Billy Epstein	Billy Eichner	Difficult People
Shirley Fee-ney-Meany	Cindy Williams	Laverne & Shirley
Ross Geller	David Schwimmer	Friends
Monica Geller-Bing	Courteney Cox	Friends
Adam Goldberg	Sean Giambrone	The Goldbergs
Patty Greene	Sarah Jessica Parker	Square Pegs
Morgan Grimes	Joshua Gomez	Chuck
Joseph Hackett	Tim Daly	Wings
Alan Harper	Jon Cryer	Two and a Half Men

Jackie Harris	Laurie Metcalf	Roseanne
Bill Haverchuck	Martin Starr	Freaks and Geeks
Richard Hendricks	Thomas Middle-ditch	Silicon Valley
Lionel Higgins	DeRon Horton	Dear White People
Alex P. Keaton	Michael J. Fox	Family Ties
Peter Lovett	John Michael Higgins	Happily Divorced
Miriam "Midge" Maisel	Rachel Brosnahan	The Marvelous Mrs. Maisel
Angela Martin	Angela Kinsey	The Office
Ally McBeal	Calista Flockhart	Ally McBeal
Ethel Mertz	Vivian Vance	I Love Lucy
Lisa Miller	Maura Tierney	NewsRadio
Adrian Monk	Tony Shalhoub	Monk
Les Nessman	Richard Sanders	WKRP in Cincinnati
Cpl. Walter "Radar" O'Reilly	Gary Burghoff	M*A*S*H
Anna-Kat Otto	Julia Butters	American Housewife
Rob Petrie	Dick Van Dyke	The Dick Van Dyke Show
Emma Pillsbury	Jayma Mays	Glee
Ray Ploshanksy	Alex Karpovsky	Girls
Samuel "Screech" Powers	Dustin Diamond	Saved by the Bell
Mitchell Pritchett	Jesse Tyler Ferguson	Modern Family
Dr. Elliot Reid	Sarah Chalke	Scrubs

David Rose	Daniel Levy	Schitt's Creek
Detective Amy Santiago	Melissa Fumero	Brooklyn Nine-Nine
Jimmy Shive-Overly	Chris Geere	You're the Worst
Jonah Simms	Ben Feldman	Superstore
Jessie Spano	Elizabeth Berkley	Saved by the Bell
Darrin Stephens	Dick York	Bewitched
Felix Unger	Tony Randall	The Odd Couple
Steve Urkel	Jaleel White	Family Matters
Bree Van De Kamp	Marcia Cross	Desperate Housewives
Abe Weissman	Tony Shalhoub	The Marvelous Mrs. Maisel
Howard Wolowitz	Simon Helberg	The Big Bang Theory
Ben Wyatt	Adam Scott	Parks and Recreation

How Neurotics are Described in the Breakdowns

A planner and a scheduler, afraid to leave comfort zone, all logic and science, ambitious, attractive in a buttoned-up kind of way, bookish, by the book, controlling, dedicated, effete (men), exacting, fidgety, gadget guru, gossipy, head of the class, hurried, hyperintelligent, math guru, nerdy, only one reality, precocious, raw foodie, rule follower, sci-fi fanboy, techie, type-A, savvy, uptight, vegan, when things don't go as planned she loses her cool, wine aficionado

Lead Body Part: Stomach

Butterflies are beautiful unless they're in your stomach. Anxiety, fret, and worry are often known to cause digestive issues. Although the Neurotic is cerebral, we don't feel emotion in our brains. Our brains are the control center for our emotions and reactions to stimuli. The brain sends signals to other parts of our body. The reason our stomach gets upset when we're panicked is because of our subconscious fight-or-flight instinct. Back in caveman days, if we needed to run from a saber-toothed tiger, we'd throw up our food to make ourselves lighter so we could run faster. If our parents didn't love us or our pack didn't accept us, *we might actually die*. We are still born with these base, powerful instincts. Neurotics are often reacting to danger that isn't there. Hence the queasy feeling for no apparent reason!

Who Are They?

Narcissists have exaggerated feelings of self-importance and love everything about who they are. Conversely, they devalue others and lack empathy as well as adaptability. A Narcissist cannot understand your worth unless you are specifically worth something to them. They are the center of their own finite, ego-maniacal universe.

They live in a bubble of grandiosity that masks an inner emp-tiness. Traditionally, while Narcissists have always existed in TV comedy, they were largely ensemble or supporting characters. Some examples are Hilary Banks (Karyn Parsons) on *The Fresh Prince of Bel-Air*, Rachel Greene (Jennifer Aniston) on *Friends*, Ari Gold (Jeremy Piven) on *Entourage*, Suzanne Sugarbaker (Delta Burke) on *Designing Women*, and Bill McNeal (Phil Hartman) on *NewsRadio*.

Interestingly, the Narcissist has evolved from an ensem-ble (supporting) character to a lead (starring) character, as social media has taken root and become an integral part of our day-to-day lives. Historically there are examples of Narcissists as the hero archetype around which a show is based. Most famous is Frasier Crane (Kelsey Grammer) of *Frasier*. However, Frasier is a spinoff of *Cheers* and Narcissist Frasier was not originally conceived as a lead character. He was born a patron in the ensemble comedy that was *Cheers*.

This evolution is noteworthy because it means actors and writers developing their careers from this point forward need to understand the nuanced transition that's occurred. Lead characters are designed much differently now than previous examples most of us grew up watching. Our society has changed rapidly, largely due to the internet and social media. The new age of television must reflect our relevant societal changes. We watch who we are.

Comedy, in particular, echoes these significant cultural changes because it trades so heavily on pop culture references. It appears our prevailing socioeconomic conditions combined with technology-driven, social media-immersed lives have made us more self-centered. Well, if not us, the characters with whom we spend time. But they say art mirrors society, right?

Nearly all half-hour comedies created from the beginning of television through 2010 or so featured an Anchor, Dreamer, or Neurotic as the lead character or characters around which a show was based. If the series featured a pair of co-leads, one of those archetypes were surely included.

If the show featured an ensemble, it's likely one of those three archetypes held a prominent position within the group. Said another way, an Anchor, Dreamer, or Neurotic (and occasionally a Cynic) were always the characters around whom the show was based. They were the leader, the traditional writer's hero, or the primary guiding force for the series' journey.

Here are a few examples: Roseanne and Seinfeld are Anchors on their eponymous shows. Lucy (Lucille Ball) is a Dreamer on *I Love Lucy*, as is Liz Lemon (Tina Fey) on *30 Rock*, and Raymond (Ray Romano) on *Everybody Loves Raymond*. Ross and Monica (David Schwimmer and Courteney Cox) are both Neurotics on *Friends*, as are Claire and Mitchell (Julie Bowen and Jesse Tyler Ferguson) on *Modern Family*.

After 2010, there was a seismic shift and suddenly most of the half-hour comedies that made it to series and stayed on the air featured Narcissists in lead roles. Evidence the following shows that have wrapped multiple seasons:

The Mindy Project stars Mindy Kaling as Mindy Lahiri, a proud Narcissist who refers to herself as such constantly. *Brooklyn Nine-Nine* stars Andy Samberg as Detective Jake Peralta, a sweet, totally lovable... Narcissist. He even has his own groupie, Det. Boyle (Joe Lo Truglio).

The Goldbergs stars Wendi McLendon-Covey as smothering, Narcissist mother Beverly Goldberg. *Girls* stars Lena Dunham as hateable-because-she's-such-a-Narcissist, Hannah Horvath. *Episodes* stars Matt LeBlanc playing a version of himself. The difference from the Joey days of *Friends*? He's now a Narcissist and the other characters refer to him as one frequently.

The Comeback came back to HBO after a nine-year hiatus. Lisa Kudrow's genius portrayal of Valerie Cherish, the ultimate Narcissist was too good not to invite to the party once more. *Web Therapy* features Kudrow's *other* Narcissist character Fiona Wallice on Showtime.

Mom stars Allison Janney as yet another Narcissist mother, Bonnie Plunkett. *2 Broke Girls* has a 50 percent chance that one is a Narcissist. She is; Beth Behrs as Caroline Channing. *Veep* stars multiple Emmy Award winner Julia Louis-Dreyfus as über Narcissist Selina Meyer. Max Greenfield's Schmidt is so into himself on *New Girl*, we don't even get to know his first name (until the end of the series).

House of Lies follows a *group* of Narcissistic management consultants headed by manipulative and immoral Marty Kaan as played by Don Cheadle. *Getting On* stars the brilliant Laurie Metcalf as raging Narcissist Dr. Jenna James, who seeks global acclaim for her study of feces. Ashton Kutcher portrays a self-loving former football star on Netflix's *The Ranch*. And lastly, *Black-ish* stars Anthony Anderson as Dre Johnson, a husband and father who is completely narcissistic-ish.

Upon intensive investigation, it appears this current trend permeates all the variables of half-hour comedy characteri-zations; single-camera, multi-camera, gender, age, broadcast, cable, premium networks, and streaming networks.

I frequently coach actors on series regular roles who struggle with how to play a Narcissist, especially as a lead. It's as if we're all still getting used to the idea of a Narcissist carrying the show. A lot of times the actor hasn't been cast this way before and doesn't have an immediate access point. It's also quite common that women, who have gone out of their way to be taken seriously in their personal lives, find it difficult to find the humor in portraying someone vapid and unsubstantial.

If that's the case, please reference Jane Krakowski as both Jenna Maroney on *30 Rock* and Jacqueline Voorhees on *Unbreakable Kimmy Schmidt* as an example of how to play a comedic and likable Narcissist. Her pitch-perfect understanding of a vapid mind and empty soul is mesmerizing.

So now that I've laid out some context, and we've updated our collective memo regarding archetypes that drive story, let's unpack the Narcissist a bit more. Narcissists are inherently selfish, and they have a rather long list of qualities that are negative; shallow, vain, spoiled, entitled, and domineering to name a few.

They have a tendency to pout and complain a lot in order to get their way. However, like a toddler, they're made content quite easily.

The Narcissist encounters obstacles just like any other archetype. The major difference is that their worldview is strongly influenced by deep feelings of entitlement. Narcissists think they deserve everything they have and everything they want. So even though they have setbacks, they are not affected by them in the same way as the other Heroes of Comedy.

When it comes to obtaining their desires, the Narcissist either has what they want, or they are certain they are on their way to getting it. This creates a happy-go-lucky buoyancy to their personality. If you think that you ultimately cannot fail in life, you're bound to be upbeat and immune to serious depression and self-doubt.

Yes, Narcissists are obnoxious. But they're also a lot of fun. Narcissists envision that they will succeed in this world no matter the odds and that steadfast belief alone may make that true for them. So, although they are shallow, Narcissists delight in not just being themselves, but being alive. They win and winning makes you feel good. They share that good feeling with their family and friends, though not much else.

Here are other qualities that most Narcissists share; they are charismatic, extravagant, happy, popular, and upbeat. These are not only generally positive qualities, they are also characteristics that are highly rewarded by society at large. Narcissists have gigantic egos, but when they're happy, they also spread a lot of merriment and good cheer to those around them.

It's tempting to judge this archetype negatively. In real life we might have Narcissists who cause us grief, or we may have worked hard to get rid of them altogether. Perhaps you grew up observing Narcissists in school and steered clear of them in the first place. If this is the case for you, I strongly suggest studying the list of actors playing Narcissists, especially in a lead role. There is a throughline in how they all approach life. Frasier, Selina Meyer, and Det. Jake Peralta are all living as if existence is an everlasting adventure. Beverly Goldberg, Mindy Lahiri, and Bonnie Plunkett love being who they are in a way that leaves them feeling deeply satisfied.

Whether they own their self-centered nature or not, Narcissists are in touch with making the world a brighter place. Whatever you might think of what they're doing, they think they're glorious. They view their judgments as sincerely valuable advice and guidance. Yes, their execution leaves a lot to be desired, but (comedically) their intention is usually not to hurt, it's to help; they're just bad caretakers.

Insults are a quicker means by which to make a point and feeling superior is their ever-nourishing manna. Don't get this confused; being judged doesn't mean you are not simultaneously being loved. Too many actors think there is a disconnect here and this is precisely where the comedy comes undone when portraying this archetype. This is where the actor's dislike for this kind of personality intercedes and the dramatic version of the given circumstances surfaces.

This is especially true for those who were raised by Narcissistic parents, particularly mothers. From this archetype's point of view, love and judgment are braided together and one does not discount the other. Narcissists do not think of themselves as mean people and you shouldn't either, at least while you're playing one for comedy!

What Is Their Strength?

The particular strength of the Narcissist is their charisma. They are magnetic and therefore socially successful. Their popularity is a by-product of the excitement they find in living. If you think of Narcissists as glib, aloof, isolated, or snooty, you're likely projecting that on to them. It may well be your own insecurities that are welling up when confronted with a person who has enough self-esteem for 10 other people.

Narcissists are happy to be in the world and that uplifts others around them. Yes, there is a price to pay in spending time with a Narcissist. Whatever you're doing, the experience is going to be about them more than you.

But on the flip side, Narcissists are great at providing their friends and loved ones with experiences they might not have otherwise had and take them places they might otherwise have never gone. Unsatisfied with the mundane, they aspire to the finer things in life. That means constantly reaching upward in life whatever their current station. The mere association with a Narcissist can easily lead any other archetype to imagine they could also have whatever they want too, if at least for a while.

2 Broke Girls is a great example of aspiration by association. The basic premise of the series is simple: two unlikely friends join forces to start a business together. Caroline Channing (Beth Behrs) is a Narcissist and her buddy Max (Kat Dennings) is a Cynic.

Working as a waitress at a greasy spoon, there is no way that Max is going to strive to be an entrepreneur on her own. However, adding a down-on-her-luck companion into Max's world changes everything for her. She remains a Cynic through and through, but Narcissist Caroline's certainty that everything will go their way if they simply start is contagious and Max buys into the proposition. Even broke, Caroline sees her life moving in only one direction and that's up the ladder of success. Living and working with Caroline, Max is uplifted despite her cynicism.

What Is Their Weakness?

I've tried hard to be an advocate for the Narcissist and highlight their winning qualities because I think they get a bad rap from a lot of actors, especially on the first read. This archetype has a lot of currency in today's marketplace and I think it's important that actors of all ages don't write off their ability to play a believable Narcissist too quickly.

At the end of the day, it may not be in your wheelhouse. It may not be a character you feel a close kinship with. But of all 10 of The Heroes of Comedy, the Narcissist is the one most commonly ignored without exploration. I see the Narcissist consistently rejected out of hand because some people don't want to be associated with these traits even though they are only acting. Hard to believe!

The Narcissist's weakness is vanity, which manifests as intolerance. When you're taken with yourself in totality, those around you pale in comparison. Lacking patience or empathy with others is definitely a shortcoming, and this is where the fun times end with the Narcissist. They are judgmental and have little concern for other people's feelings, weighted against their own needs. Fans of *Arrested Development* will recognize those traits in Lucille Bluth (Jessica Walter), who openly ridicules strangers and her own children alike:

To her daughter Lindsay (Portia de Rossi):

LUCILLE: I don't criticize you. And if you're worried about criticism… sometimes a diet is the best defense.

Regarding her son Buster:

LUCILLE: …I don't know. Maybe it's because I went off my post-partum medication.

MICHAEL:	You were still taking that? You had Buster 32 years ago.
LUCILLE:	And that's how long I've been depressed about him.

Regarding her eldest son Gob (Will Arnett):

LUCILLE:	She'd love to get at me any way she could. That's why she's been flirting with Gob. She's trying to prove that she's closer to my children than I am, but the joke's on her, because she doesn't know how little I care for Gob.

To her third least favorite child Michael (Jason Bateman):

LUCILLE:	You're my third least favorite child.
MICHAEL:	I can live with that.

In return for her palpable contempt, Narcissist and functioning alcoholic Lucille garners indifference, pity, scorn, and rage from her own kids. She never says she doesn't love her children, by the way. Her comments are born of the inconvenience of having children at all and then ranking each of them in contrast to the others.

A lot of people would say, "What's the difference?" The difference is that Narcissists perceive themselves as victims, *not bullies*, and speaking their minds about their inconveniences (even their children) is their God-given right. That is what entitlement is in a practical sense. As we will see with some further examples, not all Narcissists are so overtly reprehensible.

How Do Others See Them?

There's a range of reactions to the Narcissist from admiration to envy to disgust, which mostly depends on how nice they are. If you're the family terrorist like Lucille Bluth, you'll get bad reviews across the board. But not all Narcissists are mean. Some are quite nice most of the time. However, the rest of their tribe fears even the most grounded Narcissist when they are unhappy.

Jennifer Aniston's portrayal of Rachel Green on *Friends* is the perfect example. For much of *Friends*' original run, Rachel Green was America's Sweetheart. Her friends loved her, and the world loved her, arguably the most of all the characters. Her second season haircut even spawned an international phenomenon of its own. Named the "Rachel" after her, the character's shag is one of the most popular hairstyles in history. Rachel is also regarded as a style icon of the 1990s.

Further evidence of her immense popularity, Jennifer Aniston is the only cast member of *Friends* to win an Emmy Award for lead actor or actress in a primetime comedy series. Additionally, she won a Golden Globe as lead actress in a musical or comedy. That's quite a feat, considering the show's storylines were divided evenly among six cast members. And a lot of acclaim for a character who already likes herself plenty.

But Narcissists who are more grounded and accessible end up being the most popular girl in school, or in Rachel's case, the world. My students are often surprised to learn that Rachel Green is a Narcissist when we discuss The Heroes of Comedy and I get why. Jennifer Aniston did such an amazing job of humanizing Rachel, it's easy to forget that she was indeed spoiled and selfish. But, boy was she!

The series begins with Rachel abandoning her fiancé at the altar and seeking out her high school acquaintance Monica (Courteney Cox) for comfort. She explains, "So, anyway, I just didn't know where to go, and I know that you and I have kind of drifted apart... But, you're the only person I knew who lives here in the city." Monica replies, "Who wasn't invited to the wedding." Rachel winces, "Uh, I was kind of hoping that wouldn't be an issue."

It's funny, but it also exposes Rachel for who she is in the opening scene of the series: a complete Narcissist. She wants a distant friend to take care of her even though she didn't bother inviting her to her wedding. Having relied on her parents' money her entire life with the sole goal of marrying someone wealthy, Rachel learns to live with lesser means along with her new group of friends. She starts off working as a waitress at Central Perk, but appropriately transitions into a career in fashion later.

Structurally, Rachel Green's story arc is quite similar to fellow Narcissist Caroline Channing (Beth Behrs) of *2 Broke Girls*. They are both young women who grew up wealthy and had to learn survival skills on the fly as young adults. A sudden plunge into poverty grounded them, but their core characteristics define them as amiable Narcissists; pampered, self-centered, popular, vain, and entitled.

As noted earlier, when Ross and Rachel famously went "on a break" from their romantic relationship and Ross slept with another woman, Rachel could neither accept it nor forgive him in their immediate future. With her entitlement in full bloom, Rachel felt absolutely justified in breaking up with Ross *and* expecting him to predict and honor the terms of the breakup from her point of view. Her overwhelming judgment of Ross' indiscretion made it impossible for her to see him as the same, loving partner he was the day before, even though she was the one who instigated the separation.

Considering this popular storyline from *Friends* is a great point of reference for actors to humanize the Narcissist. We so often think of them being snobby and reaching for the finer things in life. It's easy to imagine Narcissists as complete caricatures. Sometimes they're just very relatable, vulnerable people who are yet still driven enough by their egos that they cannot acknowledge their responsibility for their own actions. Narcissists will not be humbled.

How Do Writers Use Them?

Narcissists are dramatic by nature and move through life with theatrical flair. Of course this manifests in myriad ways, from subtle to shocking. You can, however, always count on a Narcissist to put on a show when they don't get their way.

Again, in the opening scene of Friends, we meet the rest of the cast in their day-to-day clothes. We are introduced to Rachel in her wedding dress, crying. In the first couple of seasons of *New Girl*, Schmidt (Max Greenfield) was often unnecessarily shirtless. Rachel Berry (Lea Michele) was *Glee*'s resident drama queen, "Look, I know what I'm talking about! I won my first dance competition when I was three months old!" she declares in the pilot.

Haley Dunphy (Sarah Hyland) rolls her eyes and throws more than her share of tantrums on *Modern Family*. And, finally, TV's most famous Narcissist, Frasier Crane (Kelsey Grammer), will argue a point in his living room like a senator debating on the floor of Congress.

For writers, a Narcissist is like a peacock that possesses the ever-present potential to spread their glorious feathers. From the Narcissist's point of view there is little difference between showing up and showing everyone up.

What Is Your Way In?

Most of us are not full-time Narcissists, but we all have some access point to feelings of entitlement or deserving something. Use that as your starting point. A lot of actors don't view themselves this way at all, and since they may still be working very hard to make ends meet and establish themselves in their career, it's understandable that they feel the complete opposite of the Narcissist.

However, if most people dig around, broaden the parameters of their preconceived notion of the Narcissist, and don't judge the archetype, there is assuredly a personal area that's useful as a starting point. Ladies, do you expect a man to treat you a certain way on a date? Specifically when it comes to asking, paying, dressing appropriately, and introducing the topic of sex?

If so, the requirements you have for a suitor (which he has to learn from your cues in real time or else be a psychic) can be your personal way into this character. Simply substitute your feelings and point of view in that context into any given scene featuring a Narcissist and you're on your way.

Guys, do you have a personal grooming habit or a particular product that you simply cannot do without? If not that, do you expect, even as an adult, that your parents feed you or do your laundry when you visit? Do your parents help pay your bills, even school, cell phone, or medical insurance? That is entitlement, whether you ever viewed it that way or not.

Even if these specific examples don't resonate with you, use them as fodder for further exploration in areas of your life where you are spoiled or have exacting expectations of others around you. Above all else, don't fall into the trap of indicating this character's qualities. Don't think of them as snooty or stuck up, although they have been described that way.

A more current and believable Narcissist is someone who is happy to be who they are and, unless there is a problem, is having a wonderful time doing whatever it is they're doing. There is no single way to depict this archetype or any of the others.

Look for context clues to see how searing their judgment is and how scathing their insults.

If they are kinder within the scope of their narcissism, choose the qualities that support the particular version you're working with the most. If you spot a more temperamental Narcissist, there are plenty of other characteristics listed to help you develop your best mean girl or guy.

The Narcissist in a Family-Based Series: *Everybody Loves Raymond*

Doris Roberts was nominated for seven Emmy awards for Outstanding Supporting Actress in a Comedy Series for her intricately wicked portrayal of Marie Barone on *Everybody Loves Raymond*. She won four times.

Her recognition and adoration for bringing Marie Barone to life are well-earned. As a mother, and even worse, *mother-in-law* Marie is meddlesome, domineering, judgmental, spiteful, arrogant, unyielding, insulting, divisive, disapproving, and an otherwise textbook case of narcissistic personality disorder combined with a victim complex, who runs through her family's lives like a runaway freight train on icy tracks.

She is also well-read, sophisticated, talented, charismatic, an excellent cook, interested in the arts, meticulously clean, outgoing, lively, organized, and thoroughly fulfilled.

From the inside out, Marie is complicated. From the outside in, she is simply hilarious. What a precarious tightrope act it was for Doris Roberts to humanize and make lovable a rather deplorable person who suffocates everyone around her.

Marie plays her sons against each other and has since they were children; she smothers Raymond with overwhelming affection and alienates Robert. She disapproves of her daughter-in-law Debra's (Patricia Heaton)... *everything*. She is condescending, conniving, and the grand champion of passive-aggressive manipulation.

In one instance, Debra decides to spend the day cooking with Marie and her sister-in-law, Amy (Monica Horan), vowing to get along with Marie after years of constant tension. Afterward, Debra thinks she's done an amazing job being nice in the face of Marie's endless barrage of insults; she thinks she's made a valiant attempt at uplifting her and Marie's rocky relationship.

When they review the day later with the rest of the family gathered, Debra is stunned to find that Marie found the afternoon painful and everything that Debra said sarcastic. Debra is mortified that there is no reward for her monumental effort and can't find an ally brave enough to admit that Marie is the problem; the rest of the family all know better.

Defeated, Debra is left standing pathetically in the middle of the living room with nothing left to say. Marie sits her down: "Alright, alright, Debra. All right. We had... in the past, we've had our share of tiffs. But I truly believe it's because you misunderstand me. I am not interested in a relationship of artificial pleasantries and phony smiles. You never, ever have to pretend with me. I'm always honest with you, aren't I? And if I see something that you *desperately* need help with... like... cooking... cleaning... the *children*... your hair... I care so much that I have to say something, because I want to help. Oh, honey, you don't have to be worried, dear. *I forgive you for today*. And I'm *always* here to help."

Speechless, Debra turns to Raymond who simply exclaims, "Voilà!"

Marie is a master, executing her abilities with Olympic precision. Raymond grew up watching her work, so he simply knows how it goes. There is no response to her impenetrable fog of narcissism.

In *one brief monologue*, Marie is condescending, passive-aggressive, judgmental, entitled, dramatic, imperialistic, pretentious, smug, and status-conscious. She wholly victimizes herself and projects her own worst qualities onto Debra, who only wanted to get closer to her.

She deflects all blame and gives poor Debra no credit whatsoever for at least trying... *to simply be nice*. When great writing melds with incredible acting, it's a thing of true beauty.

The Narcissist in a Friend-Based Series: *Frasier*

I'm taking a small liberty here, but I will make up for it with a bit of trivia. No investigation of TV comedy Narcissists would be complete without considering Dr. Frasier Crane, as... well, let's say *totally owned* by Kelsey Grammer.

The *series Frasier* should place the *character* Frasier under the Family-Based Series header. But since Doris Roberts' delicious portrayal of Marie Barone belonged there and was too amazing to ignore, I assigned Dr. Crane's space in this book to the Friend-Based Series section, since the character originated on *Cheers* within... a group of friends.

At *20* seasons, Dr. Frasier Crane is the longest-running character featured in live-action sitcoms in television history. Frasier appeared on nine seasons of *Cheers* and 11 seasons of *Frasier*, and had a one-time showing on a third NBC sitcom, *Wings*.

In addition, the series *Frasier* held the record for the most Emmy wins for a TV series of any kind (comedy or drama) with 37 wins, until *Game of Thrones* was awarded its 38th Emmy in 2016. However, with 11 seasons under its belt, *Frasier* still holds the record for most Emmy wins for a comedy series.

Now that he's gotten the approbation he's due, let's delve into the psyche of this pompous egomaniac. Frasier is often insufferable, erudite, ostentatious, pedantic, pontifical, and haughty.

I know; you need a dictionary just to understand the words that *describe* him.

He's a lot of work, as everyone who knows him would tell you. It's pertinent that once he moves to Seattle from Boston, Frasier becomes a pop psychiatrist working at radio station KACL and has a certain celebrity status within the city.

Frasier's enormous ego needs constant reinforcement from friends and strangers alike. He regularly loses all patience with his callers who seek therapeutic advice but don't seem to take his time or knowledge seriously.

In one instance a caller wants to know what to name his new boat. He wants to call it "The Intrepid," but his wife prefers "Lulubelle." Frasier replies on the air: "Roger... at Cornell University, they have an incredible piece of scientific equipment, known as the Tunneling Electron Microscope. Now, this microscope is so powerful that by firing electrons, you can actually see images of the atom: the infinitesimally minute building block of our universe. Roger, if I were using that microscope right now, I still wouldn't be able to locate my interest in your problem. Thank you for your call."

In much the same way Marie Barone seems to loathe everyone she loves in equal measure, Frasier has open disdain for those he's vowed to treat. He wants to be taken seriously as a mental health expert, but he has a hard time taking other people's concerns seriously and will verbally eviscerate them if they bore him or take his talents for granted.

Frasier has his share of neuroses like his brother Niles (David Hyde Pierce) but Frasier isn't paralyzed by anxiety the way his fully realized Neurotic brother is. Frasier is stuffed full of bravado like a blustery piñata. If there was ever a character that was unnecessarily dramatic, theatrical, and flamboyant, it's Narcissist Frasier Crane.

In this exchange, Frasier comes home to find that his father, Martin (John Mahoney), has spilled oil on his carpet, as he and Niles try to clean it up.

FRASIER: What the hell's happened?

MARTIN: Now, don't get upset. I was oiling my chair, trying to get rid of the squeak, and I had a little spill.

FRASIER: A little spill? I just had this carpet cleaned!

MARTIN: I'm sorry, it was an accident.

FRASIER: Sure, Dad! It was an accident.

NILES: It was an accident. I saw him step on it.

FRASIER: Niles, you know as well as I do, there are no accidents! Just admit it, Dad! Your latent hostility toward me has been building through the years, little by little, until you have finally struck the Achilles heel of my décor – the Berber carpet!

MARTIN: I did not do this on purpose!

FRASIER: No? Then I suggest you dig deep into the twisted caves of your subconscious, where malicious acts abide, clothed in the robes of plausible excuses!

MARTIN: For the last time, this was not malicious. It was an accident!

FRASIER: I don't think you know the difference!

Later in the same episode, Frasier knocks Martin's beloved recliner off the balcony where the furniture is being stored while the carpet is being cleaned. Infuriated and confused, Martin asks Frasier why he'd do such a thing. Frasier's sincere reply, "It was an accident."

It takes an extraordinarily self-involved human being to react to someone's sincere, simple mistake as if it were a vicious personal attack. And then further make a similar error, seek the same sympathy and forgiveness they would utterly deny another and then be confused as to why they couldn't be let off the hook.

Grandiose, verbose, and bellicose, Kelsey Grammer's Dr. Frasier Winslow Crane is without a doubt television's ultimate depiction of a comedic Narcissist.

The Narcissist in a Work-Based Series: *Veep*

Sometimes we have to deal with Narcissists where we work. Worst-case scenario, your boss is a Narcissist. As much fun as it *isn't* working for someone who thinks they're the center of the universe in real life, it's infinitely amusing to watch others scramble to accommodate their employer's ponderous ego.

Julia Louis-Dreyfus bagged six consecutive Primetime Emmys for Outstanding Lead Actress in a Comedy Series for embodying Washington, D.C.'s greatest (fictional) Narcissist, Selina Meyer on HBO's *Veep*. (When you add in her win for playing Elaine Benes on *Seinfeld* and another win for playing Christine Campbell on *The New Adventures of Old Christine*, that makes eight Lead Actress Emmys for Louis-Dreyfus, more than any other actress in television history!)

While there's nothing wrong with ambition, it's problematic when a person strives to attain a position for which they are immensely unqualified; especially if it's the highest position in the land. And then further proceed to blame everyone around them for their incompetence and shortcomings. If you haven't met her already, please allow me to introduce you to *Veep*'s Selina Meyer.

A Narcissist with authority in the workplace is an excellent setup for conflict and relatable stories; even more so when the workplace is the White House. With ultimate power and wealth at stake, everyone on Selina's staff are effectively sycophants. All of them itch to stick with her as she ascends to the presidency. She's fully aware of that fact and it enables her to let her personal brand of Narcissism run rampant.

The rough reality is that everyone who works for her is easily replaced, which leaves Selina free to do and say just about anything she wants without fear of reprisal. She longs to be popular with no need to actually be liked. There seems to be no one she actually admires or for whom she has respect. Here is some evidence:

To her personal aide, Gary.

 Who do you think you are? Gary Antoinette? Did somebody make you First Lady? Because I don't remember marrying you, Gary! I don't remember fucking you in Niagara Falls. I think I'd remember that!"

To her senior adviser, Dan:

SELINA: Dan, you're like the closest person I've ever met to the guy in American Psycho. And I think you might think that that's a compliment, but that's just because a part of your brain is missing.

To her campaign manager, Amy.

SELINA: "What the f...fuck, Amy?! I am putting out two fires in there and I turn around to find out that you have set fire to the fucking fire truck? The level of incompetence in this office is STAGGERING!

Regarding White House aide, Jonah:

SELINA: Please God, deliver Jonah to Congress, and then give him any kind of cancer, I don't care.

To her senior strategist, Kent:

SELINA But I need to talk to the autistic, lumberjack son of a bitch... Oh, there he is. Hi, Kent!

To the White House Chief of Staff, Ben:

BEN: We're not on the same –

SELINA: Diet?

BEN: Page!

SELINA: Oh, I thought you were gonna say 'diet,' Ben.

To her daughter, Catherine:

SELINA: What in the wide world of fuck do you think you're wearing?

To her constituents:

SELINA: I've met some people, okay? Real people. And I gotta tell ya', some of 'em are real fucking idiots.

Regarding other world leaders:

BEN: I've just been kibitzing with the Qatari ambassador, Mohammed bin Nasser bin Khalifa Al Jaffar.

SELINA: Please don't have him sign the guest book.

BEN: Yeah, he comes bringing a message from China.

SELINA: Why would China go through Qatar?

BEN: Qataris love to insert themselves. They're wet-fingered.

SELINA: They're into ass play?

BEN: No, they have a gift for sensing prevailing political winds.

SELINA: I'll bet they're into ass play, too.

Regarding democracy:

SELINA: Jesus Christ, you know? You do your best, you try to serve the people, and then they just fuck you over. And you know why? Because they're ignorant, and they're dumb as shit. And that, ladies and gentlemen, is democracy.

While being interviewed by her daughter Catherine (Sarah Sutherland) for a school project, Selina reveals the moment she knew she wanted to be president was as a girl at Richard Nixon's inaugural ball. She confides to Catherine, "Daddy leaned into me and he said, 'You know, a lot of people don't like Nixon, but by God, they respect him. And that's you, peanut.'" Selina Meyer started campaigning and never looked back.

Characteristics of the Narcissist

- Blithe
- Cavalier
- Charismatic
- Chipper
- Conceited
- Condescending
- Conservative
- Covetous
- Curt
- Devious
- Domineering
- Dramatic
- Entitled
- Extravagant
- Flamboyant
- Fun
- Grandiose
- Greedy
- Happy
- Haughty
- Imperialistic
- Judgmental
- Ostentatious
- Outgoing
- Pompous
- Possessive
- Precious
- Pretentious
- Righteous
- Satisfied
- Self-Centered
- Selfish
- Shallow
- Spoiled
- Status Conscious
- Superficial
- Temperamental
- Theatrical
- Upbeat
- Vain

Narcissists Throughout the History of Television

Hilary Banks	Karyn Parsons	The Fresh Prince of Bel-Air
Kyle Barker	Terrence "T.C." Carson	Living Single
Marie Barone	Doris Roberts	Everybody Loves Raymond
Gavin Belson	Matt Ross	Silicon Valley
Elaine Benes	Julia Louis-Dreyfus	Seinfeld
Colt Bennett	Ashton Kutcher	The Ranch
Rachel Berry	Lea Michele	Glee
Lindsay Bluth	Portia de Rossi	Arrested Development
Lucille Bluth	Jessica Walter	Arrested Development
Marcia Brady	Maureen McCormick	The Brady Bunch
Alan Brady	Carl Reiner	The Dick Van Dyke Show
Peg Bundy	Katey Sagal	Married... with Children
Jackie Burkhart	Mila Kunis	That '70s Show
Christine Campbell	Julia Louis-Dreyfus	The New Adventures of Old Christine
Caroline Channing	Beth Behrs	2 Broke Girls
Victoria Chase	Wendie Malick	Hot in Cleveland
Valerie Cherish	Lisa Kudrow	The Comeback
Colandrea Conners	Antoinette Robertson	Dear White People
Gene Cousineau	Henry Winkler	Barry
Dr. Perry Cox	John C. McGinley	Scrubs
Frasier Crane	Kelsey Grammer	Frasier

Lisa Douglas	Eva Gabor	Green Acres
Kimberly Drummond	Dana Plato	Diff'rent Strokes
Haley Dunphy	Sarah Hyland	Modern Family
Endora	Agnes Moorehead	Bewitched
Quinn Fabray	Dianna Agron	Glee
Troy Fairbanks	Brandon Bell	Dear White People
Whitley Gilbert	Jasmine Guy	A Different World
Ari Gold	Jeremy Piven	Entourage
Beverly Goldberg	Wendi McLendon-Covey	The Goldbergs
Rachel Green	Jennifer Aniston	Friends
Eddie Haskell	Ken Osmond	Leave it to Beaver
Luther Hobart	Trey Eason	The Politician
Martin Hobart	Trevor Eason	The Politician
Hannah Horvath	Lena Dunham	Girls
Lovey Howell	Natalie Schafer	Gilligan's Island
Thurston Howell III	Jim Backus	Gilligan's Island
Regine Hunter	Kim Fields	Living Single
Dr. Jenna James	Laurie Metcalf	Getting On
Mother Jefferson	Zara Cully	The Jeffersons
Andre "Dre" Johnson	Anthony Edwards	Black-ish
Eden Konkler	Kelly Stables	The Exes
Mindy Lahiri	Mindy Kaling	The Mindy Project
Jennifer Marlowe	Loni Anderson	WKRP in Cincinnati

Jenna Maroney	Jane Krakowski	30 Rock
Bill McNeal	Phil Hartman	NewsRadio
Selina Meyer	Julia Louis-Dreyfus	Veep
Oliver Otto	Daniel DiMaggio	American Housewife
Thomas Pembridge	Malcolm McDowell	Mozart in the Jungle
Detective Jake Peralta	Andy Samberg	Brooklyn Nine-Nine
Bonnie Plunkett	Allison Janney	Mom
Dennis Reynolds	Glenn Howerton	It's Always Sunny in Philadelphia
Winston Schmidt	Max Greenfield	New Girl
Maxwell Sheffield	Charles Shaughnessy	The Nanny
Gabrielle Solis	Eva Longoria	Desperate Housewives
Suzanne Sugarbaker	Delta Burke	Designing Women
Jordan Sullivan	Christa Miller	Scrubs
Ellie Torres	Christa Miller	Cougar Town
Nina Van Horn	Wendie Malick	Just Shoot Me
Stephanie Vanderkellen	Julia Duffy	Newhart
Jacqueline Voorhees	Jane Krakowski	Unbreakable Kimmy Schmidt
Blair Warner	Lisa Whelchel	The Facts of Life
Charles Winchester	David Ogden Stiers	M*A*S*H

How Narcissists are Described in the Breakdowns

Born with a silver spoon in their mouth, brazen, calculated, classic rich guy, dismissive, cliché, cocky, conceited, Connecticut preppy, cunning, douchebag, fashionable, gets through life on her looks, golden boy, influential, jacket and tie hipster, larger than life, magnetic, posh, privileged, self-assured, staunch Republican, suck up, trust fund kid, venture capitalist, vindictive

Lead Body Part: Chin

It's nearly impossible to stand with your chin up and out just a bit and not feel like the world is your oyster. "Chin up!" is something you say to someone in a difficult situation in order to encourage them to be brave and to try not to be sad. We instinctively know that simply lifting our chin up brightens our mood. In a moment, we assume a better, brighter, and bolder disposition with which to greet the world. What if, then, your chin *was always up?* What would that feel like? Narcissists live their lives ready to present themselves to the world. They bow to no one. When your chin is up, your gaze automatically lowers. We immediately pull rank (gain status) when we look down on others.

REBEL

"Percocet should never be crushed, broken, or chewed unless you want it to hit your system like a bolt of lightning. Which is only a problem if you're afraid of lightning, which I am not."

Jackie Peyton/Nurse Jackie

Mantra: "I challenge"

Strength: Authoritative

Weakness: Isolated

Typical jobs: Any, but they use their position for personal gain, as a cover for illicit activity, or make their time at work more dangerous than it has to be.

Who Are They?

The Rebel sees the world through a lens of danger, intrigue, and nihilism. They don't adhere to rules set by society or feel the need to conform to the laws of common people. Bound by a moral code of their own creation, Rebels maintain a godlike vision of themselves. Always ready to thumb their nose at authority, tradition, and sacred institutions, the Rebel is ever defiant.

Rebels are secretive and very often live compartmentalized lives, sharing information with those close to them only on a need-to-know basis. Not only are they comfortable being the outsider, they prefer it. Living on the perimeter provides them with a strategic overview of their environment and prevents others, even friends and family, from learning their closely guarded secrets.

Rebels are bold; they say and do shocking things without any regard for how others might judge their actions. They move through life fully justified, even if their behavior is illegal, immoral, or reckless. Rebels get a charge from intimidating other people and have tremendous disdain for the weak.

That's a pretty intense summary! If it seems like this character has a mental illness or diagnosable personality disorder, well... they might. I'll get to how this archetype is played for comedy in a bit, but first I'll use the Rebel to illustrate parallels that exist to dramatic characterizations.

Yes, this book is about comedy and this section is about The Heroes of Comedy, but I want your time with these pages to be as useful as possible. Acting is acting. Comedy is obviously a different genre than drama, but it requires the same skills, tools, and foundational training. Given that, it's worth noting that these archetypes very much translate into drama.

It would, of course, require a whole other book to research and categorize the great dramatic programs and characters of TV history. However, the Rebel is a great archetype to exemplify how similar the memorable archetypes of both genres actually are. I'll offer this example and leave you to ruminate on how other notable dramatic characters might be categorized!

Mary-Louise Parker portrays Nancy Botwin on *Weeds*, a half-hour comedy. In a nutshell, Nancy finds herself a young widow with two sons, struggling to pay for her upper-middle class life in suburbia, and thus begins selling marijuana. *Weeds* is dark, but it is a comedy. Over eight seasons, Nancy's God complex grows right along with her escalating criminal activity. I can't describe her better than she describes herself, "I'm a bitch-ass bitch."

She spends the whole series outwitting law enforcement and other criminals alike. At various points, she: is incarcerated, her family assumes false identities, her youngest son, Shane, murders someone and displays psychopathic tendencies in his teenage years, she begins doing business with a Mexican drug cartel, and she is shot in the head by a sniper.

Just to reiterate: *Weeds* is a sitcom. Parker won a Golden Globe Award for Best Performance by an Actress in a Television Series, Comedy or Musical. *Weeds'* creator, Jenji Kohan, won a Writers Guild of America Award for Best Episodic Comedy.

Throughout eight seasons of *Weeds*, Nancy maneuvers around tremendous peril and drags her children along for the ride. Sometimes she's rightfully fearful, but most of the time she's giddy and manic with anticipation of her next forbidden conquest. For several seasons she imagines she can keep her own children sheltered from drugs and a life of crime, even as she dives headfirst into the risky life of a drug dealer. It does beg the question whether Nancy is entirely sane.

Three years after *Weeds* aired, one of television's most brilliant hour-long dramas debuted with a similar theme. *Breaking Bad* features Bryan Cranston as Walter White. In both cases, the protagonist transforms into the antagonist. In other words, the hero and the villain are the same person. Structurally, the shows are very similar.

Breaking Bad sets Walter White on a path of criminal destruction with his diagnosis of stage 3 lung cancer. *Weeds* begins with the head of household/breadwinner dead, *Breaking Bad* begins with the same figure dying. The antagonist/protagonist lead character in both instances turns to selling drugs in order to maintain the lifestyle to which they and their families are accustomed.

Nancy and Walter are both Rebels who have contempt for society, disregard for their safety, and the safety of those around them. They both think they are cunning enough to outwit the law and elevate their status in the world of illicit drugs, possessing minimal resources.

In *Weeds*, a comedy, Nancy survives the impossibly dangerous circumstances as the series concludes. In *Breaking Bad*, a drama, Walter does not. Other elements distinguish a comedy series from a dramatic one, but in this comparison, Nancy living and Walter dying is the most significant.

Now, back to our regularly scheduled comedy... Nick Offerman embodies quintessential Rebel Ronald Ulysses "Ron" Swanson, on *Parks and Recreation*. A sillier example than our aforementioned drug dealers, Ron Swanson works for the government, but hates the government.

Distant and hypermasculine, Ron is a strong advocate for privatizing all governmental functions and therefore believes that the Parks Department should not even exist. He's a Libertarian bordering on nihilist. He'd eviscerate his own career if he could somehow inflict his true belief system on the rest of the world; government is evil and should be destroyed.

His disdain for existing institutions doesn't end there. While coaching a boys' basketball team, he informs them, "Under my tutelage, you will grow from boys to men. From men into gladiators. And from gladiators into Swansons." There is a societal hierarchy in his mind upon which he rests comfortably atop.

Beneath his steely demeanor, however, we see his affection for Leslie Knope (Amy Poehler) and the rest of his tribe unfold throughout the series. And like all Rebels, we learn over time, things we didn't know in the beginning. Like, for example, Ron plays the saxophone and secretly performs at out-of-town jazz clubs under the name Duke Silver. I mentioned secretive, compartmentalized lives, right?

Jane Lynch already had a distinguished acting career before *Glee* debuted in 2009, but I think it's fair to say it is her portrayal of

Sue Sylvester that skyrocketed her to global fame and made her a household name. Sue is the cheerleading coach at McKinley High School. As a faculty member, you'd imagine her agenda might be more or less the same as the other teachers; nurture the students and create an overall safe environment for learning. Nope.

Sue is a terrifying oppressor, bent on destruction. Because her cheerleading squad competes with the glee club for the school's limited funding, she does her best to sabotage and destroy it. Sue is downright wicked, willing to get what she wants at all costs, yet she improbably has a close, maternal relationship with Becky, a student with Down syndrome.

It is revealed later in the series that Sue's older sister Jean also has Down syndrome and lives in a residential care facility. Sue is complicated. At first glance, she's just evil; the meanest of mean girls all grown up. But she is often kind. It just comes in small doses, on her own terms, and for reasons of her own choosing.

Compartmentalized life? Check. Moral code of her own creation? Check. Funny? Jane won the Primetime Emmy Award for Outstanding Actress in a Comedy Series the very first season of *Glee*. So, check plus.

What Is Their Strength?

If you consider being a total badass a strength, then the Rebel is made of titanium. Since they perceive reality itself as completely subjective to their point of view, they feel they have the final say on just about everything. They move through the world with force and authority.

Full of charisma and intrigue, people are drawn to Rebels and drawn in by them. They would make incredible leaders if they were... well, normal. Indeed, we do often see Rebels written into leadership positions, but their counterculture impulses are almost always subversive and directly undermine the goals of their core group of peers or their superior in the workplace if they have one.

However, Rebels are strong and fearless in the face of obstacles in the way of their ambition or a crisis. They will go nose to nose with anyone and never back down in a confrontation. Whether it's with their mind, body, or weapon of choice, Rebels know how to fight, defend, and fortify. It's as if they all had special ops training when they were five, while the other kids were taking a nap.

Edie Falco as Jackie Peyton in the series *Nurse Jackie* is an extraordinary case in point. A sterling example of a health care practitioner, except for the fact she has a serious drug addiction, Jackie steals pharmaceuticals from the hospital at which she works and treats patients while she's high.

She has an affair with the hospital's resident pharmacist, who additionally provides her with prescription medication, and she lies to every single person she knows. Her life is so severely compartmentalized that in the beginning of the series her co-workers don't even know she's married and has two daughters.

She removes her wedding ring upon arriving at work, in order to keep those around her from knowing anything about her life. In the opening episode, she tells her new charge Zoe (Merritt Wever) exactly what she's about: "I don't like chatty, okay? I don't do chatty. I like quiet. Quiet and mean. Those are my people." A relentless adrenaline junkie, those words become the thesis statement for Jackie Peyton's life throughout the series.

What Is Their Weakness?

James Dean characterized Jim Stark, the original Rebel in the 1955 classic feature film, *Rebel Without a Cause*. The comedic version of the Rebel, as I've noted earlier, is virtually identical. The core components are the same. Their point of view and place in the world are the same. Viewing them through the filter of comedy simply removes the anger and pain that would propel the dramatic Rebel through their journey and replaces those characteristics with superiority and condescension.

It follows then, that all Rebels suffer the same weakness: isolation. Even though they remain immersed in society, they feel cut off from it. They don't experience the same emotional connection to typical milestones and life's rituals as others around them. Birthday parties seem stupid. Weddings? Graduations? Drinks with coworkers? No, thanks.

Since they view the world around them as something to deconstruct, it only makes sense the Rebel has no access point to engage in common celebrations. Ultimately they're lonely, but they're hearty enough to withstand it.

There does, however, seem to be one thing in every Rebel's life that penetrates their dispassionate veneer. The Rebel's Achilles heel can be a substance, a time or a place or an individual who is like kryptonite personified.

In *Parks and Recreation*, Ron Swanson was so undone by his ex-wife Tammy's sexual temptations that he made a videotape warning himself to stay away from her in case he was ever tempted to reunite with her. It's worth noting Ron had not one, but two ex-wives named Tammy, which was also his mother's name. All the Tammys were a problem for Ron.

For Jack Donaghy (Alec Baldwin) on *30 Rock*, it's his mother Colleen (Elaine Stritch). Cold and austere, the mere mention of her name can send Jack swirling into a fear spiral. A typical exchange between them goes something like this:

COLLEEN: I suppose you think that they're (Liz Lemon's family) more nurturing than I am.

Mother, there are terrorist cells that are more nurturing than you are.

Be careful. I'll cry.

Karen Walker (Megan Mullally), *Will & Grace*'s resident Rebel, has a *list* of archrivals and nemeses: Most prominently Beverley Leslie (Leslie Jordan), but also Lorraine Finster (Minnie Driver), Candice Bergen (playing herself as Karen's best frenemy), Marlo Thomas, Anita Bryant, and her mother, Lois (Suzanne Pleshette).

Brooklyn Nine-Nine's Rebel, Captain Ray Holt (Andre Braugher) and Deputy Chief Madeline Wuntch (Kyra Sedgwick) were once partners and friends, but after a falling out, their friendship turned into a deep mutual hostility toward each other. Wuntch goes out of her way to undermine the 99th Precinct and appears to take great pleasure in its and Holt's failures.

Similarly, Sue Sylvester (Jane Lynch) not only makes a religious practice of trying to destroy the glee club at McKinley High, she also relentlessly strives to oust the glee club coach Will Schuester (Matthew Morrison) from his job.

Nurse Jackie (Edie Falco) is strong as steel but vulnerable to narcotics, as is walking disaster Frank Gallagher (William H. Macy) on *Shameless*. Murphy Brown (Candice Bergen) is a recovering alcoholic on the eponymous series. Victoria Flynn (Katy Mixon) has a lesser substance abuse problem, but her relationship with marijuana repeatedly lands her in trouble on *Mike & Molly*, nonetheless.

The chink in the armor of Gloria Pritchett (Sofia Vergara) on *Modern Family* is an era (place and time); her unsavory youth in Colombia. Having lived in a poor and crime-filled village, she apparently adopted some behaviors and philosophies from shady characters and frequently implies violence as a solution to problems.

On one occasion, her son Manny (Rico Rodriguez) is floating on a raft in their swimming pool. He's upset and refuses to come out even though it's making them late for his own birthday party. Out of frustration, Gloria grabs a nearby pellet gun and shoots the raft, which instantly begins to deflate.

> MANNY: You could have shot me!
>
> GLORIA: (Waving the gun) C'mon, Manny, I could have unbuttoned your shirt if I wanted to. Now, come here or sink! And I'm taking this with me in the car.

Gloria's dark side, sometimes uncontrollable, is directly related to her rough upbringing in a savage place.

How Do Others See Them?

Everyone who knows the Rebel thinks they're terrifying. Obviously not all the time, but the signals the Rebel gives off are intended to intimidate and they do. At a standing pace, their complete lack of regard for social norms is threatening to those who'd rather adhere to them. Rebels don't have to say a word to be menacing. They need merely to think a threat or ultimatum believably and their point is instantly made.

At their warmest, Rebels still have an ever-present edge. They are not the type to enjoy public displays of affection. They can be loved and loving within their immediate circle as much as any other archetype, but they work hard to maintain their reputation of impenetrability. Take a second to imagine Ron Swanson enduring a hug from Leslie Knope. Cringeworthy, right?

How Do Writers Use Them?

Rebels automatically create a status shift in scenes since they assume authority upon arrival. Everyone else's station immediately drops beneath theirs. You can see other characters around the Rebel marvel at their unwavering self-esteem. Effectively, they can pull rank within their core group any time they wish since they've established themselves as potentially diabolical or volcanic if they do not get their way.

The Rebel is a reliable source of tension, friction, or outright dread since they are unpredictable and *enjoy* conflict. The backstories writers have given this archetype are infinitely entertaining. Their aggressive set of primary characteristics must have a source. In part it can be genetic, but the degree to which it's environmental has provided hysterical insight into the psychology of this character, albeit through fictional circumstances.

Due to his family's poverty, Jack Donaghy began working at the age of 12 as a dockworker at the Port of Boston and put himself through Harvard Business School operating a swan boat. He worked as an intern for Senator Ted Kennedy and was a classmate of Michelle Obama's.

Gloria Pritchett owned a machete when she was a girl and used to compete in (and win) beauty pageants where she showcased her ventriloquist dummy Uncle Grumpy. For a time, she was wanted by the police in both Texas and Florida.

An avid woodworker, apparently from birth, Ron Swanson built his first chair at the age of five and moved in with his first wife, Tammy One, when he was only 15 years old.

Karen Walker's mother is a con artist who used Karen to scam people for money on the street.

Hot in Cleveland's Elka Ostrovsky (Betty White) escaped the Nazis in Poland as a teenager, and her late husband was connected to the mob.

There is a solid through line of Rebels overcoming extreme hardship to get to where they are in life now.

What Is Your Way In?

In order to believably play a Rebel, you must first make friends with the darkness inside of you. Not every actor wishes to do so, therefore this character is definitely not for everyone. Many actors, especially those drawn primarily to comedy have no interest in dancing with their demons. They vibe with the lightness, joy, and silliness of comedy and avoid indulging in pathos.

That's fine. That's why there is casting. Actors should know their wheelhouse and maximize their opportunities to play roles for which they are best suited. Everyone can give any character a shot and exploration is encouraged, but the goal for working actors is always to target roles in which they are most believable and comfortable. Especially when they are beginning to build their resume.

There is no winking at characters or playing *at* them for the camera, the way one might when performing a sketch or improv scene on a stage. In television and film, we must merge ourselves with the characters we portray, honestly, from the inside out.

Authenticity is a huge component in booking an actor for a series regular role. It's especially important to understand that concept for the Rebel because their primary qualities are particularly assertive and outlandish. Rebels are unflinching and enjoy intense encounters with others at close proximity. They savor prolonged eye contact.

Male and female Rebels alike have a primal quality that can border on savage and they give nothing away that they don't have to. If you're not bold, confrontational, edgy, and contemptuous of current pop culture, at least a little bit in your day-to-day life, you'll have a difficult time stepping up to the requirements this character will challenge you with.

However, there are other ways in. The comedic Rebel is not an angry person. Rebels can also be described as introspective, philosophical, and comfortable in their own skin. Maybe you're not hyper-confrontational, but perhaps you're a confident introvert. Finding enjoyment in time alone with your own thoughts will ground you in the Rebel's psyche. That can be a fine starting point and a great way to start building your personal Rebel.

The Rebel in a Family-Based Series: *Modern Family*

Including the character of Gloria Pritchett (Sofia Vergara) was masterful craftsmanship on the part of Christopher Lloyd and Steven Levitan, the creators of *Modern Family*. The show was an immediate hit largely because all the characters were so well defined from the beginning. However, as Jay Pritchett's (Ed O'Neill) second, younger, Colombian wife, Gloria is singularly unexpected.

In an otherwise typical white, suburban extended family, Gloria is exotic and embodies an entirely different cultural frame of reference from everyone else. She grew up in a dangerous, third-world environment and lived much closer to the elements and poverty than the rest of her new family.

She is aware of her physical beauty and is simultaneously at ease with it. She knows her body is an asset and shamelessly uses it to her advantage when necessary. Yet, as a mother, she is fiercely protective of her son, Manny, especially since he is tenderhearted. When she becomes pregnant with her second child and thinks Jay is not excited for the news, her true (threatening) nature surfaces, "And if you're too set on your own ways to be happy about it, I can raise it on my own. I have done it before and I can do it now. I come from a very long line of strong Latin women whose husbands are nowhere to be found!"

Since Gloria is an expert marksman, that's not entirely an idle threat. She has a disturbingly high comfort level with killing or violence, especially where animals are concerned; on one occasion she brutally beheads a rat with a shovel and leaves its head to "send a message to the other rats." When two teens egg her house on Halloween, she charges after them screaming, "You put egg on my house, I kill what you love!"

Her barely controlled Colombian temper in an urban environment is clever and there is no question Gloria provides a unique perspective on typical storylines. As the resident Rebel, Gloria Pritchett provides abundant comedy and contrast within the series.

The Rebel in a Friend-Based Series: *Will & Grace*

Karen Walker (Megan Mullally) on *Will & Grace* was initially conceived as a supporting role. However, it didn't take long before she became a prominent part of the show. In 2010, Karen Walker was ranked #23 on the TV Guide Network special, *25 Greatest TV Characters of All Time*. That ranking is low in my opinion, but I'm trying hard not to editorialize as I craft this book.

She should be number one. There, I said it. I think Karen Walker is the single most complicated, funny, intricately portrayed character in television comedy history. Even if you have another opinion, it's worth noting that Mullally received seven consecutive Primetime Emmy Award nominations for Outstanding Supporting Actress in a Comedy Series for her role on *Will & Grace* and won twice in 2000 and 2006.

She also received seven consecutive Screen Actors Guild Awards nominations for Outstanding Performance by a Female Actor in a Comedy Series and won three times in 2001, 2002, and 2003, and was nominated for four Golden Globe awards for her portrayal of Karen Walker. An incredible singer, ballet dancer and soloist, and highly trained theater actor, her work is worth studying.

Karen Walker took an administrative job at Grace's design firm simply to entertain herself. She mocks social norms from the moment we first meet her. Most secretaries actually need their jobs. Karen is wealthy and only works for Grace to get out of the house. For the longest time Karen didn't even bother cashing her paychecks because she's so wealthy that money is meaningless to her. However, in one episode, her husband, Stan, cuts down on her extravagant spending habits and Karen cashes all her paychecks at once, nearly bankrupting Grace.

Ironically, even though Karen is Grace's assistant, she has a large personal staff of her own and is conspicuously patronizing to all of them, referring to each solely by their title both in conversation and to their face: "Driver," "Butler," "Private Detective," "Pharmacist," "Back-Up Pharmacist," etc., and even refers to Will (Eric McCormack) as "Lawyer" on occasion.

Although Karen has strong leanings toward two of the other Heroes of Comedy (Narcissist and Eccentric), she is undoubtedly a Rebel at her core. Along with a requisite God complex, she is defined primarily by her disdain for the world as it is.

When Karen Walker enters a room, she immediately becomes the alpha presence. The rare times she encounters someone with equal or higher status, she is either smitten with them or aroused by them. She exalts the few people whom she finds extraordinary, like Jack, and derides others as lesser beings. She loves Will, Grace, Rosario, and her husband Stan, but in all manner of speech and behavior she clearly views herself as superior and infinitely more interesting. Here's a typical Karen musing for example, "Oh hey! Somebody got flowers. Or as I like to call them, poor people jewelry."

She thrives on power exchange, which manifests in her proclivity for sadomasochistic sexual adventures. She once made an adult movie in the role of a dominatrix. "Well, I was just out of college, I was broke. It's the oldest story in the world. Boy meets girl, boy wants girl to do dominatrix film, girl says 'naked?', boy says 'yeah', girl says 'forget it'. Boy says 'okay, then just wear this rubber maid's uniform and beat the old man with a scrub brush', girl says 'how hard?'"

She dislikes children, strict gender identification, and all other conventions that make regular people feel secure and happy. Her enemy list is a badge of honor and she wears it proudly. Between her wealth, her unseen husband, her constant drug usage, her powerful connections, her unnecessary job, and enormous ego, Karen Walker is a societal insurrectionist with some of the best one-liners in TV history; "Honey, I don't look. I'm looked at."

Karen has an alias, which she uses from time to time, Anastasia Beaverhausen, "Anastasia, like Russian royalty, Beaverhausen, like... where the beaver lives."

She is apparently armed at all times, "Well, I'm glad you finally came to your senses, Grace. I mean, I could not believe what you would let her get away with. I would just sit there cleaning my gun, thinking, 'This is an office!'"

She is sexually attracted to men and women and suspects everyone else of having same-sex yearnings, "We're all lesbians when the right guy isn't around."

She's proud of the fact that she is drunk, stoned, or a combination thereof most of her waking life, "I've got drinks piling up on my desk and a stack of pills I haven't even opened yet."

She's not shy about hitting people when she's upset, but sometimes it's exhausting, "I'm too tired to slap you. Bash your face against my palm, would ya'?"

She finds being normal painfully boring, "Wow, 10 years of game night. What a milestone. Maybe you should celebrate with a suicide pact."

Karen Walker doesn't do emotions, "Hey, hey, hey. Come on. I know what guilt is. It's one of those touchy-feely words that people throw around that don't really mean anything... You know, like 'maternal' or 'addiction.'"

She has contempt for the lower classes, "What's so great about the outside world anyway? It's just a bunch of people with their dumb dreams and even dumber kids."

She's not into vanilla sex, "You know, I just don't have time for all this getting-to-know-ya' crap. I just want somebody who gets me. Somebody who's comfortable in my world and makes me laugh and occasionally brings me flowers. And... somebody who likes kittens and the hard-core bondage scene."

She makes conflicting references regarding her own gender, "When I was a boy, I worked in a supermarket. Oh! Did I say I was a boy? Because I wasn't. I was a girl." Also, "Gosh my nails are stronger, my hair is thicker, but... I think my balls may be shrinking."

Even for a pill-popping, booze-guzzling Manhattan socialite with no regard for rules, Karen Walker takes an outrageous, anti-establishment world point of view to a higher plane.

The Rebel in a Work-Based Series: *30 Rock*

Tina Fey didn't expect Alec Baldwin to accept a series regular role on *30 Rock* when she was creating the show. She acknowledged publicly how surprised she was when he did. Thankfully that collaboration gave us the character Jack Donaghy.

Like all other Rebels, Jack is complicated. He's a socially moderate, conservative Republican who idolizes Ronald Reagan. Theoretically, Jack is Irish Catholic. but his true religion is capitalism. "Money can't buy happiness; it is happiness!" he proclaims.

"Business doesn't get me down, business gets me off." And finally, "I admire Wonka. He is a true capitalist. His factory has zero government regulation, slave labor, and an indoor boat. Wonderful."

In one fell swoop, he exposes himself as disdainful of both government and humanity but enjoys the finer things in life, even if they come at other people's expense. Jack's point of view on the world is funny, but it's definitely tinged with darkness because it also reflects how some people living in the real world actually think.

A lot of people view America as an individualistic blank slate where you can thrive if you're smart, well-connected, and able to manipulate your way to the top (hedge fund managers, lobbyists, televangelists, etc.). If you're not up to the challenge, that's just Darwinism doing its job and if you fail to thrive, it's nobody's problem but yours. The weak are weeded out for the benefit of, in their opinion, better people.

In the same way Karen Walker cares deeply for her closest friends but doesn't bother shielding them from her unrelenting and sometimes merciless judgment, Jack doles out advice and backhanded insults to his employee, friend, and protégé Liz Lemon (Tina Fey) with equal verve. Jack and Liz have an intricate and special relationship. They are both there for each other when needed, but Liz is likely to spare, or at least consider, Jack's feelings when he's vulnerable. Jack rarely reciprocates.

Anyone might incur a verbal takedown from Jack but directing constructive insults toward Liz Lemon is his specialty. "Shoulders back, Lemon. You're not welcoming people to Castle Frankenstein." He's relentless in his strong, creative opinions about Liz's appearance. "Good God, I can see every line and pore in your face. It looks like a YMCA climbing wall."

As a Rebel, Jack also has the requisite aversion for gestures of affection, immigrants, and common folk. "Hugging... it's so ethnic."

He plays by his own rulebook, which he creates as he rolls along, and enjoys sparring with his nemesis, Devon Banks (Will Arnett), with whom he has a palpable sexual chemistry.

DEVON:	Your hand's sticky from candy.
JACK:	And the worst part is, I wouldn't even want the money.
DEVON:	No, you wouldn't. Jack Donaghy taking welfare? It'd kill you.
JACK:	There's so many jobs at stake.
DEVON:	You'd have to take it. I'd make you. I'd make you take it all.
JACK:	I'd roll over and let you give it to me.
DEVON:	I'm honestly not trying to make this sound gay.
JACK:	No one is. It's just happening.

The Rebel is unequivocally the most complex of the Heroes of Comedy. Provocative and dynamic, no other archetype requires access to the Rebel's compelling darkness. The Rebel personality alone implausibly ranges from blissful omniscience to demented self-deification.

As Jack peers upon the street from his high-rise office view, he summarizes his place within existence, "From up here, I can see the whole island. A city built on the religion of capitalism and I am its high priest, looking down on the swinish multitude. And even those who hate me, the unwashed, socialist horde, the Occupy Wall Streeters and the beard-havers and the bicycle riders, even they must acknowledge me... as a god."

Characteristics of the Rebel

- Acrimonious
- Adrenaline Junkie
- Aloof
- Anti-Establishment
- Bold
- Brazen
- Challenging
- Complicated
- Contemptuous
- Cryptic
- Devious
- Difficult
- Disdainful
- Disobedient
- Edgy
- Enigmatic
- God Complex
- Hardened
- Imposing
- Indifferent
- Indignant
- Intimidating
- Intractable
- Loner
- Mysterious
- Noncompliant
- Outrageous
- Righteous
- Scornful
- Secretive
- Sphinxlike
- Steely
- Stern
- Turbulent
- Unlawful
- Unreadble
- Unsympathetic
- Unyielding
- Warring
- Wrathful

Rebels Throughout the History of Television

Barry Berkman	Bill Hader	**Barry**
George Bluth Sr.	Jeffrey Tambor	**Arrested Development**
Nancy Botwin	Mary Louise Parker	**Weeds**
Murphy Brown	Candice Bergen	**Murphy Brown**
John Casey	Adam Baldwin	**Chuck**
Denny Crane	William Shatner	**Boston Legal**
Gretchen Cutler	Aya Cash	**You're the Worst**
Jack Donaghy	Alec Baldwin	**30 Rock**
Bo Duke	John Schneider	**The Dukes of Hazzard**
Luke Duke	Tom Wopat	**The Dukes of Hazzard**
Ray Drecker	Thomas Jane	**Hung**
Victoria Flynn	Katy Mixon	**Mike & Molly**
Arthur "Fonzie" Fonzarelli	Henry Winkler	**Happy Days**
Dina Fox	Lauren Ash	**Superstore**
Frank Gallagher	William H. Macy	**Shameless**
Bertram Gilfoyle	Martin Starr	**Silicon Valley**
Jessica Huang	Constance Wu	**Fresh Off the Boat**
Andrea Jackson	Gabourey Sidibe	**The Big C**
Dusty Jackson	Jessica Lange	**The Politician**
Jessa Johansson	Jemima Kirke	**Girls**
Michael	Ted Danson	**The Good Place**
Elka Ostrovsky	Betty White	**Hot in Cleveland**
Veronica Palmer	Portia de Rossi	**Better Off Ted**
Jackie Peyton	Edie Falco	**Nurse Jackie**

Gloria Delgado-Pritchett	Sofía Vergara	Modern Family
Capt. Ray Holt	Andre Braugher	Brooklyn Nine-Nine
Max Felice Shaw	Erika Alexander	Living Single
Dr. Lilith Sternin-Crane	Bebe Neuwirth	Cheers
Ron Swanson	Nick Offerman	Parks and Recreation
Sue Sylvester	Jane Lynch	Glee
Karen Walker	Megan Mullally	Will & Grace
Samantha White	Logan Browning	Dear White People

How Rebels are Described in the Breakdowns

Authoritative, commanding, compartmentalized life, complex, emotionally distant, formidable, Gordon Gecko type, has a wild side, high status, iffy moral compass, insulated, lives an elite and unusual lifestyle, not someone to be crossed, savvy, self-sufficient, overly serious, sly, take-no-prisoners attitude, temperamental, too cool for school

Lead Body Part: Chest

When you stand with your chest out, you're basically standing like a superhero. Who wants to mess with a superhero? Leading with your chest creates a duplicity that aligns with the nature of a rebel. At once, you're projecting strength, but also vulnerability. A strong, puffed-up chest signals that someone is ready for a challenge, if not bracing for a full-out fight. Yet it also commands attention. If you walk into a room with your chest up and out, everyone will look at you and they will have a feeling about it. Perhaps admiration, perhaps fear. Either way, you don't get to blend in. Living perpetually on display makes you a target as much as an icon. Of course, the Rebel is perfectly glad about that.

Who Are They?

In the royal court of a family, group of friends or coworkers, the Buffoon is the jester. Foolish, boorish, and overflowing with an unjust amount of confidence that comes from seemingly nowhere, the Buffoon encompasses a spectrum that ranges from adorable nitwit to obnoxious bully.

None of The Heroes of Comedy are dumb or stupid, etc. Lead characters should never be thought of or developed with those words in mind. Everyone is smart in their own way. Surprisingly some people (characters) have, let's say, an expertise in remaining employed by working very little or being flat out bad at their job and keeping it anyway. Some are good at maintaining close friendships despite complete social ineptitude.

The Buffoon is definitely not the sharpest tool in the shed. Some are more aware of this fact than others. Either way, their deficiencies are only partly intellectual. Their personality and lackadaisical worldview play a big part in the Buffoon's overall low ranking in the smarts department.

Rather than dumb or stupid, think of them as shortsighted and lazy thinkers. Some Buffoons are complete slackers, meandering through life aimlessly, perhaps expressing aspirations but backing them up with little or no initiative. A perfect example is *30 Rock*'s Tracy Jordan (Tracy Morgan). He's very frank about his disdain for discipline. He bemoans, "This job is hard. I just want to be able to do what I want to do. Do you know I once shot a whole movie without ever getting out of my car?"

Even when the Buffoon is ambitious, there's always a wrinkle; they either strive for a position for which they're completely unqualified, they want maximum payoff for minimal effort, or they deify themselves for virtually every achievement as if everyone else doesn't have to work hard for what they want.

Tom Haverford (Aziz Ansari) from *Parks and Recreation* sums up the Buffoon well in this respect, "At the risk of bragging, one of the things I'm best at is riding coattails. Behind every successful man is me. Smiling and taking partial credit."

Buffoons are *childish*, which manifests as petty and insolent as opposed to *childlike*, which is earnest and unspoiled. The Buffoons who are aware of their lesser cognitive abilities usually have an inferiority complex as the cherry on their stooge sundae. The recognition of their deficits further drives their core negative traits like jealousy, stubbornness, and being famously delusional. George Costanza (Jason Alexander) on *Seinfeld* epitomizes all those qualities in just two sentences, "If I owned a company, my employees would love me. They'd have huge pictures of me up on the walls and in their home, like Lenin."

Television's original Buffoons were always best friends, sidekicks, or the ridiculous blowhard somewhere in the world of the lead characters, but they were seldom the lead character of the show themselves. Think of the original TV buffoon, Ed Norton (Art Carney) of *The Honeymooners*. Ed worked in the New York

City sewers and described his job as a "Sub-supervisor in the subdivision of the Department of Subterranean Sanitation." His career isn't glamorous, but Ed is proud of his position nonetheless. When a flustered Ralph starts to blow his top, Ed soothes him with sanitation-based advice,

"Look, just don't get upset. You're gettin' all upset now. Let's calm down and look nice when we get down there. There's no sense in getting upset. Now listen, the boys in the sewer, there, when we get upset we got a little motto, a little saying that gives us a little comfort in time of need. Maybe, I can pass it on to you. May I favor you with this little ode? 'When the tides of life turn against you, and the current upsets your boat, don't waste those tears on what might have been, just lay on your back and float.'" The Buffoon as best friend.

Then there was brilliant Don Knotts as Barney Fife on *The Andy Griffith Show*. Barney actually wrote a song that perfectly reflects his life: (Barney sings his biographical anthem to the tune of "Oh My Darling, Clementine"), "In a jailhouse down in Dixie/ Fightin' crime and riskin' life/Dwelled a sheriff and his buddy/ Pistol-packing Barney Fife./Oh my darlin', oh my darlin'/Oh my darlin' Barney Fife/He's a deadly crime stopper/What a copper, Barney Fife./Then one day there came a ridin'/ Two bad men to rob a bank/But Fife was tricky, a deadeye dickie/ Now they're locked up in the tank..." The Buffoon as sidekick.

Ted Knight created the gold standard of Buffoons portraying Ted Baxter on *The Mary Tyler Moore Show*. Like a dunce, he envisions his future in a way that's neither practical nor probable, "I'm going to be rich, Mary! I'm going to have all the things that money can buy. Happiness. Good health. Spiritual fulfillment. Then... then one day, I'm going to use my money to do something good for my country. I'm going to make a huge contribution to a presidential candidate and buy myself a political appointment.

Ted Baxter: United States Ambassador to Hawaii." Or in this case, it should be added, a future that's not possible. The Buffoon as blowhard co-worker.

Like the Narcissist, the Buffoon has moved to the foreground in our current era of television. They are now central and lead characters on many shows. In the past, we wouldn't have seen a Buffoon father, but then Phil Dunphy (Ty Burrell) became a breakout character on *Modern Family*. As a husband, dad, and professional real estate agent, Phil has to have warmth and a heart to be believable and likable. Burrell does an amazing job characterizing Phil as a good, upstanding guy and devoted family man replete with all the Buffoon's core characteristics.

Phil's a nice guy, but he is dimwitted, competitive, childish, and socially unaware. He also has an inferiority complex, which sometimes surfaces in the face of his Neurotic wife Claire's (Julie Bowen) certainty, but more often around his father-in-law, Jay (Ed O'Neill), "A relationship with your father-in-law is tough. You need to prove you can stand up to him, while being respectful. It's like walking a tightrope, which by the way I can do because I went to trapeze school."

It's also a constant with Phil that he doesn't fully realize what he's said until after he's heard himself say it. "If you show enough houses, you learn all the tricks. Every realtor is just a ninja in a blazer. The average burglar breaks in and leaves clues everywhere, but not me. I'm completely clueless," he brags into camera.

Broad City features a Buffoon, Ilana Wexler (Ilana Glazer) paired with a Dreamer, Abbi Abrams (Abbi Jacobson).

ILANA:	I want to finish a book…reading, not writing.
ABBI:	I'm gonna do one legit pull-up, for real this time.

The pair struggle to survive young adulthood in New York City. Although they're similar in many ways, Ilana is glib, cavalier, and less hopeful than her bestie. All her social exchanges range from uncomfortable to wincingly awkward, like when Abbi gets her period while on an airplane. Ilana tries to help by searching for a tampon. She crawls up to a snacking male passenger.

> ILANA: Hey! Hold on there! Could I get that pita?
>
> PASSENGER: This pita? That's almost in my mouth?
>
> ILANA: Yeah. My friend just got her period and she doesn't have any tampons and it's a first-day flow. It's really heavy and... her underpants are filling –
>
> PASSENGER: Just take it!

Buffoons are relentlessly socially awkward.

The series *Workaholics* comprises a trio of Buffoons. They're basically The Three Stooges of the 2010s. Blake Henderson (Blake Anderson), Adam DeMamp (Adam Devine), and Anders Holmvik (Anders Holm) are friends who "work together as telemarketers from 9 to 5 and live together from 5 to 9" (The actual tagline of the show). Here is the cold opening sequence from the pilot episode:

FADE IN:
EXT. GUYS' HOUSE – BACKYARD – DAY (DAY ONE)
People in swimsuits, a DJ, BBQ, and others play beer pong.
BLAKE, stands with ADAM and they drink beers.

> BLAKE: No... but they are real. It's like aliens. We haven't captured one yet, but they're out there.

ADAM: I don't know. I don't know if I believe in aliens either.

ANDERS approaches.

BLAKE: Ders, tell Adam that albino Asians are real.

ANDERS: Yeah right. They would have captured one by now.

In just a few lines, we're introduced to three straight guys who spend all their waking hours together talking about complete nonsense on page one. Larry, Mo, and Curly reborn!

What Is Their Strength?

Buffoons are passionate, if anything. It's just that their passions are often misdirected toward endeavors that are perhaps fun, but useless or excessive leisure activities. In *Everybody Loves Raymond*, Robert Barone (Brad Garrett), older brother of Raymond Barone (Ray Romano), spends his entire Buffoon life trying to get the validation and adoration that Raymond receives from their mother, Marie (Doris Roberts). He angles for her approval like it is his life's calling.

You'd think by the time he reached his 40s, he would realize that's an exercise in futility, but most of his storyline through-out nine seasons exposes him as a petty man consumed with jealousy. He summarizes his entire existence in this one musing: "Every time something good happens to me, I want to say, 'How about that, Ray?' But if something bad happens to me, I... say a prayer that Raymond doesn't do so good that day."

Robert had way funnier lines I could have chosen in order to reinforce the point. *Everybody Loves Raymond* is one of the best-written comedies in television history. But sometimes the truth hurts, and you can't produce humor without exploring the truth. Sometimes sibling rivalry lasts a lifetime, although it shouldn't, and the writers of *Raymond* depicted that trope quite thoughtfully. That said, here's Robert espousing the same truth a bit more humorously: "Ah, Ma agrees with Raymond. That's 47 years in a row!"

When a Buffoon lacks drive or enthusiasm, they fall flat for me, but that is entirely dependent on the show and the tone set by the creators and writers. Frankly, some more current TV Buffoons don't want to do much of anything and it's hard for me to find a single strength within them. I point this out to remind you that for this archetype, and all the rest, there are parameters that clearly define and encapsulate all The Heroes of Comedy, but there is no single way in which to execute them.

What Is Their Weakness?

It's hard to pick just one with this archetype, but primarily it's that they are delusional. I'll circle back to Tom Haverford (Aziz Ansari) on *Parks and Recreation* to illustrate. Tom is an entrepreneur, which is commendable. Unfortunately, he's a terrible entrepreneur because he's also a Buffoon, which means he's a social dimwit.

Within *Parks and Recreation*'s seven seasons, Tom creates a cologne called, "Tommy Fresh," he invents a high-end VIP cocktail called Snake Juice, which he debuts at a nightclub called The Snakehole Lounge, and he co-founds Entertainment 720, which he bills as a "premiere, high-end, all-media entertainment conglomerate." No one who works there knows what the company is or what they should be doing, if anything. Entertainment 720 is completely mismanaged (or rather, unmanaged) and soon goes bankrupt.

Next he opens a store called "Rent-A-Swag," where parents can rent their kids' clothing from a huge wardrobe of "the dopest shirts, the swankiest jackets, the slickest cardigans, the flashiest fedoras, the hottest ties, the snazziest canes, and more!" Rent-A-Swag was fairly successful for a time; however, it lost a lot of business when "Tommy's Closet," a similarly themed store opened up across the street. Ultimately Tom agreed to sell Rent-A-Swag to his competitor for a moderate fee and used the capital from this sale to open Tom's Bistro, a restaurant that becomes quite successful.

Tom's storyline is a great example of a character or archetype repeating patterns throughout their life because they simply are who they are. It's noteworthy that all Tom's ideas are clumsy and destined to fail except for his last. It's quite common that at the end of a series, when the writers are given advance notice of their final season, they resolve the character's persisting obstacles or send them off in a new direction.

After all his ridiculous shenanigans, it's satisfying to see Tom open a business that will endure as the series comes to a close. It would not have made sense to have his success come sooner; stories are told about trials and travails. Victories are great when they occur, but they're also sometimes a story's ending.

How Do Others See Them?

By and large, their friends, family, and coworkers see the Buffoon as predictably foolish. On the flowchart of buffoonery, this manifests in two ways: either as a pathetic slacker or a low-level thug. Some Buffoons are chronically lazy or hapless, others are actively antagonistic, and some are both.

In *Seinfeld*, George Costanza's (Jason Alexander) fiancée, Susan (Heidi Swedberg), famously dies from a toxic glue overdose because George is too cheap to buy decent wedding invitations.

The clerk at the stationery store offers the couple a large book of samples and instructs, "They're arranged in order of price. The most expensive are in the front." George immediately grabs the book and flips to the very last page. He chooses ugly, discontinued invitations for his own wedding that his fiancée openly dislikes just to save a few bucks.

While addressing the invitations, Susan becomes overwhelmed while sealing the poisonous envelopes and collapses. George returns home to find her and rushes her to the hospital where she's pronounced, "Gone" by the doctor. When the group of friends conclude together that it must have been from licking all the envelopes, George responds, "We were expecting about 200 people." Susan's unusual, untimely death is likely the most extreme consequence of a Buffoon's doltish behavior in television history. George is strangely unmoved by Susan's passing.

In an episode of *Silicon Valley*, Richard (Thomas Middleditch) buys what he thinks is Adderall from a neighborhood kid and afterward realizes he was duped. He returns to ask the boy if there was a mistake, at which point the little suburban gangster bitch-slaps him. The kid adds insult to injury by threatening to report Richard to the police for buying drugs from a minor, keeping his 50 dollars.

When Buffoon Erlich (T.J. Miller) finds out his friend was conned, he confronts the kid, who's maybe 12 years old. Erlich charges down the street toward the boy, still wearing his bathrobe, shouting angrily, "You just brought piss to a shit fight, you little cunt!" He slaps the boy across the face and hurls his bicycle over a hedge.

"Now you get in your fucking house and you get me five Adderall or I'll slit your fucking throat. You understand? I'll kill your mother. I'll rape your father. I'll curb stomp that little face so hard that your teeth will go flying! You little shit! Now, go, go, go, go, go... get me five Adderall! Right now!"

I'd be hard-pressed to find more extreme examples of *hapless* and *antagonistic* within a half-hour television comedy. They are both very dark, but then a lot of comedy is. *Seinfeld* is obviously one of TV's most beloved and critically acclaimed sitcoms of all time and although newer, *Silicon Valley* is also critically acclaimed, Emmy-nominated, and popular. Even though I'm very familiar with the shows I'm writing about, I'm sometimes taken aback by how horrible some of the characters I love watching reveal themselves to be when their worst moments are viewed in isolation.

How Do Writers Use Them?

Of all The Heroes of Comedy, the Buffoon suffers from self-inflicted anguish the most. They're not particularly bright, however, they think they know everything. Time and time again, it turns out they're wrong. Writers use them as the true classic clowns, braggarts and blowhards of comedy.

Sterling Archer (voiced by H. Jon Benjamin), of the animated espionage series *Archer*, is a perfect example of a dimwitted fool who holds himself in incredibly high regard while everyone else around him rolls their eyes. He boasts of himself, "I mean, I didn't invent the turtleneck, Lana, but I was the first to recognize its potential as tactical garment. The tactical turtleneck, Lana. The... tactleneck!" Lana literally rolls her wide, animated eyes.

Any archetype can suffer from occasional denial or have compartmentalized areas of their life and psyche that they should probably deal with therapeutically but don't. Conversely, the Buffoon's vision of themselves as smart and capable is completely discordant with the opinion of others around them and reality. They live in denial of who they actually are.

Additionally, any other archetype can behave in a foolish way or make a fool of themselves in a particular circumstance. That's necessary in comedy writing. All archetypes suffer indignities and humiliation in their journey toward their goals. It's the Buffoon, however, who can be expected to fail the most spectacularly, regularly, and by their own hand.

What Is Your Way In?

Can you remember the last time you did something that you and others around you who you respect thought was just plain inexplicable? Do you remember how you felt? Commonly people feel embarrassed, flustered, flush, and defensive when they've done something of consequence that was obviously imbecilic in hindsight.

Now imagine feeling that way *all the time*. Buffoons rarely get anything right and it's usually because they don't think things through even though they *might* have sufficient intelligence. Sure, maybe they're not Harvard material, but I think Buffoons are better understood by acknowledging their inherent laziness, even in regard to thinking.

They could do better, but they fail to apply themselves and stubbornly refuse to learn from previous mistakes. That could be viewed as lack of mental acumen, but laziness and stubbornness are personality traits, which any of us might possess. Embrace those attributes within yourself and you will be on your way to personifying this character in an honest way.

The actors who play this character well are extremely smart. As actors, we can't lower our IQs, or play dumb as a characteristic; stupidity is an external observation made by others and is highly subjective. We can, on the other hand, dial into our most graceless qualities, remember the times in our lives they dictated our actions, and relive how we felt in those moments.

The Buffoon in a Family-Based Series: *Everybody Loves Raymond*

Usually the eldest son in the family is the most revered. Sometimes, however, the baby of the family gets all the attention. As noted earlier, Buffoon Robert hunkers down in a lifelong, one-sided rivalry in which his younger brother Raymond doesn't really engage. Similarly, in *Arrested Development*, eldest brother Gob Bluth, (Will Arnett) pits himself against his younger brother, Michael (Jason Bateman), in a futile battle of wits and power within the family's business.

Gob is a professional part-time magician and the founder of The Alliance of Magicians, which had the primary function of preserving magicians' secrets. He was later blacklisted from the organization for revealing such a secret. Gob is constantly hoisting himself on his own petard.

Of note, Gob's relationship to magic is a similar trope to Phil Dunphy's (Ty Burrell) love of college cheerleading on *Modern Family*. And in *Seinfeld*, George Costanza has a particular interest in nice restrooms, which includes borderline obsessive personal bathroom habits.

In these instances, the choice of an odd occupation, extra-curricular activity, or interest set the Buffoon up perfectly to be mocked over multiple seasons. A small nugget of information can reveal a great deal about a character's overall personality.

And when it comes to personalities, Gob does not have a good one. His father, George Sr., paid little attention to Gob as a child and has no respect for him as an adult; his mother, Lucille, openly loathes him. Michael tolerates him because of his martyr complex that stems from being an Anchor in a particularly dysfunctional family.

Gob encompasses some of the very worst traits of the Buffoon; he's childish, petty, disdainful, deluded, dimwitted, and dense. He doesn't want to run the family business, but he's actively resentful that, as the oldest son, he wasn't asked. In order to appease the shareholders of the Bluth Company, Gob is temporarily made president, leaving Michael to handle day-to-day operations.

While holding his empty title, Gob gives a sexual harassment speech to employees gathered in a hallway, "… And please refrain from discussing or engaging in any sort of interoffice (bleep)-ing or si-(bleep)-ing, or finger-(bleep) or fi-(bleep)-sting or (bleep)-eeing, or even (bleep), even though *so* many people in this office are begging for it. And if *anybody* does *anything* with my sister Lindsay, I'll take off my pants, I'll shave my (bleep), and I'll personally (really long bleep)."

When it comes to dating and romance, Gob doesn't rate any higher than he does as a boss. Like most male Buffoons (and most Buffoons are men) Gob doesn't have the best perspective on women. "Illusion, Michael. A trick is something a whore does for money… or cocaine," he comments, completely unaware of his casual misogyny. He manipulatively seduces his mother's best friend and social rival, Lucille Austero (Liza Minnelli), in an attempt to convince her to sell her Bluth Company stocks back to the Bluth family. That romance does not end well.

Finally, he sleeps with and becomes engaged to Ann Veal (Mae Whitman), his nephew's former high school crush. Ann is devoutly religious and widely known for her lack of personality. When Gob decides to call things off with Ann, he breaks into her house and ends up sleeping with her instead. When he tries a final time to break up with her, the next morning at breakfast, he can't seem to get the words out of his mouth, so Ann has to be the one to say that it's over. Gob thoughtlessly says, "Marry me!" out of relief and gratitude, thinking he was off the hook. Ann takes him literally and accepts what she understands to be a sincere marriage proposal.

The only reason they don't wed is because of a failed illusion involving the resurrection of Jesus at their wedding ceremony. Gob appears at the church before Ann's friends and family (none of the Bluth's showed) attached to a glittery crucifix. "It's true that this is a magical trick. If what Jesus did was a trick. I say it wasn't!" he proclaims to applause. "It was an illusion... I am not the real Jesus! I am the *Amazing* Jesus! Yes, the real Jesus came off the cross and went into his cave a dead man. But was he crazy enough to do it handcuffed?"

He then explains that he plans to beat Jesus' resurrection by two full weeks. Ann realizes she's been had as her groom uses her wedding guests as a test audience for his magic act. Poor, foolhardy, delusional Gob never earns respect from his family, fails to find success in his career, and flubs romance in (literally) a biblical way.

The Buffoon in a Friend-Based Series: *The Big Bang Theory*

Clueless by nature, Buffoons seem to be particularly bad at romantic relationships. It makes sense since part of their profile is social unawareness, feelings of inferiority, and excessive laziness. That is not a good baseline from which to begin a courtship.

All those qualities and *many* more exist in *The Big Bang Theory*'s Sheldon Cooper, played brilliantly by Jim Parsons, who won four Primetime Emmys for Outstanding Lead Actor in a Comedy Series. He was nominated two additional years and has been nominated and won a slew of other awards and accolades for embodying the infinitely complex Buffoon.

In fact, Sheldon Cooper is so complex, he was difficult to categorize. He absolutely has traits and qualities of several other of The Heroes of Comedy. Sheldon has his share of neuroses, but he is not wholly Neurotic; he's not driven by anxiety. He can be quite odd, but the Eccentric as an archetype doesn't account for his complete lack of understanding *and disregard* of human nature. He's selfish, but not entirely shallow the way the Narcissist is. He's world-weary, but not lacking ambition like the Cynic. He possesses the boldness of the Rebel, but what he's *most* known for by his own tribe is his incredible social awkwardness. A-ha! That's it! Sheldon is a Buffoon.

I found the answer where I always find the answer to questions about characters; sides and storylines of series. I stop looking from the outside as an actor or observer and investigate the intent of the writer/creator. In this case I asked myself, "How do the writers use Sheldon?" It became clear instantly.

All the characters on the show, except Penny (Kaley Cuoco), are geniuses. Therefore, Sheldon's extraordinary IQ doesn't make him exceptional *within his peer group*. Of course he thinks it does because he's *delusional*, but it doesn't. He would be exceptional if his friends possessed only average intelligence.

Yet, they're all experts in different fields, which Sheldon constantly needs to *belittle* to make himself feel *superior*, which is a manifestation of an *inferiority complex*, which he has because he suffers from *social ineptitude* that borders on Asperger syndrome. Sheldon is scholarly but socially dimwitted. He lacks humility, empathy, and is constantly antagonistic without provocation.

More than anything else, the writers of *The Big Bang Theory* use Sheldon to bully the other characters and instigate dissension for no reason other than his sheer amusement, even with his girlfriend Amy (Mayim Bialik). Bernadette (Melissa Rauch) explains, "He doesn't know when he's being mean, because the part of his brain that should know is getting a wedgie from the rest of his brain."

Sheldon Cooper is the perfect example of a character that might be hard to properly identify and define within the pages at first glance because he's so profoundly complicated. But if you think of each character as a resource that the writers can use for a consistent purpose, you will develop insight into the words on the page that other actors do not possess.

I always encourage my students to step back from their perspective as performers and reflect on the architecture of scripted material. Almost every television show and film are formatted in a similar way. Of course actors want to dive into the psyche and emotion of a character and play, but with practice, it's easy to also start thinking about how the writer is using the character within the structure of the story. There is nothing that makes a writer/producer happier than an actor who knows exactly where they are coming from.

So when a character like Sheldon Cooper says something like, "Excuse me, no one does a better job of pretending to be a person than I do. Siri comes close, but I know more jokes," you can take their words literally and quickly assume they're socially inept. From there you can ask yourself which of The Heroes of Comedy are defined that way and find yourself with as clear an understanding of the character as the person who created it.

The Buffoon in a Work-Based Series: *The Office*

Having a Buffoon anywhere in your life comes with difficulties. Working for one, even more so. Michael Scott (Steve Carell) of the series *The Office* is the epitome of the word "dense." Michael started off as a salesman at the Dunder Mifflin Paper Company, but the series plays out with him in the position of regional manager of the Scranton branch. Michael is incredibly ill-suited for his job, as he, like all other Buffoons, lacks social awareness and is utterly clueless when it comes to comprehending basic societal norms.

Michael thinks of his staff as family and in doing so inserts awkward familiarity and inappropriate language into the workplace at Dunder Mifflin. The upside is that Michael does have a good heart. The downside is that he's a terrible boss all the way up to the point of deliberately sabotaging coworker Jim (John Krasinski) with a bad recommendation because he mistakenly believes Jim's promotion would lead to his own firing. They ultimately become co-managers.

Eternally exhausted by Michael's foolishness, Jim at one point makes a color graph to illustrate how Michael spends his time: 80% "distracting others," 19% "procrastination," and 1% "critical thinking." Jim adds that he inflated the "critical thinking" percentage so people could actually see it on the graph.

Additionally, Michael summarizes how he'd like to be viewed by his employees into camera: "Would I rather be feared or loved? Um, easy. Both. I want people to be afraid of how much they love me." Frighteningly, he means it.

Michael tends to overestimate his own importance in the eyes of his coworkers and cannot understand why they don't seem to have much fun at work, as he believes the office to be the "place where dreams come true." Partly it's because in staff meetings he says things like, "If I had a gun with two bullets and I was in a room with Hitler, Bin Laden, and Toby, I would shoot Toby twice."

Michael is also extremely irresponsible with his finances, a disturbing trait in someone who runs a company, but common in the Buffoon. It becomes such a problem that he is eventually forced to declare bankruptcy. Upon arriving at this conclusion, Michael steps out of his office, spine straight, and yells out into the general work area, "I declare BANKRUPTCY!"

Oscar (Oscar Nuñez), who's been helping Michael with his finances, senses Michael might be thinking that's all that is required. He pokes his head into Michael's office a bit later.

> OSCAR: Hey... I just wanted you to know that you can't just say the word 'bankruptcy' and expect anything to happen.
>
> MICHAEL: I didn't say it, I declared it.
>
> OSCAR: Still, that's not... anything.

Despite being a loutish blowhard, by the time Michael leaves Dunder Mifflin, he's won over the hearts of his staff and they unexpectedly do end up thinking of him quite fondly. In arguably the best episode of the series, "Goodbye, Michael," a rare but not unheard-of occurrence takes place. The show's main character exits before it is taken off the air.

Michael's separate goodbyes to Jim and Pam as he heads off to Colorado to live with his fiancée Holly (Amy Ryan) are heart-wrenching. He narrates his exit into an awaiting taxicab, pointedly reviewing to himself, "Holly's my family now. *She's* my family. And the babies that I make with her will be my children. The people that you work with are just... when you get down to it, your very best friends. They say, on your deathbed, you never wish you spent more time at the office. But I will. Gotta be a lot better than a deathbed. I actually don't understand... 'deathbeds.' I mean, who would buy that?"

Funny and poignant, Michael's final thoughts summarize his time at *The Office* brilliantly. It seems he had to retrain himself on what actually constitutes his family, as he entered his own marriage.

Fortunately for fans, Michael returns after a two-season absence for the series finale, which revolves around Dwight (Rainn Wilson) and Angela's (Angela Kinsey) wedding. With everyone he loves gathered, Michael is overwhelmed with emotion and speaks into the camera one last time, "I feel like all my kids grew up and then they married each other. Every parent's dream!" Maybe then, with two years to think about it, he didn't change his perception at all. Awkward until the very last word.

Characteristics of the Buffoon

- Antagonistic
- Bombastic
- Boneheaded
- Boorish
- Braggartly
- Bullying
- Bumbling
- Cavalier
- Childish
- Cloddish
- Competitive
- Defiant
- Delusional
- Dense
- Dimwitted
- Disdainful
- Egotistical
- Foolhardy
- Glib
- Goofy
- Graceless
- Haughty
- Indifferent
- Inept
- Inferiority Complex
- Insensitive
- Insistent
- Insolent
- Jealous
- Lackadaisical
- Lazy
- Obtuse
- Overbearing
- Petty
- Petulant
- Rude
- Self-Important
- Shortsighted
- Spoilsport
- Stubborn

Buffoons Throughout the History of Television

Sterling Archer	H. Jon Benjamin	Archer
Wayne Arnold	Jason Hervey	The Wonder Years
Erlich Bachman	T.J. Miller	Silicon Valley
Robert Barone	Brad Garrett	Everybody Loves Raymond
Ted Baxter	Ted Knight	The Mary Tyler Moore Show
Gob Bluth	Will Arnett	Arrested Development
Howard Borden	Bill Daily	The Bob Newhart Show
Det. Charles Boyle	Joe Lo Truglio	Brooklyn Nine-Nine
Matthew Brock	Andy Dick	NewsRadio
Kelly Bundy	Christina Applegate	Married... With Children
Frank Burns	Larry Linville	M*A*S*H
Eric Cartman	Trey Parker	South Park
Burt Chance	Garret Dillahunt	Raising Hope
Virginia Chance	Martha Plimpton	Raising Hope
Johnny "Drama" Chase	Kevin Dillon	Entourage
Cliff Clavin	John Ratzenberger	Cheers
Mel Cooley	Richard Deacon	The Dick Van Dyke Show
Dr. Fitch Cooper	Peter Facinelli	Nurse Jackie
Sheldon Cooper	Jim Parsons	The Big Bang Theory
Sheldon Cooper	Iain Armitage	Young Sheldon
George Costanza	Jason Alexander	Seinfeld
Count Olaf	Neil Patrick Harris	A Series of Unfortunate Events

Larry David	Larry David	Curb Your Enthusiasm
Adam DeMamp	Adam Devine	Workaholics
Phil Dunphy	Ty Burrell	Modern Family
Barney Fife	Don Knotts	The Andy Griffith Show
Dawn Forchette	Alex Borstein	Getting On
Monroe Fuches	Stephen Root	Barry
Paulie G.	Lance Barber	The Comeback
Gilligan	Bob Denver	Gilligan's Island
Vera Louise Gorman	Beth Howland	Alice
Tom Haverford	Aziz Ansari	Parks and Recreation
Pierce Hawthorne	Chevy Chase	Community
Axl Heck	Charlie McDermott	The Middle
Blake Henderson	Blake Anderson	Workaholics
Earl Hickey	Jason Lee	My Name is Earl
Boss Jefferson Davis (J.D.) Hogg	Sorrell Booke	The Dukes of Hazzard
Anders Holmvik	Anders Holm	Workaholics
George Jefferson	Sherman Hemsley	The Jeffersons
Obie Wakefield Jones	John Henton	Living Single
Tracy Jordan	Tracy Morgan	30 Rock
Dr. Bob Kelso	Ken Jenkins	Scrubs
Lenny Kosnowski	Michael McKean	Laverne & Shirley
Merc Lapidus	John Pankow	Episodes
Haskell Lutz	Wayne Knight	The Exes

Mac McDonald	Rob McElhenney	**It's Always Sunny in Philadelphia**
Ed Norton	Art Carney	**The Honeymooners**
Kenny Powers	Danny McBride	**Eastbound & Down**
Ricardo	Benjamin Barrett	**The Politician**
Matthew Ellis Ross	Cole Escola	**Difficult People**
Roland Schitt	Chris Elliot	**Schitt's Creek**
Dwight Schrute	Rainn Wilson	**The Office**
Michael Scott	Steve Carell	**The Office**
Nostradamus 'Bull' Shannon	Richard Moll	**Night Court**
Homer J. Simpson	Dan Castellaneta	**The Simpsons**
Maxwell Smart	Don Adams	**Get Smart**
Squiggy Squigg-mann	David Lander	**Laverne & Shirley**
James "J.J." Evans Jr.	Jimmie Walker	**Good Times**
Gary Walsh	Tony Hale	**Veep**
Ilana Wexler	Ilana Glazer	**Broad City**
Reese Wilkerson	Justin Berfield	**Malcolm in the Middle**
Doug Wilson	Kevin Nealon	**Weeds**
Barry Zuckerkorn	Henry Winkler	**Arrested Development**

How Buffoons are Described in the Breakdowns

Boisterous, clueless, corrupt, dodgy, flippant, full of bluster, greedy, intellectually pretentious (Lena Dunham type), jerk, opportunistic, out of touch, overbearing, pugnacious, racist, self-proclaimed genius, sexist, socially maladjusted, smug, spouts bullshit, stubborn, suspicious, thinks they have a wonderful sense of humor but jokes all land with a thud, uncharismatic, unjust amount of confidence that comes from seemingly nowhere

Lead Body Part: Forehead

Take a second and focus all the energy in your body into your forehead without furrowing your brows or scrunching up your face. Now try to look just a half of an inch in front of your eyes. You feel quite dense, don't you? If you stayed that way for much longer, you'd be on the verge of a serious headache. It's hard to think in that condition. Do it again and say a simple math problem out loud. Do you notice that your voice comes from a slightly different place? Does your neck rest differently? Your whole head might feel heavy. If you carried this shift in energy into a conversation with someone, you'd be probably feel awkward and self-conscious. This is what life is like for the dimwitted Buffoon.

ECCENTRIC

"I know all about being left in a lurch for a fundraiser. Eva Longoria and I were supposed to perform our ventriloquist act for the Everybody Nose Benefit for Juvenile Rhinoplasty when she suddenly drops out due to 'exhaustion.' I had to be both puppet and puppeteer."

—Moira Rose/Schitt's Creek

Mantra: "I imagine"

Strength: Open

Weakness: Misunderstood

Typical jobs: As an unusual person, they make a normal job equally unusual or... we simply never know what they do.

Who Are They?

The Eccentric is The Hero of Comedy that is most likely to be described by words and terms that aren't helpful for creating a fully humanized version. They are far too often identified as: quirky, spacey, out to lunch, new-agey, whacked out, zany, odd, etc.

I know what "quirky" means and most likely you do too. But if you see that word in a breakdown for a character, chances are you're going to need to interpret it with other words (better words) that are more grounded and actionable. Actors need to personalize character traits just as they would emotions. "Quirky" is a concept. If you play a character as quirky, chances are your performance will be broad and not as authentic and believable as it should be for the camera.

Better characteristics with which to work in defining your version of an Eccentric are: uninhibited, independent, opinionated, intense, and continually awestruck by everything you experience in life, regardless of your chronological age.

This is a great reminder of why understanding archetypes and mastering the ones best suited to your personality is so important. For television and film, most actors get work playing characters that are at least somewhat close to their nature in day-to-day life. Any actor with some basic training and bravery can take a swipe at playing a quirky character. Results will vary.

However, when you directly ask an actor, "Are you known by your friends and family for being utterly shameless and forcefully opinionated with a skewed view point on life that always seems different from the rest of the crowd?" you either get a furrowed brow while they try and recall if they've ever heard anything like that or a wide smile and an immediate confirmation that that is exactly how they are known by everyone who knows them well.

There's a *vast* difference between two equally trained and talented actors, one who understands the question but doesn't identify with it, and another who is defined by the question. The one who says, "Yes! That's what I'm like all the time!" is more likely than not going to be better casting, everything else considered equally.

Each of The Heroes of Comedy is clearly defined from the others but some of these archetypes have greater accessibility to a broader swath of actors. Eccentric by definition means rare, unusual, or odd. It therefore only makes sense that fewer actors can take on this archetype in a grounded, believable way. If you are not *strongly* opinionated with a history of expressing your *unconventional* thoughts in a *shameless* way, you'll have a harder time executing this character than someone who lives their life that way every single day.

If you're thinking, "Well, no one is like that *all* the time," then you're exactly the person for whom I'm elaborating on this point. Some people *are* like that *all* the time. Some people have no relationship to shame and cannot be embarrassed. Some folks are completely open to new experiences with pure curiosity and wonder and experience no fear or guardedness whatsoever.

Some people are tolerant of everyone; every race, religion, gender, or lack thereof. Not only are they accepting of everyone and everything that's different from them, they aspire to learn what they can and keep only the best parts of every experience. Curiosity, awe, and wonder remain a *large and substantial* part of daily life all throughout an Eccentric's adulthood. Is that you on most hours of most days of your life?

If yes, you're probably smiling right now simply because someone understands you for a change! While most people have glimpses of awe within their life, they don't experience all their grown-up life that way. Most people transition out of that state as they get older and integrate into whatever system their parents adhere to. Awe and wonderment then become relegated to individual, sporadic experiences.

If you aren't an Eccentric yourself, you might be marveling (perhaps even envious) that some people move through the world with little or no anxiety - ever - and seem to only attract positive people and experiences. Even when things go wrong, or the Eccentric incurs the same losses and hardships we all endure, they seem to recover with resilience. They organically navigate life's trials with ease and can utilize the incredible power of their imagination to manifest a better circumstance than the one they're in, if they so desire.

It's not that Eccentrics don't suffer or feel deeply; they do. But they possess a core set of characteristics that help them improvise through life and not take it all too seriously. None of us are given an instruction manual on how to adult. For some that's a terrible thing, causing us to feel like we were unfairly thrust into a complicated world to fend for ourselves. That point of view can cause feelings of anxiety, suspicion, dread, weariness, resentment of growing up when we're not ready, or martyrdom; core traits of other archetypes.

For the Eccentric, life is simply an adventure. They have a logical mind, but their logic is skewed by openness to all possibilities and a *hyperactive imagination*. When they see an obvious situation differently from their peers, it's not because they are less intelligent (or spacey or ditzy or dingy or nuts), it's because curiosity is a prominent defining trait for this type of person. Curiosity nullifies skepticism and the Eccentric is left free to believe anything they choose.

There is a spectrum of intellectual curiosity. Some people are simply not curious. They are closed off to the world and all its wonders. Most people have average curiosity; they wonder about the unknown occasionally but at a certain point become satisfied with their baseline understanding of the world.

The Eccentric is *never* satisfied with their comprehension of existence and enthusiastically maintains an unhindered approach to life that allows for the possibility that anything can happen at any time. Their belief systems are not set in stone and they are open to changing their thoughts on life and the afterlife at any given moment. Some might think that the Innocent is the opposite of the Cynic. I think it's the Eccentric. The Cynic feels perennially stuck where life put them largely because they lack the imagination to change the course of their life.

While the Innocent is definitely a lot more joyful about their experience of life than the Cynic, it's the Eccentric who possesses the imagination to create life on their own terms without diminishing or impeding the life or opportunities of others. Imagination is really the counterpoint to doubt (Cynic), even more so than joy (Innocent).

Does God exist? Are there other forms of life in the universe? Can a ghost haunt a house? I certainly don't know but ask an Eccentric and I guarantee you there will at least be an interesting conversation afoot.

What Is Their Strength?

Eccentrics are open to the world in a way that is similar to the Innocent, but without the gullibility or naïvete. Eccentrics are odd, but they aren't clowns or fools. This also distinguishes them entirely from Buffoons. It's enough that they are highly unusual. It would negatively overwhelm the character if they were also socially dimwitted and awkward. Eccentrics are aware that they're considered unique by all the other archetypes (not just some) and are perfectly comfortable in that position. In fact, they wouldn't have it any other way.

Since they are already the fish out of water in regard to the rest of their tribe, Eccentrics should otherwise be envisioned by the writer and performer together as sharp and stalwart. If not given a thoroughly formed point of view with which to express their unconventional outlook on life, it's very easy for this arche-type to come across as unrelatable to the audience and for lack of a better word, "sketchy."

The Eccentric approaches the world with a friendly, wel-coming attitude. They are generally not judgmental, enjoying the differences of other people, their ideas, and backgrounds. Eccentrics have to learn that people can have conflict with each other based on their inherent differences. It wouldn't occur to them to dislike someone simply for a lack of understanding them.

In contrast, there are personality types who immediately dis-like those whom they don't understand. Or perhaps they're wary of new people and experiences until a certain level of trust and familiarity is earned. Eccentrics don't need that. Trust through detached observation is a defense mechanism that can be a barrier to full participation in moment-to-moment life. That's no fun for the perennially curious.

A strong sense of acceptance combined with a vibrant imagination provides the Eccentric with a solid foundation that helps them keep their feet planted firmly on the ground in every moment in which they are engaged with friends, family, a task, or a mission. Often misinterpreted as space cadets, the Eccentric is just the opposite.

They are not *fighting* gravity; they *are* gravity. Sure, when they're alone they might stare into the clouds, contemplate the way things are and daydream. However, it's important to remember that they live in a constant state of discovery. The awe and wonderment they feel by experiencing the world can only happen with *intense focus* and *deep listening skills*.

A great Eccentric never has their head in the clouds. They have their head in the game, whatever the game happens to be. They just play by an adapted set of instructions.

What Is Their Weakness?

The Eccentric is the only Hero of Comedy with no inherent weakness. I think that's very important to consider. All their qualities lead them to have a favorable experience of life, even when things turn upside down. We cannot control other people's behavior or circumstances; we can only control our own reactions. Overall, the Eccentric has the best list of core characteristics to manage life, otherwise known as chaos, in a healthy way.

They don't have preconceived notions of how someone should behave or what an experience should be like. They love themselves and accept themselves and others for exactly who they are and aspire to be. They are not prone to disappointment or dissatisfaction. They do have the courage of their convictions, even if they're off-center, and feel emboldened to share their thoughts on anything and everything without second-guessing themselves or feeling self-conscious about what other people think of them. Pretty cool, huh?

So although the Eccentric doesn't have an *inherent* weakness, they do have one. The difference between this Hero and the others is that their weakness is conditional. It requires an external obstacle, event, or person in order to occur. Their weakness is being misunderstood.

Eccentrics are perennially misconceived by the rest of the world and therefore also often judged negatively, which is a bummer. Any given Eccentric is aware enough to understand that a personal disconnect is happening when it's happening. They know when their thought process or behavior is bewildering to someone. They aren't negatively affected by it though, until it creates an obstacle or challenge.

Being misunderstood by nearly everyone all the time can easily get in the way of important things like landing a job, finding love, or merely being deeply known by your closest friends and family.

Eccentrics are energized by other people and what they have to offer. As strong and steadfast as they are, the Eccentric is thwarted by intolerance. Once another person stops at least trying to relate to an Eccentric, the infinite loop of engagement is broken, and the connection is lost. This is when the Eccentric's sharp edges come out.

Capable of experiencing the full spectrum of emotion, as all The Heroes of Comedy are, an irritated or pissed off Eccentric can be fearsome. Remember, they don't have a filter. If they're displeased with you, you'll know about it in a very direct way.

Traveling life's path largely misunderstood by everyone you meet is equal parts liberating and isolating. When you're accepted, life is much easier. When you're not, you're entirely on your own. So while the Eccentric's weakness is conditional, it's a pretty big one.

To summarize, it's worth considering the heartiest, most well-rounded kind of person is the rarest. While, not all Eccentrics are geniuses, all geniuses are Eccentrics. Who is *like* Albert Einstein? Who reminds you of Bill Gates or Elon Musk or Oprah Winfrey? That's right, *no one*.

How Do Others See Them?

It will come as no surprise that the friends and family of the Eccentric view them as odd. We've reviewed their individuality in depth. However, I want to reinforce the heartiness and humanity of this archetype so your embodiment of them remains authentic, grounded, and well rounded.

Eccentrics are wise in their own way. They are apt to have a philosophy on life and think about the nature of why things are the way they are. They more than likely have a philosophy *of their own creation* on how to treat people and live life. Sure, it may disregard some laws, but only in favor of morality, justice, and the greater good. Having the courage of your convictions, which Eccentrics absolutely do, means you've thought about your values *in advance* of life's tests and challenges and you know with certainty who you are.

However, not everyone is wired that way. Not everyone grounds themselves in an ideology of their own creation. Some people are more comfortable joining a religion, tribe, or organization that already exists. Many people take comfort from the like-mindedness of others. A well-written and well-performed Eccentric is designed from a platform of strength and clarity that is essential for an independent thinker who embraces their identity *outside* of society's norms and the convenience of a belief system that was already in place before they were born.

Unique even amongst a diverse crowd, the Eccentric is also viewed by those who know and love them best as self-sufficient and strong. Those closest to the Eccentric might even be a bit jealous of how fulfilled they are in such a substantial way, even while struggling to achieve goals and maintain relationships. Limitless curiosity about the world prevents the Eccentric from worrying about things that haven't happened yet or dwelling on bad things that have happened previously. Their ability to remain focused on the wonders of being alive in the present moment is nearly a superpower.

How Do Writers Use Them?

Writers capitalize on the Eccentric's dynamic imagination and ability to see things in an entirely different way from the rest of the crowd. Cosmo Kramer (Michael Richards) of *Seinfeld* fame is an excellent example. *Seinfeld* features a core group of four friends living in Manhattan. Jerry (Jerry Seinfeld), Elaine (Julia Louis-Dreyfus), and George (Jason Alexander) are all three different archetypes. Jerry is the Anchor of the group, Elaine is the Narcissist, and George is the Buffoon.

I think most fans of the show would agree that the differences in demeanor between the three of them and Kramer are vastly different. As the resident Eccentric, Kramer's presence within the group is distinctive in every way. He lives his life in a state of constant wonderment and awe. He is inarguably more energized on a moment-to-moment basis than his friends. Kramer doesn't *enter* Jerry's apartment; he *explodes* in.

Jerry, Elaine, and George quibble and debate each other all the time. However, most of their conversations and disputes hinge on expected aspects of the same point. Once Kramer chimes in, it's a different story. As the resident Eccentric, he'll offer an entirely different point of view that leaves the rest of them collectively slack-jawed.

Here are a couple of examples:

JERRY: So you won't believe what happened with Whatley today. It got back to him that I made this little dentist joke, and he got all offended! Those people can be so touchy.

KRAMER: "Those people?" Listen to yourself!

JERRY: What?

KRAMER: You think that dentists are so different from me and you? They came to this country just like everybody else in search of a dream!

JERRY: Whatley's from Jersey!

KRAMER: Yes, and now he's a full-fledged American!

JERRY: Kramer, he's just a dentist.

KRAMER: Yeah, and you're an anti-dentite!

JERRY: I am not an anti-dentite!

KRAMER: You're a rabid anti-dentite! Oh, it starts with a few jokes and some slurs: "Hey, denty!" Next thing you know you're saying, "They should have their own schools"!

JERRY: They do have their own schools!

KRAMER: Yeah!

This is an excellent example of Kramer's skewed logic. He's applying the tenets of social justice and a strong moral code to a group of people who aren't being persecuted and do not need the support. Jerry is not an anti-dentite, and even if he was, making dentist jokes is certainly not in the same category as mocking someone for their race, ethnicity, or gender.

However, with utter sincerity, Kramer sees it that way. He's legitimately shaming Jerry for his behavior. He's not being sarcastic or cute and he's not kidding. He's also alone in his interpretation of this particular circumstance, yet he doesn't care and he's forceful in his defense of it.

I'm sure Elaine and George would certainly agree that if you're from New Jersey, you've been a United States citizen your whole life and you're not an immigrant who became naturalized at some point. Overall, Kramer makes sense as a member of this particular tribe, but he consistently sees things through a lens none of others would or can truly understand.

Here is one more example that reinforces the skewed logic of the Eccentric:

KRAMER: Well, my swimming pool problems are solved. I just found myself miles and miles of open lanes.

JERRY: What is that smell?

KRAMER: That's the East River.

JERRY: You're swimming in the East River? The most heavily trafficked, overly contaminated waterway on the eastern seaboard?

KRAMER: Technically, Norfolk has more gross tonnage.

JERRY: How could you swim in that water?

KRAMER:	I saw a couple of other guys out there.
JERRY:	Swimming?
KRAMER:	Well, floating. They weren't moving much, but they were out there.

I think the 'other guys' Kramer refers to are dead. Again, I'd proffer that George and Elaine would make the same deduction along with Jerry. But finding floating dead bodies in a contaminated river doesn't fit Kramer's narrative of solving his overcrowded swimming pool problem. He projected his own skewed logic onto the circumstance he encountered in the river; the dead bodies were just other guys who also wanted a roomy body of water in which to swim.

All archetypes have a distinct point of view. The Eccentric, more than any other archetype, is a great way for writers to have a character experience a situation or another person in a way that is entirely unique from all the rest of the group.

What Is Your Way In?

Some actors have a very hard time understanding and portraying an Eccentric. They often have difficulty identifying with the unusual and sometimes outrageous nature of this archetype. The Eccentric's dialogue can be very different from words some of us have ever been asked to speak, real or imagined. This highlights the point that not all roles are for all actors, but I don't think the trouble actors experience is identifying how they're personally odd or offbeat.

We all have some kind of individualistic trait or unique way of looking at something that we might use as a personalization to find our way into this character. Most people have been the odd man or woman out on at least one occasion even if they don't live their whole life feeling that way.

The reason I think most people have trouble identifying with the Eccentric is that I don't think the average person is as self-loving, strong, and free of doubt, shame, and concern for what others think of them as the character on the page. If you are, great! If this character makes sense to you, develop it, and make it as sharp and crystal clear as you possibly can.

That said, the way into this archetype on a deeper and more sophisticated level isn't to personalize being strange. The best execution of an Eccentric requires an actor to dial into complete love and acceptance of who they are as an actual human being and offer their thoughts on the world with open, thunderous enthusiasm, and no fear of resistance or pushback.

Acting is merging your skin and skeleton with the psyche of the character the writer created. Some actors (people) were not raised to say whatever they want whenever they want without criticism or ridicule. Many artists (actors and otherwise) are very talented but carry around a great deal of self-doubt, self-loathing, and stay within a predesignated comfort zone most of the time. Some people don't experience life as an open invitation to freely express themselves any way they like, any time they like with absolutely no regard to the thoughts or opinions of others.

So, it's not *weirdness* actors are having a hard time accessing in most cases, it's *absolute personal freedom*. Ironically, the archetype that is considered the most rare is also the one who is kindest to themselves and predisposed to appreciate the value in everything, even disappointment and loss.

Your way into the Eccentric is by accessing the very best of yourself and the most emotionally healthy version of who you are. Surprise. You thought I was going to break down a weirdo here, didn't you?

Consider the following: If you have shame about who you are as a person, your character will too. If you flinch at saying strange things out loud, your character will too. If you were embarrassed growing up because you were different and haven't found a way to express yourself from a loving place without being guarded or defensive, your character won't be able to believably do that. Yes, acting is pretending, but your characters can't have more personal fortitude than you do.

Sometimes characters are written as more evolved than we have had a chance to become in our lifetime. I think actors don't consider that enough. Whatever their dialogue is on the page, a character can't ultimately be more substantial than the person playing it.

Eccentrics have a very complex thought process that intersects with a vibrant imagination. That can intimidate some actors and it should. Not all of us are multifarious thinkers who also happen to have an imagination that draws equally from intellect, fantasy, empathy, strategy, memory reconstruction, and emotion. Those are truly the components of the best-crafted Eccentrics you've ever watched.

However, if you simply begin with traits like engaged, free, and empowered while leaving all judgments aside, you can begin walking the Eccentric's path. Remember, their dialogue has to be unusual. Much of the work of building this character is already done by the writer. It's then up to the actor to unflinchingly speak the Eccentric's unconventional words with complete integrity and no commentary.

The Eccentric in a Family-Based Series: *Roseanne, Malcolm in the Middle, The Middle*

Having an Eccentric family member is a bit different than having an Eccentric coworker or friend you might make along the way.

You can't choose your family. An Eccentric always adds a new dimension to their tribe, but when it's your son, daughter, brother, or sister, it's an entirely different situation. You're exposed to a unique perspective every day of your life. Whether that's annoying or amusing is for each relation to discern, but it definitely enables conflict and comedy.

This is a great opportunity not only to explore the family dynamic of the Eccentric, but to also highlight some younger characters from television history. D.J. Conner (Michael Fishman) from *Roseanne* is a great young Eccentric:

> D.J.: I haven't said anything in two days. Nobody's cared.
>
> ROSEANNE: Oh, that can't be.
>
> D.J.: Uh-huh. The last thing I said was "Cheerios."

An interesting experiment for a 10-year-old, D.J. consciously decided not to speak for two whole days to see if anyone would notice. Not only does that require complex thinking and a strong imagination, it's also pretty bold and independent for a little boy. It's also worth noting that the last previous word he said was, "Cheerios," which we can deduce was the answer to the question, "What do you want for breakfast?" And for 48 hours there was no follow up.

Not only was D.J. right about being ignored, it's also the case that when people did talk to him, the conversation was basic and routine. What a simple but very poignant way to remind your mom that no one's really been checking in with you! D.J. considered an aspect of life that no one else was thinking about, but was not, in any way foolish. Perhaps this is how geniuses begin.

Dewey (Erik Per Sullivan) from *Malcolm in the Middle* is equally unique and the same age as D.J.

MALCOLM:	Why do we have to go shopping?
LOIS:	Because you ruin everything you own. Your clothes don't just magically appear in your drawers.
DEWEY:	Mine do.

It only takes two words to illustrate that Dewey thinks, and has apparently always thought, that magic is the only way to explain how his clothes are cleaned and restocked into his dresser. Surely he'd seen his mother put clothes from the hamper into the washing machine. You'd have to think he saw her folding clothes at some point. Yet when there's an overactive imagination at work and no judgment of impractical, improbable conclusions, you end up with a skewed point of view that can land virtually anywhere.

Each member of the family is a different archetype and their nature is distinct. Each one responds to the world driven by their core characteristics. However, it's the Eccentric *alone within his own tribe* who thinks clean laundry is the result of wizardry. What does Dewey see in his mind's eye and how must he feel every time he opens a drawer to pull out a pair of pants? Very likely he experiences profound awe and wonderment going about such a mundane task.

Not only does Dewey think his clothes magically appear in his dresser drawer, he's fine thinking his brothers' *don't*. That means Dewey must also imagine that he's special amongst his three other brothers. Most kids prefer to fit in. Eccentrics prefer not to.

When I mentioned before that Eccentrics experience wonder and awe from day-to-day life, I absolutely mean that could include clean pants.

Last, but certainly not least, is Brick Heck (Atticus Shaffer) from *The Middle*. Although I earlier made a case against a certain word, I'm allowing an exception here. Brick is a walking, talking quirk. He's about as quirky as kids get and he knows it.

Campaigning for School Historian, he begins his speech to all his schoolmates in a packed auditorium, "Hi, I'm Brick Heck. Or as most of you know me, "Nerd." I spend a lot of time locked in lockers here at Orson Elementary. And that's given me a lot of time to think. You may think I'm odd. And maybe I am. I'm the kid who makes you late for recess because we have to walk in a group and I'm still in the bathroom pulling up my pants."

There is no one else in the world like Brick. Without an official diagnosis, there's a chance that the character of Brick may even be on the spectrum of autistic disorders. It's alluded to within the series and handled with considerable grace.

The Middle is an understated and extremely well-crafted show. Brick's behaviors and mannerisms are the topic of many conversations and consternation by his parents. The writers of *The Middle* explore the trials of parenting an overtly unusual child in a very subtle way and without bringing in the drama of a doctor diagnosing him with Asperger syndrome or the like. Aside from seeing the world in a way others don't, Brick has behavioral irregularities, which he struggles to control. Sometimes he repeats certain words at the end of a sentence quietly to himself.

"I just don't understand Christmas. It's like we're supposed to be happy, but how can we possibly enjoy it, knowing that it's all so fleeting? (He lowers his chin and whispers to himself) *"Fleeting..."* Later in the series, Brick develops a "whoop." Out of nowhere he may burp out a 'whoop' sound, sometimes to the frustration and concern of his parents:

MIKE: Knock off the whooping.

BRICK: The whooping? That's what this is about? I thought it was about the other thing.

MIKE: The whispering? No.

BRICK: I have to say the Pledge of Allegiance 20 times before I go to bed. (He lowers his chin and whispers to himself exiting) Pledge of Allegiance...

MIKE: Awesome.

In another moment, his two most distinctive behaviors piggy-back each other.

FRANKIE: Well... Your dad and I talked it over – not be-cause you were bugging me – and we have decided that we are going to stop and visit your girlfriend in North Carolina!

BRICK: Wow! That's great! Thanks! Whoop! (He lowers his chin and whispers to himself) Whoop. (As he exits) Whoop! (He lowers his chin and whis-pers to himself) Whoop. Whoop! (He lowers his chin and whispers to himself) Whoop.

MIKE: Yep. We're never having grandkids.

In addition, Brick is an avid reader and extremely intelligent but constantly forgets to do his homework and doesn't really care about grades. He is curious and heavily invested in learning but isn't particularly interested in any of the traditions or routine of attending school. He's obsessed with fonts and a brilliant speller but has trouble relating to other people and forming friendships. Eccentrics need tolerance from their peers in order to form connections. An easier endeavor for an adult than a child in public school.

As if that weren't enough, Brick (and Atticus Shaffer in real life) both have osteogenesis imperfecta, also known as brittle bone disease, which accounts for Brick's limp and adds to the isolation he experiences on a daily basis. While Brick is contemplative, he's not unhappy. It's important to note that while the description of his childhood is certainly less than ideal, Brick is independent and values his time alone with his thoughts and books. He's cheerful more often than not and friendly even as he struggles to further a conversation or reinforce the bonds of friendship.

Brick is a philosopher and a grounding force within the Heck household. His teachers, the neighbors, and his family would all refer to him as odd. However, he's better read than all of them and secure in his own identity in ways that elude most adults. It doesn't occur to him to be embarrassed of who he is and that makes him fierce in his own way. He's respected by those closest to him, even if he's not understood.

When his mom, Frankie (Patricia Heaton), tries to drive Brick over a bridge to help work through a long-standing phobia, he refuses. Standing outside the parked car and frustrated, Frankie asks Brick for an explanation.

> FRANKIE: I don't get it, Brick. What are you so afraid of? What do you think is gonna happen?
>
> BEAT

BRICK: We drive onto the bridge and suddenly there's a terrible cracking sound. The bridge collapses and the car is thrown into the lake. It fills with water and sinks like a big metal coffin. We struggle to get out but... under water, no one can hear our screams. We all shake with convulsions as the life leaves our bodies. Our bloated corpses go undiscovered for months, but when they're finally dragged out of the lake, they're unrecognizable because the fish have eaten out our eyeballs. (He lowers his chin and whispers to himself) Eyyyye baaallls.

Once again, the complex thinking and vivid imagination of the Eccentric motivates a detailed (and in this case) horrific answer. "What a weirdo," some would say. Yeah, until he grows up and becomes their boss...

The Eccentric in a Friend-Based Series: *Friends*

Lisa Kudrow's embodiment of Phoebe Buffay on *Friends* is quite simply the gold standard of a comedic Eccentric. There's no better case study for how to translate kooky on the page into humanely unconventional on the screen. Phoebe is alive with all the characteristics of the Eccentric and simultaneously real and relatable.

For the record, there's a good chance I'm biased. Lisa was one of my teachers at The Groundlings. I'm very blessed to have had her as part of my training because A) she's brilliant and B) she didn't teach very long. Her career took off pretty quickly after becoming a member of The Groundlings Main Company.

I completely cop to name-dropping here, but that's not the only reason I have for mentioning that I trained with her. In class with Lisa, I got to see firsthand how incredibly intelligent she is. Her notes and feedback were whip-smart and challenged everyone to work to the height of their intelligence. She was supportive, but she didn't dumb down the curriculum for anyone. She addressed the tenets of professional acting, as well as good improvisation, and guided us to immerse ourselves fully in our behaviors, mannerisms, and internal thought processes. She encouraged the truth always and guided us away from winking at our characters or playing them as an outline or a concept.

I'd watch her perform live onstage weekly and quickly thereafter she was on television. All the way through, I saw her trading on her intellect as she created offbeat characters, the best known of which is, of course, Phoebe. In class and by example she taught me that the weirder a *character* is, the smarter *I* need to be.

I learned that if you don't round out the oddity of a character with equivalent humanity, you'll lose your audience. Later I'd learn that Lisa earned a B.S. in Science from Vassar and opted out of a career in neuroscience to become an actor. So when I was thinking, "Wow! She's *really* smart," in class, I apparently wasn't just imagining it.

Friends is one of the most prominent comedies in television history. Every cast member has had leading roles on multiple series and wildly successful careers. Interestingly, only two regular cast members won Emmy Awards for their work on the show. Jennifer Aniston earned a trophy for Outstanding Lead Actress in a Comedy Series for her portrayal of Rachel Green and the second went to Lisa Kudrow for Outstanding Supporting Actress in a Comedy Series.

More than mere trivia, I think that win is significant. The show has six series regular roles and lasted 10 seasons. Owning one of only two acting trophies for playing the "ditzy" one on the show speaks to Lisa's talent, training, and clever interpretation of Phoebe Buffay. It's tougher than you might think to play the woman who writes and sings the song "Smelly Cat" at Central Perk and becomes the surrogate for her brother's triplets.

Throughout the seasons of *Friends*, we learn that Phoebe is mildly psychic, never learned to ride a bike as a child, lost her adoptive mother to suicide, and lived on the streets when she was only 14 years old. More specifically, she lived in a burned-out Buick LeSabre for a while and was married to a Canadian ice dancer for six years, who pretended to be gay and came out as straight when he asked her for a divorce. She mugged Ross years before they knew each other and she's a massage therapist by trade who doesn't pay income taxes.

That's really just the tip of the iceberg. As the resident Eccentric, the writers of *Friends* were able to give Phoebe the most jaw-dropping history, and it both made sense and remained comedic because of her nature. Although much of her early life is quite dark, Phoebe is a consistently upbeat adult. Her humanity always trumps her bizarre circumstances. She said and did so many peculiar things throughout the course of the show, but when there was a crisis, Phoebe could be wise.

In season eight, Rachel finds out she's pregnant with Ross's child even though they aren't together as a couple at that point. She tells Phoebe and Monica at Monica and Chandler's wedding. Anxious and torn between the desire to be a mother and the struggle of raising a child on her own, Rachel takes a second pregnancy test to be sure. Monica and Phoebe wait with her in the ladies' room for the results of the second test, still not knowing that Ross is the father.

RACHEL: How much longer?

PHOEBE: Thirty seconds.

RACHEL: Thirty seconds, okay...

MONICA: Did I miss it?

Rachel shakes her heads no.

MONICA: Rachel... I want you to know that if it's positive... We're gonna...

RACHEL: Oh, I know... I know.

MONICA: You do?

PHOEBE: It's time.

MONICA: Go ahead, Rach.

RACHEL: Oh, wait, you know what? I can't. I can't look at it. I can't look at it. Somebody else tell me. Somebody tell me.

PHOEBE: Okay, um... it's negative.

RACHEL: What?!

PHOEBE: It's negative.

RACHEL: Oh. Oh... well, there you go. Whew! That is, that's great. That is really great, great news. You know, 'cause of the whole not being ready, and kinda the financial aspects and all that... This is just so... the way this was supposed to be.

MONICA: Then, great.

Rachel starts crying, Phoebe hands her a tissue.

RACHEL:	Thanks. God, it's so stupid! How could I be upset over something I never had? It's negative?
PHOEBE:	No, it's positive.
RACHEL:	What?
PHOEBE:	It's not negative, it's positive.
RACHEL:	Are you sure?
PHOEBE:	Well, yeah, I lied before.

Rachel is overjoyed.

PHOEBE:	Now you know how you really feel about it!
RACHEL:	Oh, that's a risky little game!
MONICA:	Are you really going to do this?
RACHEL:	Yeah, I'm gonna have a baby. I'm gonna have a baby. I'M GONNA HAVE A BABY!
PHOEBE:	With who?
RACHEL:	Still not the time!

As Rachel says to Phoebe, it *was* a risky little game. However, it is also a once in a lifetime opportunity for Rachel to reflect on how she truly feels about becoming a mother without worrying about the reality of long-term parenting. She wants a baby. Phoebe helps her to be absolutely sure. It's a bold move on Phoebe's part, even for a close friend. Fortunately, Rachel is grateful, and it pays off.

Not all of Phoebe's ideas work out as well though. When Ross moves into a new apartment, the current tenants ask him to chip in $100 for the maintenance man's retirement gift. Having just moved in that day, Ross is indignant at the request and declines. As a result, his new neighbors think he's an unfriendly cheapskate.

Unwilling to pay on principle, Ross instead decides to throw a party to win them over. They counter with their own party for Howard the maintenance man at which Ross accidentally starts eating the cake before Howard's even seen it. The crowd turns on Ross and Phoebe interjects.

PHOEBE: Everyone, calm down. Everyone, calm down! I have something that I'd like to say. Who here likes Ross?

Ross is the only one in the crowd to raise his hand.

PHOEBE: Of course you don't like him. He didn't give you any money, he raised his own hand when I asked, 'who here likes Ross?' and he's wearing two name tags. I'll be honest with you guys. When I first met Ross, I didn't like him at all. And then once I got to know him, I saw that he's really sweet and caring and very generous. I mean, all I'm saying is don't judge Ross before you get to know him.

Alright, I mean, you know, I like all you guys now, but when I first met you… Kurt… I thought, you know, 'abrasive drunk.' Lola… 'mind-numbingly stupid.' And, okay, you guys… 'gold digger, cradle robbing perv.' So, I think you all know what I mean.

Cut to moments later, Phoebe and Ross eating chips alone in his apartment.

PHOEBE: Obviously, I didn't think they were going to start throwing things. I just thought if I kept insulting them, you would jump in and defend everyone and then you could look like the hero.

ROSS: Oh, wow, yeah... See, I did not get that.

Ultimately Phoebe had the same intention to help Ross as she did with Rachel. Her skewed logic worked in one instance and failed in another. But we can see the throughline in her thought process, which remained consistent throughout all 10 seasons of *Friends*. No small feat on behalf of the writers and the incomparable Lisa Kudrow.

The Eccentric in a Work-Based Series: *Mozart in the Jungle*

Sometimes shows built around a work environment explore the mundane. Every once in a while, we get treated to something a bit more exotic. Amazon's *Mozart in the Jungle* definitely falls into the latter category. Refreshing and worldly, the series won a Golden Globe for Best Television Series, Musical, or Comedy and its star, Gael García Bernal took home an individual trophy for Best Actor in a Television Series, Musical, or Comedy in its very first season.

Set against the backdrop of the fictitious New York Symphony, *Mozart in the Jungle* picks up with the orchestra's renowned resident maestro retiring, as a brash and unconventional conductor takes his place. Rodrigo (García Bernal) is one of very few Eccentrics to lead a comedy series. Although *Mozart* features a strong ensemble cast, the avant-garde new maestro is unequivocally the driving force of the show. Rodrigo is Mozart in the Jungle. And he is recognized as a genius.

Rodrigo is globally known by only his first name and is a child prodigy. His introduction in front of a live audience foreshadows the change he's destined to bring to the New York Symphony. Chairperson of the Board, Gloria Windsor (Bernadette Peters), welcomes Rodrigo to his new position as the previous maestro Thomas Pembridge (Malcolm McDowell) steps down.

GLORIA: And so, as one movement ends, another must begin. It is my honor to introduce you to someone special. At twelve years old he was the youngest person to ever win the Mahler Award for Young Conductors. At twenty-three, he conducted at La Scala. At twenty-five, he lifted the Oslo Symphony out of bankruptcy and placed them amongst the finest on the world stage. He has been courted by Boston, Los Angeles, San Francisco, Munich, and we got him! Please, join me in welcoming a man who only need be introduced by his first name, your new conductor and musical director... Rodrigo!

Rodrigo's eccentric nature surfaces immediately as he takes his coworkers, (in this case, world-class musicians) on an incredible adventure via his extraordinary imagination. In his first rehearsal with the New York Symphony, he introduces the orchestra members to his pet parrot, Igor, named after Igor Stravinsky. Rodrigo is elated when Igor poops on his shoe, which he thinks is a blessing and sign of good luck. As a result of a vibrant imagination, he is highly superstitious.

Rodrigo has the orchestra rehearse a silent symphony by pretending to play a piece without their instruments and later takes them on a field trip to rehearse in an abandoned lot so they can touch the earth in order to get back to basics, where he believes true beauty lies.

He has full-length conversations with dead composers like Beethoven and Mozart, whom he idolizes. He is married to an emotionally unstable violinist/performance artist, who travels the world pursuing her own career and sporadically appears in his life to torture him for becoming a sellout. Their marriage is highly unconventional, but his commitment to her is rock solid.

In life and in the show, it's rare to have an Eccentric as a boss. Although conducting an orchestra is obviously artistic and creative, it also makes the person in that position a de facto leader. The character of Rodrigo is based on Gustavo Dudamel, the real-life Music and Artistic Director of the Los Angeles Philharmonic.

The musicians he leads, the board of directors of the New York Symphony, and his personal assistant Hailey (who later becomes his lover), all have to deal with his complex way of navigating life. All the way down to the ordinary task of making his daily cup of yerba mate. Off to do research at the library, Rodrigo leaves audio instructions for Hailey on a cassette tape played on an old boom box. She sits at his desk with a nearby boilerplate, a kettle, a satchel of yerba mate, a gourd, and a metal straw. She hits 'play.'

RODRIGO: Fill it a little bit less than three quarters. More, more, more… more. It's always a bit messy so don't worry about it. The important thing is to shake it. So, now put your hand on top of the gourd. Now turn it over. Yeah? And shake. Shake, shake, shake it very hard! Shake! More. Shake! Okay, now turn it over, back. The water has to be below boiling, so 85 degrees Celsius or less. Now pour the water where the level is low, where the leaves are like a little hill. The yerba has to absorb it. Allow it. And put in the bombilla, the straw. Uh-huh. Okay. And now we wait. But don't turn off the tape. You stay there. And I will be right here. I'll tell you when it feels right. (BEAT) Hailey, why the oboe?

HAILEY: Well, uh, well... my dad suggested it because my grandfather played –

RODRIGO: (Laughs) Ah man, it's funny, you know. I'm sorry. It's a joke. It's funny because I'm not here, you know? Forgive me. Eagle! There's an eagle outside! Where's your snake? ¿Dónde está tu serpiente? Aaah! Aah! Aah! It's fascinating... an eagle in the city, you know? I can relate. Okay, Hailey, now it should be ready. Slurp in the first sip, then spit it right out. Spit it, spit it. Don't drink it! Don't drink it because it's too bitter. Wait a few seconds. Okay. Good. Now drink it. Okay... That is how mate should taste!

And *that* is a great example of what it is like to have a boss who is also the embodiment of the Eccentric.

Characteristics of the Eccentric

- Accepting
- Alert
- Autonomous
- Awestruck
- Capricious
- Creative
- Curious
- Direct
- Effervescent
- Empowered
- Engaged
- Fierce
- Focused
- Forceful
- Free
- Friendly
- Hearty
- Hyperconnected
- Idiosyncratic
- Imaginative
- Independent
- Intense
- Intuitive
- Memorable
- Nonconformist
- Open-Minded
- Opinionated
- Outlandish
- Outspoken
- Rare
- Refreshing
- Robust
- Self-Loving
- Shameless
- Shatterproof
- Skewed Logic
- Unconventional
- Uninhibited
- Visionary
- Whimsical

Eccentrics Throughout the History of Television

The Addams Family	Morticia, Gomez, et al.	**The Addams Family**
Aunt Clara	Marion Lorne	**Bewitched**
Zoey Barkow	Merritt Wever	**Nurse Jackie**
Christine Baskets	Louie Anderson	**Baskets**
Balki Bartokomous	Bronson Pinchot	**Perfect Strangers**
Beverly Januszewski	Beth Grant	**The Mindy Project**
Phoebe Buffay	Lisa Kudrow	**Friends**
D.J. Conner	Michael Fishman	**Roseanne**
Jessica Day	Zooey Deschanel	**New Girl**
Rodrigo De Souza	Gael García Bernal	**Mozart in the Jungle**
Donald "Jared" Dunn	Zach Woods	**Silicon Valley**
Darius Epps	Lakeith Stanfield	**Atlanta**
Fez	Wilmer Valderrama	**That '70s Show**
Joyce Flynn	Swoosie Kurtz	**Mike & Molly**
Holly Franklin	Kristen Johnston	**The Exes**
Latka Gravas	Andy Kaufman	**Taxi**
NoHo Hank	Anthony Carrigan	**Barry**
Brick Heck	Atticus Shaffer	**The Middle**
Keaton Hobart	Bob Balaban	**The Politician**

Reverend Jim Ignatowski	Christopher Lloyd	Taxi
Sheila Jackson	Joan Cusack	Shameless
Jimmy James	Stephen Root	NewsRadio
Synclaire James-Jones	Kim Coles	Living Single
Janet	D'Arcy Carden	The Good Place
Jeannie	Barbara Eden	I Dream of Jeannie
Lindsay Jillian	Kether Donohue	You're the Worst
Laurie Keller	Busy Phillips	Cougar Town
Cpl. Maxwell Q. Klinger	Jamie Farr	M*A*S*H
Cosmo Kramer	Michael Richards	Seinfeld
Gina Linetti	Chelsea Peretti	Brooklyn Nine-Nine
Maw Maw	Cloris Leachman	Raising Hope
Kenny McCormick	Matt Stone	South Park
Jack McFarland	Sean Hayes	Will & Grace
Dharma Montgomery	Jenna Elfman	Dharma & Greg
Daphne Moon	Jane Leeves	Frasier
Mork	Robin Williams	Mork & Mindy
Kenneth Parcell	Jack McBrayer	30 Rock
Brittany Pierce	Heather Morris	Glee
Pam Poovey	Amber Nash	Archer

Carol Rance	Kathleen Rose Perkins	Episodes
Frank Reynolds	Danny DeVito	It's Always Sunny in Philadelphia
Moira Rose	Catherine O'Hara	Schitt's Creek
Shoshanna Shapiro	Zosia Mamet	Girls
Harry Solomon	French Stewart	3rd Rock from the Sun
Sean Tolkey	John Benjamin Hickey	The Big C
Chris Traeger	Rob Lowe	Parks and Recreation
George Utley	Tom Poston	Newhart
Dewey Wilkerson	Erik Per Sullivan	Malcolm in the Middle

How Eccentrics are Described in the Breakdowns

A little off, a little strange and overzealous, absent-minded, adork-able, bohemian, colorful, dumb or just foreign, enlightened artist, ethereal, expert hacker, has theories that are brilliant but logically flawed, flighty, flower child, hippie, kooky, left of center, marches to the beat of a different drum, new age type, offbeat, people tend to misread them, quirky, space cadet, spacey, spirited, unconventionally attractive, vivid imagination, whacked out, zany

Lead Body Part: Solar Plexus

The solar plexus is a network of sympathetic nerves situated behind the stomach that supply the abdominal organs. It plays an important role in the functioning of the stomach, kidneys, liver, and adrenal glands. The solar plexus is also known spiritually as the third chakra, or the Manipura chakra in Sanskrit. 'Mani' stands for pearl or jewel and 'pura' stands for city. Thus, the Manipura chakra is responsible for 'pearls of wisdom,' well-being, clarity, and common sense in every individual. Experts call the third chakra the 'self-power chakra' — one's self-confidence, self-discipline, and the ability to achieve goals all come from it. Eccentrics are grounded like the anchor, but they draw their life force from interdimensional connectivity, as opposed to Mother Earth. Self-sufficient, curious, and imaginative, they lead with a place in the body that is both physical and ethereal.

INNOCENT

"It is a love based on giving and receiving as well as having and sharing. And the love that they give and have is shared and received. And through this having and giving and sharing and receiving, we too can share and love and have and receive."

Joey Tribbiani/Friends

Mantra: "I love"
Strength: Authentic
Weakness: Gullible
Typical jobs: Blue Collar, Service-Oriented, No Education Required. We don't often see them at work, unless the series is a workplace comedy. When we do see them at work, they're sheltered by their tribe.

Who Are They?

If The Heroes of Comedy were a family, the Innocent would be the baby of that family. Sweet, generous, and loving, the only reason not to like an Innocent is to dislike those qualities, which paradoxically, some do.

Think of a Buffoon calling an Innocent a "goody two-shoes" for committing an act of kindness. I've always found it odd, but some people are resentful and scornful of the goodness in others. We project what we know unto the world around us. If we position ourselves as victims and never find forthright integrity and unconditional love in our own hearts, it's very hard to imagine those qualities existing full time in others. But they most certainly do!

The characteristics of the Innocent are largely positive, which is a sharp contrast to most of the other Heroes. Some have mostly negative qualities and others have a balanced mix. The Innocent, however, comprises a purity of thought and lack of agenda that are completely foreign to the DNA of the other archetypes.

It's true that the Innocent is naïve and gullible, which aren't inherently positive traits, but I do categorize them as conditional by-products of a trusting nature. In other words, the Innocent is unsuspecting and sincere; they will take anybody at their word. If others around them are honest, which people ideally are, there is no problem. It's only when a predator catches wind of the openhearted Innocent and takes advantage of their kind nature that conflict arises. Otherwise, the Innocent is childlike in their disposition (as opposed to the Buffoon's *childish* nature).

The Golden Girls' Rose Nylund, portrayed by peerless Betty White, is a perfect example. Friendly, loving, honest, and utterly sincere, Rose exudes joy and overflows with generosity. However, she views the world through the eyes of a child in many ways, which frequently leaves her the recipient of Dorothy's (Bea Arthur) scathing sarcasm, in particular.

In one instance, Dorothy, Rose, and Blanche (Rue McClanahan) are caught up in a prostitution sting and mistakenly arrested for being, as Dorothy says, "hookers." While unhappy, Dorothy and Blanche manage to keep their cool. Rose, on the other hand, becomes terrified at the thought of life in the criminal justice system. She spirals out of control in a notably juvenile fashion.

ROSE: I've never been in jail. I won't make it. They always prey on the weak and innocent. The others will taunt me for trying to excel at my work in the laundry. I'll fall in with a bad crowd whose leader looks like Ethel Merman. And I'll be forced to engineer a daring prison break using my laundry cart! From that time on, I won't know a moment's peace. I'll scar my fingerprints with battery acid, and I'll run from town to town, taking jobs that people have who get bad grades in school! And then one day they'll find me, holed up in a little shack in the Louisiana bayou. And a sheriff named Bull will call my name out over a megaphone, and when I make a run for it, he'll riddle my body with bullets! Oh, *please* don't let them take me downtown. I wanna live! *I wanna live!*

DOROTHY: You're not very good in a crisis, are you, Rose?

Rose's rant is funny, but it also exposes that she knows exactly who she is within any given group. She actually refers to herself as innocent and apparently only comprehends prison life from what she's seen in television and film, just like a kid. The cherry on the credulous sundae is Dorothy's reliably sassy rebuttal.

Innocents are unique within The Heroes of Comedy in that they are the only archetype that doesn't use sarcasm to produce humor. There is a layered reason for this. Sarcasm is a jab; Innocents don't like to throw punches. Sarcasm can also be an obvious untruth. For example, Dorothy and Blanche come home with a takeout pizza box in hand. Rose is already home, seated at their famous kitchen table.

DOROTHY: Hi, Rose.

BLANCHE: We brought dinner.

ROSE: What'd ya' get?

A bucket of chicken. I hope you like it extra flat and crispy.

Innocents don't lie; they're known for being terrible at it. It goes against their nature and makes them uncomfortable. Even though the discernable falsehood that the pizza box is a bucket of chicken is also a joke that the character is making, it's an untruth nonetheless. Sarcasm is insincere speech. The Innocent rarely produces humor in that way. There is an understated elegance in simply never speaking an untruth.

All the other Heroes but the Innocent might make that flat bucket of chicken joke. Sarcasm is a pillar of American (English language) comedy. The Innocent generally doesn't have the biting wit or inclination to make a moment-to-moment snarky remark. They don't critique and they have no agenda.

Holding the pizza box in front of her and staring Rose down at the end of her nose, it's very much Dorothy's intention to mock Rose for her stupid question. In two sentences, we see Dorothy jab, fib, and judge. Rose rarely goes to that place and if she does, it's only when she's been pushed too far.

Woody Boyd (Woody Harrelson) from *Cheers* provides a similar example of the uncomplicated nature of the Innocent. Without any ulterior motives, the pure Innocent always speaks their truth in an enviably simple way. Here's an exchange between Woody and his boss, Sam (Ted Danson).

SAM: Hey everybody.

WOODY: Oh, Sam. You're just the guy I've been looking for.

SAM: Why is that, Woody?

WOODY: Because you weren't here.

Of course, our Innocents can come across as unintelligent, but they say there's more than one way to skin a cat. Rather, there is more than one way to gauge intelligence.

In his book, *Frames of Mind: The Theory of Multiple Intelligences*, Howard Gardner proposes there are nine types of intelligence. I highly recommend this book to actors and writers, as it blends psychological and educational insights together to create a unique lens through which to view intelligence and how it is determined.

As a brief aside, I've come to believe the best books for actors to read in regard to creating more interesting and marketable characterizations are psychology and self-help books. The more you understand what motivates humans to do what we do and how we function in groups, the more you have to offer on your end of the collaboration with writers.

Briefly, Gardner proposes the following categories to rank intelligence:

- **Naturalist** (nature smart; understanding living things and reading nature)

- **Musical** (sound smart; discerning sounds, their pitch, tone, rhythm, and timbre)

- **Logical-mathematical** (analytically smart; quantifying things, making hypotheses and being able to prove them)

- **Existential** (spiritually smart; examining the questions of why we live and why we die)

- **Interpersonal** (people smart; sensing other people's feelings and motives)

- **Bodily-kinesthetic** (body smart; coordinating your body with your mind, hand-motor skills)

- **Linguistic** (word smart; finding the right words to express what you mean)

- **Intrapersonal** (self-smart; understanding yourself, what you feel and what you want)

- **Spatial** (picture smart; thinking in 3D, graphic design, and mental imagery)

As an educator, it's important for me to discover ways to connect with people via the different avenues in which we are intelligent. I think it's neglectful to measure our cognitive capacity in only one way; like a totem pole on which you're either at the bottom or the top. IQ tests are utter nonsense and personality tests like the Myers-Briggs Personality Assessment are mostly unproven bunk.

If you want to know how smart you are and what you're like in practical terms, ask yourself and the people who know you best. If they love you, they'll tell you unfiltered. Boom. That's who you are.

As an actor and a writer, it's equally important that I always find the way in which the characters I personally create are brilliant. We all have something to offer and there are areas in which we all excel. We need the diversity of our collective genius within society to achieve our greatest good. More simply stated, all the characters you ever craft or portray are smart in their own unique fashion.

It's easy to think of the Innocent as dumb, but that's a degrading term, packed with a load of negative judgment. Using Gardner's methodology of discerning the various ways we exhibit inherent intelligence, I'd say the Innocent rates very highly in the categories of Naturalist, Existential, Interpersonal, and

Intrapersonal all the time, with the possibility of Musical and Bodily-kinesthetic. That's potentially six out of nine ways to be smart about life. I think that's pretty darn smart.

I included this extended analysis of what it means to be intelligent here in the Innocent's section, which comes after the Buffoon and the Eccentric. These three archetypes can be tricky if you don't have an existing kinship with them in real life. A lot of misconceptions can spring up that might lead you to the judgment that these characters are stupid because of the way they process information. They might even be labeled dumb in actor breakdowns or other character development books. Always ignore words a bully would use to describe someone. Unless, of course, you want to create an unlikable character.

If you relate to being an intelligent person with a linear thought process, you might fail to personalize the characteristics and emotional truths of these archetypes because of your unfamiliarity with them. In other words, even if you're a great actor, your version of these archetypes can collapse like a house of cards and play out like a bad sketch if you interpret them as dull, dumb, or stupid. Even the most simple-minded characters think they are clever, if not smart, in their own way.

What Is Their Strength?

The Innocent's strength, in a word, is love. I'd also include enthusiasm, but the Innocent has an encompassing unconditional love they offer to everyone they meet and every situation they encounter. In a complicated world full of anxiety, worries, and doubts, the Innocent is always able to see the bright side of just about anything.

Sue Heck (Eden Sher) of *The Middle* is a terrific example of a never-say-die Innocent. Even though Sue is always the last one picked for a team, deliberately excluded from social activities, and just plain forgotten by most people outside of her immediately family, she's a happy person.

Full of enthusiasm and ready to overcome obstacles, Sue sees only the best in everyone and a bright and hopeful future for herself. Even when she can't figure out *why* things will turn out well for her, she has an innate sense that they ultimately *will* turn out well for her. Her steadfast positivity goes beyond faith. As with all Innocents, Sue possesses an inner foundation of love and acceptance that cannot be studied or learned.

When she has to research a hypothesis for a high school science paper, she tackles the question, "Is smiling contagious?" She expects the answer to be yes, but her day-to-day observations prove otherwise. Undeterred, she turns in the following conclusion, (which Sue narrates) as she sits in class, waiting apprehensively as her instructor reads.

Sue: Is smiling contagious? After many attempts with multiple subjects, including family, friends, a Red Lobster waitress, and an unfriendly baby, I, unfortunately, was unable to prove my hypothesis. However, like many scientists before me, I refuse to admit defeat. It took Einstein 10 years to prove $E=mc^2$ and if it takes me that long to prove smiling is contagious, then I am up for the challenge.

For I believe there are some things that defy logic. French anatomist Duchenne wrote that, "Joy is expressed by the face by contraction of the muscles, but it can only be put in play by the sweet emotions of the soul." And Duchenne had a whole smile named after him! Think of the smiles over the years that have inspired a whole world to happiness: Mona Lisa's, Justin Bieber's...

Some might laugh at me, I know, just as they laughed at John Gurdon. He was told in high school that he would *never* be a scientist. *He* just won the Nobel Prize. I guess it just proves that being dismissed by people who think they know better, is not an obstacle to winning a Nobel Prize. So I will continue with my research - one smile at a time - until I prove that smiling is *contagious, because I don't want to live in a world where it isn't.*

Her science teacher finishes the paper and reflexively smiles. I doubt I could find a better example of love as a reaction to disappointment than this teenage girl's simple theory that one smile could cause everyone else in the world to do the same.

What Is Their Weakness?

The more innocent you are, the more gullible you're likely to be. Of all The Heroes of Comedy, the Innocent is by far the most likely to get taken, cheated, swindled by a snake oil salesman, or sucked in by a strong advertising hook. Their trusting nature is a wonderful thing to behold, but they often are too willing to extend trust to those who haven't earned it.

On *Cheers*, Woody develops a compulsive shopping problem simply because an 800-number flashed across his TV screen. He confesses his new addiction to his boss Rebecca Howe (Kirstie Alley) after she tries to delicately explain to him that his gifts are inappropriate and cheap.

REBECCA: Woody, I cannot accept these. People are going to get the wrong idea.

WOODY: What, that I have a crush on you?

REBECCA: No, that I like crap.

WOODY: You calling this stuff crap?

REBECCA: I'm sorry, Woody.

WOODY: No, no, I was looking for the right word.

REBECCA:	If you don't like it either, why do you keep buying this stuff?
WOODY:	Not stuff, Miss Howe — crap. I buy it because it looks good on TV. And the second they flash that 800-number, I'm dialing.
REBECCA:	Woody, this has got to stop.
WOODY:	Well, it has stopped, Miss Howe. I went over my credit limit with this crap, unless, of course, you care to advance me six months on my paycheck — could be another necklace in it for you! And if you decide not to give me the advance, just keep the necklace as your free gift.
REBECCA:	Woody, you are hooked. Listen to me. You need help.
WOODY:	I don't need help! I just need more credit!

Rebecca stares at Woody, stunned.

| WOODY: | You're right, Miss Howe. I do need help. I'm scared. Help me. Hurry. Act now! |

It's as if poor Woody absorbed every single marketing strategy employed by The Home Shopping Channel with no defense against their tactics whatsoever.

Here's an example from *Sex and the City*'s Charlotte York (Kristin Davis) that effectively utilizes the show's resident Innocent the same way, "I read that if you don't have sex for a year, you can be revirginized."

Their willingness to believe everything they see, hear, and read unfortunately leaves the otherwise *emotionally* intelligent Innocent looking like a witless dunce. Rose Nylund (Betty White) reminisces: "We weren't allowed to wear berets at my school, it was against the St. Olaf dress code. They did let me wear a paper cap, though. It was long and pointy." She makes my point.

How Do Others See Them?

The rest of the crew readily acknowledges the positive attributes of the Innocent, it's just that they're usually not super excited about being around a thousand watts of positive energy all the time. Innocents seem to always have a lot more time on their hands than the other Heroes of Comedy.

It's not that they lack ambition necessarily, but they don't put the same pressure on achieving their goals as the other archetypes might.

Innocents are fairly immune to stress and anxiety unless there is a specific problem right in front of them. They don't self-generate worry because they are so darned trusting and their thought process is simple. Remember, their job is to offer love wherever and whenever possible. That's the Innocent's number one priority. Therefore, it's their sheer positivity that often irritates the other Heroes because they don't appear to comprehend the gravity of any given crisis.

In trying to cheer up a friend or see the bright side of a plan gone awry, the Innocent very often ends up a thorn in somebody else's side. The flip side is that the rest of their tribe protects the Innocent. They are generally viewed by the rest of their group as someone who needs taking care of. Whether we see them mostly at home or at work, Innocents don't tend to have a lot of responsibility.

How Do Writers Use Them?

We already know how sweet, kind, earnest, and gullible Innocents are from the outside. Let's think about why the writer has them in the group and how they use them. Innocents speak directly, with a pure voice just like a child. They can get away with saying things that other archetypes couldn't. At least not without repercussions or starting a fight. Here is another example from *The Golden Girls*:

> BLANCHE: What was your first impression of me?
>
> ROSE: That you wore too much makeup and were a slut. But I was wrong. You don't wear too much makeup.

If Rose was being mean or trying to humiliate Blanche, this comment would cause a lot of trouble. But since Blanche asked and it was Rose's entirely sincere answer, with no intention other than to tell the truth, the conversation stopped there.

With all the other Heroes being agenda-driven and either manipulative and/or set in their ways, it's important to have a character that is pliable, open, and relaxed by nature. The Innocent is a great universal counterpoint to all the other archetypes because of their simple, uncomplicated perspective on life.

Sometimes Innocents are actual kids, like Luke Dunphy (Nolan Gould) on *Modern Family*, Joey Russo (Joey Lawrence) on *Blossom*, or Cindy Brady (Susan Olsen) on *The Brady Bunch*. Most of the time, however, they're children in adult bodies. Jason Mendoza (Manny Jacinto) of *The Good Place* is a terrific example, "I hate suits. They remind me of court. And going to court. And being my own lawyer against the advice of a judge in court. And getting immediately convicted in court..."

Such is the foundation to begin writing for them and enacting them. Imagine a good-natured five-year-old as opposed to an adult who would be savvier regarding the ways of the world. When the writer and actor best realize the Innocent, we'll know because we'll reflexively want to take care of them.

What Is Your Way In?

Playing the Innocent is your opportunity to rediscover the child inside you. Children are unfiltered, excitable, and full of energy. From birth until we enter school, we can get away with those inherent qualities running rampant. We can virtually say whatever we want. Yes, there will be a response to the stimulus we are generating, feedback, and necessary parenting, etc. But no one is ever really *shocked* by what comes out of the mouths of babes.

In order to play the Innocent well, you must connect with the child inside of you; the child who hasn't yet been told to sit down and shut up. The child who ran when they wanted to run and grabbed something dangerous they shouldn't have.

Rediscover the kid in you who has yet to be confronted with a test.

They say, "kids say the darnedest things." What they mean is, kids speak their truth unfiltered and, relative to adults, their thoughts are uncomplicated. Reach inside and find that place again to play your Innocent. To play the Innocent well, you don't dim your brain, you open your heart all the way.

The Innocent in a Family-Based Series: *All in the Family*

All in the Family, created by Norman Lear, is universally considered to be one of the best television shows of all time. The progressive series debuted in 1971, and the storylines reflect the civil rights themes of the era. As head of the household, Archie Bunker is a blue-collar, middle-class, average American Cynic who values the status quo and is played brilliantly by Carroll O'Connor. Archie is also a bigot and racist, although he certainly doesn't see himself that way.

One of Norman Lear's many genius decisions in creating this show and others was to write Archie's wife, Edith (Jean Stapleton), as an Innocent. Caustic, grumpy, and always spoiling for a fight, Archie needs some counter ballast, which Edith gleefully, giddily provides. Without question, Edith Bunker is one of the best examples of an Innocent television has ever produced. Joyful, friendly, enthusiastic, loving, and perpetually naïve, it would take someone as pure and sweet as Edith to marry and put up with a grouch like Archie.

Edith is also a mother and a friend who is so excited to accommodate and feed everyone who enters her home that she literally *runs* about the house to answer the door, fetch refreshments from the kitchen, or grab Archie yet another beer.

She personifies the word "ditzy," yet she has profound wisdom in regard to understanding people and why they do the things they do. Edith also offers often-unlovable Archie, in particular, unconditional love, even in his worst moments. For example, in this scene, Archie wakes up slumbering Edith because he's anxious and cannot sleep.

EDITH: Oh my, it's 5:30.

ARCHIE: Yeah, I know that.

EDITH: Only, you ain't sleepin'.

ARCHIE: I know that.

EDITH: You're pacin' the floor.

ARCHIE: I know that, Edith. Geesh, tell me somethin' I don't know.

EDITH: Well... there's only 63 more shoppin' days 'til Christmas. Archie! What's the matter with you?

ARCHIE: Nothin'.

EDITH: Aw, c'mon. Sit down. Somethin' must've happened to you last night.

ARCHIE: Nothin', nothin'. What are you being so nosey for?

EDITH: Oh, I ain't bein' nosey. I'm just talkin' to ya'. The secret of a good marriage is for a husband and wife to communicate.

ARCHIE: Where'd you get that?

EDITH: The Reader's Digest.

ARCHIE: Well, let The Reader's Digest condense this (he blows a raspberry).

EDITH: Archie... let me tell you something very important.

ARCHIE: What?

EDITH: I'm your wife.

ARCHIE: Who else knows this?

EDITH: Oh, everybody. And because I am your wife, if something's bothering you, I ought to know about it.

ARCHIE: Well, I tell ya' Edith, last night I done maybe the dumbest thing in my whole life.

EDITH: Are you sure? You've lived a long time.

ARCHIE: Edith... Remember last night, I told ya' I might go bowling?

EDITH: You... you, you went bowling without your ball!

ARCHIE: No! I didn't go bowling at all.

EDITH: Well, that wasn't so dumb. You didn't need your ball.

ARCHIE: Help me, Lord! Edith, I'll tell ya' what I've done. I went to a meetin'.

EDITH: Oh. Who was meetin'?

ARCHIE: Well, I ain't supposed to tell ya.

EDITH: Oh, well... give me a hint.

ARCHIE: It's a secret!

EDITH: It's a secret... Give me another hint.

ARCHIE: Where are you, Lord? Over here?

EDITH: He's everywhere, Archie.

ARCHIE: I know that, Edith. I can't tell ya, but it probably wouldn't do no harm if you guessed.

EDITH: Yeah, yeah.

ARCHIE: Yeah, well uh, see... all of the men at the meetin' were wearing sheets.

EDITH: Was they playin' trick or treat?

ARCHIE: Was last night Halloween?!

EDITH:	Oh, no... Well, then why was they wearin' sheets?
ARCHIE:	Because sheets go so good with the hoods they was wearin'... Huh? Huh?
EDITH:	Oh! I got it! The Ku Klux Klan! Ahhhhhhhh! (THEN) Ohhhhhhhh... Oh, Archie! The Ku Klux Klan!
ARCHIE:	Alright, alright, shhh... don't come apart, huh? They don't' call themselves the Ku Klux Klan. They call themselves the Queens Council of Crusaders.
EDITH:	Well, what was you doin' there?
ARCHIE:	I was sittin' there listening to a couple of the high mokey-mokes make long speeches there, you know... Down with the Jews, down with the blacks, down with the Pope, down with the UN. And they let me be a member.
EDITH:	Well, you ain't gonna, are you?
ARCHIE:	No, I ain't, but they think I am and I don't know why!
EDITH:	Maybe you said somethin'.
ARCHIE:	I didn't say nothin'! I kept my mouth shut!
EDITH:	Well, maybe it's somethin' about the way you kept your mouth shut.
ARCHIE:	Edith, don't give me your riddles and guessing games and all of that. I don't know what the hell to do. Jeez, I need-- I need help. What am I gonna do, huh? Say somethin' smart!

EDITH:	Well, just don't go there no more, Archie. They'll forget ya.
ARCHIE:	Yeah, I don't think so.
EDITH:	Oh, sure they will. You're easy to forget.

The scene continues with Archie growing more concerned about the family's safety, and the two-part episode concludes with Archie standing up to his neighborhood bigots. I present this example of Edith as an Innocent who offers unconditional love and support, but the scene also exemplifies the complexity, excellence, and continuing relevance of *All in the Family*.

When people make negative generalizations about situation comedies, I think, "Hmm, that's odd. I think they can and often do reflect the current state of our society as well as any medium. Have we watched the same sitcoms?"

Aside from issues of racism and sexism, *All in the Family* also deals humanely with Edith's transition into menopause and traumatizing attack by a sexual predator. Additionally, Edith befriends her African American neighbors, the Jeffersons, a female impersonator named Beverly LaSalle, and in the episode "Cousin Liz," the Bunkers learn that Edith's recently deceased cousin Liz was a lesbian with a life partner, Veronica.

At first, Edith is shocked at the revelation, but quickly throws her arms around Veronica and warmly accepts her as Liz's "true next-of-kin."

With a generous heart and all-encompassing love, Edith gives Veronica a family tea set Liz's spouse would have inherited. The themes explored by Norman Lear and the writers of *All in the Family* were at the time controversial and shocking. Edith's innocence played an essential part in making the hard-edged episodes not only digestible, but timelessly relevant.

The Innocent in a Friend-Based Series: *Friends*

How *you* doin'? Not everyone can pull off a pickup line that doubles as a catchphrase. Joey Tribbiani (Matt LeBlanc) is an exception. He delivered that line frequently and with aplomb. Sometimes students mistake Joey for a Player because of his recurring tagline but make no mistake; Joey is one of television's iconic Innocents.

The cast of *Friends* consists of six series regular roles, but Joey and Chandler (Matthew Perry) are paired together as room-mates and best buds. A Dreamer, Chandler leans heavily into the self-deprecating, unsettled, and needy qualities of his archetype. Again, we see the Innocent used to provide balance, in this case, for his dark cloud of a roommate. Together, Joey and Chandler parent a baby chick and a duck. They quarrel like a married couple, not entirely dissimilar from Edith and Archie Bunker.

Like all Innocents, Joey is gullible, and his ability to believe anything he's told is boundless. When he refers Chandler to his tailor to have a pair of pants altered, Chandler returns disgruntled and acrimonious. Joey learns a valuable life lesson.

CHANDLER: Yo! Paisan! Can I talk to you for a sec? Your tailor... is a *very* bad man!

JOEY: Frankie? What are you talking about?

Ross enters and pats Chandler on the shoulder. Chandler flinches as if traumatized.

ROSS: Hey. What's going on?

CHANDLER: Joey's tailor... took advantage of me.

ROSS: What?

JOEY: No way, I've been going to the guy for 12 years.

CHANDLER: Oh come on, he said he was going to do my inseam, then he ran his hand up my leg and then there was definite...

ROSS: What?

CHANDLER: Cupping.

JOEY: That's how they do pants! First they go up one side, they move it over, then they go up the other side, they move it back, and then they do the rear.

Chandler and Ross stare at Joey in disbelief.

JOEY: What? Ross, will you tell him? Isn't that how a tailor measures pants?

ROSS: Yes, yes, it is... *in prison*! What's the matter with you?!

JOEY: What? That's not... *Oh my God!*

In addition to believing everything they're told, Innocents quite frequently misunderstand what they're told. This also happens frequently with Joey. When Rachel seeks advice about dating her assistant at work, Joey steps up.

JOEY: Alright, Rach, the big question is... does he like you? Right? Because if he doesn't like you, this is all a moo point.

RACHEL: Huh. A *moo* point?

JOEY: Yeah. It's like a cow's opinion... it just, doesn't matter... it's moo.

Joey has the body of a man and the mind of a child. He likes to eat — *a lot*. He once ate the entire contents of his refrigerator in one sitting because it broke, and he didn't want any of his food to go to waste. When Phoebe (Lisa Kudrow) sets him up on a date with one of her girlfriends, she helps herself to some of Joey's french fries at dinner, prompting him to explain to Phoebe, "JOEY DOESN'T SHARE FOOD!" He has few rules and they're pretty basic.

It's noteworthy that out of such a talented cast of beloved characters, it was Matt LeBlanc who was given a spinoff with the series Joey. It didn't last long, just two seasons. I think Matt LeBlanc is a terrific actor and Joey Tribbiani is one of the most likeable characters ever on television. However, I was sure the series *Joey* wouldn't work, while a spinoff for any of the other characters could have.

When the news of *Joey* landed, my writer brain instantly recognized the difficulty of building a series around the Innocent as the solo lead character. There is no successful precedent for it. All the elements of the pilot of *Joey* played against its success. For starters, the Innocent was pulled from an ensemble to be the headliner. Hmmm.

Storytelling is about conflict, and the Innocent represents the voice and feeling of a child. Who wants to see a child handle grown-up problems? Secondly, after *Friends* concluded, the character of Joey... had no problems. The premise of the follow-up series is that Joey moves to Los Angeles *with* an acting job. He's a young, healthy, employed actor living in Hollywood. Where's the conflict?

Since he didn't have any, they assigned it to his sister, Gina (Drea de Matteo), and her son, Michael (Paulo Costanzo), effectively putting Joey in the position of problem solver and caretaker. That's exactly the wrong position in which to place the Innocent. In effect, Joey became an Anchor. The revision of Joey's archetype became the spinoff's fatal flaw. Because of LeBlanc's personal star power and placement in the *Friends'* old time slot, *Joey* initially garnered huge ratings. However, the numbers declined quite rapidly causing NBC to cancel *Joey* before airing all the filmed episodes.

I thought this example might be particularly interesting for writers. Nothing is impossible, but creating a series with an Innocent in the starring role comes with a high degree of difficulty. There is a lack of precedent for good reason.

The Innocent in a Work-Based Series: *Parks and Recreation*

Innocents simply do not have a lot of responsibility in their lives, but especially in the workplace. Andy Dwyer (Chris Pratt) of *Parks and Recreation* is an excellent example. At the beginning of the series, Andy is in a rock band that is going nowhere fast. After meeting Leslie Knope (Amy Poehler), she gives him a job as the shoeshiner at the Pawnee City Hall.

As the series progresses, Andy joins Leslie's campaign for city council as her assistant and head of security. His biggest contribution is composing the campaign's theme song, "Catch Your Dream," which includes the refrain:

'Cuz it's not enough to simply catch that dream

You gotta grab that dream and catch your dream's dream!

At the end of the fourth season of *Parks and Recreation*, April and Andy attempt to figure out what they want to do with their lives. Earnest and determined, Andy tries to think of a fulfilling career. April realizes that his list of dream jobs all have to do with law enforcement and encourages him to try to become a police officer. While acing the physical test, Andy bombs out on the personality interview:

OFFICER: So, this test will determine whether you have the right personality profile to be a police officer. Just to make sure the machine is working... is your name Andy?

ANDY: ...I don't know how to a- answer that.

OFFICER: A simple 'yes' or 'no'.

ANDY: Well, everyone calls me Andy, but my full name is Andrew, I think. So... no? Wait! Yes!

OFFICER: Let's move on. Scenario - A high school-age child asks to hold your service revolver. What do you do?

ANDY: Yes. I give it to him. When I was a kid, I always wanted to hold a cop's gun. To make that dream come true for another kid? Well, that's what being a cop's all about.

OFFICER: Scenario - You pull a car over for speeding, you find out it's your father. How do you handle the situation?

ANDY: Well, first I would be like, 'Dad... you're alive? What the hell?! Also, do you know where my catcher's mitt is?'

Andy's dream of becoming a police officer ends there. Toward the end of the series, Ben Wyatt (Adam Scott) generously gives Andy a job working with him at the Sweetums Foundation. Andy travels to England for some time because of his position. When he returns, he launches a hot mess of a children's TV show on public access, *The Johnny Karate Super Awesome Musical Explosion*

Show, where, among other surprise events, Lord Edgar Covington dubs him a Knight of the Order of the British Empire in the final episode.

From shoeshine boy to children's television host, Andy never carries much of a burden in the workplace, and he's helped by literally everyone he knows in order to stay gainfully employed. He works for both Leslie and Ben. Tom Haverford (Aziz Ansari) also offers Andy a job at his disaster enterprise Entertainment 720, but Andy turns down the offer. His wife, April (Aubrey Plaza), produces his TV show, on which all his friends appear, including Ron Swanson (Nick Offerman).

The one position Andy applies for that does come with a great deal of responsibility and would force him to make a go of it on his own, police officer, is denied him.

While it's tough to watch Andy's disappointment when he's rejected, it makes sense that a true Innocent would make a terrible cop. Andy envisions the daily routine of a policeman through the imagination of a boy and naïvely disregards the pressure and difficult decisions the job would entail. In the end, the love and support he steadily offers his friends and coworkers return to him as they all band together to keep him gainfully employed.

Characteristics of the Innocent

- Aboveboard
- Adorable
- Animated
- Candid
- Childlike
- Courteous
- Eager
- Endearing
- Enthusiastic
- Forthright
- Friendly
- Generous
- Gentle
- Good
- Guileless
- Happy
- Harmless
- Honest
- Joyful
- Kindhearted
- Loving
- Naïve
- Natural
- No Agenda
- No Sarcasm
- Positive
- Pure
- Simple
- Sincere
- Sweet
- Sympathetic
- Tenderhearted
- Thoughtful
- Trusting
- Trustworthy
- Unaffected
- Unsophisticated
- Virtuous
- Well-Intentioned
- Wide-Eyed

Innocents Throughout the History of Television

Gracie Allen	Gracie Allen	The Burns and Allen Show
Tony Banta	Tony Danza	Taxi
River Barkley	David Corenswet	The Politician
Nelson "Big Head" Bighetti	Josh Brener	Silicon Valley
Jethro Bodine	Max Baer Jr.	The Beverly Hillbillies
Woody Boyd	Woody Harrelson	Cheers
Edith Bunker	Jean Stapleton	All in the Family
Josh Chan	Vincent Rodriguez III	Crazy Ex-Girlfriend
Bobby Cobb	Brian Van Holt	Cougar Town
Mickey Deane	Robert Michael Morris	The Comeback
Luke Dunphy	Nolan Gould	Modern Family
Andy Dwyer	Chris Pratt	Parks and Recreation
Dauber Dybinski	Bill Fagerbakke	Coach
Monroe Ficus	Jim J. Bullock	Too Close for Comfort
Georgette Franklin	Georgia Engel	The Mary Tyler Moore Show
Natalie Green	Mindy Cohn	The Facts of Life
Vivian Cavender Harmon	Rue McClanahan	Maude
Sue Heck	Eden Sher	The Middle
Randy Hickey	Ethan Suplee	My Name is Earl

Louis Huang	Randall Park	**Fresh Off the Boat**
Infinity Jackson	Zoey Deutch	**The Politician**
Det. Sgt. Terry Jeffords	Terry Crews	**Brooklyn Nine-Nine**
Michael Kelso	Ashton Kutcher	**That '70s Show**
Rajesh "Raj" Koothrappali	Kunal Nayyar	**The Big Bang Theory**
Lowell Mather	Thomas Hayden Church	**Wings**
Jason Mendoza	Manny Jacinto	**The Good Place**
Tony Micelli	Tony Danza	**Who's the Boss?**
Ted Mullins	Dustin Milligan	**Schitt's Creek**
Herman Munster	Fred Gwynne	**The Munsters**
Rose Nylund	Betty White	**The Golden Girls**
Ernie "Coach" Pantusso	Nicholas Colasanto	**Cheers**
Gomer Pyle	Jim Nabors	**The Andy Griffith Show**
Joey Russo	Joey Lawrence	**Blossom**
Chrissy Snow	Suzanne Somers	**Three's Company**
Dr. Dick Solomon	John Lithgow	**3rd Rock from the Sun**
Charlene Frazier Stillfield	Jean Smart	**Designing Women**
Glenn Sturgis	Mark McKinney	**Superstore**
Morgan Tookers	Ike Barinholtz	**The Mindy Project**

Joey Tribbiani	Matt LeBlanc	Friends
Devon Woodcomb	Ryan McPartlin	Chuck
Charlotte York	Kristin Davis	Sex and the City

How Innocents are Described in the Breakdowns

Angelic, bighearted, chaste, clearly naïve, devout, driven by honor, dumb, exudes love, gullible, helpful, himbo, idiot, kid in an adult's body, last one to get the joke, light, man boy, not the sharpest tool in the shed, peaceful, the golden retriever of humans, total sweetheart, trusting, unworldly, wholesome, wide-eyed innocence

Lead Body Part: Heart

We instinctively love and are drawn to love. Too often though, we think of love as a passive feeling. We would have a healthier conception of love if we understood that love, like parenting or friendship, is a feeling that expresses itself in action. When we engage in our heart space, we find more than affection; we avail ourselves to generosity, kindness, and compassion. All these feelings move us toward activity that make life better for others. The Innocent leads with their heart. In doing so, they experience love as a verb. Just being in the presence of someone they care for is an activity for them. Loving, at least with any consequence, requires both participation and expression.

CYNIC

"That's the whole point of a surprise party. You take somebody you really love and you play 'em like a fool."
Jay Pritchett/Modern Family

Mantra: "I doubt"
Strength: Loyal
Weakness: Guarded
Jobs: Butlers, Maids, Secretaries, Receptionists, Assistants, and Servers. No Education Required. We see them at work a lot, often embittered, even if they're successful.

Who Are They?

Any of us can feel despair, pessimism, or beleaguered due to circumstances. For the Cynic, however, those traits and similar others have settled through the cracks and into the foundation. At their core, Cynics are doubtful that things are going to go their way or that their current circumstances will improve. Whatever their station in life, they are resigned to it. They wear their lack of upward mobility like a badge of honor, when really, it's a chip on their shoulder.

Television's original Cynic, Ralph Kramden (Jackie Gleason) of *The Honeymooners*, set the tone for this Hero of Comedy. Ralph is a bus driver for the Gotham Bus Company and a resident of the borough of Brooklyn in New York. Ralph is short-tempered, cutting, world-weary, pessimistic, and defined by his lack of success.

Deep down he has a tender heart, but it's rarely exposed because he tamps down his emotions until they erupt involuntarily and volcanically. Ralph, like most Cynics, is not interested in unnecessarily exposing his vulnerabilities; instead, he masks them with bluster.

The Honeymooners explored Ralph's ongoing investment in get-rich-quick schemes, which always blew up in his face. Those schemes were basically the lottery scratchers of his day and a great example of his jaded view of life. Ralph is always looking for a big payoff with little investment and then griping that a guy can't get a break. He's a man who doesn't see a way out of his meager existence unless he's stricken with good luck, which is another way of saying that he feels doubtful about realistically moving up the socioeconomic ladder.

"You just decided for me, Alice. You just decided for me! I'm going on *The $64,000 Question!* And do you know why? 'Cause I'm an expert in one of their categories: Aggravation!" he bellows at his wife, Alice (Audrey Meadows).

Ralph is grouchy, negative, and the self-proclaimed recipient of the world's injustices. He's a discontented man who thinks that one big payoff, one time, will turn his life around. He wants more and better but never defines how that would take shape or makes a consistent effort to uplift his status.

Cynics are like Dreamers without a dream. Defensively shaking his fist at the world, Ralph is the biggest Cynic of all. "One of these days, Alice, pow!" he frequently shouts at his stronger-than-steel wife as if she's the source of his endless frustration, "Straight to the moon!"

Who are you kidding, Ralph? You need her more than she needs you.

The most common misconception with this particular archetype is that they are incapable of happiness, contentment, or for that matter, a full range of all human emotions. They are. All The Heroes of Comedy are. It's just that the Cynic is forever waiting for the other shoe to drop. They've actively managed their expectations downward in order to avoid the sting of disappointment.

The Cynic has not had good luck in life or a particularly easy ride. Even if they are currently successful in their career, for example, they will go on endlessly about how grueling it was to get to where they are now. They'll tell you in great detail all about how no one ever gave them a break.

Cynic Jay Pritchett (Ed O'Neill) of *Modern Family* is an excellent case study. He owns his business, lives in a beautiful house with his beautiful second wife, Gloria (Sofia Vergara), but his default setting seems to be *cranky*. Even though he's the owner of Pritchett's Closets & Blinds, he comments on what a drag it is to attend the annual convention for his field, "Closet Con is the premiere North American trade show for the closet industry. I stopped going years ago because it's a trade show for the closet industry." Dry, world-weary, and with a tinge of bitterness, he bemoans making a small sacrifice for an otherwise idyllic life.

That is how the Cynic moves through the world. Writers take note; it would make no sense for Jay to be as well off as he is financially, have an exciting job, *and* be a Cynic. We know he made a small fortune, but with a fairly dull career, so we can understand how he might think his life lacks purpose or interest.

But does Jay love his wife and family? Yes! Does he have extremely close friendships with the men with whom he went to war in Vietnam? Absolutely. Does he experience joy at the announcement of Gloria's pregnancy? The answer has to be yes, or *Modern Family* would be a drama, not a sitcom.

This is his response, "That's the greatest news I've ever heard... I spent the day hearing what my future had in store for me, and I didn't like one bit of it. It felt like my life was ending. And now you're telling me that I get to have a new start with the woman of my dreams? I think I'm gonna cry."

It's critically important to remember that the differences between The Heroes of Comedy lie mainly in how they respond to mundane daily events, low-level conflicts, or extreme crises. The traditional major milestones of life: birth, death, graduation, leaving home, marriage, retirement, and divorce generally evoke the same (read: *appropriate*) emotional reactions from all The Heroes of Comedy.

Characteristics are what a person or character is *like;* how others would describe them or how they would describe themselves. You can also refer to characteristics as traits, attributes or their "character breakdown." What someone is like will inform *how* they express emotion, but their personality does not *limit* their ability to feel a full range of emotions and feel them deeply.

This essential truth is often overlooked, especially when it comes to understanding and humanizing the Cynic. Because most of their personality traits are negative, actors think of them as sad, joyless, or angry. It's simply not the case. They're sensitive people who are protecting themselves from pain. Cynics have either endured hardships in their lives or were never taught or given permission to express their emotions; perhaps both.

A review of the list of TV Cynics reveals that most all of them exist within a few categories. There are many middle-aged and older men; Frank Barone of *Everybody Loves Raymond*, Al Bundy of *Married With Children*, Archie Bunker of *All in the Family*, Chef Rudy of *Mom*, Martin Crane of *Frasier*, Louie DePalma of *Taxi*, Red Forman of *That '70s Show*, James Evans, Sr. of *Good Times*, Lou Grant of *The Mary Tyler Moore Show*, Mike Heck of *The Middle*, Bernie McCollough of *The Bernie Mac Show*, Fred Mertz of *I Love Lucy*, Jay Pritchett of *Modern Family*, Stanley Roper of *Three's Company*, Fred Sanford of *Sanford and Son*, and Mel Sharples of *Alice*, etc.

There are also quite a few butlers, maids, servers, and assistants; Mr. Belvedere of *Mr. Belvedere*, Berta of *Two and a Half Men*, Beth of *NewsRadio*, Max Black of *2 Broke Girls*, Geoffrey Butler of *The Fresh Prince of Bel-Air*, Benson DuBois of *Benson*, Florida Evans of *Maude*, Dennis Finch of *Just Shoot Me*, Florence Johnston of *The Jeffersons*, Carol Kester of *The Bob Newhart Show*, Carla LeBec of *Cheers*, Niles of *The Nanny*, Rosario Salazar of *Will & Grace*, and Sue Wilson of *Veep*, etc.

There are several teenage girls and women in their early 20s; Jane Benson of *The Comeback*, Darlene Conner of *Roseanne*, Julie Cooper of *One Day at a Time*, Maeby Fünke of *Arrested Development*, Santana Lopez of *Glee*, April Ludgate of *Parks and Recreation*, and Jo Polniaczek of *The Facts of Life*, etc.

Finally, there's a healthy list of middle-aged and older women; Maude Findlay of *Maude*, Selma Hacker of *Night Court*, Thelma Harper of *Mama's Family*, Dr. Eleanor O'Hara of *Nurse Jackie*, Sophia Petrillo of *The Golden Girls*, Sally Rogers of *The Dick Van Dyke Show*, Joy Scroggs of *Hot in Cleveland*, and Lois Wilkerson of *Malcolm in the Middle*, etc.

Out of the entire list of Cynics, there are no teenage boys! There is one young man in his 20s, Adam Sackler of *Girls*, and two men in their 30s; Dinesh Chugtai of *Silicon Valley* and Dennis Finch of *Just Shoot Me*.

I found this quite revealing and I hope it's helpful for you to understand the nature of this character. Of course, there are a few Cynics listed who don't fall into these categories, but out of around 60 examples, nearly all fall squarely into one of those four groups.

If art mirrors society, then what television has told us throughout history is that young men, in particular, simply aren't cynical. That by itself is quite a revelation. Women still unfortunately struggle to gain equality in all aspects of life in America and around the globe. Many psychological studies have been conducted, as well as endless research in regard to the differences between men and women and how we are raised, taught, and socialized.

More than any other group, young men are portrayed as having every reason in the world to be hopeful about their future until they become old geezers. While entirely unscientific, my hypothesis is at least worth considering, especially for actors and writers. I'm not saying younger men *should* be portrayed as Cynics more, just that it is worth considering that they *practically never are.*

I'd also add that, by and large, Cynics work best when they're particularly young or much older. Gender aside, there aren't many cynics between 25 and 50. Let's start with the teens and early 20s. *Roseanne*'s Darlene Conner (Sarah Gilbert) and *Parks and Recreation*'s April Ludgate (Aubrey Plaza) are terrific examples.

Darlene is an actual teenager on *Roseanne* and April begins on *Parks and Recreation* as an intern at the Pawnee Parks and Recreation Department, who's still in college. She's just 20 years old when the series begins. Both are moody, dark, and have a biting sense of humor. Their cynicism works because they're both very intelligent young women who see the world as an unwelcoming place.

Neither knows what they really want to do with their lives throughout much of their respective series. In both cases, however, they lighten up as they get older and their overall demeanors become brighter. They both get married and see a path toward a brighter future.

As a writer, I can tell you that their evolution toward lightness *had* to occur. It's uncomfortable to watch a young, healthy, employed, and newly married adult view the world as a hopeless place. There's nothing particularly funny about it, and it makes the character rather pathetic.

It would be one thing if Cynics were known as dimwitted, like the Buffoon, but they're whip-smart. It simply makes no sense for an intelligent person with burgeoning career opportunities and a fulfilling romantic relationship to be constantly negative. Darlene and April both remained Cynics at heart, but the characters matured and expressed their positive emotions on a more frequent basis as they moved into their mid-to-late 20s, found direction, and acquired some success.

At the other end of the telescope, there is a strong case to be made for an older Cynic, especially if they had no real success in life, and they see little opportunity for that to change. Whether you're waitressing well into your 40s like Carla LeBec (Rhea Perlman) on *Cheers*, or working as a live-in maid when others your age have retired like Rosario (Shelley Morrison) on *Will & Grace*, it's understandable that you might see the glass as half empty.

Most of the older male Cynics have strong relationships to the concept of war and/or a specific war. Whether they served in the armed forces or were simply living in the era of World War II, the Korean War, or the Vietnam War, the older guys are all very much in touch with the reality of fighting abroad and potentially dying to protect the rights of their fellow Americans.

That's a pretty serious notion for a book dealing with comedy, but it logically explains why so many Cynics are older men. They've put themselves in harm's way for the benefit of others, or if they haven't personally, they have friends who have. War is woven into their psyche.

It will be interesting to see how this perspective and tenet of the Cynic evolves in the future. America is always at war now, and we still have brave servicemen and women who fight for our freedoms on foreign soil. However, the connection between our current, perpetual wars and the general population is negligible in comparison to the generations of Americans who were adults during World War II, the Korean War, and the Vietnam War.

Americans no longer make shared sacrifices in the face of our declarations of war and occupations. None of us has to ration sugar or gasoline when the United States invades Iraq or Afghanistan, like prior generations of other conflicts. So, ultimately, what I'm wondering is if and how war will be referenced in future television comedies, if at all. There are several sitcoms that are entirely based on military life or set against the backdrop of war; *M*A*S*H*, *Hogan's Heroes*, *McHale's Navy*, *F-Troop*, *The Phil Silvers Show*, *Gomer Pyle, U.S.M.C.*, *Major Dad*, *Private Benjamin*, and *Mister Roberts*.

I know younger readers of this book won't recognize most of those titles, but it is interesting to recognize that at least 10 sitcoms about our armed services were created and broadcast over the years. Is there a way to comically depict military life in the world in which we now live? Are we personally affected by our nation's ongoing military conflicts? Something for the writers among you to consider.

That may have seemed like a major detour regarding an archetypical character, but the Cynic is the only archetype that consistently mentions a military background. In *Modern Family*, Jay helps Cameron and Mitchell build Lily a princess castle. Mitchell reminisces about how fun it was to build a bookshelf with Jay when he was a boy. Jay's response into camera, "That was my Vietnam… And I was *in* Vietnam." War refences have been a deep well from which to draw great jokes.

In a similar vein, Sophia Petrillo (Estelle Getty) of *The Golden Girls* engenders the qualities of an older female Cynic better than anyone, especially when she takes you on a trip back to her childhood in Sicily, as she does in this exchange with Rose:

SOPHIA:	Would you stop complaining? We've got it easy. Back in Sicily, I was on a game show. It was Torture.
ROSE:	What was it called, Sophia?
SOPHIA:	I just told you, Torture. Mussolini asked the questions, and you'd better have the right answers. Things like, 'Who do you like better, me or Hitler?' 'Who's got the snappiest boots, me or Hitler?' 'Who's got the cuter girlfriend, me or Hitler?' And you always had to answer, 'Mussolini.' Otherwise, they forced you to play the lightning round. And they used real lightning!

Sophia is always glad to offer a healthy dose of perspective from someone who lived her childhood under the rule of an actual fascist.

Finally, we have a whole bunch of Cynics who are servants, assistants, and servers. I've never personally known anyone with a fulltime live-in housekeeper. I've never known anyone with a butler. Maybe I need to know wealthier people. Or perhaps it's just fun, if not entirely relatable, to explore the upstairs/downstairs dynamic of *Downton Abbey* (or *Upstairs, Downstairs*, which was the precursor to *Downton Abbey* from the 1970s) in a humorous way.

Either way, there have been a slew of Cynic maids and butlers on television. It's hard to imagine seeing many more in the future because the concept of fulltime household help is so unrelatable and limited to the extremely wealthy, but time will tell.

Fortunately, with all the current options available to explore great television from the past, we can delight in the snappy takedowns, insults, and words of woe from the likes of the following.

Benson DuBois of the series *Soap*, and its spinoff, *Benson*: "Oh, there's no such thing as a broken heart, Katie. It's just a term we use to describe one of life's little disappointments that comes close to killing you."

Florence Johnston of *The Jeffersons*: "That's very good, Mr. Jefferson. You keep changing your mind like that and someday maybe you'll end up with one that works."

Lynn Aloysius Belvedere of *Mr. Belvedere*: "Mrs. King, as I told you last night, I dislike children intensely and yours, if I may say so, have peculiarly repulsive habits and manners."

Berta of *Two and a Half Men*: "Well, I spend most of my days looking at dirty toilets, and those Rorschach tests you call bedsheets."

And finally, Rosario of *Will & Grace*: "I'd wring her neck, but I don't want to be standing in a puddle of gin."

I conclude that Cynics have the best zingers. Why wouldn't they? Their primary goal is to put you in check when you're unaware of your own absurdity or God help you, deflate your ego if it should get out of hand.

What Is Their Strength?

Cynics are law-abiding people with a strong moral compass. One of the reasons they're so skeptical about life is that they play by the rules and still can't seem to get ahead. Sure, everyone fudges the truth sometimes or ignores a minor law, but Cynics are honorable citizens who value truth and justice.

They may be sour a lot of the time, but they can also be counted on to simply do the right thing when the chips are down. When the Cynic sees others cheating or slacking, it's bothersome to them because they'd much rather do whatever it is "the hard way" with integrity than achieve any kind of merit without substance.

The Cynic's single greatest strength within their tribe is loyalty. A Cynic will always protect, defend, and care for those around them when there is a real problem or crisis. Cynics have no time for or interest in petty emotional crises of the day. However, if you are in real danger, call your Cynic friend because chances are she'll cut a bitch on your behalf.

One of television's great friendships is the one that evolved between Dreamer Mary Richards (Mary Tyler Moore) and her boss and mentor, Lou Grant (Ed Asner), a Cynic. Watching them become close was both organic and heartening because they meet in the pilot of the series. They don't know each other yet. We see them transition from strangers to family over seven seasons. Here is part of Mary's first conversation with Mr. Grant from the pilot. She is interviewing for a job.

> MR. GRANT: You know what? You've got spunk!
>
> MARY: Well...
>
> MR. GRANT: I *hate* spunk! Tell ya what. I'll try you out for a couple of weeks, see if it works out. If I don't like you, I'll fire ya! If you don't like me? I'll fire ya!

Mr. Grant, like all Cynics, has no time for niceties and does not suffer fools well. He puts Mary on notice, day one, in no uncertain terms. For any reason or no particular reason, she's out if he says so. Cynics are not cryptic or mysterious at all. Nor are they passive-aggressive. They're aggressive-aggressive. They want you to know exactly with whom you are dealing.

The Mary Tyler Moore Show concludes when a new station manager fires the entire staff (except for the incompetent Buffoon and weatherman Ted Baxter). The main characters of the show all have to say goodbye to each other in the extremely touching series finale. Mr. Grant tells Mary not to get too emotional, but in their final moment in the newsroom, he relents.

MARY: Mr. Grant? Could I say what I wanted to say now? Please?

MR. GRANT: Okay, Mary.

MARY: Well I just wanted to let you know... that sometimes I get concerned about being a career woman. I get to thinking that my job is too important to me. And I tell myself that the people I work with are just the people I work with, and not my family. But last night I thought, 'what is a family anyway?' They're just people who make you feel less alone and really loved. And that's what you've done for me. Thank you for being my family.

Mary's closing words to Mr. Grant are better than any external observation with which to illustrate how Cynics make their friends and family feel; loved, protected, and cherished. Over seven years, Mr. Grant became much more of a father figure to Mary than a scary boss with the authority to fire her at will.

So many actors approach this archetype like they are an enemy within the tribe and the exact opposite is true. The Cynic will weed out the fakes and the phonies, call out pretense, and send liars and frauds packing. *They keep their tribe safe.* While they have a guarded nature, Cynics easily extend their guard to shield their friends and family from real misfortune.

Once you've earned the loyalty of a Cynic, you have a warrior by your side in the battle that is sometimes life.

What Is Their Weakness?

There's an old idiom, "Put up your dukes." It means raise your fists because a fight's coming your way. Cynics live their lives with their dukes up. They're always ready for a fight. That does not mean they always *want* to fight or that they are angry or that they are unhappy.

It means that they are guarded and prepared with a tendency toward skepticism. They are subconsciously scanning for problems before they occur and ready to snuff them out before they escalate. Better to try and douse a campfire than a forest fire.

This means that Cynics approach the moments of life with a certain degree of suspicion. They don't automatically extend trust to anything or anyone unknown; rather, they require proof that whatever is new is valid and worthy. They are comfortable living in a crouched, defensive posture.

When Carla (Rhea Perlman) becomes pregnant with her sixth child and turns down the marriage proposal of the baby's father, here is how she tells her closest friends.

CARLA: Okay, okay, you're all going to know eventually, so you might as well know now. I turned Benny down, and I'm pregnant again. So in case your math is bad, that makes six, count 'em, six kids for an unmarried woman. I don't want your sappy looks, I don't want your charity, I don't want your sympathy. As a matter of fact, I

don't even want to talk about this anymore. I
just want to be left alone to live my life. Got it?

Sam responds, "Got it," and gestures to everyone in the bar to resume whatever they were doing before Carla's announcement. After a beat, Carla's need for support wins out and she rescinds her previous command.

CARLA: What are you people made of, stone?!

The crew gladly rallies around her. With her dukes already up, Carla's instinct is to throw the first punch when she's feeling vulnerable. Her announcement to everyone in the bar is intended to squelch all gossip, inquiry, and judgment before they begin. But because she's *human* first and a *type of person* second, it takes only moments before she opens her heart and asks her true friends to take care of her.

How Do Others See Them?

As reliable and dutiful as Cynics are, they definitely have sharp edges. Friends and family of the Cynic know there will be no BS when engaging with this personality. Ultimately, however, they also know they are harmless. Cynics are not angry people. They may come across that way. So many of their characteristics are in the neighborhood of those words, but anger and true hostility or intent to harm produce drama, not comedy.

So while those who have a Cynic in their orbit might be intimidated by them, wary of them, and occasionally stung by their insults or biting remarks, they know they are safe. Cynics show all their cards all the time. They have no significant secrets and they're happy to tell you most everything about themselves through daily bitching. They wear their battered heart out on their well-worn sleeve.

So while their closest allies know they're not the person to go to for a big, warm hug, the Cynic is known to be trustworthy, loyal, steadfast, unsentimental, and honest without apology. The word "blunt" was invented for this Hero of Comedy.

How Do Writers Use Them?

Cynics provide excellent commentary. Of note, writers use the Cynic to stand outside the fray, observe the shenanigans of everyone around them, and judge. They're almost like a sports-caster up in the booth watching the players of a game tear into each other while they remark on points scored from a distance.

In contrast to the Anchor, the Cynic isn't going to get involved in someone else's circumstance unless they are dragged kicking and screaming. Similar in that both archetypes are intelligent, straightforward, particularly sarcastic, and grounded, the distinction is the Cynics' defensiveness and guardedness.

With the Cynic emotionally detached from events even within the group, they are free to observe and comment without the drive to teach and help course correct the way the Anchor might. They will say something is a bad idea once and then walk away. A well-written Cynic will take a meta view of what's going on in their world and not get caught up in the frenetic energy and hyperreactivity of most of the other Heroes, even the Anchor.

This does not make them indifferent. It's part of their wisdom. They've lived long enough (or their soul is old enough) to intrinsi-cally understand that a heightened emotional response to daily events does no good. If anything, unchecked emotions will likely escalate a problem and make it worse.

Mike Heck (Neil Flynn) on *The Middle* and *Louie* (Louis C.K.), on his eponymous series, are both Cynics and both characters are fathers of younger kids. Both are also great examples of men who espouse all the qualities of the Cynic, including their humanity and heart. Just because people are not particularly emotional, doesn't mean they are unfeeling. If a person doesn't have a similar reaction to an event as everyone else in their tribe, they are not necessarily indifferent. They would call it "having a healthy perspective."

Writers use the Cynic as the voice of doubt. Yes, they are very hard to win over. It takes a lot for them to trust and be convinced a good thing is a good thing and that it will last. However, their pragmatic nature and "wait and see" attitude is perfect for taking down an idiot with an insult in one particular moment or society as a whole.

With their emotions in check and their keen eye on the lookout for trouble beneath an arched brow, Cynics are great guardians of the status quo.

What Is Your Way In?

If you don't have an automatic sense of this character or an immediate entry point, there's a very good case you might also judge them as mean, angry, or unhappy. If that is case, let's start there. None of those statements are true. There is no anger in comedy or comedic characters who are defined by sadness. On occasion a Cynic can be mean, *but so can anyone.* They are not defined by meanness, and they don't think of themselves that way.

A better understanding of the Cynic is someone who feels limited by their circumstances, even if the circumstances seem great from another's point of view. The Cynical servers, Carla on *Cheers* and Max on *2 Broke Girls*, for example, don't have exciting or lucrative jobs. Nor do the butlers, maids, or assistants I mentioned before. They're employed, but they don't have a lot of hope they'll move up in society. Resigned is therefore a better one-word description than sad or angry.

Jay Pritchett (Ed O'Neill) on the other hand, has a great life on *Modern Family*. He's wealthy with a successful business, great family, and beautiful wife. Why is he so cantankerous then? Jay, Carla, and Max all react to life the same way. Money and security don't seem to make the difference.

From his point of view, Jay's spent his whole life being dutiful for the benefit of others without much in the way of thanks. He never pursued his personal ambitions. Instead, he dedicated himself to the welfare of his family. In other words, he felt resigned to a storyline of his life from which he saw no way out.

Frasier's cynical dad, Martin Crane (John Mahoney), has the very same outlook. Martin is a former cop, wounded in the line of duty, and a widower. He feels he's fought with life his whole life. In his later years he finds himself living with a son that he has a very hard time relating to and has virtually nothing in common with.

Frasier's apartment is beautiful, and Martin has a personal physical therapist and friend in Daphne Moon (Jane Leeves), so what's there to bitch about? Frasier's difficult, sure, but he's there for his father and loves him. Everyone should have it so nice in retirement.

But that's not how a Cynic looks at it all. They feel stuck where they are in life and cannot see how to change their destiny. Interestingly, we almost never hear about what they'd want instead. We only hear about what they *don't* like about what they *do* have. "Let me tell ya about my son," "Let me tell ya about my wife," "Let me tell ya about my upbringing..."

If you've ever been in that place or felt similarly, that is one way you can personalize yourself into the Cynic. For all their intelligence, what the Cynic doesn't understand is that the grass is not necessarily greener on the other side.

They aren't able to ignite their imagination and envision specifically what kind of life would be better and then manifest it for themselves. Cynics perceive their status like it's a hand they were dealt and it's their duty to play it out.

In truth, they could just as easily get up from the table, walk away, and find another game to play entirely. Once you understand why they grudgingly stay put, you understand the sedentary nature of the world-weary Cynic.

The Cynic in a Family-Based Series: *The Bernie Mac Show*

There is a lineage of cynical men at the helm of their families throughout sitcom history. Cynic and extreme blowhard Ralph Kramden (Jackie Gleason) was husband to Alice (Audrey Meadows) on *The Honeymooners*, although they had no children. Carroll O'Connor played embittered blue-collar Cynic Archie Bunker with a wife, Edith (Jean Stapleton), who together had one adult daughter, Gloria (Sally Struthers), and a son-in-law, Mike (Rob Reiner). Mike Heck (Neil Flynn) is a gentler if not somewhat more emotionally accessible Cynic dad on *The Middle* with three younger children, Axl (Charlie McDermott), Sue (Eden Sher), and Brick (Atticus Shaffer).

Bernie McCullough (Bernie Mac) had a bit of a twist thrown into his home life. Married without kids of his own, he and his wife, Wanda (Kellita Smith), take in Bernie's two nieces and nephew when his sister is sent to rehab in Chicago and can't care for them.

The Bernie Mac Show is an extremely well-written sitcom that holds up over time. Larry Wilmore, widely known for his appearances as Senior Black Correspondent on *The Daily Show* among many other notable credits, created the show and won an individual Emmy for penning the pilot.

While *The Bernie Mac Show* is not as widely known as others mentioned in this book, it's a particularly great example of how a Cynic functions within a family dynamic. We meet Bernie McCullough while he's learning what it is to be a parent on the fly in real time. Add to the setup that Bernie Mac was an incredible performer, a force to be reckoned with, and a true Cynic born out of stand-up, and you have an amazing case study of this archetype navigating modern family life.

Bernie felt he got no gratitude and, more importantly, no respect; a trope that started all the way back in vaudeville, ran through Rodney Dangerfield (a comedian whose thesis statement was, "I get no respect!"), and continues on through Murray Goldberg (Jeff Garlin) griping about the way things are or aren't from his armchair in *The Goldbergs*.

Bernie sees himself as another victim of circumstance with no way out. Once again, we see a beautiful wife, beautiful house, and flourishing career (his character was also a successful stand-up comedian). Such a life would make most people quite happy, but Bernie was eternally frustrated and discontented.

The format of the show has Bernie talking to all of America (by breaking the fourth wall and speaking directly into camera). In this brief shout out, he makes his view of parenting perfectly clear. "America! You know you ain't safe! Nobody's safe. They're in your neighborhoods... Your schools... Your homes. Cold-blooded criminals. That's right, I'm talking about your children. They're Public Enemy No. 1!"

Of course he's being facetious, but it's also true that he finds the kids in his house a constant splinter underneath his skin. Of course kids can be exhausting and aggravating, but they can also be joyful, wondrous, and fun. They can help adults rekindle their childhood. Bernie never sees any of that. He's so focused on having the life he had before taking in his nieces and nephew, he's unable to imagine a different way of living with the kids included.

Bernie is smart and successful, but he's stymied by stubbornness and a lack of vision. From the outside, it often seems Cynics are unnecessarily choosing their own misery. However, if you ask them what the problem is, their answer is always going to be, "Other people." While they understand different folks are going to function different ways, the ever-intolerant Cynic lacks the patience and imagination to understand why. They never developed the coping mechanisms needed to interact with differing personalities without exploding.

The Cynic in a Friend-Based Series: *Sex and the City*

Although she softened as the series progressed, Miranda Hobbes (Cynthia Nixon) was *Sex and the City*'s resident voice of doubt and discontent. Nixon took home both an Emmy and a SAG Award for her work as a career-minded lawyer with extremely cynical views on relationships and men. And life.

"It feels good to be sarcastic," Miranda proclaims. It's the thesis statement for all Cynics, but Miranda actually said it out loud. Within a group of friends, Cynics are the tough-love givers and the cold-as-steel truthtellers. Miranda describes her core group of girlfriends thusly: "How did it happen that four such smart women have nothing to talk about but boyfriends? It's like seventh grade with bank accounts."

Anchors are also great at setting others straight and giving good advice, but they're more inclined to apply a life lesson, attach a moment to a greater theme, or in some way teach somebody something. Cynics, on the other hand, give feedback that is almost always on point, but your emotional reaction is your problem.

They won't pull a punch and they don't care how you feel after they've said what they have to say. Cynics are shrewd, sharp, and sardonic. In one sentence, Miranda sums up her entire philosophy on romance, "The only person who should have to pay for your *last* relationship is the person in your *next* relationship." It's easier and faster for them to get to the point with an insult or biting retort. It's like a doctor giving a patient a shot. Sure, it'll sting, but then you're vaccinated.

Miranda's boyfriend (and later husband) Steve (David Eigenberg) once asked her, "What's wrong with corduroy?" Her reply, "I don't have enough time to tell you what's wrong with corduroy."

When Steve proposes marriage to Miranda on bended knee after finding out they're pregnant, her stunned reply is even sharper. "What are you, fuckin' crazy?" she asks while he holds out an engagement ring. Although Miranda did end up marrying Steve and having their baby, her initial reaction was horror. She could initially only see what was wrong with the whole situation. In this quick exchange, she processes her fate with her best friend, Carrie (Sarah Jessica Parker):

MIRANDA: Oh God, Carrie, is this my baby? I mean, what am I waiting for?

CARRIE: Sweetie, do you want to leave?

MIRANDA: No. I can't have a baby. I could barely find the time to schedule this abortion.

That's about as real as it gets. Whether she's talking to her friends, her lovers, or even talking herself through a crisis, none are immune to her blunt pessimistic take on life. Cynics expect doom and disappointment. Whether that's what will manifest is up to fate. A Cynic would just say they're being realistic.

The Cynic in a Work-Based Series: *Cheers*

Carla Tortelli (Rhea Perlman) of *Cheers* fame has decided that the world is divided into the "haves" and the "have nots." Viewing her life as one filled with misfortune and no upward mobility, she's put herself squarely in the have not and *never will* camp. She's representative of all television's great Cynics who work in service positions: butlers, maids, secretaries, waiters, waitresses, hosts, and maître d's, as well as receptionists and personal assistants.

Not every one of those jobs is filled by a Cynic, but many are, and Carla is arguably the best and most biting of the bunch. Rhea Perlman won four Emmy Awards for Outstanding Supporting Actress in a Comedy Series for her portrayal of Carla. She earned her trophies with insults, scathing takedowns, and witty exit lines that could rarely be topped. Was she mean? Some would say yes. Diane Chambers (Shelley Long) would *definitely* say yes.

> DIANE: I'm having a bad day. Aren't I allowed to have a bad day?
>
> CARLA: Sure, you've given us plenty. Keep one for yourself.

But Carla would probably just say that life is hard and she's realistic about it. And that being nice just for the sake of being nice is a weakness you can't afford when you constantly have to defend yourself against a cruel and merciless world. Carla would also say she's exhausted. When *Cheers* begins, Carla has four children and as the show ran its course, she has four more by three different men.

Carla stands alone as television's only single mother of eight embodied by a Cynic (*Cheers* worked two of Perlman's three real-life pregnancies into her character's storyline). Carla's lack of fortune with romance and her overwhelming responsibility caring for eight children while serving cocktails for a living is a perfect recipe for a character's sharp and doubtful outlook on life.

Already divorced at the onset of *Cheers*, Carla becomes pregnant post-divorce by Nick Tortelli (Dan Hedaya), the father of her four previous children, making them the parents of five together. Several years later she marries a mediocre ice hockey player, Eddie LeBec (Jay Thomas), after they discover she is pregnant with twins.

Carla and Eddie remain together until he is killed by a Zamboni while attempting to save the life of a fellow cast member of an ice show. At Eddie's funeral, Carla learns that Eddie has another wife and had fathered other children. While touring with the ice show, he got another woman pregnant and married her.

Not only was Eddie a liar and cheat, but also a polygamist! And dead! That's pretty serious subject matter for a sitcom to explore, but it's part of why *Cheers* was such a great show. The preposterous and the possible always merged in the storytelling.

It's not just good writing, but brave for *Cheers*' creative team to push Carla's bad luck in love to the farthest limits: betrayal and death. She shouldn't be a Cynic for nothing. It's worth noting how rare it is that a character's spouse dies on a half-hour comedy. Carla was absolutely affected by Eddie's passing, but her hardened exterior (her Cynic core) was a logical mask the writers used to bypass showing the audience the grief you'd normally expect to see from someone who just lost a husband.

There was poignancy in the episode that featured the news of Eddie's death, but for the sake of comedy over tragedy, he died in a penguin costume getting run over by a slow-moving ice-scraping machine. It was established that he toured so often that Carla barely even saw him anymore, and she was aware the relationship was troubled. Further, two wives showed up at his funeral and had a hair-pulling fight over who he loved the most. And if that weren't enough, Eddie's other wife, Gloria, looked, sounded, and behaved just like Carla.

All of life's trials and travails — even the death of a spouse — can and have been dealt with in the vessel of situation comedy. Choosing the right moment *and the right archetype* for the most difficult stories is what elevates a good comedy to an iconic cornerstone of pop culture.

In other words, Carla's cheating husband can die in season eight of 11, and the audience can accept it through a comedic lens. Sooner would have been too tough. Other archetypes like the Innocent or even the Dreamer losing their spouse would be possible but harder to keep comedic at any point in the life of the series. The specific point of view that each of The Heroes of Comedy bring to a series cannot be underestimated.

Here are some examples from Carla's point of view of how a Cynic keeps her friends' egos in check:

NORM: I want something light and cold.
CARLA: Sorry, it's Diane's day off.

FRASIER: I've been taking stock of myself.
CARLA: Not exactly AT&T, is it?

CLIFF: It's a little-known fact that 42% of deaths in America are caused by accidents in the home.
CARLA: So were you.

| LILITH: | Well, I'm off. I don't know what the future holds. Whatever happens, I only hope I can realize my full potential. To acquire things the old Lilith never had. |
| CARLA: | Like a body temperature? |

| NORM: | I'm going to pitch it to my supervisor tomorrow, but I tell you, I'm a little nervous about putting my butt on the line. |
| CARLA: | How do you think the line feels? |

| FRASIER: | May I suggest something that seems to have worked for many of my patients? |
| CARLA: | What? Changing doctors? |

| REBECCA: | To my sweet baby, Robin. We may not have much, but we have each other. |
| CARLA: | Then you don't have much. |

| SAM: | Do I look like a guy who is about to do something stupid? |
| CARLA: | Always. |

| DIANE: | Hey everyone, guess why I'm here? |
| CARLA: | Generations of inbreeding? |

Whatever other activity they may be engaged in, great Cynics are also polishing their stand-up routine, using their family and closest friends as continual fodder for material.

Characteristics of the Cynic

- Acerbic
- Astute
- Beleaguered
- Biting
- Caustic
- Condescending
- Critical
- Cynical
- Droll
- Dry
- Dutiful
- Embittered
- Entertaining
- Guarded
- Humorous
- Indifferent
- Intolerant
- Irreverent
- Jaded
- Loyal
- Observant
- Perceptive
- Pessimistic
- Quick-Witted
- Reliable
- Resigned
- Salty
- Sarcastic
- Sardonic
- Sassy
- Short-Tempered
- Shrewd
- Snarky
- Snide
- Spiteful
- Street-Smart
- Unapologetic
- Unwavering
- Wise
- World-Weary

Cynics Throughout the History of Television

Frank Barone	Peter Boyle	Everybody Loves Raymond
Mr. Lynn Belvedere	Christopher Hewett	Mr. Belvedere
Jane Benson	Laura Silverman	The Comeback
Berta	Conchata Ferrell	Two and a Half Men
Beth	Vicki Lewis	NewsRadio
Max George Black	Kat Dennings	2 Broke Girls
Stevie Budd	Emily Hampshire	Schitt's Creek
Al Bundy	Ed O'Neill	Married... with Children
Archie Bunker	Carroll O'Connor	All in the Family
Geoffrey Butler	Joseph Marcell	The Fresh Prince of Bel-Air
Chef Rudy	French Stewart	Mom
Dinesh Chugtai	Kumail Nanjiani	Silicon Valley
Darlene Conner	Sara Gilbert	Roseanne
Julie Cooper	Mackenzie Phillips	One Day at a Time
Martin Crane	John Mahoney	Frasier
Louie DePalma	Danny DeVito	Taxi
Det. Rosa Diaz	Stephanie Beatriz	Brooklyn Nine-Nine
Roz Doyle	Peri Gilpin	Frasier
Benson DuBois	Robert Guillaume	Benson
Florida Evans	Esther Rolle	Maude
Nurse Carla Espinoza	Judy Reyes	Scrubs
James Evans, Sr.	John Amos	Good Times

Dennis Finch	David Spade	Just Shoot Me!
Maude Findlay	Bea Arthur	Maude
Reginald "Red" Forman	Kurtwood Smith	That '70s Show
Monroe Fuchs	Stephen Root	Barry
Maeby Fünke	Alia Shawkat	Arrested Development
Murray Goldberg	Jeff Garlin	The Goldbergs
Lou Grant	Ed Asner	The Mary Tyler Moore Show
Reggie Green	Marque Richardson	Dear White People
Selma Hacker	Selma Diamond	Night Court
Thelma Mae Harper	Vicki Lawrence	Mama's Family
Mike Heck	Neil Flynn	The Middle
Miranda Hobbes	Cynthia Nixon	Sex and the City
Florence Johnston	Marla Gibbs	The Jeffersons
Julius	Terry Crews	Everybody Hates Chris
Carol Kester	Marcia Wallace	The Bob Newhart Show
Reuben Kincaid	Dave Madden	The Partridge Family
Ralph Kramden	Jackie Gleason	The Honeymooners
Beverly Lincoln	Tamsin Greig	Episodes
Santana Lopez	Naya Rivera	Glee
Louie	Louis C.K.	Louie
April Ludgate	Aubrey Plaza	Parks and Recreation
Bernard "Bernie" McCollough	Bernie Mac	The Bernie Mac Show

Garrett McNeil	Colton Dunn	Superstore
Fred Mertz	William Frawley	I Love Lucy
Alfred "Paper Boi" Miles	Brian Tyree Henry	Atlanta
Susie Myerson	Alex Borstein	The Marvelous Mrs. Maisel
Norman Newlander	Alan Arkin	The Kominsky Method
Niles	Daniel Davis	The Nanny
Dr. Eleanor O'Hara	Eve Best	Nurse Jackie
Thomas Pembridge	Malcolm McDowell	Mozart in the Jungle
Sophia Petrillo	Estelle Getty	The Golden Girls
Jo Polniaczek	Nancy McKeon	The Facts of Life
Jay Pritchett	Ed O'Neill	Modern Family
Sally Rogers	Rose Marie	The Dick Van Dyke Show
Stanley Roper	Norman Fell	Three's Company
Adam Sackler	Adam Driver	Girls
Rosario Salazar	Shelley Morrison	Will & Grace
Fred G. Sanford	Redd Foxx	Sanford and Son
Joy Scroggs	Jane Leeves	Hot in Cleveland
Mel Sharples	Vic Tayback	Alice
Eleanor Shellstrop	Kristen Bell	The Good Place
Astrid Sloan	Lucy Boynton	The Politician
Sam Sylvia	Marc Maron	GLOW
Carla Tortelli	Rhea Perlman	Cheers

Lois Wilkerson	Jane Kaczmarek	**Malcolm in the Middle**
Sue Wilson	Sufe Bradshaw	**Veep**

How Cynics are Described in the Breakdowns

Always has a dark cloud hanging over their head, been there/ done that, believe it when they see it, brash, cantankerous, cranky, dowdy, frumpy, goth, grouchy, hardened, has a caustic wit, irascible, no time for bullshit, no-nonsense, nonplussed, ornery, racist, reluctant, rough around the edges, stoic, tell-it-like-it-is type, tough, unimpressed, waiting for the other shoe to drop, war veteran

Lead Body Part: Back

As the saying goes, we carry the weight of the world on our shoulders. However, folks don't generally talk about shoulder pain from collecting life's layered burdens. We feel weariness in our backs. If we're sedentary, our lower back can take the brunt. If we overuse our muscles, our upper back might get strained. Either way, Cynics know what it is to carry a load and where we carry it. There's another saying; "Get your back up." It means to become annoyed and defensive. And another, "Your back against the wall." We say this when we're cornered and don't know which way to pivot. We can all feel this way in a moment, but this is the posture with which the Cynic moves through the world.

PLAYER

"The only reason to wait a month for sex is if she's 17 years, 11 months old."

Barney Stinson/*How I Met Your Mother*

Mantra: "I lust"
Strength: Confident
Weakness: Noncommittal
Jobs: Their work has an inherent sex appeal.

Who Are They?

The Player has an insatiable appetite for sex and an astonishing propensity to discuss their needs and conquests freely with friends, coworkers, and family. Everyone has sexual desires; they're natural. Most people in general and all the other archetypes tend not to discuss their sexual exploits in graphic detail. In contrast, the Player has absolutely no problem with frank sex talk whatsoever. Further, it's almost as if recounting their intimate adventures after the fact is an extension of the encounter itself!

If they weren't also charming, lively, and charismatic, we'd find the Player completely creepy. However, with enough winning qualities to balance out their complete lack of filter when it comes to private matters, we not only enjoy their company, we're very likely titillated by them.

Sure, we'll call them out on their vulgarity, but the truth is the Player brings an aura of arousal with them wherever they go. If you know one personally, you have to admit the Player is a non-stop good time whether you're the object of their amorous intent or not.

Most people would be a Player (at some era in their life) if they thought they could get away with it. Sex is primal. It feels good and we're hard-wired to seek it out for a variety of reasons. Most people suppress their urges, sexual and otherwise, to some degree because of the myriad demands placed on them by society. When you layer on cultural restrictions, religion, learned shame, body insecurities, and the worship and celebration of outward physical beauty, it becomes even more difficult for people to fully realize their maximum sexual potential.

For whatever reason, it's not that way for the Player. They prioritize sex simply for the sake of pleasure and release without compunction. In an endless cycle of validation, the extraordinarily confident Player pursues, captures, and savors their prey. If you know you can walk out of the house and get laid at any time of your own choosing, you're experiencing the world differently than most people. It's also very likely you walk around 24 hours a day feeling like you've got an edge on life. There's probably a glint in your eye. Why wouldn't there be?

You might think someone who lived that way would have to be classically good-looking or beautiful... hot. Not necessarily. Looks aren't a factor as much as a strong game and the right mindset. The Player may be great looking, but they may also be average. They might be older. *Much* older.

Albert "Pops" Solomon (George Segal) on *The Goldbergs* is a widower and grandfather who possesses a highly active libido and an eye for the ladies. His daughter, Beverly (Wendi McLendon Covey), tries to keep him in check, but to no avail.

BEVERLY: Mom's been gone for 10 years. He's dated at least five different women a week. That's over 2,000 women!

You're saying something that's good. But you're saying it like it's bad.

Even if Beverly is exaggerating by 90 percent, that's not a bad scorecard for an octogenarian. So, what if a Player is still in his prime but seriously flawed? Can he score in spite of his sorrows? If he has a system and an eye constantly open for an opportunity, then, yes.

The series *Californication* is a character study of an addict, Hank Moody (David Duchovny). An alcoholic and substance abuser, he's also a shameless womanizer. *Californication* chronicles Hank's life and career as a frustrated novelist who misses the mark with his ambitions but hits it with the ladies. If he has a philosophy on life, it's built around his views on sex. Some would say Hank is a pig, some might say he's wise. Perhaps both are true. Whatever the case, here are 10 favorite Hankisms:

1. Are you sexually harassing me right now? Because if you are, I think I'm gonna have to report you. For giving me a serious boner.
2. I probably won't go down in history, but I will go down on your sister.
3. Friends don't let friends bang each other's soulmates.
4. I'm just like my father. You know, there isn't a woman that I've met that I haven't fallen in love with for 10 minutes or 10 years.
5. A morning of awkwardness is far better than a night of loneliness.
6. I may be easy but I'm not sleazy.
7. No man should ever have to bear witness to his 'O' face.

8. Fuck around all you want, I'm no Judge Judy. But don't string a woman along for a major chunk of her childbearing years. That's not cool.
9. Hang out with your wang out, but remember, no gloving, no loving.
10. Don't you sometimes wish you had two cocks? I do.

Whatever else Players are or are not, they are perpetually hedonistic. They filter their experiences of life through a lens of sensual self-indulgence. They make decisions based on how good something might make them feel in a moment and worry about the consequences later. They are drawn to romance like a moth to a flame.

What Is Their Strength?

If love is a battlefield, the Player is armed with confidence, charm, and charisma. Charisma is defined as "compelling attractiveness that can inspire devotion in others." It almost sounds like a superpower. For the Player, it is. Think about that for a second. What must it be like to be able to compel others to be enamored with you? The Player would say it's fantastic.

There's an old idiom, "He could charm the pants off you." In the Player's case, it's not a metaphor. Smooth, suave, and intense, the Player is dialed into their ability to influence others. Anyone can *hope* to get lucky. The Player creates their own luck when it comes to courting. They envision the outcome they want and assume victory. Most of their strategy is certainty.

One of television's greatest Players, Samantha Jones (Kim Cattrall), essentially purred her way through *Sex and the City*. Like a hungry kitty cat, she lapped men up like milk from a saucer. She's a self-proclaimed try-sexual (she'll try anything once), and although she's gorgeous, it's not her looks that ensnare men as much as her hypnotic intent. Players understand the power of desire. We all want to be wanted and Players shamelessly exploit that universal truth.

Of course, for the sake of comedy, Players are bound to make bad choices and/or extend their promiscuity past appropriate boundaries. A perfect example is when Samantha sleeps with her good friend Charlotte's (Kristin Davis) brother, prompting an angry Charlotte to call Samantha's vagina "the hottest spot in town: it's always open."

In Samantha's case, that's more of a testimonial than an insult.

What Is Their Weakness?

Although they thrive in the presence of others, the Player's "no strings attached" attitude leaves them perennially noncommittal and ultimately lonely. More often than not they're tortured by true love. They're either afraid of the expectations others will put on them if a lasting relationship develops, or they've been hurt by love before and never, ever want to go through the pain of a breakup again.

On *How I Met Your Mother*, Barney Stinson (Neil Patrick Harris) reluctantly reveals the reason for his promiscuity to his friends when an old and embarrassing videotape surfaces. On the tape, he is singing a romantic ballad to his first love in a desperate attempt to keep their romance alive. As it turns out, he wasn't always a scoundrel.

Previously a peace-loving hippie, Barney consciously becomes a Player in order to avoid another broken heart after his first one. Before he knew the rest of the group, Barney was working with his girlfriend and love of his life, Shannon, in a coffee shop. They planned on joining the Peace Corps together and travelling to Nicaragua.

After Shannon fails to show up for their departure, Barney discovers she is cheating on him with a businessman named Greg. An obvious womanizer, Greg tells Barney the key to getting women is having money and suits. When Barney realizes there's no hope left for him and Shannon, he flees the coffee shop distraught. As he walks alone crying, he is randomly handed a brochure for a suit sale. A light bulb goes off. He transforms himself into a clone of Greg, the man who took Shannon away from him and never looks back.

As Barney wraps up his origin story to the gang, he additionally reveals that he's just seen Shannon that very night, eight years later.

> BARNEY: ...And then she told me about her life. She and Greg dated for a while and then split up. Here's the real kicker — Shannon's a mom. She has a little kid named Max. That's crazy. That could have been my kid. Instead, what do I have? My whole life's some money in the bank, some suits in my closet, and a string of one-night stands.

Barney tears up.

> LILY: Hey... C'mon, I mean, just because your life went one way and hers went another, doesn't make your life any worse.

> BARNEY: My life rocks.

> LILY: Huh?

> BARNEY: Money, suits, and sex? These are tears of joy! I could be cooped up in some tiny apartment changing some brat's poopy diapers, but

instead I'm out in the world being awesome 24/7/365! (He looks toward heaven) You let me dodge a bullet, Big Guy. Plus, here's the mini-cherry on top of the regular cherry on top of the sundae of awesomeness that is my life... after Shannon and I talked, *I nailed her!*

Even for flamboyant Barney, his friends find it hard to believe that, without emotion, he just hooked up with his first true love. However, Barney proves it to be true with a phone video recording of their lovemaking. He summarizes the evening like a master of ceremony.

BARNEY: Ladies, gentlemen, Ted... This has been a wonderful evening. I got great dirt on all you guys. I got Ted to tell the re-return, I *finally* nailed Shannon — told her I'd call her tomorrow — ah, yeah, *right*! And I rediscovered just how awesomely awesome my life is. Peace out hombres!

He exits.

Barney, like many other Players, pities his friends who lead less exciting lives. He may even consider them chumps. Yet time and again those same friends are in meaningful and/or lasting relationships that provide fulfillment and strength. Through all their bluster and indulgence, the Player is afraid of commitment. They're afraid of the complications and perils of romantic love. What they tout as independence is merely a smokescreen for their deep-seated insecurity.

How Do Others See Them?

The Player's friends and family see them for exactly what they are. The polite way of saying it is "loose." The not so nice way of putting it is "slut" or "man whore." Not my words...

The characters around the Player have to react to their nature and behavior, otherwise there's no point in the Player flaunting their exploits. The reactions can range from shock to admiration to sheer horror, but a reaction there must be.

Also, those around the Player are likely voicing concern and suggesting *some* sense of boundaries even when they're calling them out. They may be judging, but they are also trying to teach their horned-up friend a thing or two about how to treat people. The Player alone among The Heroes of Comedy thinks that it is okay to objectify people.

Here's a quick example from *Saved by the Bell*. Jessie (Elizabeth Berkley) tries to nudge her boyfriend, A.C. Slater (Mario Lopez), in the direction of male evolution.

JESSIE: Slater, haven't you heard of the women's movement?

SLATER: Sure. Put on something cute and *move* it into the kitchen.

Yes, it's a typical male chauvinist remark and whether it's funny or not is debatable. There is no question, however, that it is a source of conflict, which is necessary for both story and comedy. But treating people like disposable pleasure devices is not gender-specific. *Sex and the City*'s Samantha explains the concept to her friend, Carrie (Sarah Jessica Parker), "You can't date your fuck buddy... You're going to take the only person in your life that's there purely for sex, no strings attached, and turn him into a human being? Why?"

The Player's point of view and subsequent behavior make perfect sense to them. "It feels good and I want to do it, so I'm going to do it. No particular upbringing, religion, moral code, societal judgment, or shame will stop me," they might say. It's like they're trying to fill an unnamed void while willfully avoiding evolution. With such extreme self-indulgence, it's no wonder that the Player's acquaintances see them as shiny, shallow, and underneath the steamy facade, sad.

That pathos even applies to young Manny Delgado (Rico Rodriguez) on *Modern Family*. A lot of students wonder how Manny can possibly be a Player, since the primary qualities of that archetype are so... let's say, mature, and he's so young. I'll take that on here, since it's asked about a lot and the answer also provides another layer of insight into the Player's psyche. When *Modern Family* originally aired, Manny is 11 years old and still in elementary school. It would have been inappropriate for a network, family show to depict a kid scoring all the time.

So rather than write Manny as chronically horny, they made him a hopeless romantic. From the very beginning of the show, Manny wants to be in love and has no reservations about seducing older women. His first date is with a woman he meets online. She didn't know Manny was a kid until she saw him, but he knew she was an adult. He didn't care.

Manny says into camera: "Her name is Whitney. I met her in an online book club. We both like vampire fiction and the romance of eternal life."

Whitney (Kristen Schaal) is devastated when she arrives at the Pritchett house and realizes Manny's age because she thought that he might be the *man* of her dreams. Gloria (Sofia Vergara) and Manny console her over tea as she composes herself.

WHITNEY: This is so humiliating. I am sorry.

GLORIA:	It's okay.
WHITNEY:	He just seemed so mature online. How could I be so stupid?
MANNY:	You're not stupid. Stupid is not following your heart and taking a chance on love.
WHITNEY:	I mean, what kind of 11-year-old talks like that?!
GLORIA:	Manny's an old soul.
MANNY:	Here... here's my handkerchief.
GLORIA:	You see what I mean?

In another instance, Manny prepares an intimate and unwelcomed candlelit dinner for his baby brother Joe's nanny. He slides a menu to her across the table. On the back of it is a poem he's written: "With silken hair and supple, olive skin and hands that wash the laundry of my kin..." She stops reading once she sees where this is going and tries to let him down easy, but Manny is relentless.

NANNY:	Aw, Manny...
MANNY:	You still have 12 lines to go. Spoiler alert — I love you!

So, there you have it. Manny is definitely a Player, just a young one. Always dressed in a pressed guayabera shirt or a tailored suit, he's perennially outfitted just like all other players. He has a look that says he's prepared for any opportunity, and the kid has moves. Manny's the classic Latin lover we often see as an adult but rarely get to glimpse as a child.

How Do Writers Use Them?

Writers use the Player to titillate the audience and bring overt discussions of sex into the environment. As previously mentioned, everyone has sex, but not everyone wants to talk about it. Enter the Player.

From flirtation to fornication, the Player wants to have sex, replay sex they've had, brag about sexual conquests, and strategize about how to get even more sex. Whether it's to electrify a situation that might otherwise be boring or to shock, the Player provides writers with permission to get more intimate or flat-out nasty than they might otherwise comfortably be able.

The Player not only is forthcoming about their exploits, they act as something between a surrogate and therapist for others around them when it comes to their sex lives. All the other archetypes are inherently reserved when it comes to talking about the details of their romantic escapades. The Player is great at drawing out intimate details from others who would not ordinarily spill the beans.

The premise for *Who's the Boss?* revolves around a male housekeeper, Tony (Tony Danza), who works for a single mother, Angela (Judith Light). However, its Angela's mother, Mona (Katherine Helmond), the Player, who encourages Angela to move in the handsome, full-time housekeeper.

MONA: See, my instincts tell me this is the man for my grandson. And it doesn't hurt that he's a hunk.

ANGELA: Mother, I'm not looking for a hunk, I'm looking for a housekeeper.

MONA: Why not? He'll do floors, he'll lift furniture... Can I come over when he lifts?

From her point of view, hiring Tony was like having your cake and eating too. Angela and Mona are both single women, so why not have a hot guy around the house to ogle while he's doing manual labor? A strong throughline within the series is Mona trying to get her uptight daughter Angela to loosen up and find romance after her divorce.

Mona is a steady instigator of the sexual tension that evolves between Angela and Tony over the series' eight seasons. A great example of how the Player's amorous nature isn't limited to their own encounters, but also affects others.

What Is Your Way In?

A lot has been said about sex both in general and in this particular section of the book. The range in which sexuality is portrayed on television runs the spectrum of flirtatiously innocent to downright raunchy. Regardless of what is on the page, it's up to you, the actor, to be first and foremost, brave.

You must expose your carnal desires in an honest way. In order to play the Player with integrity, you must let the audience see you authentically sexually charged, not merely pretending, suggesting or worse, indicating. Especially within (but certainly not limited to) scripted comedy, actors sometimes have a difficult time conveying their raw sexuality openly or to a great enough extent, depending on what is in the script. True arousal seems to some to belong in the domain of drama. A more serious matter, if you will.

But great shows have been created and great stars made by those who aren't shy about turning themselves on and letting the world watch. A good Player is a true exhibitionist. They like it when other people see them in heat.

As an actor, your first priority is to be comfortable in that regard. All characters are sexual, as are almost all people, but the Player lives in a sexually charged space most of the time. Exposing your true primal urges is a vulnerable affair and not everyone is up to the task, even very talented, well-trained actors.

There are different reasons why people don't want to expose their sexuality for a camera, so there is no one way to guide an individual actor to that place. It simply boils down to awareness and an internal review for each of us; do I like the idea of *actually* arousing myself through my imagination for others to witness or not?

It's not wrong if the answer is no. If you're certain you don't like the idea of exploring the erotic intent of a character, then this archetype isn't for you and it's that simple.

If the answer is an easy yes, you should know that you're very much in the minority and you should do whatever you can to capitalize on this in your career. Specifically, make sure you have reel footage that shows off your willingness and ability to unleash your sexual energy. Make sure your inherent boldness shows up in your headshots.

If raw sensuality is a known strength for you, make sure everyone knows. Sex sells. Show business is sexy. Have fun using it to your advantage.

For most people, in my experience, the answer is closer to this, "I'd be game but no one ever really sees/casts me that way, and I don't have a lot of experience playing a character like that." The majority of actors, especially those who focus on comedy, generally don't feel like sexy beasts on a day-to-day basis. Real life is where this character begins, however.

Some of us are bestowed with sexual prowess and shamelessness in sating our sensual appetites. For most, however, it's simply a matter of practice. If you never try flirting, you'll never be a great flirt. If you never take a chance and hit on someone, you'll never get lucky. If you never overcome being shy about exploring your sexual impulses, you'll never be bold about indulging in them.

Obvious statements but far too many actors have somehow acquired the notion that if they are flirtatious within business interactions or expose an air of sexuality in their daily life, they won't be taken seriously. Especially women, which I understand thoroughly, but I think is a real shame. For the record, I am a lifelong feminist and I actively fight for equal rights for *everyone*, end of statement, full stop. I'm not advocating that women or men use sex as a manipulation to get ahead.

I am pointing out however, that far too many actors, most of whom are at the apex of their sexual years, entering an inherently sexy business often come across as entirely asexual! I do advocate *often* that my students ignite *some* amount of flirtation and *at least* a *tiny* percentage of sexual energy into their performances and careers, because it's actually weird when there is none detectable *at all*.

Walking the earth with your intellect as a guard against anyone seeing you as a sexual entity is wholly unnatural. A lot of folks have it the wrong way around. If you don't know what I mean, go to Paris.

The Player may or not be your wheelhouse, but if you step up to this character, be brave and expose your lust without filter or hesitation. What have you got to lose?

The Player in a Family-Based Series: *Two and a Half Men*

The Player has the shortest list of examples of all The Heroes of Comedy. Even shorter is the list of examples of Players in a family-themed show. It makes sense. Playing the field is on the opposite end of the spectrum of traditional family life. *Two and a Half Men* traded on this inherent conflict by forcing the two dynamics together and becoming one of the most financially successful sitcoms in television history.

Divorced and broke, Alan Harper (Jon Cryer) is forced to move in with his Player brother, Charlie (Charlie Sheen), along with his young son, Jake (Angus T. Jones). Hence the show's title, which summarizes the premise succinctly, two and a half men. Alan and Jake rely on Charlie, but they're trying to have a typical father/son relationship in the household of a modern-day Caligula.

Charlie lives a life of utter debauchery in full view of his 10-year-old nephew. Charlie is a shameless womanizer, drug abuser, and classic playboy who lives in Malibu with a fulltime housekeeper and smokes cigars. He engages in every flavor of intercourse, including revenge sex. He's perhaps the worst possible example of a man for a boy growing into his teen years. At least they speak about it openly:

JAKE: Oh, come on. Why can't I live with you guys?

CHARLIE: Oh, Jake. Do you have any idea how much I have to clean up my act when you're here on weekends?

JAKE: What are you talking about? I see you drink, gamble... you have strange girls sleep over.

CHARLIE: Uh-huh. Drop in unannounced on a Wednesday and you'll be scarred for life.

Whether *Two and a Half Men* suits your particular taste in comedy or not, it's worth noting what a simple but effective premise it deployed to become a massive hit, lasting 12 seasons and garnering 46 Primetime Emmy Award nominations. The series did not reinvent the wheel when it comes to executing a multi-cam sitcom by any stretch.

What it did do, brilliantly, however, is combine specific comedy archetypes in a way that was entirely original in television history. This is important to consider for writers, especially because it's hard to come up with an entirely original premise for a show while keeping it relatable to a broad enough audience to make it sellable in the marketplace.

It's much easier to twist the prism with a fresh combination of archetypes and generations, while still basing a show in a household or office environment, than it is to create a high-concept show that's never been done before or has no reference point in television history.

The core foundation of *Two and a Half Men* is about as simple as it gets — three people living in a house together. The vast majority of scenes over 12 seasons take place within said house with recurring characters coming and going.

It worked so well and lasted so long, however, because of the unique juxtaposition of archetypes. Uncle or not, a Player shouldn't be co-parenting a kid. But Lee Aronsohn and Chuck Lorre thought it would make a great, and perhaps lucrative, comedy series, and they were right. Keeping the premise simple and utilizing The Heroes of Comedy in a never-before-seen configuration is not the only recipe for success, but it's sure an easy one to follow.

The Player in a Friend-Based Series: *Golden Girls*

"There is a fine line between having a good time and being a wanton slut. I know. My toe has been on that line."

— Blanche Devereaux

Portrayed with endless vigor by Rue McClanahan, *The Golden Girls'* Blanche Devereaux is one of television's most iconic Players. Set in Miami, *The Golden Girls* is a multi-joke per page laugh machine featuring four previously married women who live together in retirement.

It astonishes how much humor the writers of *The Golden Girls* were able to mine from Blanche's promiscuity. Since she spends most of her time with her friends and peers, the jokes about her rigorous love life fly fast, furious, and unfiltered.

The Golden Girls are mature women who've lived a lot of life and there aren't any kids around, so when it comes time to comment on Blanche's nightly, naughty exploits, they really let her have it. I'm no prude, but I'd sometimes blush at how often Blanche was called a slut to her face, directly or indirectly.

Here's just a handful examples:

BLANCHE: I can't believe you said that! Oh, if I weren't a lady, I'd deck you.
DOROTHY: You try, and I'll have you on your back so fast you'll think you're out on a date.

BLANCHE: You know what I hate doing most after a party?
ROSE: Trying to find your underwear in the big pile?

DOROTHY: Is that all you care about? Money and applause?
BLANCHE: And sex. For which I usually *get* applause.

BLANCHE: Why I couldn't... I'd feel like a... like a...
DOROTHY: Like a backstabbing slut?

BLANCHE: What do you think of my new dress? Is it me?
SOPHIA: It's too tight, it's too short, and shows too much cleavage for a woman your age.

DOROTHY: Yes, Blanche. It's you.

BLANCHE: I do love the rain so. It reminds me of my first kiss.

DOROTHY: Ah, your first kiss was in the rain?

BLANCHE: No, it was in the shower.

TRUDY: Well, that's that. How does it feel to have your butt whipped?

BLANCHE: Well, sometimes I find it strangely titillating, but... Oh, you were talking to *her*.

BLANCHE: My goodness, what would the neighbors think if they saw two men lying in my bed?

SOPHIA: They'd think it's Tuesday!

BLANCHE: I feel like I did when I was a virgin!

SOPHIA: You mean the feeling isn't going to last long?

BLANCHE: Are you implying I lost my virginity at an early age?

SOPHIA: I'm just saying you're lucky Jack and Jill magazine didn't have a gossip column.

BLANCHE: I'm not going to stand for this! Not in my own house...

SOPHIA: Take it, Dorothy.

DOROTHY: But I bet you'll *lie* down for it!

BLANCHE: Sophia, by placing this pearl necklace between my bosoms, does it make me look like I'm a

	sex-starved slut who is in need of a man to bed?
SOPHIA:	Yes.
BLANCHE:	Good, then pearls it is.

And to think that is just a sampling! However, those sharp comments and cheap shots wouldn't have worked if Blanche wasn't a strong, sexually fulfilled woman who exudes confidence and has good humor enough to let the zingers roll off her back. That's real craftsmanship and collaboration between the writers and the actor. And like all other actors who play this archetype well, Ms. McClanahan had the personal courage and wherewithal to show the audience her unbridled lust honestly.

It's also worth noting that watching Rue McClanahan portray Blanche through seven seasons is a masterclass in character development. Everything about Blanche is synchronized perfectly. A mannered and manicured Southern belle, there's no denying she is just plain horny all the time. However, she also very much appreciates romance, seduction, and the charms of a true gentleman. Whether it's foreplay, sex, or potential love, she is *always* prepared.

Blanche is perpetually dressed in clothes that flow. She doesn't enter a room, she floats in; she has a certain fine carriage of her hips and head when she walks. Past her Southern accent, there is a lilt in her vocal performance that tells the story of her upbringing just outside of Atlanta, Georgia. If Blanche is awake, her bosom is on display, whether she's standing or sitting down. She's made it both her job and her mission to be beautiful at all times, and she does it with panache.

Some would say Blanche Devereaux is just one of so many wacky sitcom characters on a broad sitcom with a laugh track. Anyone who'd say that is either A) not an actor, B) undereducated, or C) simply sheltered. There are people like Blanche in the world and they're interesting, if somewhat over-animated. They are women who command attention and respect. Rue McClanahan won a Primetime Emmy Award for Outstanding Lead Actress in a Comedy Series playing Blanche.

On the page, the character is looser than a baby tooth, but Ms. McClanahan humanized Blanche with a ravenous libido, personal flair, and most importantly, a warm Southern heart.

The Player in a Work-Based Series: *Cheers*

Samuel "Mayday" Malone, better known as Sam (Ted Danson) of *Cheers* fame, is the epitome of a hypermasculine jock turned bar owner. Prior to opening *Cheers*, Sam was a relief pitcher for the Boston Red Sox. He is a recovering alcoholic and drives a little red Corvette.

In playing Sam Malone, Ted Danson dials into a primal sexual energy that is so palpable, it at times overrides Sam's intellect and makes him seem dumb, even though he absolutely is not. Even when he's flustered, furious, or frustrated, Sam is always prepared to manipulate circumstances to his advantage.

This exchange with Rebecca Howe (Kirstie Alley) is a great example:

SAM: You know, I'll tell you something, lady. There was a time when I was considering making love to you, but now it's out of the question. As a matter of fact, you know, I wouldn't make love to you if asked me, if you *begged* me, to make love to you, I wouldn't. Go ahead. Just ask me. Just try. See what happens.

REBECCA: Would you make love to me?

SAM: Well okay, but just once.

He's almost like an idiot savant with his innate ability to remain focused on his urges at all times. Just when it seems he's a meandering moron, he's actually setting a trap.

Like *Cheers*, *Californication* is helmed by a womanizing substance abuser, Hank Moody (David Duchovny). The bulk of *Californication* shows Hank immersed in his drug addiction while *Cheers* keeps Sam in recovery most of the time. Although after yet another split in his on-again-off-again relationship with Diane (Shelley Long), Sam falls off the wagon and begins drinking excessively at one point. Later, in the second to last episode of *Cheers'* 11 season run, Sam joins a support group for sexual compulsives.

It's noteworthy that in both Hank's and Sam's case, the chronic need for impulsive sex is an obvious symptom of psychological issues and treated as a condition with serious consequences. Sure, they both make a lot of glib jokes about getting laid, but they are both tormented men and dealt karmic retribution for their lackluster treatment of women. It's acknowledged by themselves and those around them, that their behavior is unhealthy and requires treatment.

Sam was in love with the idea of being Sam Malone — former baseball star and barman in the great city of Boston, Mass., and the only relationship he ever fully committed to without reservation was his relationship with Cheers. After proposing multiple times to Diane, she agrees, and they decide to get married amongst their friends in the bar. During the wedding ceremony, they decide against it and call the wedding off temporarily so that Diane can pursue her writing career, which will take her away from Boston for six months.

It's a bittersweet and poignant moment. The mood foreshadows Long's departure from the show, and we get the sense Diane is not coming back, despite her declaration that she will. She says to Sam, "Next time, let's have our wedding somewhere else."

In truth, Long did not renew her contract and left the show. However, the writers had to resolve the departure of Diane Chambers, the character. There didn't end up being a next time, but in that moment, as Diane is leaving, you almost get the sense that Cheers was always in the way of Sam connecting fully with someone. As if he always knew Cheers would be there for him as a solid backup with no questions asked. Diane seemed to know that, too.

Sam spent the next six months on the sea, sailing on his yacht. When he returns, we find he's sold Cheers to a corporation but still wants to work there, tending bar. Of course, as the show's star, there needs to be a reason for Danson to be present. But in returning to Cheers, Sam's psychology and true reason for being remains intact. Even if he can no longer be his own boss, he still chooses to be with Cheers. Oops, I mean *at* Cheers. Three seasons later, Sam buys Cheers back.

A lot has been written and discussed regarding Sam and Diane's epically spotty romance. It seems in the end, that Cheers was the great passion of Sam's lifetime and the one relationship from which he could never walk away. Although he got close to marrying several times throughout *Cheers'* eleven seasons, he never did.

After six years of separation, Sam and Diane reunite in the final episode. Not only is Sam finally going to marry Diane, but he plans to move to California with her, leaving Boston and Cheers behind. But just before they fly off to California together, they both begin to have doubts about their future and call off their relationship one last time. Sam returns to Cheers, which offers no surprise to Norm (George Wendt).

> NORM: But, um... Sammy, can I let you in on a little secret?

> SAM: Sure.

> NORM: I knew you'd come back.

> SAM: You did?

> NORM: You can never be unfaithful to your one true love. You always come back to her.

> SAM: Who is that?

> NORM: Think about it, Sam.

Norm exits. A Player until the very end, Sam remains uncommitted with his options open and he's happy that way. He stands alone in Cheers in the final moment of the last episode, looks around lovingly and says to himself, "Boy, I tell ya... I'm the luckiest son of a bitch on earth."

With the help of his friend's wise observation, Sam finally realizes his primary romance has never been with *any* woman. There is a knock on the door from a potential customer. Sam waves him away through the window, "Sorry. We're closed."

Characteristics of the Player

- Addicted
- Aggressive
- Animalistic
- Audacious
- Bold
- Bravado
- Carnal
- Certain
- Cocky
- Commanding
- Conceited
- Confident
- Explicit
- Fearless
- Flirtatious
- Forward
- Grand
- Hedonistic
- Horny
- Lecherous
- Lewd
- Lustful
- Manipulative
- Narcissistic
- Predatorial
- Primed
- Provocative
- Randy
- Risqué
- Romantic
- Seductive
- Self-indulgent
- Sensual
- Sharp
- Single-Minded
- Smooth
- Superficial
- Unreserved
- Vain
- Wanton

Players Throughout the History of Television

Vinnie Barbarino	John Travolta	Welcome Back, Kotter
Edie Britt	Nicollette Sheridan	Desperate Housewives
Bud Bundy	David Faustino	Married... with Children
Phil Chase	Donald Faison	The Exes
Sandra Clark	Jackée Harry	227
Larry Dallas	Richard Kline	Three's Company
Manny Delgado	Rico Rodriguez	Modern Family
Blanche Devereaux	Rue McClanahan	The Golden Girls
Daisy Duke	Catherine Bach	The Dukes of Hazzard
Dan Egan	Reid Scott	Veep
Dan Fielding	John Larroquette	Night Court
Ginger Grant	Tina Louise	Gilligan's Island
Brian Hackett	Steven Weber	Wings
Charlie Harper	Charlie Sheen	Two and a Half Men
Florence "Flo" Jean Castleberry	Polly Holiday	Alice
Samantha Jones	Kim Cattrall	Sex and the City
Sam Malone	Ted Danson	Cheers
Henry "Hank" Moody	David Duchovny	Californication
Sue Ann Nivens	Betty White	The Mary Tyler Moore Show
Mona Robinson	Katherine Helmond	Who's the Boss?
Dwayne F. Schneider	Pat Harrington Jr.	One Day at a Time
A.C. Slater	Mario Lopez	Saved by the Bell

Albert 'Pops' Solomon	George Segal	The Goldbergs
Sally Solomon	Kristen Johnston	3rd Rock from the Sun
Barney Stinson	Neil Patrick Harris	How I Met Your Mother
Cheryl Tunt	Judy Greer	Archer

How Players are Described in the Breakdowns

Athletic, breezy, built, charming head turner, cougar, dashing, feisty, fit, handsome but smarmy, horn dog, hot, hypersexualized, inappropriate, no boundaries, persuasive, physical, revealing in their dress, roguish playboy, rugged, seductress, slick, slippery, super-hot, swagger, touchy-feely, velvet-voiced, womanizing ladies' man

Lead Body Part: Mouth

You might have expected genitals or private parts to be high-lighted here. That certainly wouldn't be out of step. A Player is in constant pursuit of sexual conquest, so of course they're deeply in touch with arousal and physical pleasure. However, when I say to an actor, "Read those lines and lead with your penis or vagina," most feel lost. If, on the other hand, I say, "Read those lines knowing the favorite part of your body is your mouth," it's nearly impossible not to ignite sensuality. The mouth is an erogenous zone. It is associated not only with sexual acts, but a variety of sensual experiences as well. With our mouth we can delight in taste as well as carnal desire. Bringing focus to your lips and tongue can be far more intimate, tantalizing, and licentious than dialing into your groin.

The Heroes of Comedy Quick Review

Anchor

They *are* stable. They *seem* bossy. They *feel* burdened.
Practical and responsible, Anchors keep their tribe grounded.
Activate the parent within you.

Dreamer

They *are* immature. They *seem* screwed. They *feel* hopeful.
Desperate and vulnerable, Dreamers are uniquely unsatisfied.
Activate the aching desire you feel for your dreams to manifest.

Neurotic

They *are* meticulous. They *seem* uptight. They *feel* insecure.
Anxious and cerebral, Neurotics organize to self-soothe.
Activate the thoughts that keep you up at night.

Narcissist

They *are* selfish. They *seem* glamorous. They *feel* entitled.
Flamboyant and shallow, Narcissists feel deeply about trivial things.
Activate your inner diva.

Rebel

They *are* commanding. They *seem* intimidating. They *feel* superior.
Potent and enigmatic, Rebels disregard typical laws and morality.
Activate your demons.

Buffoon

They *are* dense. They *seem* oblivious. They *feel* out of step.
Dimwitted and unrefined, Buffoons are their own worst enemy.
Activate your feelings of inferiority. Then add feelings of superiority.

Eccentric

They *are* unique. They *seem* bizarre. They *feel* engaged.
Curious and lively, Eccentrics revel in the human experience.
Activate your sense of awe and wonder for the miracle that is life.

Innocent

They *are* naïve. They *seem* kindhearted. They *feel* happy.
Amiable and pure, the Innocent is the perennial child of their tribe.
Activate your deepest feelings of love and share them with
everyone.

Cynic

They *are* brusque. They *seem* agitated. They *feel* content.
Realistic and weary, Cynics are loyal but do not suffer fools well.
Activate all of your doubts, weariness and negative perceptions.

Player

They *are* charismatic. They *seem* loose. They *feel* antsy.
Charged and sensual, Players are happiest on the hunt.
Activate your libido.

Which Hero Are You?

For most actors, I suggest developing three archetypes found in
the breakdowns that you are most likely to play and become the
best there is at playing that type of character. Identify them, label
them, name them, and flesh them out for yourself. Some actors
are so well-suited for one archetype, that's all they need to focus
on. They can build a whole career on playing just one type of
person. Some actors comfortably play more than three Heroes
well. There is no exact rule. But the realities of casting tell us that
each actor has a definable range that makes the most sense.

Working actors nail down their wheelhouse. They know how they will be cast within breakdowns and develop characterizations in advance of auditions.

For example, if you play a Dreamer well and that character matches your look and vibe and you know that, you shouldn't be starting from scratch every time you portray that Hero. You will approach that type of character the same way every time you step into their skin. In fact, you should be able to teach others how to play your strongest archetypes because you've developed them so thoroughly. Ideally you understand the thought process of the Heroes you match most closely so well, you can *think in character* without distraction.

Your characters should be constructed from a combination of techniques you've learned as an actor. Maybe The Heroes of Comedy are your starting point for on-camera character development. Perhaps you've had prior training you can fortify with the specificity and immediate definition of The Heroes of Comedy.

Either way, include observations of people you know in real life and constant examination of others around you. Add your understanding of human behavior and psychology, plus your analysis of roles you've seen played successfully in television and film. You learn by studying the work of those who are working.

However you describe your characters, they need to be thought through and designed to be attractive to an audience, worthy of fans, interesting, and frankly, intricate enough to outshine other actors.

In addition, always choose words like the ones listed below to round out your character development and make sure you are creating someone the world will want to spend time with!

Aside from their clearly categorized, core traits, *any* of The Heroes of Comedy can be: Activated, Amazing, Appealing, Arresting, Audacious, Awesome, Bold, Brilliant, Captivating,

Charismatic, Colorful, Dauntless, Dazzling, Delectable, Delightful, Desirable, Dynamic, Energetic, Engaging, Entertaining, Enthralling, Fascinating, Fiery, Flirtatious, Forceful, Gutsy, Hilarious, Intoxicating, Intrepid, Intriguing, The Life of the Party, Lively, Lovable, Magnetic, Mesmerizing, Outrageous, Passionate, Present, Provocative, Scrumptious, Sensational, Sensual, Sexy, Snappy, Spirited, Steamy, Strong-Willed, Titillating, Uproarious, Vibrant, Vital, Vivacious, Winning.

To further flesh out your personal version of The Heroes of Comedy, answer the following questions for each one you'd like to develop or understand on a deeper level. The goal is not to write extensive backstory. The idea is to round out the point of view of a certain kind of personality.

- How does this Hero describe themself?
- What is this Hero's function in the show? How do writers use them?
- Why would an audience sympathize with this person?
- If this Hero is not sympathetic, how do they remain part of their tribe?
- What is this Hero's greatest fear?
- What is this Hero's biggest flaw?
- Who needs this Hero the most in this world and why?
- What is this Hero's dominant ambition?
- Where does this Hero get their self-esteem?
- If they are lacking self-esteem, why?
- How does this Hero dress and where do they buy their clothes?
- What is this Hero's kryptonite?
- How was this Hero raised?
- What was high school generally like for this Hero?
- Is this Hero satisfied with their current circumstances?

- What does this Hero resent the most?
- How does this Hero describe the world?
- How is this Hero funny in isolation?
- Did this Hero go to college? If so, where? If not, why not?
- Has this Hero had their heart broken?
- What does this Hero think happens to us when we die?

PART 3

WHAT THE ENTERTAINMENT INDUSTRY EXPECTS FROM YOU

"You are perfectly cast in your life. I can't imagine anyone but you in the role. Go play."

Lin-Manuel Miranda

7

The Casting Process

Actors, both new and very experienced, often have misconceptions about the casting process and how it works. With technology evolving and changing the industry's flow in significant ways, I thought a review of how it *actually* works is in order. It's quite simple and not at all mysterious. However, if you don't know, it can seem like finding your way through a hedge maze.

Before I go into detail, I want to start with a broad overview so everyone really understands how the system functions. I genuinely want you to succeed within it. It's much harder to do that if you think things that aren't true. In fact, too many actors who are already here are operating with outdated information.

I personally know thousands of actors, some very successful, who don't have a clue about how agents and managers (representatives) communicate with casting and producers. I'm on a mission to fix that. The following information is neither subjective nor my opinion. It's acquired knowledge about the day-to-day functionality of show business that every actor should know. Let's dig in.

First and foremost, it's important for actors to understand that television and film careers largely develop online. **The entertainment industry is almost entirely digital**. Let that sink in first. Casting directors and producers rely on images, video, and links to relevant information that are current and can be transferred instantly when asked for. Casting through Skype, Zoom and other teleconferencing platforms is becoming more common. How comfortable you are auditioning through the camera on your computer or phone will factor into your ability to book work.

There is very little chance your work on a stage will directly result in casting opportunities in Los Angeles. Stage training is valuable. There will always be a few actors who get a break because they appeared in a quality show. I'm aware of that. I just want newer actors especially to be realistic about how much performing live will factor into career opportunities. I have tremendous personal value for the thousands of hours I've spent performing live theater. In the digital age of Hollywood, however, that is not how most casting directors find new talent.

I just want to set the table, so to speak, and dispel the myths that exist about booking professional acting work. If you take these observations to heart and set yourself up properly from the beginning, you have a distinct advantage over other actors who don't. In this era of show business, establishing your online presence is your first job. It will also be an **ongoing** job as you acquire credits, new footage, and evolve into a stronger actor or new age range. Now onto details and specifics.

Hard copies of headshots have been eliminated for the most part. When an agent submits an actor to a casting director, they do it digitally, online. Casting directors send actors' auditions to producers digitally so they can be viewed on computers or cell phones. That's right. A producer might hire you while they are on an active set, watching auditions on their phone.

If producers want more information about an actor, they generally go to the actor's IMDb profile online to get it or ask casting. Either way, your IMDB profile will be the point of reference. Any and all information that can help someone else make the decision to hire you needs to be available online. This includes resume, headshot, and reel footage, all of which should be up-dated every single time there is a change.

Casting transactions occur online, and most daily com-munications are made through email. Actors maintain their professional profiles on **Actors Access** and **Casting Networks** for TV and film work. Casting offices release breakdowns elec-tronically on these two platforms. Agents and managers submit actors through Actors Access to **Breakdown Services**. FOX TV and Film Casting and a few other production entities use the Casting Networks platform. For a brief time FOX TV was exclusive to Casting Networks but no longer. Like all other studios they can and do use Breakdown Services.

If there's a pitch to be made for an actor, it's most commonly done by adding a note when they are digitally submitted by their agent online. The industry no longer needs agents to call casting to make them aware of new talent. As detailed above, actors present themselves online for the industry's consideration. Casting and producers make decisions about whether to call you in for an audition based on what they see on your Actors Access profile, Casting Networks profile, and your IMDb profile.

Phone calls don't factor in as much as they did in prior eras of show business. Actors often think that their representative will pitch them to casting. While that may happen, it's rarer than it used to be and likely won't happen for newer actors build-ing credits at the co-star level. Agents generally don't *promote* actors, they *submit* actors. This is especially true when you're just starting out.

Larger agencies and managers may be able to promote their clients when it comes to guest-star roles and series regular roles. But developmental actors are expected to promote *themselves* with professional photos, strong reel footage, and by forming industry relationships in whatever way they can. Your agent is only required to submit you for roles that you are appropriate for and negotiate contracts in good faith. Nothing more.

It's not their job to take care of you, encourage you, teach you, or validate you. The same is true for casting. Depending on the person before you, they *may* be nurturing and helpful. If they are, it's because that is their personal nature. It's not because either job description includes teaching actors anything about how the casting system works.

Just know that, in summary, an agent's job is to submit actors throughout the day as roles are released on Breakdown Services/ Casting Networks and negotiate contracts when actors they represent get hired.

Casting directors work for production, and their job is to offer several actors who could *all* do a great job in the role to producers. The producers view casting's selections and choose one actor that best suits their taste. Callbacks have virtually been eliminated, therefore your first take needs to be bookable. Again, you may be invited to a callback. Some producers value live interaction with actors. You should simply be aware that callbacks are broadly considered "old school." In order to be successful and have a positive relationship with auditioning, I want to manage everyone's expectations. It's always a disappointment to not book a job for which you auditioned. Actors in the digital age of Hollywood now need to be prepared for not having a callback as a way to gauge if they are close to the mark. Knowing for yourself that your script analysis, character development and audition skills are honed to a competitive level is essential for your emotional wellbeing. Validation that you're getting it right is not likely to come from the industry at large, only from experienced teachers and mentors within a credible training program. In order to maintain a healthy mindset, booking a job cannot be the single way in which you gauge how well you're doing. When you know your training is sound and your technical skills are solid, you can offer your best performance and let all other expectations go.

Hopefully this detailed outline of the digital age of Hollywood will keep you sane in the fast-paced world of auditioning. With the influx of information hurling toward casting directors online, they attend live shows far less than they used to. They have more than enough talent at their fingertips, viewable online in their office. What shows up for you online when they look? In addition, top casting offices now cover multiple shows. Before Hollywood went digital, they likely only covered one series at a time, maybe two if they were casting a pilot. This heavier workload, which is newer in the scheme of things, keeps them in their offices longer and makes it difficult for them to attend live performances, even if they're so inclined.

In summary, actors don't often meet directors, writers, or producers through the audition process anymore. If you're going to get discovered in Hollywood, you're far more likely to get dis-covered through a screen than performing on a stage. All of your time, energy, focus and training should lead to excellent on-camera skills if you're serious about booking acting work.

> *"You're not going there to get a job. You're going there to present what you do."*
>
> — *Bryan Cranston*

The Casting Office

Most casting appointments are brief. If you have a worthy ques-tion, one that will really help you do a better job in the moment, you should ask it. Otherwise, you step onto the mark and your audition is recorded.

The universal assumption is that your first take is your best one, unless there is an obvious gaffe. There may or may not be a second take with notes. Actors should not have any expectation that there will be collaboration within the audition process. There may or may not be. However, it is not up to you to decide or appropriate for you to have a reaction if there is or isn't.

After your audition is recorded, casting will say something like "Thanks for coming in," and you're done.

If you did a particularly outstanding job, they may let you know. But they also may not. After all, they're not the ones who will make the final selection. Casting directors don't have the final say on what actors to hire; producers do.

I've observed casting directors who are free with their thoughts and opinions. Some like to play, laugh, and cheerlead the actors who come into their office. Conversely, I've observed others who seem to have a policy of only saying, "Thank you," at the end of auditions no matter what. They're nice folks. They probably just don't want to get wrapped up in the emotions of actors who come into their office one after another throughout the day. Again, casting sends approximately six actor auditions to the producers, any of whom might be the booker. I know from my time working in casting, I tried not to get invested in any particular actor getting the role because the final choice wasn't mine.

Actors want clues, feedback, and validation on auditions. While I'm empathetic to that need, it's important for actors to embrace the degree to which the system is not set up to give them that. Nothing casting directors say or do has any great meaning and you shouldn't assign it any.

If you *need* anything at all from an audition experience, your head is in entirely the wrong place. If that's the case for you, you are working at a basic level against seasoned pros. Of course you'd like the job. So do all the other actors auditioning for it.

However, in daily practice, most auditions are simply a matter of a casting director recording you or you self-taping your audition and that is the end of the experience.

You make your offer, as do several others, and one actor will be chosen for the role. If you think your agent or manager might call casting for feedback, you're imagining a Hollywood that no longer exists. Yes, some upper level agencies can selectively get feedback on certain clients for certain experiences. Generally speaking for co-stars and guest-stars, it's simply not the case that anyone will give you feedback regarding your audition.

Actors are often shocked at the lack of collaboration, ad-justments, and overall communication when auditioning. Adjustments still happen, but infrequently. Callbacks still occur, but infrequently. It's your job (even if you're just entering the business) to know the current TV and film landscape, research and understand the material for which you're auditioning and prepare an audition suitable for the show, show creators, and network, if applicable.

I understand this can all sound very impersonal for some. Others prefer the efficiency of casting actors this way. It does save valuable time. Either way, it's reality. I see actors moving to Los Angeles wildly unprepared for it every day. I wish it was all more collegial. But at the risk of sounding like everyone's dad, "You youngsters live in a digital world. Embrace it!" In fairness, every industry on the planet that can streamline through tech-nology has done so. Why should the entertainment industry be any different?

Do theater if you like. Improvise your heart out if you love it. But if you want to work in TV and film, embrace the idea that your talent — the best of what you have to offer — needs to be viewable online. No one can help you advance within the system without links to your **on-camera** work. If you haven't booked any yet, the expectation is that you create it for yourself. Agents and managers will tell you to *make sure* you have improv training on your resume. Ask them exactly why. Ask them when they last saw an improv show. There's an extremely high probability they haven't been to one in about a decade. Perhaps they've seen a *sketch* show that was written, directed and rehearsed, but that's quite different. If that's the case and it was in Los Angeles, they probably attended a show performed by the Groundlings Main Company or Sunday Company. Those are both excellent show-cases for actors, but it's worth noting they are not improv shows.

This summarization can feel daunting, especially if you're starting out. But time and time again, actors have thanked me for pulling back the curtain on the mysteries of show business. It's hard to get a clear, unbiased road map you can use to plan your artistic journey. I'm an artist and entrepreneur; I like helping actors understand career building as much as I like coaching the work.

Knowledge is power. Yes, you'll have to put in some effort, but at least you know where to direct your time and money to create your own best odds. If you give your representatives the right tools, they can offer them to casting and producers on your behalf. From there, your chances of success skyrocket!

"Be so good, they can't ignore you."

— Steve Martin

8

The Audition Code

Pro-Level Audition and Self-Tape Technique

The Audition Code is a 10-point protocol for industry-standard auditions that establish you as a bookable actor. Everyone knows they need to audition well. Not everyone knows exactly what that means. Let's unpack it.

It's important to understand that auditioning is actually its own *genre* of acting.

The actor is isolated on a mark with no obvious point of reference for scaling, volume, tone, etc. Actors inherently want to connect, but the distance between the actor and reader can make that difficult. Auditioning can feel like freefalling in space unless you have training and practice. This is what **audition technique** classes are for and they are essential for actors breaking into the business.

There are elements of theater in audition technique; imaginary environments, space work, and acting your best against a reader who is acting just a bit. It's technical; you must understand working with the camera, be comfortable with your body on a mark while maintaining your frame, and be able to use your script gracefully as needed.

Questions arise that aren't about comedy or acting choices: Do you enter or exit? Stand or sit? Mime actions? Is space work allowed? Should you add a tag? Answer: Yes, no, maybe.

It depends on context. There is not one answer to any question you might have about what to do in auditions that applies 100 percent of the time. Auditioning well is as much an art as writing and acting themselves. There are sensible guidelines, but within those guidelines, you'll need to learn to make commonsense decisions that keep you safe and steady on the mark.

Booking professional acting work is almost solely done by video auditions that are submitted to producers. Strong audition skills have always been important. However, it's never been more important to audition well than it is now and going into the future.

Cold reading and audition technique are invaluable training you should get before you enter casting rooms or self-submit auditions. No one within the audition process will give you guidance on what you should do with the material or feedback on whether what you did in relation to the camera was appropriate.

Although auditioning can feel deeply personal for us, it's not for anyone else. It isn't a special occurrence for other members of production. It's a daily, recurring transaction to find the right actor for each role. Producers hire actors who feel seasoned, steady, and permanent. If you want to work, it's imperative you become those things. It's not difficult to get there if you have the right knowledge.

1) Confidence

I could have either put confidence at the beginning of the list or the end of it. It's critically important that you *lead* with confidence; that you bring real ease and self-worth into your auditions from the get-go. Yet actors don't *earn* true confidence until they've mastered the other aspects of professional-level auditioning.

So, I'll start with confidence, with a nod to its rightful place at the end of a list of other skills.

If no one ever told you this clearly, I'm telling you now; actors are hired as much, *if not more*, for their overall demeanor and confidence when **auditioning on a mark** as they are for their inherent talent.

No one else is in charge of your audition experience. You are.

It's no one else's job to make you somehow better or help you feel comfortable. Conversely, no one should have the power to make you feel badly about you or your work. If you leave auditions feeling poorly about yourself or what happened in the room, it's probably not because you're untalented. It's much more likely you are merely unprepared for how quickly auditions can go by and how vulnerable you feel when there is no validation for your efforts.

I always tell my actors that auditioning shouldn't feel like a trip to the principal's office. A bit of nervousness from excitement is a good thing. Shrinking because you're not sure exactly what is expected of you is a guarantee you will not be called back into that office. Casting directors should not feel like authority figures to you. Being called in for an audition should neither feel like a favor nor a stroke of good luck.

It may seem counterintuitive, but part of your job as an actor when auditioning is to take care of how the room feels. When we walk into an office — any office — we set the temperature with our attitude. Each new actor who walks into the room sends signals that convey how capable they are of walking onto a set and integrating seamlessly with the existing cast if hired.

We can elevate the mood or destroy it. If we bring in fear, the room feels awful. If we bring in joy, we will be remembered for that always. Do you love auditioning and think you're great at it? Whatever the answer, it's obvious. If it's not "Yes!" right now, that's fine, but you should work toward it.

So much emphasis, especially for comedic acting, is put on stage training, but the only way you're going to book work is to audition for it. Auditions are technical and pointedly exclude all the things that make improvising and working on a stage fun: other actors, an audience, and laughter that validates your work.

If you have any negativity or uncertainty about auditioning, that is assessed by casting before they can gauge your talent. It's unlikely you'll be moved on to producers if you're uncomfortable at the start. Casting directors are not just assessing acting ability, they're being paid by the production to screen out unqualified candidates. Just the same as anyone interviewing a candidate for any other kind of job.

To that end, too many actors audition with some degree of fear or doubt about what they're doing. This reads and you're kidding yourself if you think it doesn't. Casting directors watch actors all day every day of the week. They know which actors have appropriate audition skills and which do not. They can easily tell the difference between actors who have only worked onstage and those who have trained themselves for on-camera work. No amount of talent can overcome lack of audition practice.

If you're not sure about how to stand, where to put your hands, how to hold your script, how to read from it if needed, or where to put your eyes, you're going to feel terrible and you are wasting other people's valuable time. If you're insecure, scared, or unsure about what you're doing on the mark, you are, by definition, disempowered.

If you lack personal power and true confidence, it's hard for you to win the room. Any discernable awkwardness makes it difficult for producers to hire you and for casting directors to call you back.

It's okay to be new and have no credits yet. Actors get hired for their first gig every day of the year. But only if they present themselves to their potential employers as a well-trained peer. How do you get to that place if you're new or have only done improv or theater? Audition training. It's a specific kind of acting training you need after you've had your core acting training. Los Angeles has the best on-camera audition teachers in the world.

We exist because most acting departments in theater schools and conservatories don't address auditioning at all, or if they do, not to industry standards. Definitely not enough to make actors competitive when they make a move to a major casting market.

When it comes to comedy, many people train at the well-known improv schools. That training will help you cultivate your comedic voice, but those venues don't address acting for the camera, cold reading, auditioning, or any career building skills *at all*.

Auditions for professional acting work shouldn't feel like a guess. They should feel like a well-thought out offer from the actor to the writers and producers. Ideally your auditions are executed with pride and certainty about how you think the part should be played given your deduction of the script. In other words, with training and practice that leads to confidence!

2) Commitment

An actor seems confident when they are completely committed to all their choices, characterizations, physicalizations, and the imagined environment they must create when auditioning. When an actor says a line they don't connect with or understand, it shows. When their space work is vague, it shows. If there's uncertainty about how to play the character, it shows.

Actors know they are being recorded when a camera is present, but they often fail to acknowledge that means the camera is *zooming in* on their performance in a pretty tight frame. Auditions are watched on video playback with actors in a close-up shot. There is nowhere to hide any potential lack of commitment on your end.

Watching an actor's video audition isn't that much different from watching TV or a movie. The **booking performance** seems just like the final shot, minus the set. Can you imagine watching your favorite show with the lead actors *guessing* if they're playing the part right? What if they had some physical comedy written into the scene and only *halfheartedly* invested in the actions? It would be hard to watch. Same with auditions. A winning audition isn't simply "better" than others that were not selected. It feels like watching the show.

Great auditioners are bold actors. That doesn't necessarily mean they are making *bigger choices* than other actors. It means, for the most part, that they are simply committing *fully* to *all* the elements the final performance will have *within the audition*.

This can make a lot of actors feel like they are doing too much or going too big. What's really happening is that your instincts are kicking in, flooding you with subconscious doubt. There's a little voice most of us have when auditioning that's yelling, "Hey! This is supposed to come off 'real,' but there's no people, furniture, or walls here! What the heck do I grab onto for support? How do I anchor myself in this space?"

Acting is pretending. No matter what, we are on a journey of make believe when we play a part. But it can feel awkward to pretend *everything* and auditions ask us to do that: pretend there is a set, pretend multiple actors are there speaking to us even though it's only one reader, pretend there are objects in our hands that are not there, etc.

So much imagination work is asked of actors while they are auditioning, that it commonly causes suppression of the joy of acting itself.

When we're not having fun, we're in a losing position. We seem uncommitted. It's extremely difficult to fully immerse ourselves in an invisible world we have to create within our mind's eye. And when we do, it sometimes causes us to drop the best acting we might have to offer. Our mental energy can get diverted to sustaining imagined things and we fall off our storytelling.

Further, we must commit to our comedic choices, plus the great homework and script analysis that will make our auditions athletic and competitive. In other words, what our character wants in the scene, their agenda, etc. This leads to stakes, which are often underplayed in auditions for all the reasons I've mentioned here.

Whether you are auditioning in a casting office or self-taping an audition, offer a solid, specific take born of great homework. Leave it at that. Don't second-guess yourself or think about what could have been in the car ride home. Commit to *yourself*.

Unless there is some reason you are trying *not* to, you are performing to the best of your abilities every time you perform.

You are as good as you are in every moment. Beating yourself up or wishing you had another chance does not make you better. In fact, that mindset can quickly make you worse. Class and practice are not just for initial learning. Smart actors continue to train after they begin working.

In order to book, and keep booking, we must commit to auditioning itself. We must learn to enjoy it on the whole as part of the process. If you can give your very best performance in an audition, acting anywhere else is easy!

3) Activation

Auditions don't feel great when you're catching up to them. I'm sure any actor who has already begun auditioning can relate to this. Part of great overall audition technique is total preparedness on the mark. Here's exactly what that means in day-to-day practice.

When casting brings you in to audition, they'll greet you and perhaps ask if you have any questions. Occasionally there is greater conversation to be had but often not. Either way, there is a transition from you being you to you being the character in the scene that happens very quickly. While this is obviously what will occur in an audition, actors are often taken aback at how fast it transpires.

It's important to have performance energy and your moment before immediately available. Actors only have a few seconds to sink into character along with their emotional state at the top of the scene. It takes training and practice to animate yourself internally and ground your body externally in the context of an audition.

There is a duality that you're trying to achieve on the mark that is very similar to any professional-level athlete who is about to begin; overall, you should be energized and relaxed. Those words may seem like they don't go together at a glance, but upon reflection, they certainly do.

They are the components of poise and indicators of experience. If a lawyer is defending me in court, I'd like them to be energized and relaxed. If I need an operation, I'd like the surgeon to be energized and relaxed. We need energy to maintain stamina throughout the scene and for our performance to be exciting to watch. We need relaxation for focus and to maintain our physical composure. Without it, our bodies might flail, shrug, and shuffle in the frame.

Auditioning tends to flatten actors out. That feeling of catching up happens mostly when actors are inexperienced auditioners. We can feel when we're not emotionally ignited from the beginning. We can tell when we're not really engaging the reader. It feels like we're talking *at* them, not *to* them. We can easily feel lost in the vacant space of a mark.

The worst part is, we can almost always feel that it's happening; we know we're a beat behind, but once we've begun, it's too late to do anything about it. We're screaming for a do-over in our heads, but more likely, we finish and we're out the door. The good news is that your audition probably wasn't as bad as it felt. The bad news is that it's probably only fine compared to the person who booked.

Learning to activate yourself and your choices on the mark in three seconds or less takes time and guidance. Actors don't automatically do that. It's not natural even within all the imagination work we incorporate into our acting. Our core training, stage training, or improv training doesn't prepare us for a moment specifically like that. In the real world, we need to have our best performance handy at the time of someone else's choosing. That doesn't mean you are rushed. It just means it's your responsibility to take care of yourself.

Activating ourselves without time or privacy can be difficult. Great performances don't come from the head, they come from the heart and the gut. We need to breathe and find our best voice in "3, 2, 1... action." Our vocal performance should come from our diaphragm, not our throat. It's easy for an actor to reduce their potential precisely when they should be showing off.

When I worked in casting, I saw countless actors who underestimated the pace and technical qualities that are specific to acting *only* in auditions. They thought it was just about scouting talent. Some actors learned and adjusted while others remained a beat behind not just once, but throughout their whole careers.

Gauging their auditions only by their talent and core training, they never understood or accepted that there were learnable aspects of auditioning that might have changed things considerably. Their talent couldn't overcome bad audition habits they probably didn't even know they had. It's exciting for me to teach actors how to be as funny, lively, and great when they are standing still on a mark as they ever have been playing freely on a stage.

4) Cold Reading Technique

This is a common term that, in practice, has multiple meanings that are similar, but not exactly the same. Generally it means using the script for performance with little time to prepare. When it comes to auditioning well, cold reading is an essential skill that has a more narrow definition. It means using your script comfortably and strategically when you audition.

Actors audition for TV and film roles in Los Angeles with their script in hand. While not required, it's universally preferred. In other markets, actors are told to come in memorized and be fully off-book. I teach all over the world, so I want everyone to feel heard when it comes to this topic. Wherever you are, and whatever the expectations from your casting community, I guarantee you that learning to cold read well is invaluable to you.

Knowing how to cold read makes auditioning far less stressful. Even if you're told to audition off-book and are great at memorizing, at some point in your career, you will have to refer to a script while offering your best performance.

If you auditioned from memory and booked a job, there may be rewrites that you don't see until you're on set. Maybe there are script changes right before you sit down for a table read. The truth is that throughout the process, actors don't always have the luxury of time to prepare for performance the way they like or to commit dialogue to memory. Not having more time with the material will never be an excuse to offer a subpar performance.

In practice, cold reading means using your script only if needed and still offering your best acting and strongest connection to the reader or other performers. In other words, the pages don't get in the way of anything. Casting can still see you, they can see your eyes, see your work, and the scene itself still feels alive.

When actors don't cold read well, they dip in and out of character and engagement as the scene progresses. It's jarring if they forget a line and have to find it in a script, and they aren't staying marked within the pages as they go along. In comedy, poor cold reading can easily wreck the timing, rhythm, and pace. In a professional casting session, no one will cue you in if you drop lines. Actors are expected to be prepared and familiar with the material but not necessarily fully memorized unless told otherwise.

I don't want anyone confused about the function of cold reading professionally. You will be told — and rightly so — not to be buried in your script.

If you use it too much, you seem unprepared and shy. Sometimes actors use their script even when they don't need to just because it's there! It's in your hands, you're standing on a mark, maybe a little anxious, nerves kick in, and it's natural for your eyes to read words off a page. It's almost like they get pulled to the paper like a magnet. Part of cold reading practice is simply holding the script and resisting the urge to look unless you need to in order to pick up your cue. You should use your script when auditioning only when needed and you should use it gracefully.

Cold reading while auditioning has a psychological component to it as well. A lot of actors feel like it's cheating, feel like it's in the way of their best performance, or react like they've done something wrong if they use their script in front of casting. All casting directors and producers want from actors are solid, professional auditions that showcase your abilities to their fullest. That may or may not include referring to your script.

When I speak to groups about this, at least one actor invariably puts up their hand to double-check what I'm saying. They likely heard some version of a story about a casting director screaming at their friend for using their script in an audition or workshop. Maybe true, maybe not. I'll tell you this: I've employed more than 200 different casting directors and associates to teach workshops at my studio. Many of them are good friends of mine.

The information in *The Comedy Code* is current and cultivated from my peers who cast the top shows and films seen around the world. That's not what typically happens. If anything, the actor got busted for using their script too much. In other words, they weren't cold reading well. Actor horror stories **never** translate into good advice for other actors.

I promise you from a lifetime of experience in this field, production is not thinking, "She used her script, so she's bad, he didn't use his script, so he's good." They will judge you on *how* you hold your script and *how* you use it, if you use it. And I further promise you that if you enter acting as a career, you *will* use a script while performing in front of people who can hire and fire you.

If you hold your script in a "death grip" you will seem tense and inexperienced. White knuckles aren't a good look on anyone in a casting office. If you use your script *after* you really needed it, that will cause problems. Actors who aren't practiced in solid cold reading skills tend to use their script reluctantly. They will use it but only after it's clear they've gone up on the lines. This has a halting effect on the performance. It's like everything stops for a millisecond and then resumes when the actor finds their next line.

The reason casting wants you to audition with script in hand is so you can thrive and *help yourself* if needed. Good cold reading means you know exactly where to look in your script if you feel your words starting to fade *before* you need them. Working actors have their cold reading skills down to a science so they can be proactive about sparing their audition experience any awkwardness.

I can ice cold read a script very close to the final version of the performance. Most working actors can. I don't say this to boast. I say this so that those of you who are new to acting know how to gauge what is expected of you. It's also a good reminder for those of you already working within the system. Few actors say that their cold reading skills couldn't be improved upon.

Actors want to book work. I understand and empathize with the disappointment when they don't. That said, frequently when I diagnose their auditioning skills — particularly their cold reading ability — it's often clear there is much work to be done on their end to become competitive.

There is a great deal of misinformation about when/how/if to use your script when auditioning. I hope this clears it up. Scripts are tools for actors to succeed and should be respectfully treated as such. They shouldn't be rolled, folded, or stuffed in pockets. You should bring them with you to professional auditions, use them gracefully, and only when necessary.

It's best if you integrate the script into your performance since you will be holding it. Whether they refer to it or not, actors who are great at cold reading make the script virtually disappear. They're comfortable with it in their hand and perhaps transform it seamlessly into various objects like a clipboard, magazine, or chart. When it's done being that object, it transforms right back into a script that feels like an extension of their body.

If you want to become a great cold reader, the simplest way to get there is to read out loud every day. Practice scooping up as many words as you can with your eyes, saying them outward and getting back into the script *before* you need to. Focus on keeping the energy and momentum as you go.

Use your thumb as a guide as you go down the page to stay marked in the area your eyes need to get to. Turn the pages *before* you get to the dialogue that's on the next page. Memorize your opening and closing lines so that you're anchored, and be as familiar as you can be with the rest of the dialogue. And if this applies to you, practice giving yourself permission to use the script any damn time you feel like it because you're not a child who's doing something naughty when you look! Use your script whenever you want, in front of whoever you want. Just use it well and wisely.

In other words, practice getting ahead and *staying* ahead of the moment you need the words that just popped out of your brain.

5) Imagination Work

Actors incorporate imagination work throughout the creative process to create characters or find their way into circumstances they have not personally experienced. For drama, that could mean portraying a serial killer (hopefully none of you are serial killers). For comedy, it could simply mean playing a spouse believably if you aren't yet married or a parent if you haven't had kids.

Personalization is usually the best foundation on which to build a performance, but when what's on the page is outside our frame of reference, we must ignite our imagination. That's a basic review of imagination work as applied to acting in general.

When it comes to auditioning, though, actors have to imagine a lot more than characteristics or labels that exist in the script. We have to imagine the environment in which the character exists while standing on a mark in an office or studio. We have to imagine objects that aren't there and use our imagination to speak to the reader as multiple people.

If that wasn't enough, we must also use our imaginations to compensate for spatial disparity. You may audition in a very small space like a trailer set up on a studio lot. But what if your character is making a speech in a high school auditorium? I have auditioned with the reader and camera up to 10 feet or so away and I've auditioned with a camera so close to my face I could barely overcome my sense of personal space violation. You won't know how the room is set up for you until you arrive. Whatever the parameters of the actual space, a solid audition includes the actor treating the space as if it were the size and scale of the character's environment.

That may mean you need to project, it may mean you need to scale your volume and emotions down to, in effect, bring the reader closer to you. When actors reach out into the space between themselves and the reader either physically or emotionally, it comes across as desperate and records poorly. Hands reaching out, palms facing up, shoulder shrugging, etc., are all ways our bodies react to having too much space around us. That's just the short list.

In an effort to connect and engage, actors will also collapse forward at the waist, bend their knees, or lean their whole body forward, starting with the top of their head. All these movements propel your body out of the proper framing and degrade your audition. It's hard for producers to watch actors on recorded playback who can't anchor themselves on a mark.

When you work on a set, you'll be blocked on a mark and expected to act in a camera-friendly frame without moving about or gesturing through your performance. It's fair for producers to think you won't be able to still yourself on a set if you can't ground yourself within an audition. I've mentioned this elsewhere within this book, but it bears repeating — especially when it comes to comedy — actors are overtraining themselves to work on stage and undertraining themselves to audition well and work on camera. They're different mediums with vastly different parameters for success.

Imagining your character's physical world creates a better audition for you and increases your chances of working. Quite literally think of how your scene will look once it's been shot and aired. Where is your character standing or sitting? How far away are other characters in the scene? How open or cramped is the environment?

When you work out these details through your imagination, you are creating a fourth wall (invisible wall or conceptual barrier) for yourself. This fourth wall serves to keep you grounded and *actually make you feel safer* when you are placed on a mark. Your body believes what you tell it if you imagine it clearly. If you believe there are walls around you, there is furniture in front of you, and the reader is three feet closer to you, your body will organically settle down and find the scaling you need for a successful audition.

That terrible feeling of self-consciousness because you're standing on a mark with a camera pointed at your face will go away. If you're auditioning in a larger space, you won't feel like you're standing in the middle of nowhere. Watching the playback of your audition will feel refreshing for producers.

When an actor is able to build out the scene in their mind's eye, it can feel similar to watching the final product. Auditions are more professional and commanding when the actor sees the details of their surroundings in their imagination as clearly as they would on set.

6) Micro-blocking for the Camera

Once you've established the space for your audition and contained yourself within an imagined environment, the next step is to block any specific actions or movements. Mapping out the geography of the scene in advance will help your audition tremendously. I call it micro-blocking because it's very much like a scaled-down version of blocking for the stage. Instead of blocking a horizontal, three-dimensional plane, you're blocking a two-dimensional, vertical plane. You're blocking the frame in which the camera sees you.

Do you enter the frame or exit? It helps to work that out in advance. Do you have any physical actions? Have you thought through whether they will appear in your frame? Generally, auditions are shot from chest to the top of the actor's head; a bust shot. Actors unfamiliar with audition technique might just assume the camera will capture all their actions or that casting will follow them with the camera. Usually not.

If big actions are written into the scene, casting will automatically widen the frame because they know what's coming. You won't have to ask (in fact, you shouldn't ask). Otherwise you're in a fairly tight frame. Producers want to clearly see you and see your performance.

Next you should know where your eyes will land throughout the scene. There is always a reader, maybe another person in the room and the camera. For professional auditions you don't look into the camera unless specifically instructed to do so. Depending on the scene, you may need to indicate multiple people or reference the location of objects or areas. You do this with your eyes.

It's essential that you don't dart your eyes around the frame when you audition or work on camera. Busy eyes are distracting, and it reads on playback as if the actor is performing to the air, not the reader. Further, you should never roll your eyes on camera. It looks terrible, it's indicative, it disengages you from the scene, and for the most part, it's not done by working actors.

Finding stillness when you're performing for the camera can feel paralyzing to some. It's easy for actors to develop a running monologue of what *not* to do when auditioning. That can be stifling. I guide my students toward what *to do* and remind them of it consistently until they are working at professional standards. (A lot of them will be chuckling at that last sentence. I remind them... often.)

It can take time to cement the tenets of acting for the camera, but it's well worth the effort. When you are able to control your body as an instrument while performing, your emotions, intentions, and characterization are magnified and focused. That's when you are viable, even a star. It's not about freezing your movement, it's about channeling your energy so it comes out through your eyes and voice. When your energy is conducted properly, your body tends to not *want* to move in ways the camera dislikes.

It's important that actors who want to work in TV and film conquer the impulse or habit to move vaguely or with static in the frame. The camera blows up and exaggerates even minor movements. If your eyes are roving around the frame it looks much more like you're ranting to yourself out loud than talking to someone. It can look absurd. Even seasoned actors will come across as green (new) if they don't have a comfortable relationship with acting for the camera.

Understanding how the lens captures your performance is essential for when you ultimately book work. Hot sets are intense, fast-moving environments, and you want to be prepared when opportunity comes your way. Blocking your movements before you step in front of the camera, even small movements, *even your eye movement,* can make the difference between you becoming a bookable actor or not.

7) Vocal Targeting

Without realizing they're even doing it, actors tend to fill the whole room with their voice even if they're not speaking loudly. Their vocal performance spreads across the space they're in, which produces a theatrical feel to the audition. To be clear, I'm not talking about choices that are too big or projecting too much volume. I'm talking about vocal engagement and connection. Your vocal performance needs a target or landing point. When you're auditioning, it should be the reader.

I'm making the distinction between talking *to* someone and talking *at* them, which comes across as broad (bad) acting, regardless of volume. If your voice spreads evenly across the room at any volume, it's clear that you aren't breathing or speaking properly. You're not engaging your diaphragm and bringing your intentions to the reader. This makes you appear inexperienced to casting and producers whether that is the case or not.

A lot of actors haven't had any voice training at all, and it shows. Some have had a little bit but still need frequent reminding whether they are "on voice" or not. Ideally, actors speak with their diaphragm engaged and breathe through their dialogue. In reality, without breath and voice training, many actors actually *hold their breath* on the mark, breathe improperly, and misplace their voice in their throat, head, or mask.

When you speak from your diaphragm, it's like engaging your abs or your core while talking. When you do that, your words are generated from your belly, flow through your torso (gut and heart) on your breath, and then articulate from your mouth. All kinds of great things happen when you're speaking that way!

Primarily, your voice has more resonance and sex appeal. Who doesn't want that? You become more authentic and trustworthy. You appear more authoritative and substantial; very important for actors who want to be believed. Your performance becomes more athletic and you start to "pop" without trying or pushing. Your presence is magnified. Overall, you seem more like a person of integrity. You suddenly seem significant.

When those things happen for you, they also happen for your character. You will only be able to target your voice the way I've referred to, if you know how to control it. Even just a basic understanding of where your diaphragm is located will help. Once your speech is properly supported, you can then take the next step toward directing it. You can isolate a single person within a crowd and put your words right on them and no one else.

If this concept seems abstract, I'll offer a universal example to which most of you can relate. Did you ever get in trouble with your mom or dad in public? If you ever got scolded in front of other people, you know exactly what I'm talking about. Could anyone around hear what your parent was saying? Yes. Was anyone confused about *exactly* who they were talking to? No. You were their vocal target in that moment. Your mom or dad could have distributed their voice more evenly based on whoever else was around. However, they instinctively did not.

Their words pierced you like an arrow, and they probably didn't even have vocal training. Were you embarrassed for getting chastised in front of strangers? If so, then bullseye! Like a heat-seeking missile, an activated voice impulsively singled one person out of a crowd and changed how they felt in an instant. Just what you should do when you're acting.

We were born with smart, beautiful voices. They're ours to lose. So, speak well. It's life-changing. Finding your voice is not an extra chore for actors to nail down. To me, it's the best part of being an actor. My size, shape, and age are all things I have no control over. They are what they are. But I can play with my voice.

I can merely tell you something or I can speak a word painting. Once I learned to speak from my center, I started living in my center. That's synonymous with living in your personal truth. When I speak, people listen. I'm taken seriously in any environment. That's a big deal for a kid who recognized people by their shoes until he was in high school. It doesn't mean I always get what I want. But I have earned a lifetime of respect and trust from my students and peers. I doubt that would have happened if I held my breath while I was talking to them.

I'm getting personal here because I know how important it is to present ourselves to the world boldly. Not only do actors endeavor to speak for a living, we can expect an unusual amount of attention if we gain success. Speaking well versus poorly makes a considerable difference in regard to your bookability and how seriously people take you upon meeting you.

We are all born speaking from our diaphragm and breathing properly. The confines of life, how we are raised, what our school experience was like, the permission we were given to speak freely, or lack thereof growing up, all play a part in diminishing our strongest voice. Stress takes away our strongest voice.

Your vocal mechanism is made up of a series of muscles. Your diaphragm is a muscle. Like any other muscles in your body, they grow stronger when exercised properly. Conversely, they grow weaker with misuse and can even become damaged. Since I speak for a living, I have to use my voice properly or it will be gone before the weekend. Professional singers will tell you the same thing.

I won't go further in depth on the specifics of voice training. In another era, actors wouldn't even get signed by an agent unless they had significant voice training from a notable institution or well-known instructor. We don't live in that time anymore, so I integrate guidance on how to better utilize vocal power when I teach. If you have voice training, great! Bring it to the party! If not, consider this section and see how you might strengthen your vocal technique. I can always help you speak better while teaching other aspects of the craft.

8) Scaling Your Audition

Now that you know how to land your vocal punches, so to speak, let's factor in scaling and projection. This includes volume but isn't limited to volume. Scaling your auditions properly includes factoring in the genre, tone, and personality of the project.

If you're auditioning for an existing TV show, it's easy to learn the tone if you don't already know it. We live in a world where we can look up anything. Episodes or even trailers for shows can be found easily online.

For pilots or films, you can still find guidelines from indicators like genre, what the breakdowns say, and looking up the prior works of the writers and producers. It's easy to research who is behind a new project and assess their tone and sensibility. In most cases, it doesn't vary wildly from one project to another.

There is likely to be a throughline in the sensibility of their body of work. For example, Chuck Lorre's sitcoms have an identifiable sensibility (*Dharma & Greg*, *Two and a Half Men*, *The Big Bang Theory*, *Mom*, etc.) Michael Schur created *Parks and Recreation*, *Brooklyn Nine-Nine*, and *The Good Place*, which all make sense together. Tina Fey created *30 Rock* and *Unbreakable Kimmy Schmidt*. Her future productions will invariably include her trade-mark brand of witty, sketchy-in-a-good-way, subversive humor.

Knowing your show creators will help you scale your performance accurately. This is also where experience controlling your voice comes in handy. Identify whether the show is single-camera or multi-camera; the scripts for single-camera sitcoms are single-spaced, multi-camera sitcoms are double-spaced. An audition for a multi-cam sitcom will require more projection than most other auditions. Actors on set will be performing in front of a live studio audience. As noted elsewhere in this book, multi-cam sitcoms are theater! It makes sense to scale your multi-cam auditions with that in mind. You'll be working in front of an audience.

A drama or single-cam comedy or dramedy will likely be scaled more intimately. But that's not true 100 percent of the time. Many single-camera comedy writers love larger-than-life characters. If you think of *The Office* when you think of single-camera comedies, I understand. However, most shows aren't quite that dry and underplayed. *The Office* debuted in 2005, which is a while ago now. Television has changed considerably since.

I suggest studying the scaling of the myriad other single-cam comedies shown across a wide variety of platforms. Here's a list of suggestions: *Veep*, *Silicon Valley*, *The Marvelous Mrs. Maisel*, *Russian Doll*, *Schitt's Creek*, *The Goldbergs*, *Black-ish*, *Superstore*, *GLOW*, *Grace and Frankie*, *Jane the Virgin*, *The Good Place*, etc.

A lot of the performances on these shows are more charismatic, emboldened, and outright frenetic than most people think. Some of the premises of these shows are totally outrageous. Some are absurdist comedies, others are dark comedies.

It's important to consider then that the same guest role on each of these shows might be played differently. For example, any of these series might feature a guest part of a relative to one of the lead characters the audience hasn't met before. Even if the breakdown was *exactly* the same, I'd imagine a different *scaling* when it comes to auditioning for each different show.

Let's explore by writing an imaginary breakdown:

Abby: Late 30s, wild child. Lives in a van and drives across country seeking adventures. She is (lead of show's) cousin. They were close growing up, but Abby now only shows up occasionally and only when she wants something. She's fun but unpredictable.

So yes, you'd want to first develop the character for yourself and break down the scenes. But when I apply the same breakdown to different shows (a guest star breakdown might look very similar on completely different shows), I see right away that my audition of Abby would not be the same for *Russian Doll* versus *Superstore*.

Given the *exact same words* to describe Abby, I'd make her more cryptic for *Russian Doll* and the *scaling* in the audition would be more intense and intimate. *Russian Doll* is a dark comedy that addresses issues of mental illness and existentialism in a direct way. Whatever the dialogue, I'd know Abby was probably showing up with complicated family history in tow. The show is dark therefore the character would likely need a layer of darkness. She'd be something like Jessa Johansson (Jemima Kirke) on *Girls*.

My audition for *Superstore* would be much brighter. I'd lean into the comedy more. Abby would also show up here with complicated family history. Regardless of the show's tone, that's why any writer would introduce a flighty family member later into a series. But my *scaling* would be much different from *Russian Doll*. Abby on *Superstore* would *literally speak louder and faster*. The overall pacing of the dialogue would be tighter; no pauses or beats. She'd be crisp and direct within her eccentricity. She'd have worldliness without secretive undertones. She'd be something like Jenna Maroney (Jane Krakowski) on *30 Rock*.

So... the exact same breakdown gave me a Jessa and a Jenna. Again, *Russian Doll* and *Superstore* are both single-camera comedies. Why such an enormous difference? Tone and scaling. Both of which need to be addressed before you step on the mark to audition. Hopefully this example illustrates how important it is to know the producers you're auditioning for and what the material they're writing is like.

This is also the best way to highlight that you are ultimately auditioning for producers. Casting directors are an essential part of production and a conduit to working regularly. You need relationships with them built on trust that comes from consistent good work. They might also give you guidance and invaluable information during the casting process. They are advocates for the show and its production team. In the end, however, producers make the final decision on who gets cast. They want to know you get their show. If it doesn't seem like you do, why on earth would they hire you?

9) Physicalization

A lot of actors ask about physical actions and space work when auditioning. I've referenced physicality earlier, but I think it's important to elaborate here. All actors need to understand there are no universal rules that you can apply to every circumstance you will encounter. Nothing is written down as policy. However, there are practical guidelines that will always have to be metered with common sense.

There are many myths about what is acceptable to casting and what is not. These notions are born out of fear and not at all helpful to actors seriously working on a career. Sure, maybe one casting director from another era declared, "No space work in my office, ever!" I would also bet $10 million that actors did space work in auditions in his office before and after that proclamation and were moved through to producers and brought into that office again.

It's fair to want to know how things work, but don't reduce yourself to the point of powerlessness by thinking that miming a bit of physical action in an audition will make someone mad at you. Producers want to hire talent who feel like stars, even for smaller roles. When they watch auditions, they'd like to see scenes played as much like they would be played in the final version that is shot on camera for broadcast. Sometimes you just stand or sit, sometimes that includes miming and space work.

Yet physical actions are not all equally important. A good rule of thumb is to gauge whether the scene *makes sense* to watch if you don't offer the action. With sitcoms, you should also gauge whether the comedy written into the scene relies on physical-ization. Is the scene still *funny* without the action?

Don't get caught up on basic actions the writer has included for general continuity and flow, like whether your character sits down in the middle of the scene. If that's the only physical action, ignore it. Casting will either have you stand or sit all the way through the audition. Sometimes they'll let you decide whether to sit or stand. What is never, ever, *ever* important is that you sit down when that action comes up in the script. You're not doing a play.

Your audition is not theater or even a piece of entertainment. It's a job interview so producers can see if you have translated the **character** and **story** they wrote accurately. Further they want to see if you understand the **tone** of their show and can work well **on camera**. No one gets hired for a television or film role because they pretended to stir cake batter well in an audition. Likewise, no one got dismissed out of hand if they were the right match on all counts for the part and didn't stir the cake batter well or *at all*.

Here are words on which to hang your hat: Live in the scene. Physicalize as necessary and edit your space work and actions to the bare minimum. If you are miming an action, commit to it totally. While you may need to incorporate physical actions, auditions for TV and film are never about physical actions. They are about characters and their relationships. Don't forget that just because you're pretending to deal with an object that's not really there.

I have coached people for countless auditions at this point in my career. Many of them because the actor needed guidance on what to do physically regarding actions. Here are a couple of examples so you can develop your own sense of what is important and what is not.

One was a big guest star role for a character who was competing with the lead of the show in a marathon. There was a lot of dialogue, much of it referred to the marathon, and all the scenes were to be shot outside while the two guys were running alongside each other.

Did I advise the actor to lightly jog in the audition? You betcha. The conversation about competitive running seemed bizarre if the actor was just standing there. But notice I said *lightly* jogging. If he jogged as hard as the character would be running in the scene, it would be distracting. This is a great example. A producer needs to know the actor auditioning is in shape and can run. But he's not going to get hired for running as hard in place as he would be running while shooting the scene. Producers need to see the history between these guys. It made sense to suggest the marathon, but not make the whole audition about running the race.

Another example is a scene where a couple (both leading roles) is washing their dog that was sprayed by a skunk. The smell is horrible. They're both soaking wet, kneeling over the tub. They talk about getting the smell off the dog with tomato juice, but other important aspects of their relationship come up. Serious ones. Like the fact that he doesn't think what she does for living is all that important. Sounds sobering, and it was, but it was also an audition for a sitcom, not a drama. The scene neither made sense, nor was funny to watch if the actors didn't kneel and realize the dog. At times they spoke to the dog. It had to have a presence, or the scene just made no visual sense.

Also, the ridiculousness of the skunk-sprayed dog made the conversation more comedic. The actors going in for these lead roles were not in a contest to see who could pretend to wash a dog the best. They needed to show their comedic chops and that they understood the personalities of this particular husband and wife.

More important than the physical action, they needed to tell the producers they could fight funny and land just the right tone for this particular show. Producers are thinking, "Do these actors seem like they understand marriage, and do they get why this couple stays together even though they argue like teenage siblings?" Those qualities are what those actors needed to highlight. After that, it then made the most sense to offer a very edited and committed physicalization of the dog in the bathtub.

Let's finish by contrasting mediums. For an improv scene on stage, you'd want to wash the dog *in a funny way;* exaggerate the washing and rinsing, deal with the dog as if it's unruly, get splattered when the dog shakes the water off its coat, etc. For an on-camera audition, you'd wash the dog in the *simplest, most realistic, least distracting way to your performance.* Of course a different on-camera scene might have you wrestling with a dog in a bathtub. *But that would be a different scene!*

I hope common sense would lead you to the difference between the two. If you were alone in the bathroom with the dog and the dog was going nuts, of course your actions would be different. But if you're talking to your spouse about her career choice, I'd hope you wouldn't go overboard washing the dog. The dog is not the point. Television auditions are not theater and watching them shouldn't feel like watching stage work.

Some of you might be thinking, "But I've been asked to pretend to pitch a tent, jump in a lake, and run through an obstacle course in auditions. The *whole audition* was about space work and physical actions!" Sure. Me, too. Those were probably either commercial auditions, non-union auditions, or both. Auditions for SAG-AFTRA TV and film projects all adhere to the guidelines I've laid out in this section. Fair enough if you want a second pair of eyes on what you're doing so that you're sure it looks appropriate. Come and get coached! But what I've detailed in this section will guarantee you meet the industry's standards across the board.

10) Resolve

Finally, your auditions should end well. All auditions stop. Not all of them feel resolved. Sometimes actors fade out by the end of the scene, they lose their stamina or, for some undefined reason, they throw the last words away or mumble them under their breath. Be careful that your energy and volume don't bottom out once the scene has arced.

The end of your audition is arguably the most important moment. It's at least as important as your opening. Either way, it's the last producers are seeing of you. Make it count.

You need to continue to live through the last moment of the scene in character. Casting regularly lingers a second or two after the last line of dialogue is spoken to capture your character's last moment on camera. It's really the job of the actor to conclude the audition, not the casting director!

Yes, their finger is on the stop button, but generally they're offering you an opportunity in the final second or two to continue thinking, feeling, and exit if necessary. Perhaps for a sitcom, you might add a tagline. If you let the camera catch you dropping out of character, it's quite uncomfortable. It's equally disconcerting when actors freeze and hold at the end of an audition.

Auditions generally end in one of two ways: either your character has the last line, or the other character has the last line. It's a bit easier to end well when you have the last line. It's literally the last line of the scene. Simply think through where your character is headed in the next moment. Are they staying? Leaving? Giving the other character a look? Totally over the whole situation? Whatever the case, live that truth through and keep thinking in character.

If the other character has the last line, I advise my students to write themselves a final line and simply *think* it in response. The line may be funny or not. That's not the point. It's just the next logical thing your character would say if they had the chance. This will help ensure you continue thinking in character. It's a small detail, but it makes an enormous difference on playback. It's the difference between your character coming across as authentic or sketchy. It's the difference between real acting and indicating the moment. You can throw off the attitude of, "Well, eff you, buddy!" Or you can think that thought authentically as you stare down the reader.

If you're offering the *idea* of "Eff you!" I can almost guarantee you will A) roll your eyes; B) shrug your shoulders; C) nod or bob your head in a goofy way; D) play the moment for comedy, not truth; E) not know what to do with yourself the very next moment if the casting director doesn't call cut; or F) all of the above. The term for indicating the idea of a thought or emotion while acting is "attitudinizing." It means you're adopting an attitude just for effect. It's showing, not living.

Sketchy.

If you're emotionally dialed in and *thinking*, "Eff you!" in character, *feeling* what the words imply and *landing* that thought in the reader's eyes, you will resolve your audition with impact and make fans out of casting directors and producers. If they keep rolling for another second or two your instincts will organically take care of you because your body is engaged in real thought and genuine emotion. You will have remained grounded and engaged through the very last moment of your audition.

Great on-camera acting. Nailed it!

"Honesty isn't enough for me. That becomes very boring. If you can convince people what you're doing is real and it's also bigger than life - that's exciting."

- Gene Hackman

9

What's "Too Big" for Comedy?

M any actors auditioning for comedy have a fear of going "too big." The result very often is an audition that is lackluster and not dynamic enough to make an impression. By and large, comedy casting offices are not inundated with actors chewing up the scenery and doing way too much. If anything, it's the opposite; actors aren't making specific and bold enough choices to muscle out the competition.

Understandably, actors want a way to gauge whether they are doing too much, too little, or just enough. There is an answer, but it's not one-size-fits-all. Several factors overlap to create the target you're looking to hit: The tone of the show, whether it's a single-camera or multi-camera sitcom, the character you're portraying, and your personal, individual level of training and experience. All those elements factor into what *your* audition should be, versus anyone else's.

I've covered the differences between single-camera and multi-camera sitcoms. For both I've observed, living in Hollywood my whole adult life and working in casting for part of it, that for either format, actors who book are memorable and remarkable, not just competent. Let's dig a little deeper into what exactly that means.

I'll elaborate on a point I made earlier that seems obvious but is often overlooked. Not all actors have the same training and ability to sustain heightened characters. You can be extremely talented, but if you haven't *practiced and been given feedback* on portraying characters who have heightened, flamboyant or intense personalities, you are less likely to book that type of role.

Characters can range from totally organic to outrageously theatrical within either kind of sitcom. The question therefore is not, "What role were you born to play?" It's "What roles are you *trained* to play and how *comfortable* are you playing them long term?" Knowing the basic tenets of acting is only step one to becoming a bookable actor. The next level up is refining your wheelhouse to precision.

Actors can easily come across as broad if they are trying to portray a character that is written beyond their skill set and/or outside of their comfort zone. Ironically, underplaying the potential of a lead role can produce a broad performance. In daily practice, casting directors mostly encounter broad acting that is born of uncertainty, doubt, and lack of total commitment, not overblown choices. Actors who go into casting offices and over-perform with no believability in their work do exist, but they are few and far between. It's far more awkward and uncomfortable to witness an actor who's unsure of their choices than it is to watch a committed actor take a big swing, even if they miss.

We all start with basic training, but quite simply, some of us continue to grow and master our skills while others do not.

Here's an analogy: A chef doesn't open a restaurant after they've just conquered the basics of cooking. They grow their abilities and more likely than not, hone in on crafting certain kinds of cuisine within the broader category of "food." When they do open a restaurant, there's one question asked and one question only. The bank will ask it in order to provide a loan; financing the prospect depends on the answer. Friends and family will ask this question. Customers will ask it.

Not only will the chef have the answer, the chef will be *proud* of the answer. The question is, of course, "What *kind* of restaurant?" Inherent talent and years of training get distilled into a brand that is identifiable. The brand can still have range, but it definitely isn't, "I'll cook whatever ya want!" At a glance, we can process what we're getting when we take a seat at that chef's table. There is a menu and options are honed and refined. There is a balance of what the chef enjoys making most and what customers in the marketplace want.

"Good food" is too broad a construct to succeed in a saturated culinary marketplace. Same with "good actor." People want to know what *type* of thing they're getting when they are exploring choices. This is true in all regards. We think of safety and gas mileage when buying a car, but those are the basics and the standards regulated by law. Does the color, shape, size, brand, and interior design of a car matter to you? Probably.

Overall professional quality may be an achievement for the artisan, but for the customer, it's a given. I'm pretty sure no one in the history of being asked "Where do you want to go for dinner tonight?" answered, "Anywhere is fine as long as the food is cooked competently." We are not impressed that someone who opened a restaurant is a great cook. It's expected of all restaurants. We relate to restaurants in terms of type, style, decor, cost, and whether they are established or new. Do they have existing reviews to which we can refer?

The same is true for how the entertainment industry considers actors. That is how casting works, and this is how actors should think. Being professionally trained and not needing any guidance when auditioning or working on sets is a given. Beyond that, actors must identify in whatever way is comfortable for them what specific needs they serve within casting.

Actors are born with some degree of natural talent and inherent ability. The critical question becomes, how do you insert yourself into a system already in motion and stand out within it? Largely the answer to that question is identifying your wheelhouse and training to become the best *whatever-that-is* that casting will meet that day. Understand what you do best within the broader category of good acting and maximize all potential outcomes of those attributes. When you think, practice, and work this way, the question of whether you are too big or not will evaporate.

Additionally, the best actors in comedy are using their entire bodies as instruments and have delicate control over every movement they make on camera. Across the board, these actors have solid voice and speech training and are perhaps incredible singers, maybe dancers. They understand that how a performance sounds is every bit as important as the emotional and intentional choices they make. They know how to scale their volume, energy, and characterizations to match the quality of a production with little to no instruction or feedback.

As stated, what constitutes broad acting in common practice is not overacting or chewing the scenery. It's too much physical movement on camera while the actor's internal choices are too safe and expected. Darting your eyes around the frame, talking with your hands, moving your head while speaking, blinking too much, raising your eyebrows on camera, and failing to breathe properly are the components of broad acting. Indicating is broad acting; for example, putting your hand on your chest when your character refers to themselves in first person is broad.

Consider the work of Tituss Burgess as Titus Andromedon on *Unbreakable Kimmy Schmidt*, T. J. Miller as Erlich Bachman on *Silicon Valley*, Max Greenfield as Schmidt on *New Girl*, Wendi McLendon-Covey as Beverly Goldberg on *The Goldbergs*, or Jane

Krakowski as Jenna Maroney on *30 Rock*. These are all actors working on single-camera sitcoms who make enormous character and emotional choices while their bodies support them as reliant and unflappable frames.

While some people find multi-camera shows inherently broad, that's usually the wrong word. It's more accurate to say that multi-cams include a theatrical component that no other genre of scripted series on television has. The term "broad," when applied to acting, implies that the performance is either generalized or lacking substance over style.

More simply, it's used to describe bad acting. Most people think of an actor being too broad because they are too loud or somehow too much. For whatever reason, some folks project that description to all multi-cam sitcoms. Yet it simply cannot be the case that every performance on every single multi-camera sitcom in television history is unbelievable and lacking substance. Some of the best and most successful actors in the world are sitcoms actors.

When it comes to taste, we can each like and dislike whatever we want. However, I do want to set the record straight on multi-cams specifically, which can sometimes get a bum rap. A bad performance can turn up anywhere. Broad doesn't mean loud, it means the actor is offering an outline of a character; a caricature. A broad performance can occur just as easily on a simmering procedural drama or moody feature film about young vampires in love.

Megan Mullally portraying Karen Walker on *Will & Grace* and Michael Richards portraying Cosmo Kramer on *Seinfeld* come to mind as cases in point. They are incredible actors who maximized their *personal* skills as well as their *character's* depth and potential. There's just no intelligent, respectable way to assess them as bad actors offering broad performances.

Were they theatrical? Yes. **As much as they could get away with!** They performed their television shows in front of a live audience. The question is, why *wouldn't* they be theatrical? What they offered was winning because they spoke the absolute truth from their character's point of view with every word. They each rested comfortably within the skin of an intricately crafted character. Both maintained complete commitment to every moment they spent living their respective character's life. As examples of so many other outstanding comedic performers, they are in fact, brave actors who elevated beloved shows. Broad has nothing to do with it. Broad is not the droid you're looking for.

Actors on multi-camera shows have to narrate the story crafted by the writers and be honest in every word they speak and action they take. In addition, they must also account and hold for audience laughter. That, combined with performing in a large space, means the theatrical nature I outlined lands largely on scaling and vocal performance. Great sitcom actors, more often than not, have great voices and are well-trained on how to use them. In some cases, weaponize them. A lot of musical theater actors thrive on multi-cam sitcoms.

Here's a comparison for consideration: Will Arnett is amazing as Gob Bluth on *Arrested Development*, a single-camera comedy, as is Patricia Heaton portraying Debra Barone on *Everybody Loves Raymond*, a multi-cam. If pushed to say which performance was "bigger," I'd say Arnett's. In reality though, I wouldn't call either big. It's a meaningless term that keeps actors from maximizing their own potential. The fear of "going too big" is little more than an excuse actors make in order to feel safe and limit expectations of a great performance by others. Thank goodness Jane Lynch wasn't afraid of "doing too much" when she and the writers of *Glee* created Sue Sylvester. I'm equally glad Rainn Wilson didn't fear going "too big" when depicting Dwight Schrute on *The Office*.

I could cite dozens of other examples, but the point is, every show of either format has its own personality, tone, and a mix of characters that are grounded and heightened. Actors on hit comedies are among the highest paid actors in the world. If you want those jobs, I cannot stress how important it is to train yourself properly for them and then be fearless showing off your skills. Comedy is inherently unsafe. Your odds of booking are better when you explore the edges. The middle of the road is the surest place to get run over.

So, what's too big for comedy? Not necessarily volume and certainly not bold, definitive choices. Surprisingly to most, it's a collection of very small things that tell producers you don't have enough training to realistically book the work for which you're auditioning. It's unmotivated movement, eye rolling, sighing, un-aware smiling, and incomplete commitment to dialogue and stakes. If you're not auditioning with certainty, clarity, confidence, and crisp on-camera skills, you can quite easily come across as "too big" by offering the performance *way too little* and playing it *way too safe*.

PART 4

BREAK DOWN SCRIPTS SO WELL YOU GET HIRED

"The more you do your homework, the more free you are to be intuitive. But you've got to put the work in."

— Edward Norton

10

iCAMERA Intro

iCAMERA is my simple, effective, and powerful method of executing professional-level script analysis quickly and consistently. It's a clear rundown of the most essential actor homework you want to nail down before stepping in front of the camera. I teach to the standards of Hollywood. That means not only do I graduate funny, solid actors; I create efficient and skillful actors who book work and make positive, lasting impressions within the industry.

Actors are booked for their ability to do three things well:

1. Deduce essential elements of story and character from sides that are absolute and not subjective; the **facts** of the scene.

2. Add their unique interpretation of how to best express those elements, which is subjective.

3. Execute their work with total confidence and clarity in regard to what constitutes both a solid on-camera performance and a professional in-person or self-taped audition.

The turnaround time to produce great auditions for television and film is rigorous at best, punishing at worst. In order to realistically book work, actors have to know how to look at sides and make sense of them by the very next day, sometimes the same day. It doesn't matter whether it's a couple of lines or nearly half the script.

Improv, sketch, and theater training are a great foundation for comedic performers, but it's only the starting point of working on sets and auditioning well. Especially since callbacks are virtually nonexistent in Hollywood and actors are tasked with self-submitting their auditions more and more often.

You either know what a great audition is, or you don't. Everything in between is a just a guess you can't afford to take. Working actors are definitely not guessing. They have the knowledge I lay out in this book. Audition technique and script analysis skills have never been more important to an actor than they are today. This truth will only increase moving into the future.

For the most part, agents and managers email sides to actors in the evening with appointment times for the next day. Of course there are exceptions, but in order to be competitive, actors must be prepared to crush their auditions without much time to prepare. Aside from teaching group classes, I coach actors privately. Sometimes for guest or recurring parts but most often for series regular roles. I have prepped hundreds of actors on upwards of 12 pages to play a lead in a sitcom with less than 24 hours' notice for us both.

Sure, it can feel pressured, but honestly not so much when you know what you're doing and that you possess a skill set that works consistently. It helps on a deep level to know for sure that you're meeting the writer on their terms and fully understand the heart, soul, and essence of their characters, not just "taking a swipe" at the role.

Script analysis breaks down into two columns: deduction and interpretation. Think of deduction as assessing the facts of the scene. The facts are not only the character's names, jobs, location, role in the family, etc. The facts of the scene also include personality type, the story of the scene, and even what the character wants. Actors often think the latter elements are "up for grabs" and they're not. Facts don't change. The story of a show doesn't change from actor to actor as they audition. Neither does a character's scene objective. You can be plain wrong about what a character wants, though.

Think of it this way: If 10 different people read a book, the book still tells the same story. Different people may *feel* differently about it. The book may speak to each person differently. Yet *The Great Gatsby* will always be a story about Jay Gatsby and his obsession for Daisy Buchanan set against a backdrop of excess in the Roaring 20s. It will always be a cautionary tale of the American dream taken too far. If you read the book and don't deduce some version of that summary upon analysis, you've missed the mark. Similarly, when you read a script or a scene, there is a story the writer is telling that is unchangeable.

When I worked as a casting director, I saw how often actors were dead wrong from the very beginning about what the character even wanted in a scene. Too many auditions were awkward to watch because the actor simply didn't have script analysis skills appropriate for television and film or audition technique training. They thought for some reason they could step right off a stage and onto a mark without training their abilities for the camera. It was like watching a train crashing in slow motion.

Ten different guys might audition with 10 different variations of what the same character wants. Yes, each actor should make his own contribution to the role, but no, there shouldn't be 10 different ideas of what the character is working toward.

Casting doesn't merely involve finding a good, or even the best, actor for the part. Part of what casting directors and producers are gauging when they hire actors is their ability to deduce what's in the script accurately. Bringing the character and story to life fully with an exciting interpretation is the *next* step. The first step is syncing up with the writer.

Working actors understand that interpretation intersects deduction. How you might get something to change and how you feel about what is happening to your character is totally open to interpretation. How *you* portray a cynical character compared to another actor is open to interpretation. Whether the character is a Cynic or another archetype altogether is *not* open to interpretation. That would fall under deduction.

Ideally, what a character is like from the page is something everyone sees the same way. We need to deduce or conclude that from given information (the breakdown, the dialogue, what the character says they are like). The same can be said for assessing what a character wants in a scene.

The deduction (the "what" of a scene) should be universal. The interpretation (the "how" of a scene) is where the art of acting is actually applied, and choices can vary.

Since I developed my writing skills prior to my acting skills, I have always looked at scripts through the lens of the writer. I think that is what makes my voice as a teacher distinct from other acting coaches. All my guidance and direction on how to maximize the potential of a character or scene (or both) comes from inside the scene and nowhere else.

I don't create backstory that may clash with the writer's biography of a character. Far too often actors suggest options that have no support from within the pages.

A common example is a scene that features a male and female friendship. A lot of actors will assume or add an element of romance in the subtext. There's nothing wrong with chemistry, but if the words and actions aren't there for support, you can't just make assumptions. Maybe the pair falls in love, maybe they don't. Maybe they do years down the road. If two characters are attracted to each other romantically and that's the story the writer wants to tell *right now*, it's highly likely they will say so out loud or simply kiss by the end of a scene. Simple.

Additionally, there is not a lot of subtext in television or film. It's extremely literal for the most part. That may come as a big surprise to many and it gets a reaction whenever I say it. The definition of subtext in regard to acting amounts to *hidden* meaning. Comedy, in particular, works when *nothing* is hidden. All cards on the table. The characters navigate one another with their ids exposed. More often than not, The Heroes of Comedy articulate what they're like and verbally justify their actions. That's the exact opposite of the words and actions being driven by subtext. Subtext suits allegorical and metaphorical projects best.

A lot of the confusion I see actors experiencing while breaking down scripts is due to their efforts to infuse literal work with deeper meaning. If that's what the work requires, then sure, think about what the character is hiding. Investigate what they're thinking but not willing to divulge. However, the smarter and more appropriate agenda most of the time is to understand the complexities of human behavior more substantially and cultivate a broader palette of emotions that are immediately accessible.

The ability to consistently discover the substance and humanity of a character who reads light on the page is a skill well worth mastering. Understanding the complexity of interpersonal relationships will make you a powerhouse actor. NOW we're talking. THAT'S when you're going to start making money, doing what you love.

Add in a clear vision of what the character immediately wants in the scene and assume it's a high mountain to climb to get it. You're going to need to burn calories to incorporate your varying strategies and tactics to achieve your goal. A strong vocabulary of intentions will help you there! Great acting is athletic. Dynamic performances don't come from actor's heads; they come from their hearts and their guts.

I have performed thousands of hours of live theater. Yet even onstage, and even when portraying larger than life characters, I always considered the whole story first. Then I would consider individual scenes within the context of the greater story. Then I would assess what my character wanted in a scene only after I had context around that mission.

I *know* I'm an actor and a writer, but I *identify* as an entertainer and a storyteller. That's how I present myself to the world, whether I'm teaching, performing, or speaking to a crowd. I'm less apt to be wrong when my goal is to uplift, engage, and delight. I always honor the bigger picture, even when I have an immediate task at hand.

Characters in scenes are best tackled that way. Get the story first. Acknowledge the surrounding context. Yes, you are auditioning for a part, but you're not likely to get it without embracing the whole. Think of who your character is in their world. How are they seen by others? How do they handle conflict? Create it? Think of how they help generate story.

When you show up as an actor hoping to get something right, you've got little chance of getting hired. When you make consistently bold offers that honor the writing and you tell interesting stories within your performance, you just might.

If you're wondering exactly how to do that, keep reading. My practice, my mistakes, my studied observations, and my triumphs comprise these thoughts on how to produce great, honest comedy. I've been told they help. I hope they help you.

I Want What?

Identifying what a character wants is one of the first priorities for actors when breaking down a scene. You need to know what your character is working toward so your performance will have energy and engagement. You might encounter a scene with no drive, featuring characters just chit-chatting away, but rarely.

Most everything that is broadcast or streamed is constructed with characters overcoming conflict; a hero or group of heroes going on a journey. That means they want something. Whatever that something is, there's not much of a story if achieving it is effortless.

After accurately assessing your character's want, you next strategize on how to get it and imagine how you will feel as you work to earn it. A want statement is also referred to as a goal, objective, desire, agenda, mission, etc. The terminology might vary, but their definitions are the same.

You should be specific, detailed, and accurate about what your character wants in the scene. Think moment to moment, from their point of view, not a broad or general overview from outside of the scene. A well-crafted want statement will infuse you with performance energy when you need it later.

For example, if you were given a three-page scene about a couple on a first date who were set up by a mutual friend, it would be woefully insufficient for your scene want statement to be, "I want love." It's true, that's why you're on a date. But it's broad. Wanting love is also both characters' super-objective. Most people in the world want romantic love. That's a universal theme, not a scene want statement. Want statements are also vastly superior when they include a specific point of view. Not all people (characters) react to a first date the same way.

Depending on what else the scene tells you, each character may have a goal within the scene that includes romance but other elements that are more specific. For example, "I want Bill to treat me like a queen tonight since I'm doing Rebecca a favor by going out with him." His want statement might be something like, "I want my blind date, Leslie, to comfort me from my horrible breakup last week."

These examples are specific, funny, and they reflect a true understanding of story and scene. Anyone can gauge that people on a date want love, companionship, or sex as a result. That's not script analysis, it's common knowledge. Want statements need to address the dynamic, personal ambitions of the characters and specific plot points that exist within all scenes.

Identifying what your character wants in a scene is relatively easy. However, there are many ways in which an actor can be off in determining their character's goal. The most common problem is that the want statement is too broad. The second most common problem is that the want statement is far too academic and impersonal for the close, casual relationships the characters likely have.

Actors can easily generate a want statement that is accurate but not active enough to help them play the scene at the professional level. In other words, you can easily be *not wrong* about what your character wants, but not quite right either. Passive framework around what your character is *really* trying to achieve can leave your interpretation lacking heart, soul, and emotion.

Ideally, all your discovery sets you up for a fun, athletic performance that will get you noticed. Great want statements acknowledge that your character likely wants to change a relationship dynamic because of an immediate need that drives the dialogue with emotional activity from a clear point of view. Your goal is to find what's important and personal to your character in each scene and how that desire is connected to the other character's willingness to help you acquire it.

Want statements are not a matter of semantics. They are a pathway to powerful, personal, and laugh-out-loud funny performances. The difference of just a few small words can either make your character sympathetic, even heroic, or unintentionally leave them (and you) feeling cold and withdrawn from the action. Acting in film and television isn't about relaying information or characters *telling* each other things. The characters are trying to *change* or *challenge* each other's opinions, attitudes, beliefs, moods, and behaviors. Acting is an emotional and intentional contact sport.

Actors play what they say. We like to think we'll get in front of the camera and offer an exciting, lively take regardless of how we phrase our choices. I work with so many actors who say, "I know what I want to do (or am doing) with this script and character, I just can't put it into words."

I understand and empathize with that. Most obviously, I teach comedy. A fuller description of what I teach includes how to be a working, professional actor who can unpack their work easily and artfully.

You can't just comprehend the basics of the dialogue and action in a scene and therefore assume your performance will be strong enough. If a casting director, producer, or director wants to collaborate with you, you need a concise actor's vocabulary with which to answer questions and translate adjustments within seconds.

If we misidentify or misperceive what our character wants, we won't have a shot at booking. If we can't articulate or describe a performance in an exciting, active way, the chances of it being fun to watch or bookable are slim.

I'm going into great detail in this section on how to craft killer want statements. My goal is to empower you with knowledge that isn't found elsewhere. It takes practice to weaponize your words. But as you read on, remember that it's not just about better word choices over weaker word choices. It's about what more powerful words challenge you to do as an actor.

If your homework itself reads like a great story filled with conflict, relationship difficulties, and absurdity, your performance will be ablaze. If your homework sounds like a general observation of what is happening to someone else from a distance, your performance will likely be dull.

The scale of vitality and life force required to act in sitcoms, and for the camera in general, can be deceptive, especially when you are auditioning your work.

Believe it or not, how you define what your character wants in a scene makes a *huge* difference in whether you ignite all your best acting training when you need it most. It's the difference between telling your body that it should prepare to have a casual chat with a friend, or that it's going on a mission to change the way a friend behaves with less than two minutes on the clock.

You should know that reinforcing these guidelines for want statements and the impact of the work underneath them is largely how I get my actors booking. Exciting agendas animate us internally while grounding us externally. Great actors have emotional fireworks exploding inside while they stand unflinchingly still for the camera. The more emotionally alive you are, the more likely your body will anchor itself and remove physical static without you having to think about it.

I believe that words matter, and I've mastered making the most of them. The right ones can transform an adequate actor into a comedy beast who can blow the competition out of the water, any time in any environment.

With that, let's examine where we might go right and where we might go wrong in stating what we want.

One Want Per Scene

Find and focus only on one want per scene. Nearly all characters in all scenes want ultimately just one thing. They may mention or discuss more than one topic within conversation, but scenes are generally only a few pages long. In terms of scene structure, several pages of a script are really only enough time to handle one significant plot point. Sometimes actors get this confused and say things like, "At the beginning of the scene he wants "Thing A," but it changes halfway through and he goes after "Thing B."

That is almost never the case.

There is usually only one primary concern on a character's mind during a scene. Anything else that's mentioned merely has to do with context and continuity. Your goal is to find and summarize your character's main desire within the scene and expend your energy getting it.

Think of it this way: If you want to borrow money from a friend, you're likely to say hello and get a read on their mood first. You might start with friendly chit-chat and ask about their day. Using this simple scenario as an example, you would *not* say, "My character wants to know about his friend's day first, then it changes, and he asks for money."

The opening conversation is a prelude to asking for the money, not a separate want. It's the same context we would incorporate in real life. Depending on the scene, the opening dialogue may even be a strategy or tactic that leads your character to asking for the money. For example, you might compliment your friend or build some excitement about this new idea you have that could use some financial backing...

Nonetheless, the primary want for your character in this scene is getting a loan from a friend. That's where all the energy, interest, tension, conflict, and comedy lie. Focus and intention are diffused if you have multiple agendas within a scene. Since almost all scenes are only a few pages long, we channel our energy into one predominant drive.

Your Want is Your Personal Thesis Statement

Ideally, your character's want statement is written in one clear sentence that becomes the foundation for the rest of your discovery. It's like formulating a thesis for an essay. It might take some practice to quickly write concise, well-crafted want statements, but I guarantee you it's worth the time to practice.

It will help if you put your want statement and all your homework in first person right away. Script analysis by nature can have a clinical feel to it. Our cellular memory can react to dissecting a script or doing "actor's homework" like we're back in school being tested and graded. Who needs that?

What we want to generate as performers is artful, entertaining direction for ourselves. Our homework should enable us to interpret story, character, and the fabric of our character's relationships accurately and energetically. We want to break down scenes so well that we play them like champions! Our job as actors is to collaborate with writers in bringing a fictional character to life. So, don't say, "He wants..." or "She wants...." Say, "*I* want..."

When you claim what is happening to yourself as opposed to "him" or "her," you are creating an immediate advantage for yourself. You're marrying yourself to the character and the material, which helps you to humanize the role from the inside out. The closer you put yourself in your mind's eye to being the character or being the one who gets cast, the better chance you have of that becoming true.

It's helpful to personalize your agenda immediately by equating how you would feel in the same circumstances. When you're acting well, you are stepping into the shoes of another human being and, with empathy, becoming their spokesperson. You know what it is to want something. Give that need, desire, yearning, or ache to your character.

Imagine yourself really saying your character's words to your own boss, parent, child, spouse, friend, etc. How bold would you have to be? How would it make you feel? Is it easy for you to say what your character is saying in real life? Take ownership of the person you're playing then imagine and ignite the feelings that go along with their mission. Right from the beginning.

My choices are better and stronger when I start living the life of my character from the second I receive a script. I don't analyze from a distance and then attach myself to the work later. I activate myself emotionally on the very first read. I don't need to know anything about the circumstances before I dive in.

If nothing else, I know it will *always* be a story about someone who's trying to change something in his immediate environment because *that's what stories are*. There will be an emotional journey within that endeavor. I'll feel good if I get what I want, I'll feel bad if I don't. Such is the trajectory of nearly every scene you will ever act.

Whatever the outcome, I know that acting is feeling varying emotions and igniting varying intentions as scenes unfold and arc. The moment I clue into what the scene is about, I activate internally and start to experience the life of the person on the page. Said a simpler way, I'm acting all the way through my homework from the moment I start. I strongly encourage performing, playing, and personifying throughout your analysis!

It's All About Specificity

Next, your want statement should include words of action, emotion, and specific labeling of other characters. Declare what you want with passion, in your own words, the way you would speak. Remember, you're not being quizzed. Breaking down a script should not produce anxiety or a fear response. You're not trying to "get something right."

You are creating a starting point for a charged performance that will allow you to play in the big leagues and outperform your competition. You are offering your interpretation of a fictional life that ultimately must feel exciting and real.

The scene always tells you what your character is going after. I often see actors searching for their want statement as if it is something abstract or outside of the pages they are working with. It's as if they think playing, "I want my friend Jonathan to loan me money," is too obvious or there's some secret agenda beyond that they can't quite put their finger on. Nope. If your character asks their friend for a loan by the end of the scene, a loan is what they wanted. Simple.

Beyond specificity, a great want statement also includes an understanding of the depth and history of the relationships in the scene and the psychology of the character. It goes beyond merely assessing the goal and captures the life of the character you're embodying. It includes an understanding of what drives them at their core and the difficulty or ease they will encounter in their attempt to get what they want, *based on who they're dealing with.*

Stay Positive!

You should always write your want statement in the positive. Think of exactly what you're trying to achieve given the context of the scene and your dialogue. Are you trying to get a physical object from someone? Are you trying to teach somebody a life lesson? Are you trying to change someone's mind about something?

These are all things that require an expenditure of energy and an exertion of will. They include another person and something you are trying to do. Your assumption should always be that your character wants to be wherever they are unless they are being detained or face a consequence worse than their fate in the scene if they leave.

Actors sometimes focus their performance on what their character *doesn't* want as opposed to what they *do* want. That will certainly throw the scene in a strange direction and definitely step on the comedy. When you write your want statement in the negative, you will play yourself out of the scene.

If you genuinely think your character doesn't even want to have the conversation they are having, your energy will inevitably be low. It's quite likely you will also send an undercurrent of hostility through the scene. The predictable result is that your character will come across as distant and unsympathetic.

It's neither fun nor funny to watch someone *wanting to do something else*. It is funny to watch someone overcome an obstacle they *wish they didn't have to*.

So, *don't* play what you *don't* want. The stakes will be low, the energy will be low and you will fail to engage your scene partners and the audience. This is important because acting is all about storytelling and engagement.

Writers don't write roles or scenes in isolation. They write films or episodes of an ongoing series in order to tell a fully realized story. Actors forget that sometimes. Especially when auditioning. Standing alone on a mark is a very lonely and vulnerable place to be. All the attention is on you, the camera is on you and the pressure is on you. It's easy to feel in that moment that the entire experience is about you.

However, the truth is, it's not. The role for which you are auditioning is just one component of an entire production that could ultimately require the efforts of hundreds of individuals from start to finish. It is imperative that all the choices you make as an actor don't merely support the character and scene, *but the overall story and project as well*.

Stories involve conflict, and conflict requires engagement. If you play what you don't want, i.e., I wish we *weren't* having this discussion, I'd rather *not* be doing this, I wish he'd just *shut up and go away*, etc., you're actively weakening the story and making choices that are not interesting to watch. As long as you are speaking to someone, you are by definition attempting to achieve something, even if it's to placate someone or keep peace.

General Concepts Play Poorly

Great want statements avoid general words or concepts like, "I want him to understand..." "I want to prove to her that..." "I want to let her know..." "I want him to get it in his head that..." "I want her to accept...", etc. These apply to most every conversation. Have you ever had a conversation with anyone where you *didn't* want them to understand you?

Actors use lackluster words like these in their want statements all the time and they always make the performance weak. In order for you to understand me, all that needs to happen is for me to be clear and you to be intelligent enough to comprehend my words. Pretty dull, huh?

If I want you to know something, I can just tell you. No energy or emotion is required. Frankly, no acting is required. If I said to you, "Hey! Do you want to watch two people exchange knowledge with each other?" you'd think I was nuts.

Yet time after time, when I ask actors about their choices — what their character wants in the scene — they offer some version of a want statement that merely summarizes what one character wants the other to know. Unacceptable! Your character is *always* doing something more dynamic and interesting than simply telling someone something.

If understanding, knowing, or comprehending what is being said is your stated want, your performance will be lacking.

Everyone who says anything, anywhere, anytime wants to be understood. When you apply your logic and reasoning within a discussion, you are making a point. When the other character responds with their logic and reasoning, they are making their point in response.

That's just another way of saying people are talking to each other!

Obviously! Here's what you're trying to uncover: What *exactly* is your character trying to *change* via their conversation? Exactly *when* do they want that change to happen? Whose *help, support, or cooperation* do they need to get it? What *efforts* are you *igniting* to *manifest* the change you want? The answers to those concerns create the underpinnings of valuable want statements.

Acting is not about moving words back and forth, it's about moving an audience of potentially millions to either laughter or tears. We have to dig deeper and find a relatable human goal that's worth throwing energy into. I don't burn calories getting folks to simply understand me. However, wrestling someone from their long-held point of view to see the world another way — *my way* — might as well be an Olympic event.

If You Want to Prove a Point, Become a Lawyer

Further, if you want to prove you're right to me or "get me to admit" something negative about myself, I guarantee you that I'm just going to feel attacked. Who wouldn't? Try applying that tactic to a couple in real life or on television: A) I want to *prove* to my husband that he is wrong about how to discipline the kids. B) I want my wife *to admit* she could be a better mother.

Yikes! Maybe that couple needs to level up their parenting, but *proving* your spouse is wrong and getting your spouse to *admit* their failings is dramatic and just plain mean. Stay far, far away from those words in want statements as well. If you think something negative about me and want me to know it, it's on you to say so. If you think something negative about me but want me to acknowledge and say it about myself, you're being extremely passive-aggressive, cowardly, and unkind. That applies in real life as well as fictional life. It's vicious to assess an unflattering trait in someone and coax them into admitting it about themselves.

Proving, telling, letting someone know, getting someone to understand, agree, admit, or acknowledge all have no heart. I can't impress enough the importance of learning to consistently frame your character's desires in a more humane, active and emotionally intelligent way.

Remember the Love

Sitcoms are about tribes of people who love each other. Even when they drive each other crazy. Your want statements need to express the love and history that exists within the relationships between characters, even when there is discord. So how do you create warmer and more active want statements? Easy. Play around with the verbs!

Example:
What if the character opposite yours in a scene was completely freaking out over a parking ticket?

There's a huge difference between assessing your mission in the scene with "I want him to calm down and understand that a parking ticket is no reason to become hysterical," versus "I want to help my best friend Oscar manage his sudden panic attack over his parking ticket because neither one of us can move on with the day until he chills out."

The verb "understand" is completely passive. Here's the definition: "to perceive the meaning of; grasp the idea of." It sounds cerebral and it is. Understanding happens in your brain and is a dull action to watch.

If my friend is freaking out right next to me and my goal is for me to tell him that he doesn't need to, that would leave me looking strangely passive, frozen even, like a zombie. Two guys on a street, one overflowing with chaotic emotion and the other *explaining* that the reaction is unnecessary is a rather sad scenario. If you were to play a scene like this with the goal of making Oscar *understand* something, you would seem fairly heartless.

The verb "manage" on the other hand, is active. Here's the definition: "to succeed in accomplishing, sometimes despite difficulty or hardship."

Wow! What a huge difference. We've gone from "perceive and grasp" to "succeed and accomplish despite difficulty or hardship."

The latter is more in line with a hero going on a journey. Just one word, "manage," says we're going to have to engage, work, change, overcome obstacles, and feel multiple emotions. Merely understanding sets you up for a forgettable performance.

Watching someone perceive the meaning of someone else's words is no fun! It's not dynamic and in most cases, as with this simple example, it's not even an appropriate course of action. Your friend needs help changing back to normal! Now! From you!

We *involve* ourselves with our friends, family, and coworkers with whom we're close. Your want statement should include your desires *in relation to the other person*. An active want that requires exertion of will is always written into the scene. Changing someone's disposition is *always* more interesting than one person offering another an explanantion.

Your character is not a witness. They are an active participant of life in motion.

They are a driving force full of emotions that ebb and flow like the tide. They love the people they spend time with. What they want generally includes the cooperation of those people. Therefore, their desires aren't abstract; just the opposite. They're consistently, awkwardly precise and unbearably intimate.

Overcoming Obstacles

What your character wants in a scene intersects with the conflict of the scene. Getting to the heart of what your character truly wants in the scene helps develop stakes. An extremely common note to actors is that the stakes of the scene could be higher. This happens when actors are merely relaying information as opposed to trying to change someone else's disposition. More often than not, what the character wants in the scene is usually quite hard to obtain. Especially since it requires cooperation from someone else who is reluctant. Sometimes it's even impossible. Wanting something you cannot get creates both conflict and comedy. Most want statements are some version of these basic desires:

Difficult:

- I want the other person in the scene to give me something they have and want to keep.

- I want the other person in the scene to join in an activity, event, or scheme with me that they currently resist.

- I want the other person in the scene to change a behavior or emotion that has to do with an immediate and/or un-usual circumstance in which we've found ourselves.

- I want the other person in the scene to change their opinion about something that's equally important to us.

- I want the other person in the scene to know me well enough to predict my tastes and preferences.

Impossible:
- I want the other person in the scene to be a person they've never shown themselves to be.

- I want the other person in the scene to change a strong and long-held belief about a particular person, philosophy, or political affiliation.

- I want the other person in the scene to evolve immediately.

Most of the time what your character wants in a scene is for the other character to be a different person than they actually are, if only for a moment. It's important to always bear in mind the consent and cooperation your character needs from the other members of their tribe in order to get what they want.

Play Your Character's Scene Objective, Not Their Super-Objective

It's also important that you don't inadvertently mistake your character's super-objective for their scene objective. Your character's super-objective is their overarching goal for that particular era of their life. The term sounds important, even fancy... *super*-objective! Like it might be more important than what your character wants in any given scene, but that's not the case. Super-objectives are broad by definition. And broad is exactly what we *don't* want.

Here's an example most people get: in a romantic comedy, it's generally the case that the super-objective of both of the leads is to fall in love and get married. Hence the super objective is like an awning that shades the season of a character's life.

If you think of all the events that happen in a romantic comedy that comprise a fun and gripping story, they have very little to do with lovey-dovey feelings. The scenes usually lead up to the wedding at the end. The movie is apt to be mostly about what's going wrong beforehand; disapproving mother-in-law, obstacles to making it to the altar on time, bad wedding singer, etc., until things are resolved in the end, even though they were difficult throughout.

Those events unfold in individual scenes. Those scenes put the characters in situations where they have more urgent and immediate tasks to manage than basking in their romance. More likely, they're trying to *fix* something, *save* a moment, *challenge* someone's ideas, or *teach* someone they care about that they are doing whatever they're doing absolutely, positively wrong!

Those kinds of agendas are deeply personal and achieving them burns a lot of fuel. Everything that happens to a character in a story has weight just as it does for you in life. It's not for us to judge why they want what they want or how much. It's our job to always identify the specific mission our characters have lit upon, empathize with it, and empower it with hope, electricity, and maybe even mania.

Here are some more examples of super-objectives that actors sometimes offer as scene want statements. By now I hope you can see how woefully general and incomplete these are as the foundation for an exciting, fun, and powerful performance.

"I want love," "I want success," "I want power," "I want sex," "I want peace in my own house," etc. Those are not scene want statements. They're broader life goals that take more time than one scene allows. These wants may be accurate to the life of the character, but their lack of immediacy and inclusion of other characters leave them, well... wanting. (See what I did there?)

Want Statement Review

Answering the following questions will help you find clarity and stakes in your want statement. It will also help you practice including the other person or people involved. The other people in the scene with your character hold the key to them attaining their desires. Embracing this tenet will lead you to active choices that support an energetic performance.

What Is the Story of the Scene?

Trust the script. It always tells you what your character is going after. It is a want or desire that is complicated by the need to involve someone else who is perhaps judging or denying you. Feel that desire in your gut and acknowledge the tension that comes with risk. Articulating our desires leaves us vulnerable, emotional, and utterly human.

Our characters should be affected similarly. Don't put your script under a microscope and study it like it's an exam, even though we call it homework. Do your best to step into the shoes of another human being and, with compassion, become their advocate. What is the story being told within the scene?

- What's happening right now and why?
- What labels apply to the relationships?
- How do all the relationships feel right now?
- What can others give me or help me with?
- Are they resisting? If so, why?
- How do I hope this moment will end?
- When do I want my request fulfilled?

When you fully empathize with the character and imagine their moment-to-moment reality, you will find a more dynamic mission to embark upon than just telling someone something or proving a point. You'll see that, time and time again, your characters are stepping up to tough, challenging conversations with people they love, need, and respect.

There is some truth to the fact that they may not want to have some of those discussions. However, life doesn't let us off the hook. We don't get to avoid the people we love and still keep them fully in our lives. We have to say messy, complicated stuff to each other. It's unavoidable. We need to manage smaller moments of life in the present to gain our greater ambitions later. Our relationships play a significant part in how we level up in all eras of our life.

It's often the smallest, most immediate goals involving those within our inner circle that scare or stymie us the most. What your characters want in scenes is ultimately the same as what we all want in life; to find the courage to say what we want, when we want, how we want and still be loved unconditionally for who we are once we've said it.

Conflict

After you've zeroed in on what you want in the scene, the next step is to explore the conflict involved in acquiring it. I addressed conflict to some degree as it applies to invigorating your want statement, but now let's tackle it head on. Stories are told about problems, not tranquility. Leo Tolstoy wrote what's become a literary classic, *War and Peace*. He got the order of events exactly right. Conflict first, *then* resolution.

Almost every scene in every television show or movie you've ever seen has conflict. Obviously there is a range from trivial to catastrophic, but we don't stare into screens to watch polite exchanges that leave everyone the same as we found them. We watch to see villains, society, nature, or our inner demons create problems and heroes overcome them. We watch to see what's going to go wrong, not right.

When there is no conflict in a scene, it's most likely because the audience is being introduced to the world the writer has created. Conflict-free scenes almost always come at the beginning of a film or, in the case of television, the first scenes of a pilot. For the record, conflict-free scenes aren't necessary. You can open with a bang and keep going from there. It's just worth noting that if you can't find any conflict at all in a scene, this might be why.

Global disaster movies are a great example here. By and large, they all have the same template; whether the world is going to be destroyed by asteroid, volcano, tidal wave, earthquake, tsunami, solar flare, tornado, flood, zombie apocalypse, or alien invasion, we need a core group of citizens to represent all of humanity.

More often than not, we meet the hero of the bunch leading a Zen life, eating a nutritious breakfast at home just before they receive news that imminent doom will erase them and their loved ones from existence. This no-conflict introduction gives us a chance to meet the characters of a film and see them free of distress for at least a little bit because they will be in great distress for the rest of the film.

In television, the parallel is the pilot episode of a series. There will still need to be a story with some kind of conflict, but since we need to get to know the series regulars, there may also be scenes with minimal or no obstacles. This allows us to meet the lead characters, become acquainted with their world, learn how they function within it, and who they generally engage with.

It's our job as actors to maximize the conflict in our work, which attaches directly to heightening the stakes. The problem, obstacle, or disagreement will be apparent in the script. Does the conflict revolve around an object? A person or group of people? A desire? Your ego? How to execute an idea? How to keep yourself or someone else true to an ideal?

More often than not, at least several of the above coalesce to create the greatest potential dissension within the scene.

The pages always tell you what to do (trust them), they just don't tell you *how* to do it. Sometimes actors have a difficult time finding the stakes in comedy scripts because the circumstances can be silly, petty, and absurd. I understand that, but if you ever feel that way, it's a judgment call on your part. I'm sure the writer thought they were creating an obstacle, issue, or hurdle for the character that is difficult to overcome from the character's point of view.

I promise you that The Heroes of Comedy do not evaluate the moments of their lives with external judgments of that sort. What they're in touch with is having the hopes of their lives ful-filled or dashed, working through overwhelming discomfort, or navigating a psychological obstacle. A fight between roommates over shared shelf space in the refrigerator can be as important in that moment to each of them as a king declaring victory on a battlefield.

With that example on deck, let's work towards maximizing the conflict in a seemingly meaningless situation. Space in a refrigerator for your food vs. someone else's food really isn't a big deal in the scheme of things. But if two people are fighting over it, it's a big deal to them. Why?

As both a writer and performer, I evaluate and exploit conflict via three different avenues:

- External Dilemma
- Archetypal Psychology
- Unconscious Emotion

External Dilemma

The external dilemma is easy to gauge. It's simply any problem that arises in the course of life. It could be a broken blender, a letter bringing bad news, a car that won't start, a person coming down with a cold when they have somewhere important to go, a text from a friend who's in jail, etc. In this example, it's the need for space in a shared refrigerator. That's a real thing that people who live together have to navigate. One person wants to divide the space up one way, the other person wants it done a different way. Or perhaps one thinks they require more space than the other. Hence, a foundational conflict that anyone passing by would observe.

Archetypal Psychology

One of the many and powerful uses of The Heroes of Comedy is that they all come front-loaded with a worldview that informs you how they will react when engaged in conflict. There are predictable reactions that are consistent for each archetype. Once you study and become familiar with the inner workings of each, you will start to innately know how to discharge them into a scene. These predictable responses are born out of the psychology of a particular kind of person. Each Hero is defined by set core characteristics.

Real people in our actual lives and fictional characters on TV all have predictable behavioral responses. They may surprise us, but rarely. It's not to say they aren't unique, merely known. Part of the reason we keep people in our lives, let alone offer our trust to them, is because we can predict their behavior at least most of the time. We wouldn't feel safe around them otherwise.

A Neurotic might become high-strung, tense, and persnickety in this situation because the other person doesn't understand their method of organization that they are *sure* is the best and most efficient. An Innocent, on the other hand, might pout like a child to get their way. A Buffoon would respond like a dimwitted bully and fight tooth and nail for equal space just on principle, even though they never food shop or cook at home. If you know these people or characters, you can anticipate these reactions.

When you understand The Heroes of Comedy, you can easily heighten the tension and excitement of watching a scene like this. It's funny to watch a Neurotic lose their composure over something so trivial. The problem remains what it is, but the character's psychology starts to unravel in a *specific* way that makes sense according to how they see the world. Different kinds of characters (people) perceive the same events differently based upon their psychological profile.

When you sculpt and sharpen your wheelhouse archetypes, the ones most suited to your casting and the ones you play most authentically, you have a distinct advantage in the marketplace and a lot of your competition falls by the wayside.

A lot of actors come and go from the industry without ever really knowing what they play well for on-camera purposes. Improv and stage training are helpful to a degree, but you don't necessarily get the accurate information and industry feedback necessary to build a television and film career. Actors Comedy Studio stands alone in teaching strong script analysis skills, audition and self-taping technique, as well as character development suited for the camera.

Unconscious Emotion

Lastly, I like to examine the unconscious emotion that characters experience when they don't get their way. Have you ever blown up about something and not know why? Ever wake up sad when nothing bad happened? These are unconscious emotional reactions that you might process and work through later or maybe never at all. But in a given moment we might be the hostage of these feelings that make us feel or seem unhinged. Sometimes our behavior is illogical and makes no sense. When that's the case, it's likely because our emotions have been heightened to the point that they are overriding our intellect.

We have emotional triggers within us, and we don't have any control over them when they're set off. One day you might let the division of refrigerator space roll right off your back. You might even say, "Just tell me where to put my stuff and it'll be fine." And it truly would be. But on this day, you're standing your ground and planting a flag.

I'll talk more about emotional work in scenes later, but for now let's explore the idea that your characters are susceptible to *unconscious* emotional reactions that don't make any sense to them in their moment-to-moment life. How exciting! You can't think your way into that space. It's volatile, electric... a little bit dangerous. What lives below the surface in the deep waters of the subconscious mind is what connects us all and has the potential to make a simple disagreement between friends a rather fascinating study of interpersonal relationships.

Any of The Heroes of Comedy (or any person in real life) might feel threatened by someone wanting more than their share of space, *even if they don't need it*. What the hell is that about? *Your* insecurities are triggered because *I* buy food in bulk and need more room in the fridge? You betcha!

Our unconscious emotional responses are usually the source of our own discontent, not the *actual* difference between getting the high shelf or the low shelf in the refrigerator. Issues of respect, self-esteem, feeling heard, valued, and understood come up. Your childhood comes up. Your neuroses and insecurities surface despite your efforts to rein them in. The end result is that emotions you can't quite explain in the moment take hold of you and transform a petty squabble over an icebox into a battle for veneration.

In considering the reality of unconscious emotion driving us through moments of our life, I'm drawing a contrast between feelings that we *are* in touch with *as they're occurring*, and feelings we *are not* registering until *after they've occurred* or *maybe never at all*. This can be as simple as liking something without thinking about why.

What's your favorite flavor of ice cream? Why? Who knows? Maybe it's because of the way your DNA dictates the way your palate registers taste. Maybe your grandma gave you that flavor a lot as a child, you love your grandma, and you associate the two. Opinions and preferences are often the product of unconscious emotion. Opinions and preferences are assessments we make partly through intellect. We also form them based on feelings, or emotions with which we are not immediately in touch.

What is a phobia? An *irrational* fear (emotion) of something that we can't explain logically (unconscious). To be clear, if you have a fear of dogs because you've been bitten by even one, that's not a phobia. That would be a rational or learned fear. An irrational reaction to a stimulus is another way of acknowledging unconscious emotion. Spiders? Snakes? They're important creatures in our ecosystem. Why do so many people have a knee-jerk negative reaction to them? A few are poisonous but most not.

General psychology, opinions, and phobias are all ways in which humans demonstrate unconscious emotion. Most actors are taught emotional exploration and practice ways to remain open emotionally within their work. Method actors, in particular, are guided into and through emotional experiences to broaden their palette.

In my experience, they are often not taught the distinction between what emotions a character would be in touch with as they are evolving moment to moment, and what they might feel unconsciously from the very same moments because of their personality. Mastering the distinction produces breathtaking results in an actor's work and increases conflict.

Here's the simplest example of this point: A lot of guest roles are for some type of business professional in the world of a series regular. Let's say a favorite character of yours has to go to the doctor. Just making the doctor busy versus relaxed — because most doctors truthfully are busy — will take your audition to another level. Even if we're totally focused on the person we're with in any given moment, the surrounding pressure and demands of our day are ever-present. This should be true for your characters.

We cycle through unconscious emotions simply because life is complicated, and we have a schedule to keep. Ever have a nice, relaxing lunch with a friend but after an hour (*two* hours?) you feel a very real change in your body? It's not just a matter of acknowledging that time passed in your mind.

The emotions change in your gut because the relaxation and fun you've been experiencing are over and you're headed toward the remaining challenges of your day. You felt glad, happy, and calm during the bulk of the lunch, but anxiety unconsciously crept in toward the end. For great actors, that happens to their characters, too.

There is an emotional intelligence in understanding that as we go through our day, our mood shifts constantly, and a great deal of the time we don't know why or have time to think about it. There is a level of sophistication that is added to an actor's work when their characters operate with the same bandwidth. The greater commitment to your character's neuroses, tastes, opinions, and fears, the greater the conflict. The more unconscious emotion you infuse into your character's life the more you are giving other actors to respond to.

With that said, we endeavor to eliminate qualifiers from our homework, analysis, and description of our work. Phrases like "kind of..." "sort of..." "a little...", etc. are all *terrible* ways of articulating choices in a scene and work toward reducing conflict when your certain goal is to maximize it.

Your character will have a problem at hand with which they must contend. They also have baggage and flaws. They're probably the product of either weak or overbearing parenting. They have issues at home, work, and within their friendships. They have more to do *that day* aside from the conversation they're having at any given moment.

So be sure to bring the hustle, flow, and general angst of life into a scene to increase conflict and heighten stakes. Your baseline for a professional-level performance should never be zero tension. Most characters aren't completely without cares or worries, even when there isn't a specific problem on deck. Whenever we do see a character "relaxing" on television, it's depicted as a rare occurrence and even then, it doesn't last long. This is television's way of telling *you*, it wants you to upset the apple cart.

Arc of the Scene

The arc (apex, climax) is the pivotal moment for your character in a scene. The arc of the scene is *directly* attached to your want statement. It's the exact moment you stop working for what you want and contains the most radical change of emotion. The arc is where your character either gets what they want or accepts that they aren't getting what they want, at least right now. You've either won or you've lost.

You identify the arc simply by asking two questions. The first is "Do I get what I want in the scene?" Whether yes or no, the next question is "*Exactly* when do I stop working or fighting for what I want?" That precise moment is the arc.

The arc of the scene always lands *between* lines. The assessment of what your character wants in each scene must always include the amount of cooperation the other characters in the scene give or withhold. The want *statement* should then be worded with as much specificity as possible. Another character will tell your character within their dialogue whether they are granting or denying your request. What you want in the scene directly involves others or you wouldn't be talking to them.

To circle back to want statements for just a moment, I'd like to reinforce that if your want statement is broad and not inclusive of the other characters, you're failing to train yourself to consistently play *up* to the arc of the scene. You are also almost certainly not having conversations that are as grounded and authentic as professional-level work requires. "I want power" could be an aspect of what a character wants, but it includes the cooperation of no one, at least as stated.

It *implies* you want power over the other people in the scene, but it inherently excludes whether they have any say in the amount of power you have or not. Actors who work from broad want statements that are actually super-objectives tend to be selfish performers, intentionally or not.

If the framework around an actor's scene work is that their character doesn't need anyone's *immediate* help with anything, they tend to speak to other characters like they are props. The performance comes across as preachy or inauthentic or both. If you want to book on-camera acting work, you need to experience the moments of a fictional character's life, not illustrate their broader agenda that could take an entire era of their life. A scene can only arc if the characters within it have immediate wants and desires that are either given or thwarted *by each other, right then and there.*

The reason scenes arc or build with an upward trajectory most of the time is because conversations include various components of speech that naturally cause the discussion to escalate: pretext, context, negation, inquiry, information, proposal, promotion, disagreement, challenge, defense, support, tangents, addendums, interruptions, check-ins, and summaries.

Since the scenes you act involve telling a larger story with a point, a plot, a build, a journey, and resolve, it's helpful for you to always think of your conversations as being constructed this way as well, because they are. We naturally build, banter, and barter when we speak. Our conversations organically build to crescendo.

If a character on a comedy series walks into their boss's office, asks directly for a raise and the boss says, "Of course, you deserve one," there would be no story. More likely we'd see the employee weary and overworked first. They'd discuss the raise with a friend, partner, or coworker before asking. The audience would see the risk they felt in making themselves vulnerable by requesting a raise.

Asking for more money based on the quality of our work is directly attached to our self-esteem and comfort level initiating potentially uncomfortable conversations. When the character finally asks their boss for a raise, the scene won't be interesting if the answer is a foregone conclusion either way. The scene arcs because of the uncertainty of the outcome and the tension within the request.

All the elements of conversation I mentioned above come into play; pretext, context, proposal, negotiation, summary, etc. The character would lay out reasons why they thought it was time for a raise. They might have an amount in mind. They may be willing to settle for less than that amount but have a number in mind that's a dealbreaker, etc. The answer could be a definitive yes or it could be an absolute no. It could be yes, plus added responsibility moving forward. It could be no, pending the result of a trial, test, or probation of some kind.

There are several realistic answers. The scene arcs as we work our way toward that answer. When your character gets what they want or realizes they won't, that exact moment is the arc of the scene. The response to your want will be clear based on the boss's *final* verdict. The arc of the scene for you is crystalized *in between* lines because it is brought about by something you hear, not something you say.

Whatever your character was feeling throughout the scene, this pivotal moment contains the greatest emotional shift. The arc *adds* celebration or defeat to the mix. All the other feelings you've had throughout the scene are still alive in your body but diminished. Your work is done. For better or worse, the tension is broken. Your obstacle is overcome.

Some emotion is instantly added; various layers of joy or disappointment. Some emotion is instantly erased; anxiety, fear, hope, determination, insecurity, etc. Even if the answer is no, the bulk of the emotions you experienced getting to that moment — the arc — mostly melt away. Traces of them are still there, but they've been overwhelmed by new emotions that sync up with victory or failure.

Even if you didn't get the raise, the obstacle in this case, the first step was summoning the courage to ask. You did that, no matter the response. *Asking* your boss for a raise is the plot point for this scene. The answer is relevant, but more so for the following scenes than this one.

What your character does with the answer is for another moment. The purpose, point, plot, story of this example is to *ask*.

That is the actionable verb from which to form this scene's want statement. The arc of the scene is the ultimate response to that very human, vulnerable want. The simplest summary is that in some regard, every scene has a winner and a loser. Play up and into the challenge until a victor is declared.

What's left of the scene after the arc is the resolve (denouement, resolution). Think of the resolve as words spoken mostly for context or continuity. They still matter though. In real life and in fictional life, context and continuity are extremely important. It is worth noting, however, that because they aren't attached to your character getting what they want, they are infused with a different energy. Consistently recognizing the arc of the scene will help you handle these lines with appropriate care.

Actors innately know that the lines of dialogue that come after the arc aren't attached to the main desire or plot point of the scene. Without realizing it, they often underserve those lines and inadvertently "throw them away." Be careful to never do that. It can lead to a crummy ending, even if the rest of the performance was great.

Remember the end of the scene is not only the result of your character's want being fulfilled or denied, it's also the last moment casting directors and producers see you. You don't want to instill the habit of fading away at the end of your scenes. You don't want to swallow your last words or mutter them under your breath.

Disappearing at the end of the scene is a common way new and even very experienced actors take themselves out of the mix when it comes to final casting decisions. Mostly actors are unaware of the degree to which their energy drops in the resolve. The lines can easily lose a target and just be said aloud without direction or clear purpose. It's awkward to witness and in one quick moment, a great actor can appear inexperienced.

Sometimes actors feel that comedy is asking for forced or pushed energy. They're usually just shy and have insecurities about their own personal, comedic performance abilities. The more common concern is an actor simply not sustaining their own energy level within their performance or audition all the way through their version of the scene. If you drop out at the end of the scene, casting and producers will drop out on you. Be careful you never fall into that category!

Moment Before

Scenes have a strong tendency to start with life in motion, not right at the top of the character's day. It's therefore important to assess where your character is geographically and emotionally before the scene begins. This is a pretty simple task. The break-down and scene almost always tell you where your character is physically, within their world. Gauging your character's emotional state before you speak in the scene is also not a great challenge, just an important step.

What I often do that is helpful for actors is attach the value of a clear moment before to a working actor's life. When you audition, you go to a location, sign in, and wait in a lobby with other actors until it's your turn. There may be the hustle of a busy work environment, friends who want to talk to you, nerves, or other elements that can potentially be distracting. When your name is called, you only have about 10 steps until you hit the mark.

Typically, casting will greet you in a friendly manner and per-haps ask if you have any questions. If you don't, they'll say some version of "Let's go ahead then!" Three, two, one and... you're au-ditioning. Less than six seconds ago you were sitting in a lobby chair. Now the camera is rolling, casting is reading with you and, unless you're interviewing for a lead role, the audition is over in a matter of seconds and you're heading back to your car or the curb to wait for your ride-sharing service.

What was your moment before again? Were you completely grounded in the emotion and imagined environment you worked out for yourself? Did you change emotionally throughout the scene? Or did the scene go by in the blink of an eye as you felt the great choices you made flatten and evaporate into thin air? Did some part of you want desperately to give another take because you weren't even breathing during that one? Did you feel less than satisfied when the casting director simply smiled and said, "Thanks," when you were finished?

We can answer those rhetorical questions with yet another one. Did you actually *use* your moment before?

If you felt anything other than great about your chance at booking a job, the answer is probably no. Simply knowing what your character is feeling before the scene begins and grounding yourself on a mark, igniting the emotion fully, and immersing yourself within the imagined geography of the scene in an audition are very, very, *very* different things.

This is why I detail the elements of a great audition in The Audition Code section. Auditions go by very quickly after a long lead-in. You get the material the day before (maybe less), either way you have to prepare for the audition, get yourself to the audition, sign in, wait, etc.

It's extremely important to walk into your auditions focused, energized, and ignited. Some actors think of this as coming into the room "in character." That may work for some and not for others. There is no rule about it. I think it's more organic and wiser to simply be clear on your emotional starting point and not ever be too far away from it as you're waiting to offer your work.

If you are anchored in a clear emotion when you start a scene, and you can see an environment vividly in your imagination, the chances of your overall audition going well increase exponentially. If you're untethered from the beginning, it's harder to recover or feel like you've done the job you wanted to do.

When you take full advantage of your moment before, you are more likely to keep the timing, rhythm, and pace of the scene and not fall a beat behind. You are more likely to feel emotionally alive and diverse throughout the scene. You are more likely to respond with your lines because you are listening deeply to the reader and not merely kicking out lines because it's your turn to say them. Professional-level work requires a clear, fully realized emotional state that reads for the camera. It's an easy concept to embrace. It's also easy to let that moment slip by. If you do, you won't get it back.

Your moment before when you hit the mark isn't just something you know. It isn't just a box to check off on the actor's homework list. It's something you absolutely need to consistently ignite yourself into action, especially in auditions. In order to activate, you need to have focus, awareness, and attentiveness as you begin.

Even in class, I tell my students to ignite performance energy once they stand up from their chairs. I want them to practice entering the scene emotionally charged and with their imagination churning in the time it takes to walk eight steps. That's what real life is like and I want them to be prepared for it.

You probably already knew what an actor's moment before was. Even if you didn't, you could probably deduce the meaning. It's fairly self-evident. Hopefully these thoughts impart the value of utilizing it to catapult your work to pro-level takes, when one take is all you might get!

Emotional Bandwidth

How your character feels about their tribe, circumstances, self, their life, and their place in it is essential to portraying a well-rounded human being. It's also crucial to fulfilling the comedic promise of a scene. Emotional turmoil is an enormous part of keeping an audience engaged and it also makes people laugh. Feelings are funny when they are felt honestly and change feverishly.

People commonly think of storylines and dialogue in television comedy as predictable. In truth, they often are. If the audience gets ahead of the scene, they can tune out because they know what's coming. If, however, the actor performing a scene — even one with an obvious outcome — is traversing a multitude of emotions as they scramble toward a resolution, the audience is still titillated, engaged, and amused. A performance instilled with emotional spontaneity can feel fresh and exciting even if you know how the moment is likely to end.

Emotional availability and volatility are specific aspects of the craft that distinguish good actors from amazing actors. Yes, the most iconic actors and characters from the history of television comedy are just plain funny. It's equally true that they are iconic because they have tremendous emotional bandwidth. They feel things deeply, quickly, and honestly. They have access to a full range of human emotions and don't mask or filter them in any way. They are brave and don't guard their hearts.

If the character's feelings are real, that means the actor's feelings are real as well. That's precisely the point where pretending ends and immersion begins. When your work is emotionally fulfilled, you're doing a great job *no matter what else is happening*. Sure, there may be adjustments or refinement ahead of you, but acting is living not observing, simulating, or outlining.

Aspire to always lead with your emotions when you perform.

We think we watch sitcoms to laugh. To some degree that's true. More than that, we watch to feel. Countless people around the world rewatch sitcoms from the first to last season — in some cases, hundreds of episodes — multiple times. I doubt the same is true for *Law & Order: SVU*. You don't get to the last episode of *Friends*, *Frasier*, or *Everybody Loves Raymond* from the very beginning more than once just because of quality jokes. We keep The Heroes of Comedy in our lives because they make us feel uplifted, accepted, and just plain better.

The jokes are the responsibility of the writers. They're in the dialogue and the audience will laugh or not as suits their taste. Characterization is important, and actors must strive to fulfill their character's core traits. But the writers also created the character and defined what they are like. Their dialogue — the way a character speaks — is in the hands of the writers. It's *extremely* rare that anyone improvises dialogue in an ongoing series.

The *single* aspect of the work that is solely in the hands of the actor is how emotional each experience is for their character. Yes, we still have to honor context. For example, we don't send our character into hysteria if there's no logical reason for it in the scene. However, it is a common issue that an extreme emotional state like hysteria *is* written into a scene, and actors aren't able to fulfill hysteria's potential. Limits suddenly surface. Without wanting or meaning to, actors show the extent of their comfort zone. It can't be small if you want to book professional-level work.

The greatest misunderstanding about acting in comedy is how reliant it is on emotional turbulence. Every scene requires emotional bandwidth from the characters within them. Performers must make the effort to wring every justifiable ounce of emotion from the character's experience as possible. Actors often feel or assume their performance will be too big if they get too emotional. If you show, telegraph, or indicate your emotions, yes, your performance will come across as too big because indicating emotions is the definition of bad acting.

If you experience feelings authentically, there is no limit to their depth. Actors NEVER get the note, "Dial back the emotion." They may get feedback on how to execute or adjust their character's emotional state. But no one in all of Hollywood ever says to an actor, "This would be much better with less feeling."

Emotions exist within us internally and can be fairly chaotic. They come and go in layers, many at a time. Sometimes mismatched, unrelated, and confusing, which is yet another emotion. But we know how to mask and channel our feelings, if not control them entirely. We do that in our personal lives every day.

How often do you feel something strongly and the people around you don't necessarily know? Feeling out of control does not mean you are out of control. Thrusting your character into the deep waters of unrestrained emotion absolutely does *not* equate to broad or bad acting. Conversely, weak acting is easily defined by a lack of emotional depth and variety.

You should never be afraid of anything while you're performing. But if there is anything to fear, it's certainly not that your performance is infused with too much emotion. How can that even happen? The wrong emotion for the scene? Yes. Your emotions need to align with what's happening to your character. Indicating emotion without feeling it authentically? Happens all the time. Can't fake it. Gotta keep it real. Good note, one note? Sure. That means an actor is attached emotionally to the material but anchored in only one primary emotion and not experiencing a journey. The performance lacks emotional diversity and nuance. Okay for drama, won't work for comedy.

If you're not changing emotionally throughout a scene, you're not... changing. If you never leave your initial emotional state, it appears the experience means nothing. The other characters apparently did not affect you in any way, which leaves you un-sympathetic. When there's no impulsive emotional reaction to incoming stimulus, it's like watching an actor perform a mono-logue within a scene.

We laugh at things that occur more quickly than they typically should, including feelings. The greatest comedic actors we've ever had explode into their emotions with shocking magnitude and are hardly thought of as too big or too broad. If anything, they are considered geniuses of the genre. Witness: Robin Williams (*Mork & Mindy*), Lily Tomlin (*Grace and Frankie*), Jim Carrey (*In Living Color*), Martin Short (*Saturday Night Live, SCTV*), Lucille Ball (*I Love Lucy*), Carol Burnett (*The Carol Burnett Show*), Phil Hartman (*NewsRadio*), and Catherine O'Hara (*Schitt's Creek*).

When I break down scenes, I brainstorm all the possible emotions I might feel given the circumstance in the scene, the moment before the scene begins and the moment after it ends. On average, a character in a four-page scene can easily ex-perience 30 or more distinct emotions. Occasionally less, but often more.

We read in a linear fashion so, yes, I might list them in order from the beginning of the scene to the end, but I don't assign emotions to specific areas or lines. Do what provides you with your best results, but I personally don't want my actor's home-work to feel like a test. I want my investigation and interpretation to set me up for success. I don't want to ever feel like I need to land on a certain emotion on a certain line. I just want to know what the options and parameters are so I can play.

I further want to challenge myself to find emotional possi-bilities that other actors perhaps aren't seeing. I also trust that emotions ebb and flow in layers and that we are designed to change our emotional state instantly. Our emotions reflect what we're experiencing. One way to define acting is a person playing a character who exists within a story. Stories need to engage and entertain. They inherently do that by detailing how things change for the characters. If events are everchanging that means emotions are too. *You therefore cannot be too emotional in your work.* You can be too expressive or demonstrative depending on the style and tone of the series but that's a different matter. Actors never get called out on simply being emotionally vital.

Great comedy leaves you vulnerable because it asks you to experience your emotions honestly and quickly. There is no slow burn. You cannot guard yourself and expose yourself at the same time. There are no emotions in quotes. You're not "disgusted" by what your partner just did in bed. You're **disgusted** by what your partner just did in bed. You're not "kind of" desperate to sign a lease on a new apartment. You're **desperate** to sign a lease on a new apartment.

A desperate person is at the end of their rope and, frankly, dangerous. He's gnawing on his last bit of hope and about to gulp it down to fuel his last wild swing at his *severe* desire, utilizing *all* his strength. If I was in the presence of someone who felt desperate, I would automatically feel concerned, alert, alarmed, charged, etc., *without their saying a word*. What a powerful scene that would be. It's okay if you can't get to every extreme emotional place possible, but you should know that's what leading on-camera comedy actors do. They maximize their emotional bandwidth.

Sometimes actors need help identifying the emotion written into the scene or igniting within themselves. Of course, I can help them do that. Other times actors know exactly what the character should feel and how to excite that feeling in their own body but simply get relaxed and forget that *emotions are inherently big.*

They shove their way into the moments of your life without asking permission first. They sit where they want inside of you and put their feet up on your psyche. Our reasoning mind has to constantly assuage our bullying emotions. That's what therapy is: learning to understand and manage our feelings that dictate our behavior. Emotions are like boy kings; they have tons of power and nothing to restrain them. They're capricious and lead with entitlement. So, if you thought acting in comedy was a way to play, laugh, and *not* to feel, you couldn't be more wrong.

Emotional freedom is of paramount importance to a sitcom actor because the reality is feelings come first. We like to think we move forward in life because of thoughts and plans, but the truth is we only take action on our goals if we *feel* like it.

Relationships

When you audition for a role in television or film, your goal isn't merely to bring your character to life; you must also actualize the relationships your character has to the other members of their tribe.

It's obvious that your character has relationships, but it's easy for actors to overlook how each relationship distinctly feels. Not every couple has the same kind of marriage. Some characters have complicated relationships with their boss that could use better boundaries, others are indifferent to their boss. Siblings in sitcoms almost always engage in some sort of rivalry. It's easy to spot the difference between actors who offer their detailed take on that common trope and those who play the concept of sibling rivalry with no attachment to the true nature of a particular dynamic.

Gauging and embodying the texture, tone, depth, proximity, and history of your character's relationships are key elements to booking on-camera work. It's a challenge to begin with but magnified when an actor is auditioning for a lead role. Imagine any character from one of your favorite sitcoms. If you like the show and like the character, you probably like the way they engage their friends and family. In other words, you also like their relationships. (I like Liz and Jack's *relationship* on *30 Rock* as much as I like each individual character). Now imagine working backwards from what you know and love about the show to the day the actors first auditioned for the role. The actors were each on a mark alone reading with a casting director.

The casting directors who audition actors and the producers who hire actors are looking for more than just a solid performer who understands the character. They are also assessing whether the actor is striking the right note in their relationships to the other members of their tribe. It is evident by the actor's vibe and intonation whether their relationship work is on point. Producers need to see that you understand the qualities of the primary relationships your character has within the show.

It's easy to see what the relationships in a script are. It takes practice and personalization to make sure they have the right feel. If you're thinking, "How will I know if I'm doing that?" The answer is training in script analysis for television and film. It's different from theatrical script analysis and, frankly, most actors who want a career in front of a camera don't have enough of it.

You can offer a terrific take on a husband's characterization but read as if you don't really love your wife. This occurs often with improvisers who haven't had ample on-camera practice. The producers can't even consider hiring you as that husband if there is tension or dismissiveness where there shouldn't be. You can be the funniest actor auditioning for a mom but come off as distant and cold when the character is being sarcastic with her kid.

If your audition sides involve a fight with a roommate, even an intense fight, it doesn't mean you hate your roommate. It's more likely that you love your roommate, the way the group loved each other on *Friends*, but are feeling irritated, righteous, and blindsided by something they've done. The fight is comedic when there is a foundation of love and shared history beneath it. That history likely includes good times, birthday parties, important milestones, helping each other through breakups and losses, etc. Typical life stuff.

The script tells you everything. There are no secrets shrouding the information necessary to produce a great audition. You just need the right skills to extract the key clues from the pages. Once you know how to break down scripts, it's like reading with magic glasses. Answers that were never there before suddenly appear!

Sometimes actors get stymied, especially if they are auditioning for pilots (new shows that haven't aired yet), by what the relationships between the characters are like. I can always find the answer within the dialogue and I can teach others to do the same. Before we refine relationships with nuance, however, we begin with a simpler step.

The relationships between lead characters on *every* show are either built on a foundation of affection or admiration. If the characters have a history together, always assume there is affection between them. If there is no evidence of affection between the characters, they probably don't know each other and are just meeting. This happens often in pilots. If characters haven't known each other long enough to have formed a loving bond, they admire each other instantly. You do not have to love or even like someone to admire them.

Case in point: *Cheers* opened with Sam and Diane not knowing each other. By end of the pilot, Sam hired Diane to work at Cheers. Why? She said yes. Why? The answer is the same. Even though they gave each other quite a hard time upon introduction, Sam admired Diane's intelligence and she admired his charisma. They grew to love each other and then fell in love with each other.

In the pilot of *The Mary Tyler Moore Show*, Mary is just moving to Minneapolis and in need of a job. She interviews with Mr. Grant at the WJM television studio. When they meet, he's gruff, over-bearing, and inappropriate. But at the end of the interview, he offers her a job. Why? Because she's authentic and earnest. Admirable qualities in a job candidate. She takes the job. Why? He's blunt to a fault but honest. It's clear you'll always know where you stand with Mr. Grant. Honesty in an employer is admirable. I'd work for that guy. So would Mary. He went on to become her mentor and great friend. Their affection and love for one another blossomed out of mutual admiration.

Maybe you're thinking of a character on a show that no one seemed to really like. Gunther on *Friends* or Newman on *Seinfeld*, for example. Those are recurring characters, not leads. That's a big distinction. It's fun to have someone the whole group likes to kick around. If you ever encounter a character that no one seems to like or admire, it will be quite clear on the page and you can manifest that relationship accordingly.

More often, the confusion tends to stem from actors not being able to navigate the line between heightening conflict and lean-ing into the affection or admiration you hold for the other person. As I say throughout this book, stories are about obstacles. The problems within the stories create tension within the relation-ships. We must always bear in mind that we can love someone very much and be very unhappy with them at the same time. The same is true for your characters.

Whatever else happens, their commitment to each other can't be broken. Sitcom relationships are elastic. We need to see them stretch, but we don't want them to snap. Ross and Rachel had an epically tumultuous relationship on *Friends*. But even when they couldn't be together romantically, they remained friends. Their care and love for each other was never severed.

Characters also have relationships to things other than people. We have relationships to pets, objects, memories of the past, and our hopes and dreams of our future. So do our characters. The Heroes of Comedy often talk about other people in their lives who aren't present in the current scene, things they've done in the past, and things they've yet to do but want to.

If your character has a noteworthy shirt, mug, or ring, you need to identify the emotions and history involved with those objects. Especially while auditioning, you need to acknowledge how you feel about the other characters you mention who aren't there. Does your character feel the same way about their mother and their mother-in-law? Their father and their stepfather? The way you say someone's name can tell a whole story. Make sure you're always telling it.

Everyone knows we have memories and dreams. Actors don't always fulfill the emotional connection we have to them in their work. We don't just *have* thoughts in our heads, we have *relationships* to the thoughts in our heads. Our memories stay with us throughout our lives and we define ourselves by them in part because of the way they make us feel.

New ambitions can be very much like making a new friend you feel like you've always known. Making a commitment to a long-term goal is no less significant than making a commitment to a person. In ways, it's more intimate because the whole association exists within and relies entirely upon you for fulfillment. Our dreams thrive or wither based solely on our feelings.

So, yes, we definitely have relationships with them. Make sure your characters do too. When actors reference members of their tribe, favorite objects, their high school prom, their retirement plans, career ambitions, etc., and there is no emotional connection, it's apparent and a missed opportunity. There's a vacancy of feeling precisely where there should be a shift.

Even further, we have relationships with religion, spirituality, personal philosophies, ideals, and standards. These may or may not be mentioned directly in scenes, but still worth considering.

When you consider all the relationships that are referenced in any given scene, the number can climb rapidly. Maybe there's only one other character in the scene, but you talk about several others. Your birthday is coming up, so you reminisce about how last year's celebration bombed because someone in your tribe mucked it up. That leads to a plan about what you'll do this year instead and you hope it will be better. What will you wear? Your favorite (lucky) party outfit, of course. If it's a significant birthday (30, 40, 50, 60, etc.), you might have a certain relationship to that particular milestone. You can see where I'm going.

You do not need to investigate your character's relationship to a person, place, or thing that is merely placed into dialogue as a joke. You, the actor, just need to understand the reference and why it's funny. Pop culture references are used in comedy all the time. Here's an example from *Veep*: On her departure from the United Kingdom, Selina Meyer says to her staff, "Okay, let's get the merry old fuck out of merry old England. Okay, I need to be driven to the airport at *Diana* speed. Okay, just more carefully though, please." If you get this joke, great. It's dark but very funny. If you don't get it, I'll help. It's a reference to Diana, Princess of Wales, and her untimely death from a car crash. Her driver was speeding to flee paparazzi.

Selina didn't like England. That's an opinion she formed while there. She does not have a relationship with England, and there is no work for the actor to do there. More importantly, Selina doesn't have a relationship with Princess Diana. It's a pop culture reference that the character is aware of because it is a commonly known historical fact.

Sometimes actors include references of this nature on their list of relationships to explore and it's not necessary. In fact, it would get in the way of the joke if it read on any level like Selina had a personal relationship with Princess Diana. Her death was tragic and if it seemed like Selina had any kind of connection to it other than common knowledge, the already dark joke would just seem cruel.

I'll remind you again here as I do throughout the book that auditioning can leave actors particularly vulnerable and isolated. Even if you've done great work exploring your relationships in the scene, it's easy for that effort to evaporate if you lose focus while on the mark. If you haven't been working through how all your relationships *feel*, you're missing essential work that is necessary to be competitive. If you're a working actor who gets opportunities to interview for lead roles in comedy and aren't booking, this is definitely something to examine.

If you didn't know that the texture of your relationships— literally *how you talk to other people* in the scene — was a big part of how producers assess whether to hire you, now you know. Yes, you are auditioning for a single role, but that character belongs to an ensemble that must mesh. Casting is not just matching an actor with a role. It's matching several actors' portrayals of different characters in a show *to each other*.

A sitcom audition isn't a test you take to prove you're funny. Your goal is to portray a person who has a distinct nature within their tribe with a clear understanding of their connections to others within that tribe. Furthermore, it's your duty to assess their status in the hierarchy of their world.

There is a way to know for certain whether you are close to that target or not. You just have to look at the script the way the writers do. You don't have to be a writer, just think like one. And it's easier to learn than you might guess.

Scripts are not as open to interpretation as most actors think. Writers sell shows with a pitch that can be boiled down to a logline. One sentence. The characters all have biographies. They're defined. Any investigation into how the writer sees the relationships unfolding within the story brings you closer to becoming a valued collaborator on their project.

Actions

For actors, the words *actions* and *intentions* are interchangeable. Quite simply, they are verbs; activating words that you can apply to every sentence of dialogue in your scene. Clear intention in what you say creates nuance and distinction in your performance. Verbs are all about what we are *doing*, so they also help support an athletic, energetic, and ultimately memorable performance.

Your character speaks in a scene, but to what end? They want something. Intentions are how they get what they want. I previously reinforced how emotions are everchanging in a great comedic performance. In a similar way, intentions should change constantly too. Emotions and intentions work in harmony together. You can think of emotions as "incoming" and intentions as "outgoing."

Certainly we feel emotions inside our body, but they are stirred, manipulated, and heightened by stimulus hurling toward us, *incoming*. Someone says something, something happens, and it touches us emotionally, if only slightly.

We react to what comes at us by speaking purposeful words or taking a result-oriented physical action, *outgoing*. Our behavior is influenced by how we feel. We only say or do something because we want something to happen. *How* we speak and *how* we behave has everything in the world to do with how we *feel*. Emotions and intentions work in synchronicity.

You might not have a particularly strong feeling behind everything you say or do, but make no mistake; our words and how we say them, our actions and how we execute them, are invariably colored by how we are feeling in each moment.

Clear intent underneath your lines helps enhance your performance in a number of ways. Distinct intentions inform each sentence of dialogue you speak, which give your words power and unmistakable purpose. Intentions enable your character to work toward what they want in a scene with precision, specificity, and clarity.

You should always know *why* your character is saying whatever they're saying. That's a different statement than saying you should *understand* what they're saying. You should know what motivates the words to fall from your character's lips. Knowing the intention for every line of your character's dialogue enables you to answer the question, "Why did you say that?" When you can answer that question for every word you speak, you're in an incredibly powerful position as an actor.

You may assume it's always an easy question to answer. Mostly it is. But when an actor speaks a line of dialogue and they're not connected to it in any way, it's extremely obvious. It reads like the actor is just connecting the verbal dots until they get to something they'd like to say better. If you're lacking a relationship to something you say in a script, it's because you're not clear on the intention. You don't have a handle on what you want to happen because you said it.

When you get to the point that you can easily and consistently articulate why you're speaking all of your dialogue within your scene, you have quite likely become a master of the craft. Once you are able to attach the significance of all the words in your scene to your want statement, you own the scene entirely. It's like you're holding it in the palm of your hand.

If, in addition, those intentions are distinct and varying throughout the scene, not much else can be asked of you. One way of defining what it is to be a truly great comedic actor is: one who is switching up emotions and intentions rapidly while maintaining their characterization.

Comedy teachers who are worth about a nickel bark, "Louder, faster, funnier!" at actors as if that might help. What are you going to do, scream quickly in an odd way? That won't work. It's a cheap attempt at guiding actors to what is actually an elevated level of execution. You wouldn't tell an ice skater, "Higher, faster, spinnier!" and expect a substantial result. What those folks are trying to say, but can't, is that the internal mechanisms of The Heroes of Comedy operate at a high rate of speed. That's true at a standing pace and exacerbated by dilemma.

Absorbing what's coming at you rapidly on a deep level and strategizing how to respond to it moment-by-moment, produces a sort of mania all its own. We laugh at emotional nudity and intentional karate. Funny is the byproduct of an ego exposed at an accelerated rate. That said, if "Louder, faster, funnier!" works for you, then so be it.

Diversifying your intentions throughout a scene makes it more exciting to watch and opens up comedic opportunities. Sometimes lines of dialogue are funny because they are also well-written jokes. The words you speak can also be funny because of an unexpected or clever intention underneath the line.

Cultivating a broad, diverse vocabulary of intentions makes you a superior actor. The reasons actors book work or don't go way past assessing whether they are good or bad. That's rarely the discussion. The vast majority of actors who are brought into the audition room by casting are good, well-trained, experienced performers. They wouldn't be there at all if that weren't true.

So, let's start with the premise that the actors auditioning for a role are only there because they are more or less equally qualified. It's fair to wonder if there's anything more you can do than simply act the part honestly and hope for the best.

There is. Actors can set themselves apart by applying intentions in a smart, strategic way. Not all actors you are competing against have learned the power of utilizing intentions to create a stronger, more dynamic performance. Many others who know what intentions are ignore intentional exploration as part of their actor's homework when prepping. In most cases, I advise actors to do whatever works best for each of you. When it comes to practicing intentions, I think it's neglectful not to explore them if you want to compete for work at a professional level.

If you haven't been introduced to intentions, we're taking care of that now! If you know what they are, how to use them and simply don't, you're ignoring a powerful tool that can uplevel your work significantly. Deploying great intentions helps you book!

General or repetitive intentions are what make a performance or audition executed by an otherwise good actor weak. It is extremely easy and all too common to say four lines of dialogue in a row with the same intention underneath all of them. That will make a performance boring and forgettable very fast. With just a little effort, the same four lines could have different intentions underneath that complement each other, fit the context of the moment, and strategically support your want statement.

Switching intentions as you travel through your dialogue will also enhance the musical nature of scripted comedy. Some actors coach with me privately just so I can help them assign sharper and wittier intentions to their dialogue. When you're auditioning at the network/studio level for series regular roles, every percentage point helps. Clever intentions underneath the lines for each sentence is one way I can make an audition performance stronger 100 percent of the time.

Here's an example of strategically used intentions: Let's say this scene is about a middle-management boss tasked with firing an employee who is also a friend. For the sake of context, it's a given that the boss is genuinely sorry to have to let the employee go. They like each other. We'll just deal with Boss' four opening lines:

"Bill, it looks like we're going to have to lay you off. Just so you know, it wasn't my decision. The word came down from corporate. I'm really sorry."

Boss opens the scene with four separate sentences. Since we know these two are friendly, it would be very easy to generalize all this dialogue with an apologetic tone. "Apologize" could potentially be the intention under all four lines. Someone hit the snooze button!

While that would be at least accurate for the scene, it's not engaging enough to book. Anyone could read those lines and apologize all the way through them. It would be an extremely weak opening to an audition. Casting would certainly not move it forward to producers. I've worked in casting. Please trust me on this. I promise you we'll still "keep it real." With that, let's explore better options!

1. Bill, it looks like we're going to have to lay you off.
    Some intentions that apply only to this line of dialogue and not the other three are: *brace, introduce, ease.* Other options include: *empathize, announce, steady, fortify,* and *apologize.* Comedic choices include: *pout, discover, whine,* and *complain.*

2. Just so you know, it wasn't my decision.
   Contextual: *defend, clarify, absolve.*
   Comedic: *halt, mourn, unload.*

3. The word came down from corporate.
   Contextual: *inform, elaborate, explain, justify.*
   Comedic: *blame, condemn, throw under the bus.*

4. I'm really sorry.
   Contextual: *apologize, commiserate, conclude.*
   Comedic: *pity, grieve, guess.*

Mixing these intentions underneath the lines will give your performance hustle and dimension other good actors may not be offering.

In review, you can't get away from this being a story about a boss who genuinely regrets having to let an employee that they like go. You can't deny their status. With the full scene, you would see what kind of people they are, and you won't be able to get away from their core characteristics, either.

It's worth noting that intentions are heavily influenced by characterization. If Boss is an Anchor like Michael Bluth on *Arrested Development*, the more practical and direct intentions make more sense. If Boss is a Neurotic like Amy Brookheimer on *Veep*, intentions that support that archetype's insecurity and anxiety would make the most sense. If Boss is a Buffoon like Michael Scott on *The Office*, you would go with the intentions I listed as comedic.

If you didn't understand how some of the intentions I listed might play, let me explain. I imagined how different Heroes of Comedy might get through that moment. Anchors ground people, Neurotics worry, and Buffoons are socially dimwitted. They would not know how to fire someone with grace even if they liked them. They might *guess* that "I'm really sorry," is the right way to end a termination.

Michael Scott said many idiotic things on *The Office*. He also said his fair share of typical things any boss might say. In either case, Steve Carrell made all his moments believable by dialing into sharp, atypical, and everchanging intentions. The actions under his lines were filtered through his primary characteristics.

Incorporating intentions is not the only way, but it's a great way to offer the writers and producers a performance that surpasses their expectations and showcases your unique con- tribution to the overall project. Emotional flexibility is one way you can excel as an actor. Sharp, smart, surprising intentions that align with the moment they're spoken but still offer a surprise is true artistry.

iCAMERA Quick Review

What is the story of the scene? It's the story of...

I WANT

What does your character want that involves the cooperation of one or more other characters?

CONFLICT

What is the external conflict in the scene? The archetypal conflict? The unconscious emotional conflict (fears, phobias, historical resentments, etc.)?

ARC

Where does the scene arc? Exactly what moment in the scene do you stop moving toward your want/goal/agenda/demand/ desire?

MOMENT BEFORE

What is your character's moment before? Where are they in the world? What is their exact emotional state before speaking? Exactly when is their first emotional change?

EMOTIONAL BANDWIDTH

What are all the emotions your character experiences within the scene? What is your emotional journey?

RELATIONSHIPS

What is the complete list of people, places, objects, memories, hopes, and philosophies referred to in the scene that your character has a relationship with? How is your character changed emotionally when they are mentioned?

ACTIONS

Are your intentions underneath the lines changing throughout the scene? Are they interesting or expected?

"Words are the model, words are the tools, words are the boards, words are the nails."

– Richard Rhodes

11

The Secret Power of Operative Words

Operative words are the key or root words of a sentence. They are the compulsory words for communicating your thoughts. When stressed or given emphasis, these words provide clarity of intent and lead to the truth of your communication. Operative words are contained in narrative or action lines, but most importantly for actors, they are also found within dialogue.

Most of the references to operative words in performance dialogue involve the study of Shakespeare. I looked high and low for resources that would help modern actors and writers level up their practice with operative words and could not find anything of value. So I created this section from scratch. Actors and writers alike will have an edge on their competition with a deeper understanding of expression through precise inflection.

Let's play with a simple sentence: The dog peed on your rug.

Changing emphasis gives this sentence very different meanings.

The <u>dog</u> peed on your rug.
- This emphasis contrasts the dog to something or someone else. It clarifies the subject of the sentence, which is the dog.

The dog <u>peed</u> on your rug.

- This emphasis reveals that the dog peed on the rug, as opposed to another possible bodily function. It highlights the verb, which is what the dog did.

The dog peed on <u>your</u> rug.

- This emphasis illustrates that the dog peed on a specific person's rug versus someone else's. Highlighting the possessive pronoun assigns ownership.

The dog peed on your <u>rug</u>.

- This emphasis indicates that the dog peed on the rug as opposed to something else. It clarifies the intent of the sentence by highlighting the object.

Identifying operative words is particularly important for comedy as they help uplift the musical nature and embedded joke structure of comedic dialogue. The context of the situation and flow of conversation help you identify the correct operative words and connect you more accurately to the subtext.

Becoming crystal clear as to *why* you're saying what you're saying will help you make smarter and crisper choices in regard to your intentions, strategies, and tactics. Consequently, your work will become more specific and dynamic.

Operative word exploration can even lead to sharper character development. If, for example, an actor deliberately chooses to redirect emphasis to words that are *not* operative, they are creating a certain kind of person. Maybe bolder, maybe more dimwitted, maybe more self-effacing than typical. It depends on the context, but the point is actors who have strong acuity with language are able to play with it to their advantage.

When a speaker puts emphasis on the right words, both communication and comedy are enhanced. It helps us hear not just the words, but the greater point that is being made. So, while operative words exist and are important in all kinds of communication, they have a heightened importance in comedy; even more so within multi-cam sitcoms. Operative words elevate the comedy on single-camera sitcoms, but that format doesn't have an audience to contend with.

Multi-cams are shot in front of a live, studio audience. An obvious goal is for the audience to laugh. Not every line of dialogue can double as a well-crafted joke. Often writers sneak in funny sounding words, specific references, or colloquial phrases to get laughs. Other times actors are able to tickle the audience simply by speaking well! When dialogue is delivered with clarity, intent, and accurate intonation, we are engaged, if not mesmerized. It's kind of like casting a spell on the people listening.

When an actor hits all their jokes in a comedy performance and nails all their operative words as well, it's magical. The main cast of *Will & Grace* is particularly adept at doing this, for example. Their cadence and speech patterns are elevated, synchronistic, and akin to singing. Comedy, especially comedy performed for an audience, is musical. There's no way around it. Setting up jokes and punchlines that create audience laughter, which factors into the timing, rhythm, and pace is in every way comparable to the rests, stops and tempo of a song.

It's been a tremendous joy to see actors play with this tool. I am endlessly amazed how one read of a line can get no response, but adding emphasis to *just one word* can bring the house down. That's power. And it's available to anyone.

We've all heard operative words spoken since birth. Nursery rhymes are likely our first exposure to them. Singers hit operative words in songs. Rap, hip-hop, and beat poetry all rely on word emphasis. Nurses, doctors, and military personnel rely heavily on operative words to get an urgent message across instantly. ("I need X, Y & Z... *stat!*)

We organically use them ourselves in daily speech. When we say a sentence out loud and it comes out wrong, we instantly know it. There is now finally an accessible way to better understand something we all practice but to which we never before had a practical reference guide. Hitting your operative words will literally make you funnier and people will regard you as smarter. Mastery of language skills implies both intelligence and wit.

It's a bit of an art form to deduce operative words properly. Sometimes there is not one in a given sentence. Sometimes there are several. There are no bulletproof rules that apply 100 percent of the time. Within dialogue, context and intention can force words to become operative that grammatically should not be. Here are some guidelines that will lead to the correct choices nearly always. Every single one has an exception. So have fun, but don't overthink it!

Adverbs and adjectives are operative most of the time because it's their job in language to modify, (*change, specify, highlight, emphasize*) other words. Think of them as intensifiers that also increase the emotional possibilities within a scene. Leaning into your most important words will give your acting greater vitality and spontaneity!

Since adverbs and adjectives have an active task to bring us into clearer understanding of what's being said to us, it makes sense they would claim emphasis!

An **adverb** is a word or set of words that modifies verbs, adjectives, or other adverbs.

Examples:
I was <u>unjustly</u> fired today.
(*unjustly* is an adverb that modifies the **verb** *fired*.)

Well, isn't she <u>especially</u> clever?
(*especially* is an adverb that modifies the **adjective** *clever*.)

This marriage is happening <u>all too</u> quickly for my taste!
(*all too* is the adverb group of words that modify the **adverb** *quickly*.)

An **adjective** is a word or set of words that **modifies** (i.e., describes) a noun or pronoun. Adjectives may come before *or after* the word they modify.

Examples:

That was a meaningless text.
(*meaningless* is the adjective that describes the **noun** *text, beforehand.*)

Dylan's mother is evil.
(*evil* is the adjective that describes the **noun** *mother, afterward.*)

She looks magnificent in that dress.
(*magnificent* is the adjective that describes the **pronoun** *she.*)

Colloquialisms are often operative and garner emphasis as a whole phrase.

A **colloquialism** is a word or phrase that is used mostly in informal speech: a colloquial expression.

Examples:

Oops. <u>My bad</u>.

<u>At the end of the day</u>, breakups are always hard.

I know breakups are hard, but <u>what are you gonna do?</u>

Dude, quit <u>harshing my mellow</u>.

You handled that <u>like a boss</u>.

<u>Don't make a mountain out of a molehill!</u>

Are you going to <u>spill the tea</u> about your date last night?

Words that are used to compare or contrast are almost always operative.

<u>One</u> of us has to do it. Is it going to be <u>you</u> or <u>me</u>?

I'm either going to <u>stay in</u> or <u>go out</u>.

Honestly, I don't know whether to <u>kill</u> you or <u>kiss</u> you.

Prepositional phrases generally don't contain operative words because they can be done away with if necessary.

A **prepositional phrase** is a group of words consisting of a preposition, its object, and any words that modify the object. Most of the time, a prepositional phrase modifies a verb or a noun.

Here is a full list of prepositions:

- aboard
- about
- above
- across
- after
- against
- along
- amid
- among
- around
- as
- at
- before
- behind
- below
- beneath
- beside
- between
- beyond
- but
- by
- concerning
- considering
- despite
- down
- during
- except
- following
- for
- from
- in
- inside
- into
- like

- minus
- near
- next
- of
- off
- on
- onto
- opposite
- out
- outside
- over
- past
- per
- plus
- regarding
- round
- save
- since
- than
- through
- to
- toward
- under
- underneath
- unlike
- until
- up
- upon
- versus
- via
- with
- within
- without

Examples:

I'm <u>digging</u> out my <u>retainer</u> *from the garbage.*

If you were there and had visual context, you could see the person had their hands in the garbage. It's not necessary to say, so the words *from the garbage* can be eliminated altogether.

The <u>book</u> that was *in the sauna* is <u>swollen</u> *from the steam*!

Again, if the scene took place just outside a sauna, you could say, "The book is swollen." If another character exited the sauna and a blast of steam bellowed forth, we'd get why the book swelled up. This sentence has two prepositional phrases; *in the sauna* and *from the steam*. Since both can be removed and the sentence still makes sense with visual context, we find no operative words there!

There are times you will find an operative word in a prepositional phrase. The English language is complicated. When you add in slang terms and common phraseology, things can get tricky. Remember, these are guidelines, not absolute rules.

When new people, objects, or concepts are introduced into the story, they are likely to be operative *only the first time they are mentioned*.

If they are referred to thereafter, they will very likely *not* be the operative word again, even though they may be the continued topic of conversation. This is important because writers use words repeatedly for comedic effect. It would be incorrect to assume that because a particular word is the focus of a conversation that it is perpetually operative. Often, comedy teachers will define repeated words as operative words. This is incorrect as I exemplify below.

Example:

"Hey everyone, I'd like you to meet <u>Ken</u>. Ken will be working here <u>temporarily</u>. I know it may get <u>a bit</u> confusing since we now have <u>four</u> Kens on staff. To review, Ken <u>Carlson</u> is the <u>accounts receivable manager</u>, Ken <u>Maccabee</u> is our <u>janitor</u>, Ken <u>Kimoto</u> is our <u>CFO</u>, and <u>this</u> Ken will be our <u>receptionist</u> for the time being. <u>His</u> last name isn't <u>super</u> important because <u>he</u> won't be here <u>long</u>."

As you can see in this example, the aforementioned rules of adverbs, adjectives, and comparison apply when deducing the correct operative words. All the Kens are being contrasted by last name and job title. The new Ken is being compared to the other three Kens as temporary and unimportant versus permanent and necessary. *Temporarily* is an adverb. *Super* is an adjective. *A bit* is an idiom that modifies confusing. There are also three prepositional phrases: *on staff, to review, for the time being*. Notice there are no operative words contained within them.

If there are no adverbs, adjectives or new ideas, objects, or concepts being introduced within the dialogue, then the subject or the verb of the sentence are likely to be operative.

Examples with subjects/nouns as operative:

Here is the <u>robot</u> you asked for!

Where are my <u>glasses</u>?

That is Beth's <u>PowerPoint presentation</u>.

Examples with verbs as operative:

The car <u>crashed</u> into the telephone pole.

I'm <u>eating</u>!

You wanted to <u>see</u> me?

Single words followed by a comma at the beginning of a sentence are not operative.

Commas instruct a slight pause when speaking, similar to a rest in music. In contrast, periods, question marks, and exclamation points indicate a complete resolve and stop to each thought or sentence. Don't let the natural pause or emphasis created by a comma trick you into thinking those words are operative. They're not. They may still warrant emphasis, but generally those words alone are not the overall point you are trying to communicate.

Examples:

~~Look~~, if you <u>really</u> want me to leave, I <u>will</u>.

~~Well~~, that's <u>not</u> what I <u>ordered</u>.

~~So~~, if it's a <u>yes for you</u>, it's a <u>yes for me</u>!

12

Heart

HEART is an emotional thesaurus that features 550 words of emotion, placed in five general categories. HEART is an acronym for Happy, Exasperated, Amorous, Repulsed, Troubled.

In order to maintain emotional depth and diversity throughout your writing or performance, it's essential to have a strong vocabulary of emotions. HEART will help you quickly and efficiently explore your character's emotional bandwidth.

If you can't say it, you won't play it. Finding just the right word for the moment can make all the difference in a performance.

I thought about the emotions actors need most quickly, based on reading and coaching tens of thousands of scenes, and compiled them here. Generally, characters in scripted comedy are feeling a version of those five category headers. Building your vocabulary of emotions as you refine your craft will make all your script analysis and actor prep go much faster!

With HEART, all you need to do is detect the general emotional state you're sensing and within that column you'll find precise words that will give your performance bold definition.

The difference in your acting or writing is like watching a film on an old television versus a 4K ultra-high definition screen. Competitive actors have a large palette of emotions always at the ready. I highly recommend keeping this resource handy!

Happy	Exasperated	Amorous	Repulsed	Troubled
Absorbed	Adamant	Adoring	Abominable	Abandoned
Accepting	Aggressive	Affectionate	Afflicted	Agonized
Accomplished	Ambivalent	Aflame	Aggrieved	Alone
Adequate	Annoyed	Amped	Aghast	Angry
Adroit	Apathetic	Ardent	Agitated	Anxious
Agreeable	Bad	Aroused	Alarmed	Apologetic
Almighty	Bored	Attached	Appalled	Ashamed
Amazed	Challenged	Attracted	Astounded	Bashful
Arrogant	Competitive	Awakened	Awkward	Betrayed
Astounded	Confused	Berserk	Bereft	Bitter
Awed	Conspicuous	Bestial	Besmirched	Blindsided
Awesome	Contrite	Bonded	Chagrined	Boiling
Beautiful	Determined	Captivated	Chilled	Broken
Blissful	Different	Carnal	Choked	Burdened
Bold	Diffident	Charmed	Contemptuous	Cautious
Brave	Discouraged	Covetous	Creeped out	Cheated
Calm	Distracted	Desirous	Daunted	Cold
Capable	Disturbed	Devoted	Dejected	Combative
Cheerful	Divided	Dirty	Demoralized	Condemned
Childish	Dubious	Enchanted	Depressed	Cruel
Clever	Envious	Engorged	Despicable	Crushed

Happy	Exasperated	Amorous	Repulsed	Troubled
Comforted	Exasperated	Erotic	Despondent	Culpable
Competent	Exhausted	Fervent	Detestable	Deceitful
Confident	Fatigued	Fervid	Disappoint-ed	Defeated
Curious	Flustered	Fevered	Disapprov-ing	Desolate
Delighted	Foolish	Fired up	Disbelieving	Despairing
Divine	Forced	Fond	Discomfited	Destructive
Dope	Frustrated	Frisky	Discontent-ed	Devastat-ed
Dynamic	Full	Fuckable	Disdainful	Diminished
Eager	Greedy	Gung ho	Disen-chanted	Distraught
Earnest	Guilty	Hard	Disen-thralled	Dominated
Easy	Harassed	Heavenly	Disgruntled	Embar-rassed
Ecstatic	Hesitant	High	Disgusted	Empty
Electrified	Homesick	Horny	Disheart-ened	Endan-gered
Energetic	Hungover	Hot	Disillusioned	Enraged
Engrossed	Ignored	Hot and bothered	Dismayed	Evil
Excited	Indifferent	Hot blooded	Dismissive	Forsaken
Fascinated	Inferior	Hot to trot	Dispirited	Frantic
Fine	Insulted	Hungry	Disquieted	Frightened
First rate	Intimidated	Hyped up	Dissatisfied	Fucked

Happy	Exasperated	Amorous	Repulsed	Troubled
Fortunate	Irritable	Hypersexual	Distressed	Furious
Free	Jealous	Infatuated	Distrustful	Grief-stricken
Gay	Jumpy	Itchy	Disturbed	Hardened
Glad	Lazy	Jacked up	Downcast	Hateful
Good	Loaded	Jazzed	Dumbstruck	Heartbroken
Gratified	Lousy	Jonesing	Fearful	Helpless
Great	Mean	Languorous	Fed up	Horrible
Groovy	Melancholy	Lascivious	Gagged	Hostile
Helpful	Miffed	Lecherous	Gloomy	Humiliated
Honored	Negative	Lewd	Gob-smacked	Hurt
Hopeful	Nervous	Libertine	Grave	Hysterical
Impressed	Nosy	Licentious	Grossed out	Idiotic
Impulsive	Nutty	Longing	Gutted	Immoral
Innocent	Obnoxious	Lovestruck	Horrified	Incensed
Inspired	Obstinate	Loving	Icky	Inconsolable
Interested	Odd	Lubricious	Ill at ease	Infuriated
Intrigued	Off	Lustful	Jaundiced	Insane
Joyful	Opposed	Lusty	Loathing	Isolated
Keen	Paranoid	Moved	Misgiving	Left out
Kind	Parsimonious	Naughty	Nauseated	Lonely

Happy	Exasperated	Amorous	Repulsed	Troubled
Loved	Peeved	Out of control	Offended	Low
Loving	Perplexed	Overexcited	Opposed	Mad
Meditative	Pissed off	Passionate	Out of place	Maudlin
Mischievous	Precarious	Pervy	Overcome	Miserable
Mystical	Pressured	Pretty	Overwrought	Obsessed
Nice	Prudish	Prurient	Pathetic	Outraged
Open	Put out	Raging	Pessimistic	Overwhelmed
Optimistic	Puzzled	Rampaging	Petrified	Pained
Peaceful	Quarrelsome	Randy	Pitious	Panicked
Perfect	Queer	Raunchy	Put off	Paralyzed
Pleasant	Rebellious	Ribald	Queasy	Persecuted
Pleased	Restless	Ruttish	Repelled	Petrified
Priceless	Ruffled	Salacious	Repugnant	Powerless
Proud	Sheepish	Satyric	Revolted	Provoked
Rapturous	Shocked	Scurrilous	Revulsed	Rageful
Receptive	Skeptical	Sex-crazed	Ruffled	Regretful
Refreshed	Sneaky	Sex-starved	Saddened	Rejected
Relaxed	Snide	Sexual	Sadistic	Remorseful
Reliable	Sore	Sexy	Scandalized	Resentful
Relieved	Startled	Snug	Self-conscious	Sad
Reverent	Stingy	Steamy	Shameful	Scared

Happy	Exasperated	Amorous	Repulsed	Troubled
Rewarded	Stuffed	Stimulated	Shocked	Screwed
Righteous	Stunned	Stirred	Sick and tired	Servile
Sated	Stupid	Tempted	Sickened	Solemn
Satiated	Surprised	Tender	Soured	Sorrowful
Satisfactory	Tense	Toasty	Squeamish	Spiteful
Satisfied	Tentative	Tumultuous	Stung	Strangled
Secure	Tenuous	Turned on	Tormented	Stupefied
Settled	Testy	Turnt	Tragic	Suspicious
Silly	Tired	Unchaste	Turned off	Terrible
Smug	Undecided	Unleashed	Unamused	Terrified
Splendid	Uneasy	Vital	Uncomfort-able	Threatened
Superb	Unpleasant	Vivacious	Unhappy	Thwarted
Superior	Unsettled	Wanton	Unhinged	Trapped
Sure	Upset	Warm	Uninspired	Ugly
Sympathetic	Useless	Wet	Uninterest-ed	Vehement
Tenacious	Vexed	Wicked	Unnerved	Violent
Thankful	Vulnerable	Wild	Weary	Vulnerable
Wonderful	Weepy	Wired	Woeful	Withdrawn
Worthy	Worried	Worked up	Wretched	Wrecked

13

Spark

SPARK is an intentional thesaurus that features 550 verbs, placed in five general categories. SPARK is an acronym for Stimulate, Pivot, Aid, Reason, Knock down.

The other category of words actors and writers need to have handy are verbs. SPARK will help you quickly and efficiently assign intentions to your dialogue line by line. In addition, you can use this section to find general strategies for your character to employ in their attempt to gain their scene objective.

Changing the dynamic under each of your lines is imperative so that your performance will have color and variation. Since your character only really wants one important objective per scene, the lines are often redundant.

Characters reiterate what they want in a scene until they get it or realize they are not going to. Varying the delivery of your dialogue is therefore essential. Similar to HEART, all you need to do is assess the general idea of the action you're looking for and within that column, you'll find many alternatives.

It's highly satisfying when you know there's a word that defines a moment and you have it at your fingertips. SPARK will help you easily diversify your intentions or actions throughout your scenes, which in turn keeps your performance dynamic and athletic.

Stimulate	Pivot	Aid	Reason	Knock Down
Alarm	Absolve	Abet	Accept	Abolish
Alert	Acquiesce	Accommo-date	Address	Abuse
Allure	Acquit	Acquaint	Affirm	Admonish
Amaze	Adapt	Adore	Allow	Afflict
Anger	Adjust	Advocate	Analyze	Affront
Approach	Allow	Amuse	Anticipate	Antagonize
Arouse	Amend	Appreciate	Appeal	Attack
Astound	Avert	Approve	Apply	Badger
Awaken	Backpedal	Arrange	Appraise	Baffle
Beguile	Buck	Assist	Assess	Bait
Bewitch	Cheat	Augment	Authenti-cate	Befuddle
Boost	Collude	Award	Bargain	Belittle
Bribe	Con	Baby	Beg	Berate
Cajole	Conceal	Befriend	Beseech	Blame
Charge	Concede	Bless	Bid	Bushwhack
Charm	Confess	Bolster	Bluff	Censure
Cheer	Confide	Boost	Brainwash	Challenge
Coax	Consent	Carry	Calculate	Chastise
Command	Correct	Caution	Clarify	Chide
Court	Cover	Celebrate	Classify	Coerce
Criticize	Dare	Cheer	Concern	Condemn
Delight	Defy	Coach	Confer	Conde-scend

Stimulate	Pivot	Aid	Reason	Knock Down
Dictate	Disclose	Coddle	Confirm	Confound
Direct	Discover	Collaborate	Consider	Confuse
Disgust	Divert	Comfort	Consign	Criticize
Dominate	Dodge	Commend	Contest	Crucify
Dramatize	Duck	Conciliate	Convince	Crush
Embroil	Endure	Congratu-late	Deduce	Curse
Enchant	Entrust	Cultivate	Defer	Damn
Endear	Evade	Cure	Depict	Deceive
Enflame	Finalize	Defend	Describe	Defame
Engross	Fix	Demon-strate	Detail	Defraud
Enmesh	Focus	Disencum-ber	Detect	Delude
Entertain	Impress	Ease	Determine	Demean
Entice	Improve	Educate	Develop	Demonize
Excite	Indoctrinate	Elect	Diagnose	Denigrate
Frighten	Induce	Elevate	Differentiate	Deny
Frustrate	Indulge	Elucidate	Digest	Deter
Generate	Innovate	Enable	Dissuade	Devastate
Goad	Install	Encourage	Divine	Disconcert
Govern	Intervene	Endure	Draw	Discourage
Humor	Invent	Enhance	Dwell	Discredit
Hurry	Involve	Enlighten	Elicit	Disgrace
Hypnotize	Join	Equip	Engineer	Dishearten

Stimulate	Pivot	Aid	Reason	Knock Down
Ignite	Launch	Excuse	Entreat	Dispirit
Incite	License	Facilitate	Establish	Displease
Influence	Liquidate	Familiarize	Estimate	Distress
Inspire	Manuever	Favor	Evaluate	Entrap
Interview	Mask	Feed	Examine	Eradicate
Intrigue	Master	Foster	Fashion	Eschew
Lead	Maximize	Free	Filter	Execute
Lobby	Mimic	Furnish	Formulate	Exploit
Lure	Minimize	Further	Frame	Force
Magnetize	Mislead	Give	Gauge	Gag
Marshall	Misuse	Gladden	Grade	Harangue
Mobilize	Modify	Grant	Graft	Hassle
Mortify	Muster	Guide	Handle	Henpeck
Mystify	Obtain	Hallow	Identify	Hoodwink
Nauseate	Offset	Help	Illustrate	Humble
Offend	Oppose	Hire	Imagine	Humiliate
Pamper	Originate	Honor	Implicate	Hurt
Panic	Overhaul	Impart	Insinuate	Hush
Participate	Overturn	Introduce	Inspect	Impair
Perform	Perfect	Liberate	Inventory	Indict
Pray	Permit	Lighten	Investigate	Insult
Preach	Persuade	Listen	Justify	Judge
Preoccupy	Prevail	Locate	Learn	Kill
Promote	Purge	Maintain	Lecture	Lambast

Stimulate	Pivot	Aid	Reason	Knock Down
Propel	Purify	Manage	List	Lampoon
Propogan-dize	Qualify	Mend	Litigate	Libel
Provoke	Quench	Mentor	Log	Malign
Pursue	Ratify	Motivate	Manipulate	Muffle
Rally	Rebuke	Notify	Mediate	Nullify
Recreate	Recall	Nourish	Moderate	Obliterate
Recruit	Reconcile	Nurse	Nag	Orphan
Repel	Rectify	Nurture	Navigate	Overlook
Repulse	Redirect	Offer	Negotiate	Patronize
Sedate	Reject	Officiate	Observe	Perplex
Seduce	Rejoin	Orchestrate	Obsess	Persecute
Shake	Release	Orient	Organize	Prosecute
Shock	Relegate	Orientate	Outline	Quash
Sicken	Relent	Parent	Perceive	Ravage
Smack	Remedy	Placate	Peruse	Read
Snare	Renege	Please	Plan	Reprehend
Spellbind	Reorganize	Pledge	Pontificate	Repress
Spoil	Resist	Plug	Press	Reprimand
Spur	Rethink	Promise	Process	Ridicule
Stage	Retract	Promote	Prod	Scold
Startle	Retreat	Rave	Prompt	Shame
Stir	Revamp	Relieve	Propose	Shun
Stretch	Review	Sanctify	Recognize	Slander

Stimulate	Pivot	Aid	Reason	Knock Down
Strip	Revise	Satisfy	Reiterate	Slur
Suggest	Revitalize	Save	Sample	Smother
Summon	Revolt	Secure	Scan	Spoil
Surprise	Settle	Simplify	Scheme	Spurn
Symbolize	Subscribe	Sober	Screen	Squash
Tame	Surrender	Sooth	Scrutinize	Squelch
Tantalize	Synthesize	Spoil	Structure	Strike
Tease	Threaten	Still	Study	Stymie
Terrify	Tolerate	Strengthen	Substanti-ate	Suppress
Test	Transpose	Support	Tease	Swindle
Tickle	Trick	Thank	Tempt	Tarnish
Titillate	Uncover	Unburden	Theorize	Thwart
Trouble	Update	Understand	Think	Torment
Unify	Upgrade	Uplift	Urge	Torture
Uproot	Veto	Validate	Vacillate	Trammel
Woo	Volunteer	Vindicate	Verify	Tyrannize
Worry	Win	Warn	Wheedle	Victimize
Worship	Withdraw	Witness	Wrangle	Vilify

PART 5

EVERYTHING THAT MAKES US LAUGH

"Be funny whenever possible, even if some people don't get it."

Laughter comes from a variety of sources. A well-written joke is always going to find a welcoming audience. Particularly good writers love to play with the nuance of language and craft witticisms that tickle our ears.

Physical humor is a way to crack people up. Writing comedy also means thinking about what might be going on in the background of a scene. A well-placed prop that is never addressed by the characters in a scene can become iconic.

In this chapter, I'll classify and define the myriad ways humor is created in scripted comedy. Actors can use the clear definition of what is intended to be funny within the scene to be sure that they're playing the comedy for everything it's worth. Conversely, writers can use this section as a checklist to make sure they're exploiting all avenues of humor when they're writing comedy.

14

Jokes

A joke is a display of humor in which specially chosen words are used to make people laugh and is not meant to be taken seriously. Jokes can ultimately take a variety of forms. Here are examples, all of which are from the award-winning smash hit, *Parks and Recreation*.

Classic Joke

A classic joke generally has a neutral and believable setup and ends in an unexpected or farcical punch line. The setup and punchline can be shared by different characters or a character can set themselves up for their own punchline.

Example:

LESLIE: Well, Paunch Burger just recently came out with a new 128-ounce option. Most people call it a gallon, but they call it the Regular. Then there is a horrifying 512-ounce version that they call Child Size. How is this a child-size soda?

KATHRYN: Well, it's roughly the size of a two-year old child, if the child were liquefied. It's a real bargain at $1.59.

One-liner

A one-liner is just that. It gets the job done in just one sentence.

Example:

> TOM HAVERFORD: Sometimes you gotta work a little so you can ball a lot.

Turnaround Joke or Reversal

A turnaround joke is a misdirect. It leads the audience toward an assumption, then contradicts it. Turnaround jokes are mostly executed in two sentences. *Examples*:

> RON SWANSON: That's Swanson family mash liquor, made from the finest corn ever grown on American soil. It's only legal use is to strip varnish off of speed boats.

Sometimes it only takes one:

> APRIL LUDGATE: I wasn't listening, but I strongly disagree with Ann.

Triplet

Triplets are jokes formed by words, phrases, or whole sentences that come in threes. A three-part joke includes a slight build of tension that one-liner and turnaround jokes don't. Here are three examples, just to honor the spirit of things.

> RON SWANSON: I once worked with a guy for three years and never learned his name. Best friend I ever had. We still never talk sometimes.

| ANDY DWYER: | I'm fine. It's just that life is pointless and nothing matters and I'm always tired. |
| LESLIE KNOPE: | We need to remember what's important in life. Friends, waffles, and work. Or waffles, friends, work. It doesn't matter. But work is third. |

Shocker

Shockers are intended to jar the audience unexpectedly, usually pushing past the boundaries of good taste. Since shockers use foul language, deal with off-color subject matter, and test the audience's tolerance for humor regarding race, gender, sexuality, etc., it's best to use them sparingly and only after you've let your audience know in advance they're in safe, smart hands.

Example:

| BOBBY NEWPORT: | I guess my thoughts on abortion are, you know... let's all just have a good time! |

Meta Joke

Meta jokes are essentially jokes about a previously established joke, a joke within a joke, or a character winking at society while they're speaking either directly to another character or into the camera. Meta jokes often play on traditional joke templates and provide a reversal of expectations. For example, "An Irishman walks past a bar."

We're used to hearing both about people who walk *into* a bar and jokes about Irish folks drinking too much. This simple but effective meta joke combines two time-tested tropes and assumes the audience is smart enough get the streamlined, all-in-one setup and punchline.

A similar concept is breaking the fourth wall. When fictional characters reflect on their own behavior from a previous scene into the camera, meta humor is being created.

Example:

> LESLIE KNOPE: No matter what I do, literally nothing bad can happen to me. I'm like a white, male U.S. Senator.

Catchphrases

A catchphrase is a phrase used repeatedly by a character, usually to the point that it becomes their slogan.

Example:

> DONNA MEAGLE AND TOM HAVERFORD: Treat yo' self.

Tag

A tag is an extra joke after the last big joke of the scene, also known as the blow of the scene. It may be written as an added chuckle for the audience or it may be improvised.

Example:

> BEN WYATT: Let's do it to it, my dudes!

15

Sight Gags

ight gags encompass all visual humor. They can take the form of a funny handshake, a t-shirt logo, a mislabeled birthday cake, or anything else the writer can see in their mind's eye. Great comedy writers exploit every opportunity to produce humor; that definitely includes props, pratfalls, funny signage, text messages, and anything else that might decorate their characters' world.

Physical comedy is anything the writer asks the actor to do with their body. The simplest manifestation is simply standing, sitting, kneeling, or lying down in a peculiar way. A physical comedy bit could include a regular high-five or an elaborate one.

In scripted comedy, some characters have become known for their grand entrances like Jack McFarland (Sean Hayes) on *Will & Grace* and Cosmo Kramer (Michael Richards) on *Seinfeld*. Both actors are able to use their own bodies to execute a common function like walking into a room for comedic effect.

Slapstick is physical comedy taken to further extremes. It escalates physical comedy from typical actions to clumsy and sometimes dangerous actions, coupled with humorously embarrassing events.

Lucille Ball performed a lot of slapstick comedy on *I Love Lucy*. She famously got a job at a chocolate factory wrapping candy on an assembly line. When it starts moving too fast, she struggles to keep up and an iconic television comedy moment was born.

Another time she puts too much yeast in her homemade bread. The yeast causes the bread to rise to an absurd degree and it flies out of the oven like an unstoppable Chinese flying dragon.

When Lucy gets drunk while shooting a commercial for Vitameatavegemin, a nutritional supplement, Ms. Ball executes arguably the best-known bit of slapstick comedy in television history. Drunk, slurring, and confused, her ability to execute her commercial pitch deteriorates rapidly and hilariously.

Although slapstick has its roots in vaudeville, that doesn't mean it's relegated to bygone eras of television. Current comedies still employ slapstick comedy to this day. Zach Galifianakis plays Chip Baskets, a classically trained clown on the series *Baskets*.

When he takes center stage in a rodeo arena and gets dropped by a charging bull, that's slapstick; outrageous, improbable, and violent. *Crazy Ex-Girlfriend* offers its star Rachel Bloom ample opportunities to show off her slapstick skills. *Workaholics*, *Broad City*, and *Modern Family* also ask their lead actors to partake in slapstick from time to time.

16

Humorous Situations

Sometimes the situation itself is the source of comedy. That can either mean a typical situation begins to rapidly spiral downward or The Heroes of Comedy find themselves in an unusual situation. Since almost all series deal with the reality of day-to-day life for their characters, they will inevitably have storylines and episodes centered around birthdays, holidays, graduations, romantic dates, and other common life milestones.

There are infinite ways any of these ordinary occasions can go off the rails. Here's an example from *Roseanne*. In "White Trash Christmas," Roseanne and Dan Conner receive a passive-aggressive note from their homeowners' association urging restraint in exterior holiday decor. The ever-rebellious Conners take this request as the ultimate challenge to snub authority and respond by creating a Christmas display that takes tacky to new, dithering heights. "The wise men are supposed to be adoring the baby Jesus, not leering at Mrs. Claus," says Roseanne's mortified mom.

Setting up Christmas lights is typical fare all over America and many other parts of the world. An otherwise mundane activity can easily be turned into a storyline for an episode. The reactions we have to everyday occurrences can be fodder for all kinds of comedy.

The episode "The Comeback Kid" features one of the laugh-out-loud funniest moments of *Parks and Recreation*. Leslie Knope and her entire campaign staff are scheduled to make a campaign speech at an ice hockey rink. They enter from the wings and stride out onto the ice along a red carpet that only gets them halfway to the makeshift stage. Tom informs Leslie they ran out of money for a longer carpet. With a small crowd watching and "Get on Your Feet" by Gloria Estefan blaring over the loudspeaker, the group has to make their way to the stage by crossing the ice in dress shoes.

The journey is short but perilous. The entourage has to baby-step their way to the podium, desperately fighting to stay upright. They finally make it but not without casualties; Andy face plants onto the ice and Ron gets peed on by Andy and April's three-legged dog, Champion, that he's carrying. Once there, it takes the entire group to lift Leslie onto the stage.

Humorous situations might build slowly and deliberately like Roseanne and Dan's well-thought out visual assault on the neighborhood. The opposite can also happen when our Heroes suddenly encounter an unexpected obstacle like Leslie and her campaign staff. It's also funny to see things snowball wildly out of control. A rapid escalation of worsening events is always sure to amuse an audience.

The creative team behind *Frasier* often wrote intricate physical comedy into their series. Perhaps the best example is contained in the episode, "Three Valentines." David Hyde Pierce executes a masterclass in slapstick comedy as Niles. The scene features Niles alone in Frasier's apartment with his father's dog, Eddie. It has no dialogue and it's more than five minutes long.

The scene begins when Niles decides to iron a crease out of his pants while waiting for a date to arrive. He sets up the ironing board next to the couch. While ironing, he notices a loose thread.

He retrieves scissors from the kitchen. As he returns to the ironing board, he starts to run but catches himself as we see him "hear" his mother's voice cautioning him, "Don't run with scissors!" He slows to an awkwardly stiff walk, clutching the scissors like a loaded grenade.

When he cuts the thread, he nicks his finger. A Neurotic through and through, Niles faints at the sight of his own blood. He collapses onto the couch. When he comes to, a moment later, he realizes he's left a blood stain on Frasier's sofa. Back to the kitchen for spot remover, holding his barely injured finger over his head to prevent more blood loss.

He returns and dabs the spot with a cloth. It seems he's in the clear until he catches another glimpse of his barely bleeding finger. He faints again, spilling the entire contents of the spot remover onto the couch. He returns to the kitchen, screwing the top back onto the near empty bottle of spot remover while holding it over his head. He puts it back under the kitchen sink and checks his food, which is simmering on the stove.

He smells the dishes he's preparing and while doing so, smells something coming from the living room. He returns to see the iron has toppled onto his pants and is burning through them. The very next moment, they burst into flames before his eyes. He first tries to douse the fire with the spray nozzle on the iron, but to no avail. When that doesn't work, he tries to tamp the fire out and then folds the pants into a ball to smother it. He burns himself and reflexively tosses them onto the couch, which is doused in flammable spot remover.

The couch lights up like a torch. Niles runs to fetch a fire extinguisher. He tries to aim it at the couch, but the high-pressured extinguisher seems to have a mind of its own. He sprays the entire apartment, himself, and Eddie. By the time he regains control and directs the extinguisher toward the couch, it's empty.

Niles is finally able to douse the fire with the contents of the pots he had simmering on the stove. He opens the door to clear the smoke and fumes from Frasier's apartment. As he frantically waves his arms, the oven mitts he'd put on to carry the hot pots fly off his hands and he again sees his bloody finger. With the fire out, he faints a third and final time (a triplet of fainting). This is a sterling example of a writer imagining what a character can do, not just say, that will leave viewers in stitches.

Surprise

Have you ever played with a jack-in-the-box? Its only goal is to surprise you. If you haven't experienced one, a jack-in-the-box consists of a box with a crank. When the crank is turned, a music box mechanism in the toy plays a melody. After the crank has been turned a sufficient number of times (such as at the end of the melody), there is a "surprise." The lid flips open and a googly-eyed clown or jester pops out of the box.

A theory as to the origin of the jack-in-the-box is that it comes from the 14th century English prelate, Sir John Schorne, who is often pictured holding a boot with a devil in it. According to folklore, he once cast the devil into a boot to protect the village of North Marston in Buckinghamshire from his villainy. In French, a jack-in-the-box is called a "diable en boîte" or literally, "devil in a box".

One has to wonder why this is a universally recognized children's toy. It doesn't teach you anything. It doesn't ignite imagination. You play with it alone. A jack-in-the-box is designed so that you can create your own tension bubble as you simultaneously wait for it to explode.

Really, it's a toy that teaches your brain to produce anxious thoughts for no good reason. But then we laugh within the relief. The jack-in-the-box is a metaphor for life's intricate dance between sorrow and humor. With time, tension increases, our worst fear is realized and when we live through it, we chuckle.

Surprise can take so many forms within scripted comedy. As noted earlier, it can simply be in the form of a joke; a punchline we did not see coming, a triplet where the last word or phrase in the series is unlike the prior two, a reversal where there is an immediate contradiction within just two lines.

An unexpected visitor can arrive, a text message can pop up on a phone, or a group of friends can organize a good, old-fashioned surprise party. Any time a character's expectations are upended within their world and they're surprised, the writers are setting up a comedy adventure. The surprise can range from miniscule to monumental.

In an episode of *Schitt's Creek*, Alexis' boyfriend, Mutt, shaves off his beard; a relatively small surprise. However, the writers created conflict and story out of one seemingly small action. When Mutt kisses Alexis awake *sans* beard, she's horrified, displeased, and even starts crying. Mutt is taken aback by Alexis' extremely adverse reaction, so she offers, "Your beard is, like, my favorite thing about you."

Thinking they had something much deeper, Mutt is shocked to realize how shallow Alexis can be. By the end of the episode they break up. This is an excellent example of incorporating surprise to comedic effect and driving story. While Mutt shaving his beard off is the initial surprise, his action creates subsequent surprises. Alexis and Mutt learn a lot about each other, what they want out of a romantic relationship, and what they're willing to offer and compromise (or not) within a romantic relationship.

Here's an example of a monumental surprise from *Everybody Loves Raymond*. After taking an art class, Marie gives Raymond and Debra a sculpture she created. The towering piece is covered by a cloth in Raymond and Debra's living room. Marie defines her piece as spiritual and abstract, but upon reveal it closely resembles a set of labia. Surprise!

Raymond notices first and hints to Debra, "Isn't it a bit too... lady-like?" Once he points it out, Debra can't unsee the comparability. Marie is particularly proud of her efforts, which creates tremendous tension. The family needs to break the news to her and get the sculpture out of the house without hurting her feelings but doesn't know how. In the meantime, Raymond simply covers the artwork with a garbage bag. When Marie walks in and sees, she's devastated and arranges to have it donated to the local church auction.

When two Sisters arrive to pick it up, they're horrified by the piece and ultimately inform Marie that the sculpture is "inappropriate." Marie finally faces the awful truth that her sculpture resembles female genitals and declares, "Oh, my God! I'm a lesbian."

Surprise and the varying reactions from the different points of view of each of The Heroes of Comedy can produce a simple joke or an entire storyline.

A broader example of how to drive story with surprise would come by way of the Grim Reaper. *The Good Place* opens with Eleanor Shellstrop learning that she's dead. "Cool. Cool... I have some questions," she responds upon learning she's no longer amongst the living. The series moves forward in the afterlife, after opening with life's greatest surprise.

Russian Doll is another comedic series that examines our existence here and hereafter. The series follows Nadia Vulvokov, a game developer who repeatedly dies and relives the same night in an ongoing time loop. It's shocking enough to find out you're dead once. Surprise! You're dead again. And again and again and again...

We laugh when we're surprised but also focused. Surprise keeps audiences attentive. As in the examples above, it can even form the foundation for a series' entire concept.

18

Observations

Observational comedy is often associated with stand-up comedy. Simply, a great stand-up comic can find a humorous, unusual, or absurd twist to everyday life situations. They make fun of our collective consciousness, so to speak. *Seinfeld* is not the only, but is arguably the best example of a television show adapted from an observational stand-up comedian's stage material. If not the best, then certainly the most successful. "Do you ever wonder why..." If your answer is "yes" to however that sentence ends, you will probably laugh in recognition.

The Heroes of Comedy help us understand how different personality types think and feel as they experience the world. The differences in our DNA and life stories don't result in entirely unique human beings the likes of which the world has never known. Our differences merely create varying opinions on how to engage in life's typical circumstances. Collectively, we have differing points of view regarding the same things.

Since this is true for us, it's true for our characters. Simple observations on how to deal with life create comedy. Here's an example from Eleanor on *The Good Place*: "I know it sounds crazy but if it weren't crazy, they wouldn't call it a 'leap of faith.' They would call it a 'sit... of... doubting.'" This joke works as well in a stand-up routine as it does within character dialogue. It's a simple observation about something we've all heard before with a thoughtful twist of the prism.

Here's another example made by Darius on *Atlanta*: "I would say 'nice to meet you', but I don't believe in time as a concept, so I'll just say we always met." Within a conversation, Darius is also offering an observation. Not every person would have such a thought in real life. It follows that neither would every character, only a certain type. In this case, an Eccentric. Point of view is everything when defining characters clearly, whether writing or performing them. The observations made by The Heroes of Comedy offer significant clues as to who they are.

Dreamers, for example, are particularly prone to self-deprecation. They don't make fun of themselves *exclusively,* but of all The Heroes of Comedy they do it the most. Self-deprecation is also an example of observational comedy. It's just directed inward. It's an observation you make about yourself. When Nick Miller on *New Girl* finds himself underdressed for dinner, he calls his friend for help, "Where are you, Schmidt? This is place is fancy and I don't know which fork to kill myself with." In the same moment, Nick is both his target and audience.

19

Parody and Satire

Parody and satire are other forms of observational humor. They're similar, but not exactly the same. Let's define them clearly with examples.

A parody television show or film is a composition that *imitates* the style of another composition for comic effect. Often that style is exaggerated and applied to an outlandish or inappropriate subject. *Police Squad!, Reno 911!, Archer, Wrecked, Scream Queens, Angie Tribeca, Childrens Hospital*, and *Eagleheart* are terrific examples of parody television series.

Police Squad!, Reno 911!, Archer, Angie Tribeca, and *Eagleheart* all skewer cop/crime shows, both scripted and reality. *Scream Queens* spoofs horror spoofs. *Childrens Hospital* is a black comedy series that parodies medical dramas. *Wrecked* is a send-up of the dramatic series *Lost*.

A satirical television show or film incorporates the use of humor, irony, exaggeration, or ridicule to expose and criticize people's stupidity or vices. This cutting form of observation is often employed in the context of contemporary politics and other topical issues.

South Park, The Simpsons, Family Guy, Futurama, American Dad!, King of the Hill, The Boondocks, BoJack Horseman, and many other animated shows are satirical. An animated series, like *The*

Simpsons, can be as relatable as any given live-action show. Many times throughout its record-breaking history, a given scene from *The Simpsons* could be shot and performed like a typical live-action sitcom without a second thought. Yet animation affords *The Simpsons* the ability to have Homer work at a nuclear power plant and live nearby without suffering any real-world adverse effects. The simple premise of *The Simpsons* allows for near endless commentary on American culture.

The Office, Veep, Silicon Valley, Episodes, Entourage, and *Extras* are great examples of live-action series that are born of satire. Parody pokes fun at a style or genre, especially if it should take itself too seriously. Satire asks us to look at our collective cultural failings and laugh while we're wincing. Satire is humor that mocks human weaknesses and absurdity.

The Office examines the mendacity of the working class in Middle America through a lens of irony. *Veep* mocks American politics while *Silicon Valley* lampoons the tech industry. *Episodes, Entourage,* and *Extras* all exploit the folly found in show business.

The Daily Show, The Colbert Report, Last Week Tonight with John Oliver, and *Full Frontal with Samantha Bee* are also examples of scripted, satirical television comedy. Their pseudo-news format allows the hosts of these series to report and comment on real news stories while simultaneously mocking the political class, the pundit class, and citizenry.

20

Wit

Some jokes are witty but not all. Some writers are great linguists, but not all. Wit implies particularly clever observation and/or exemplary craftsmanship with language. I've given examples of solid jokes that are classic and broadly accessible. However, some shows succeed because the minds behind their creation are sharper than average. Well-read, clever writers have a broader palette with which to word paint. Dialogue can be utilitarian, or it can rise to poetic heights.

It takes sagacity, as well as broad knowledge of pop culture, to write for certain shows. For example, not every great comedy writer could write for *Veep*. Not only does the series eviscerate America's political class, which requires intricate knowledge of how the United States government works, but the verbiage is also quite dense, multilayered, and cosmopolitan. The humor ranges from urbane to esoteric.

I'd say the same for *Silicon Valley*, *Frasier*, *30 Rock*, and other comedies that rely heavily on intricate semantics and worldliness to produce humor.

Here are a few examples:

Veep

MIKE: I had an aunt who transitioned twice. She was trapped inside of a man, and then that man was trapped inside of another woman.

RICHARD: Oh, like a turducken.

The Office

ERIN: Hey, I never told you my Christmas wish.

ANDY: Ah, okay.

ERIN: It's about you.

ANDY: That's not what it should be, it should just be like a trinket or something.

ERIN: It's that I wish Jessica was dead.

ANDY: Y-you... wait, you mean you wish she wasn't here or something?

ERIN: I wish she was in a graveyard! Under the ground. With worms coming out of her mouth.

ANDY: Hey, you know, you can't say that, okay? That's my girlfriend that you're talking about. You and I are not together anymore. You need to get over it! Take your wish back.

ERIN: Too late! It's already been wished! And you promised it would come true. You wrote it in an email! So, which one are you? A murderer or a liar?

Silicon Valley

HENRY: Gavin, you've staked the entire future of this company on the Signature Box Three. Where are they?

GAVIN: Well, the last two months have been challenging. The Chinese were petulant. The North Carolinians proved very entitled. And I held out hopes for our experiment in the Yukon Territories. But as it happens, the Inuit are surprisingly adept at collective bargaining. But fear not, I am in the early stages of a new plan. Did you know that some of America's most capable, motivated laborers are, at this moment, awaiting execution?

Some jokes and shows are simply more sophisticated than others, incorporating layers of surprise, advanced language skills, and worldliness underneath crackling dialogue.

21

Banter

Banter is generally thought of as being comprised of wit; conversational sparring, so to speak. A common conversation can be made funnier by fine-tuning the words and creating an exacting cadence when spoken aloud. *30 Rock* features great banter, particularly between Liz Lemon and Jack Donaghy.

Here's a classic example:

LIZ:
Why didn't anything ever happen between us?

JACK:
Good God, Lemon. If you're trying to conjure my mother's ghost, you could just shake a jar of coins while praising Jimmy Carter.

LIZ:
No, I'm not saying I wanted something to happen, but why didn't something happen? We've spent a lot of time together. We've been drunk together, and day drunk together, and on the rebound at the same time. And also, you're kind of a slut.

JACK:
I did sleep with Jenna a lot in season three.

LIZ:
If I was a different person, would you have hit on me?

JACK: I understand what you're getting at, Lemon. There was a particularly youth-oriented priest in my childhood parish who went after everybody but me. Even Fat Ralph, and he ate his boogers. I felt so unpretty.

LIZ: No, this isn't about appearance, Jack. Did nothing ever happen between us because I'm not fun?

JACK: Good God, Lemon. Obviously, our relationship, however you define it, mentor/mentee -

LIZ: ...Sister-ployee/work oracle...

JACK: ...Is more interesting than some dating scenario. And obviously, to ruin what we have with a tawdry, yet expert sexual encounter would've been a mistake.

Great banter generally includes palpable sexual tension, lightning pace, and innuendo.

22

Puns

Puns are another (potential) example of wit. Puns are the humorous use of a word or phrase so as to emphasize or suggest its different meanings or applications. For example, "She had a photographic memory but never developed it." In one sentence, multiple meanings of the key words, "photographic" and "developed" are explored.

A pun can also employ the use of words that are alike or nearly alike in sound but different in meaning. For example, "That last joke about developing a photographic memory was really punny." Puns have recently come to be known colloquially as "Dad jokes."

Phil Dunphy is responsible for a lot of those on *Modern Family*. In this example, Phil tries to lighten up his niece, Lily, by showing off an intricate duck village he's constructed in the driveway. "I drew up plans for a Duckingham Palace, but I can't find them. So I guess we'll just have to wing it," he muses. Lily isn't impressed.

23

Callback

A callback is simply a joke made by bookending a reference from earlier in the scene. Here's a great example:

In the Mother's Day episode of *Everybody Loves Raymond*, Marie and Debra have a quarrel and stop speaking to each other. Raymond, Robert, and Frank gather in Raymond's kitchen bemoaning the lack of a festive mood and, of course, food. Debra enters with her hands full of bedsheets. The kids brought her breakfast in bed, which didn't go so well.

DEBRA: Just what every mother wants to do on Mother's Day; wash the butter out of her sheets.

Debra heads to the laundry room. Marie peers through the kitchen door.

RAYMOND: What are you doing, Ma?

MARIE: Hello. I was just flipping through your baby books… recalling the agony of your delivery. And I was wondering if I was going to get a visit from you on Mother's Day.

RAYMOND: Yeah, um, Mom, of cou- I'm taking care of a few things here, that's all.

MARIE:	Well, of course, by all means, take your time. You obviously have other priorities... on Mother's Day.

Robert hands Marie flowers Raymond intended to give her.

ROBERT:	Here you go, Ma. These are for you.
RAYMOND:	Hey! What are you talking about?
ROBERT:	Happy Mother's Day!
MARIE:	Oh! They're lovely!
RAYMOND:	They're not from – stupid!

Debra enters from the laundry room.

DEBRA:	Listen, Ray...

Marie and Debra see each other. The air grows thick with tension and everyone falls silent.

FRANK:	Korea...
MARIE:	Okay, well, I'm going back across the street.

Marie grabs Robert by the ear.

MARIE:	Who's coming with me?
ROBERT:	I'll go with you, Ma.
MARIE:	Anyone else?
FRANK:	She ain't my mother.
DEBRA:	Go ahead, Ray.
MARIE:	Raymond?

RAYMOND: Look. I shouldn't have to choose, okay? This is not my fight. Can't you two just start talking already? C'mon, it's Mother's Day! Can't one of you two mothers just say something? Dad, please, can't you help me out here?

FRANK: What, are you kidding me? Maybe Deb'll come around at some point, but we'll never get anything out of Sitting Bull over there.

RAYMOND: Debra, please, c'mon. Just do it for me. (Beat) Great, great, great, you see? Here's the problem, okay? You think it's just her. Well, I'm gonna say it. We all know if my wife wasn't so snippy all the time - yes, I said snippy - none of this would've happened!

FRANK: You'd be snippy too, if this one was yammering at you all day long. You got nothing to complain about.

RAYMOND: Hey, how do you know what I've been going through over here, okay? I actually have to live with her, alright? So don't start with me because you don't know what the hell you're talking about!

Frank stands ominously.

ROBERT: Wow.

FRANK: Let me ask you something, pal. What have you had, a tough week? Well, I've been living with your mother since... before you were born.

RAYMOND:	Debra wouldn't let the twins tell a knock-knock joke.
FRANK:	She's right! Knock-knock jokes stink!
RAYMOND:	Look, that's not the point. Mom came over with her friends to show how cute the twins are telling a knock-knock joke, and Debra couldn't even give her that little bit of joy.
FRANK:	Well, who the hell is Marie to come barging in demanding joy when Deb is wrestling with the damn kids?!
RAYMOND:	She didn't have to be so rude!
FRANK:	Rude is the only thing that gets through to her! How do you think I got the way I am? I USED TO BE A GENTLEMAN!
RAYMOND:	Never! You were never a gentleman! You never gave mom any respect! You're just as bad as Debra!
FRANK:	Hey, that's a fine way to talk to a father!
RAYMOND:	Fine, you don't like it? I don't talk to you at all!
FRANK:	I don't talk to you at all!
ROBERT:	Hold it, hold it, hold it, SIT DOWN!
RAYMOND:	Fine! I will sit down!
ROBERT:	(To Debra and Marie) Look what your fight is doing to the family! It's Mother's Day, and you're ruining it. This day is supposed to be for

appreciating each other, not shutting each other out. We should not be wallowing in hate. We should be wallowing in a beautiful brunch of Belgian waffles and berries. And sausages... of both link and patty. Now, I know when we're angry and hurt we can only see the negative in the other person. But you two people know deep down how you feel about each other, how you care about each other and how much... how much you love each other.

Beat.

FRANK: I'm sorry, Ray.

RAYMOND: Me too, Dad.

ROBERT: Not you guys!

FRANK: Yeah.

RAYMOND: Yeah. C'mon, How about it, Debra?

FRANK: What do you say, Marie? Can we eat?

Marie and Debra both exit without saying a word.

Robert joins Raymond and Frank at the kitchen table. Another beat.

ROBERT: Why is there butter on your sheets?

An excellent way to end a scene that was about so many other things going on within that family.

Irony

Irony describes situations that are strange or funny because events unfold in a way that seem to be the opposite of what we expect.

Nurse Jackie is a great dramedy series that is born of irony. Jackie Peyton is a New York City nurse at All Saints' Hospital. She is married with two daughters but having an affair with the hospital pharmacist. She's a drug addict who is responsible for prescribing and administering medication to others. She has an irreproachable code of ethics to care for those in need, but she lies to her husband, children, friends, coworkers, and family without hesitation. She disregards obvious and inevitable consequences of her own personal behavior.

Who Jackie *is* versus who she *presents* herself to be are two entirely different women. As the series progresses, Jackie collapses both emotionally and physically. She increasingly becomes the person in need of care as she fights to keep her position as a nurse. The caregiver succumbs to the disease of addiction, damages every relationship she has, and ultimately comes to rely on the bits of mercy those close to her have left to dole out or not.

Nurse Jackie is a brilliant example of a show that examines what seems like an ordinary American life but is upended in epic irony.

24

Specific References

Adding specificity to any kind of reference will always add humor. For example, a character can simply say they're going to the store to pick up some dog food as they exit.

However, labeling the store and the dog food is a stronger option. There are examples of both fictional and real references of stores, brand names, etc., throughout television and film. Sometimes products are deliberately placed on-camera and referenced within dialogue because they sponsor or finance the project.

The same character who said they're going to the store for dog food can say they're going to the "Corner Barkery" for some "puppy paninis" (fictional as far as I know, however, I'm quite sure both exist somewhere in the world).

Another option is to incorporate a real store name within the dialogue to create humor. We can rewrite that same moment this way:

HER: I'm heading out to Walmart. Do you need anything?

HIM: It depends. Which one?

HER: What do you mean which one?

HIM: If it's Walmart Express, no. If you're going to the Supercenter, yes.

HER: I'm going the Campus Convenience store. It's closer.

HIM: You can't go to that one. That one's for students.

HER: It's not only for students. Anyone can go. It's closer.

HIM: Fine. I don't need anything then.

HER: You obviously need something.

HIM: If you're not going to the Supercenter, it doesn't matter.

HER: I can go to the Supercenter if you want me to.

HIM: I don't want you to. You asked me if I needed anything, I don't!

HER: You just said you do!

HIM: You're not going to the right Walmart!

HER: I can go to any Walmart!

HIM: Alright, then I need a new lawnmower!

HER: What?! I'm not getting you a lawnmower. I meant like, "Do you need Axe Body Spray?"

HIM: I have Axe Body Spray. The lawnmower died. We need a new one.

HER: You know what? I'm sorry I even asked.

HIM:	Well you're gonna be even sorrier when you get there and everyone's looking at you like, "Hey, why is that old lady going back to college?"

In this case, not only did I use a real store name and product name, I exploited them for their comedic potential. It's funny that Walmart stores have several variations that don't all serve the exact same needs. A lot of folks can relate to this type of conversation. So we get a specific reference and really a whole scene that blossoms from one character simply heading out to the store.

25

Obscure References

Obscure references are not only funny, they elevate comedy. *Frasier*, both the series and the character, were infamous for arcane references. They can be made in regard to a person, place, or thing. In addition, language itself can veer toward the obscure with sharp construction and word choices.

KATE: Dr. Frasier Crane! Kate Costas.

FRASIER: Kate, what a pleasure!

KATE: Likewise. I've been listening to the tapes of all your shows. I love what you're doing!

FRASIER: Really? Well, thank you very much! I like to think of my show as a haven for the tempest-tossed in the maelstrom of everyday life.

KATE: Wow. You really talk that way.

Not everyone is going to understand what "tempest-tossed" or "maelstrom" mean, but you don't necessarily need to know the dictionary definition of the words to get the point of the joke. Context leads you towards Frasier's overblown point. He sets himself up as a pompous windbag upon meeting someone and she calls him out on it instantly. Frasier's arcane vocabulary is integral to his laughably haughty nature.

26

Pop Culture References

Pop culture references are references to specific people; politicians, celebrities, fictional characters, etc. They also include references to newer elements of the times in which we live. Pop culture references are very relatable and make the audience feel included. Sometimes celebrities or fictional characters are the target of a joke and sometimes their names are incorporated into the humor simply because they're broadly known.

Here are a few examples.

The Big Bang Theory

SHELDON: Oh, on the contrary. I found the Grinch to be a relatable, engaging character and I was really with him. Right up to the point that he succumbed to social convention and returned the presents and saved Christmas. What a buzzkill that was.

Will & Grace

JACK: You hurt the feelings of my male fiancé - or "Boyancé," if you will.

WILL: I guess that makes you "Gay-Z."

Veep

DAN: Listen, I don't know if I'm ready to be a daddy to anyone who's not a sexy boho jewelry maker struggling to pay off her college loans, y'know?

AMY: I appreciate the soul-searching.

DAN: But if you wanna go dutch on the abortion or something, just hit me up on Venmo. Oh, and make it public – shows I'm a gentleman.

In these examples, we have a fictional character, real celebrities, and a nod to a newer way we use technology to transfer money used to produce humor.

The brief passage from *Veep* also includes the reality that social media and finances intersect on the Venmo app. Dan is concerned about his image and he conveys his narcissism in a very current way. That reference would not have been possible in a prior decade of television. Venmo also has the benefit of being a pretty funny word on its own.

Student debt is also referenced; a topic that wasn't so broadly discussed 10 or even five years prior. An awareness of pop culture, the climate and temperature of our time, and its influence on us culturally is essential for up-and-coming comedy writers.

27

Hyperbole

Hyperbole is simply a matter of pushing exaggeration to absurd extremes.

Here are a few examples:

Modern Family

CAMERON: Meryl Streep could play *Batman* and be the right choice!

30 Rock

JENNA: Oh, don't be so dramatic. That's my thing. And if you take it away from me, I will kill myself and then you.

Glee

SUE: Well played, sir. I underestimated you. All right, here's what happens now. I'm going to head on down to my condo in Boca, brown up a bit, get myself back into fighting shape, then I'm going to return to this school even more hellbent on your destruction. Get ready for the ride of your life, Will Schuester. You are about to board the Sue Sylvester Express. Destination? Horror!

28

Wordplay

Wordplay is simply having fun with language. It can include elements previously mentioned but also funny-sounding words, double entendre, analogy, similes, and overall silliness.

Here are few examples from *Will & Grace*:

In this example, Karen is helping Jack prepare for a gay spelling bee.

KAREN:	Oh! Here's a good gay word. "Doily."
JACK:	Doily?
KAREN:	Doily.
JACK:	...Doily.
KAREN:	Doily.
JACK:	Could you use it in a sentence?
KAREN:	He went... doily down the street.
JACK:	Oh, doily... D-O-I-L-Y!
KAREN:	Right!

Malcolm meets Karen and is immediately enchanted. He's holding a paper sack filled with melting ice cream sandwiches. Will notices.

> WILL: Your package is dripping.

> MALCOLM: What can I say? I like her.

A dysfunctional simile filtered through a specific point of view is always an opportunity for a great joke.

> KAREN: It's not something you can just run away from like a hotel bill or a crying baby.

The creators and writers of *Will & Grace* are particularly adept at creating *fun* within their character's dialogue, as well as funniness.

29

Fighting Funny

Let's keep this simple: anger and pain generally do not produce comedy. Scripted comedies often feature serious or poignant moments. Those isolated, occasional conversations veer toward drama. Poignancy, sadness, and sentimentality humanize The Heroes of Comedy by allowing them to experience loss and heartbreak.

If the tone of the scene is intended to be dramatic, then it will be obvious, and actors should act the scene accordingly.

However, if the goal of the production is to produce comedy in any given moment or scene, the actor needs to leave out the anger and pain. I'm carefully defining this distinction because many actors can fight well dramatically but miss the mark when asked to maintain the stakes within a comedic confrontation.

Fighting funny is difficult for some because they never saw funny fights in their household while growing up. As children some of us only saw our parents fight with anger or maybe abuse or violence.

Some parents never fight, at least not out loud. This teaches kids to stifle feelings and harbor unspoken resentments, which isn't funny at all. When this happens, kids are not taught forgiveness or how to laugh at conflict once it subsides. When my students have a hard time seeing what's funny about a scripted fight or argument, I can deduce a lot about their upbringing.

There's no judgment, it just lets me know what we need to work on. If there is no point of reference to fighting with some level of humor involved at least some of the time, we can understand why it would be hard to think of fighting as funny at all.

When my parents fought, they were sarcastic, and they would insult each other. Sometimes it was intense. Other times my brother, sister, and I thought it was hilarious. My parents were hilarious. My mom had a razor-sharp tongue and didn't take crap from anyone. My dad couldn't yell without laughing. It was like he thought somewhere in the back of his mind that fighting at all was so unnecessary and preposterous that he couldn't take it entirely seriously, even while he was doing it.

Sometimes my brother, sister, and I would watch. Sometimes we'd join in and maybe take sides. Sometimes our dog, Boone, would bark at my dad while our parents fought, and we'd encourage him to bark more. I was sometimes allowed to make fun of my parents while they were in the middle of a fight and get away with it. I did not know how valuable this was to my developing comedic point of view until I met others who marveled that there could be anything remotely funny about a family fight.

I'm sure my parents had fights we never saw. I'd bet they included anger, tears, and bitter silence. I think the fights we did see my parents have were about petty things and they were born out of *frustration* more than deep-seated *anger*. Hence we were able to comment, chime in, make jokes, and laugh at them. Of course, not all fights are funny. But growing up with the perspective that they certainly *could* be helps me help others along with the concept.

Leaning into all other emotions *around* anger and pain allow us to fight funny. Frustration, fury, even rage, can all be played for comedy. If someone has become infuriated, it's funny because they've lost control to some degree. People out of control, hysterical people can be laughed at. If you've lost control, you're feeling multiple emotions by definition, which dissipates anger.

We can still produce comedy when we're irritated, perturbed, disgusted, pissed off, or appalled. Exhausted, unhappy, disappointed, troubled, and incensed all work, too. Just not anger alone. Emotions are not played in quotes. There is no "comedy" anger. Your real anger is just not funny.

The *perimeter* of your real anger is though. If you want to charge into a heated scene, exploit the comedic value and fight funny, you have to dial into what lies on the outskirts of your anger.

Here are two favorite feelings that help a lot; righteous and indignant. When you're feeling righteous, you're taking the moral high ground. That means you're feeling mad, plus superior. That's funny. When you're feeling indignant, you're insulted, and your sensibilities have been offended. That means you're feeling mad, plus disgruntled. That's also funny. Are you starting to notice that the synonyms for anger even *sound* funnier?

Righteous indignation is the emotional driving force of phrases like, "How dare you?" and "Do you know who you're speaking to?" Are people who say things like that angry? Perhaps, but other emotions come in front of the anger and are more prominent within the moments. They are more likely characterized as livid, frenzied, offended, abhorred, and vehement.

What about pain? It's the same thought process as anger. If the writer, even in a comedy, wants the character to experience hurt, then let in the pain. If the scene is supposed to be funny, however, and sharp comments are flying, highlight other emotions. Shock is a great response to an insult. Disappointed, displeased, disillusioned, discouraged, bummed, and defensive can all be played for comedy. Often in comedic fights, the characters are amused, bemused, tickled, floored, stymied, or utterly baffled.

Of course, it depends on the context of a particular scene, but these are the words you can draw upon to consistently raise the stakes in a heated confrontation and keep the comedy intact. There are no victims in comedy. Once we feel real anger and real pain, we've surrendered humor to the circumstance at hand. The moment has defeated us and there's nothing funny left about it.

Fighting is necessary and can even be healthy. Our tempers may flare but at least there is communication, and where there is communication, there is hope. There is something truly absurd about humans trying to get their words out when emotion has overtaken reason. Consider that when you're tasked to fight funny.

Also remember what you want. Do you want the relationship to be better afterward? However bad it gets between characters, there's a very good chance they still want to stay in each other's lives. Aside from emotions, you'll need to employ strategies and tactics to enable that to realistically happen.

If you fight with anger or hate, you can drive a wedge into a relationship that might be hard to repair. What's underneath the fight can seem vicious if you're not careful. Hostile tones can imply you want to be done with someone, but you just don't consciously know it yet or how to say so if you do.

Similarly, once you're hurt, the fight's over. You may still have words left to say but emotionally, we check out once we've dialed into our pain. The scene feels over even if there's dialogue left on the page once a character is taken by anguish.

Even the worst fights can be laugh out loud funny or at least contain moments of humor. Just adhere to these two guidelines: love the person you're fighting with and there are no victims in comedy.

30

Sarcasm

Most simply stated, sarcasm is insincere speech. In daily conversation and scripted dialogue, sarcasm manifests in two distinct ways. It can take the form of words that convey the opposite of what would seem their obvious meaning. Remarking, "Nice car!" to someone who just pulled up in an old jalopy is sarcastic. It's obvious to most you are not being sincere.

It's also possible to produce sarcasm with a positive intent and negative language. This commonly, but not exclusively, occurs within subcultures, for example. If one drag queen says to another, "Bitch, you look sickening!" it's definitely a compliment. The words "bitch" and "sickening" are not usually regarded as positive, but in the right context they're just the words you'd want to hear. In both examples, the typical or literal meaning of the words are reversed, thus creating sarcasm.

Sarcasm can also manifest through tone or inflection without transposing the meaning of words. If someone you dislike walks into the breakroom while you're eating lunch and you say, "Ohhhhhh, hiiiiiiii..." in an obviously unenthusiastic way, you're igniting sarcasm. "Oh, hi" is an appropriate way to greet someone entering a room unless your tone conveys otherwise. In this case, we're not juxtaposing the meaning of the words, we're juxtaposing the tone or intention beneath the words.

Sarcasm is a quintessential part of humor in America and English-speaking countries. We use it liberally in daily conversation and comedy writers season their dialogue with it like it was table salt.

Other cultures certainly employ sarcasm but it's worth noting, that globally speaking, it's not always acceptable social discourse. In some parts of the world, casual sarcasm is considered quite offensive. There are cultures across the globe that never broadly adopted sarcasm as a means of communication.

Sarcasm is not a product of language; it's a means of expression. It can be used in harmful ways, as all forms of communication can. However, it may also be used to produce humor. Students of comedy should be crystal clear on exactly what sarcasm is and be practiced in its execution. As a comedy coach, I find that far too many actors and writers do not have a clear definition of sarcasm; they cannot always detect it within dialogue.

To quickly review; irony applies to situations and circumstances. Parody is spoofing of genres. Satire is cultural and social criticism or mockery. Sarcasm applies to people and speech; a situation or scenario cannot be sarcastic. As with irony, parody, and satire, sarcasm depends on the listener or reader to be in on the joke.

To wit, this exchange from *The Big Bang Theory*:

LEONARD: For God's sake, Sheldon, do I have to hold up a sarcasm sign every time I open my mouth?

SHELDON: You have a sarcasm sign?

As smart as he is, Sheldon doesn't get sarcasm. This makes sense because it's not for the literal-minded or socially dimwitted. Sheldon is both. Sarcasm comprises wit, intricate layers of intention, ambiguous emotion, duplicity, and *possibly* humor.

Sarcasm can range from blunt and easy to detect to nuanced and difficult to identify. It all depends on the messenger and their mastery of sarcasm as a linguistic tool. If you're great at it, you might assume everyone else is too. They're not.

Over the years I've come to realize that sarcasm, in and of itself, is never discussed, taught, or practiced in isolation for its own merits. Yet it permeates our collective sense of humor. It's so common that we've grown to take for granted that everyone gets it and can execute it if they want. However, that's not even remotely true. There are several different reasons we're all not actually on the same page when it comes to sarcasm.

First of all, our brains are wired differently. Some folks, like our friend Sheldon, just don't get sarcasm, even though they're otherwise intelligent. People with autism or spectrum disorders tend to not be able to register sarcasm. Some of us are simply not great at unpacking subtle cues from facial expressions or tonal inflections.

Others detect sarcasm clearly when they hear it but find no joy in being sarcastic even if they can be. Their primary person-ality traits don't support engaging in sarcasm as conversational sport. If you don't like something, you don't practice it. If you don't practice something, you're not as good at it as others who do. Simple.

Finally, some people have only a hurtful relationship with sarcasm. They shy away from it because it was a component of a traumatic communication dynamic growing up.

I can't teach comedy without addressing sarcasm, because it exists in *every single comedic television show and film ever created*. My antennae have gotten pretty good at sensing when an actor dislikes being sarcastic or fears imagined consequences for speaking in a biting way, even while acting. I frequently offer actors permission to be as sharp in performance as the sarcastic words that are written on the page.

Whether you've ever considered it or not, sarcasm is something we all have a *relationship* with. Our feelings about sarcasm and how it fits into our communication skill set is highly personal. We likely spend time with others who have a similar relationship with sarcasm as ourselves. It's too prevalent in our collective cultural frame of reference to be ignored.

We subconsciously find comfort in being around others who have similar styles of communication as ourselves. Most of us take for granted that our core group of friends "more or less talk the way we do."

In reality, we choose whom to spend time with based on subliminal assessments of how spending time together *feels*, which includes compatibility in regard to interpersonal communication. Ergo, if someone constantly uses biting sarcasm in their speech and you don't use it at all, you're less likely to spend time with that person. You're not on the same wavelength in either communication or humor. If you're getting hurt or offended when they think they're being witty and hilarious, you're not a match. Who's to blame? No one.

Sarcasm is fascinating because as a mechanism of communication it can be benign or brutal. The intentions underneath a sarcastic remark can range from teasing to teaching to tormenting. Depending on the delivery, sarcasm can make you feel loved or loathed. How it lands for each of us can change with our mood.

Sarcasm is derived from the Greek word, "sarkazein," which means "to tear flesh." So from the get-go, it seems we understood sarcasm to be at least a jab, possibly more. There is a low-level hostility within sarcasm. Saying the opposite of what you mean and expecting someone else to extrapolate your intent is passive-aggressive, albeit just a tiny bit. Even when it's all in good fun, there is a bit of contempt thrown in for good measure.

Most people assume they know what sarcasm is and can detect it in conversation and dialogue. However, that's not necessarily the case. A 2006 published study[1] on sarcastic messaging found that roughly half of the participants could not accurately provide an example of a time they used sarcasm. They either provided no answer to that question or answered with an example that was not at all sarcastic.

Notably, respondents frequently mistook direct insults as sarcasm. For example, one respondent wrote that they had told someone, "You really need to stop letting things blow your head up because you're not that cute." Those words are not sarcastic. They form a straightforward insult.

Participants also mistook outright lies for sarcasm. Another respondent wrote, "My roommate told me he lost a lot of weight and I told him he looked skinny, but he doesn't." This person was not kidding with their roommate. They were not letting them know they did not see the weight loss with their inflection underneath the words. She or he was under the impression that a *white lie* you'd tell to spare another's feelings was an example of sarcasm. It is not.

I think this reflects the relationship we each have with sarcasm that I mentioned earlier. Some people only acknowledge the sting of sarcasm and none of the wit or playfulness. So much so, that they don't always identify it correctly. They only recognize sarcasm as something hurtful or untrue.

Additionally, this study confirms my observation that too many of us have only a vague of idea of how to define sarcasm.

---

1   Rockwell, Patricia. (April 2006). "Yeah, right!": A Linguistic Analysis of Self-reported Sarcastic Messages and Their Contexts. Presented at the Language and Social Interaction Division of the Southern States Communication Association at the annual convention, Dallas, TX.

Since sarcasm is an essential building block of comedy, all actors and writers should have a crystal-clear understanding of what sarcasm is and isn't. The difference can absolutely impact your ability to forge a comedic career.

I've witnessed copious amounts of students avoiding the direct nature of sarcasm when it comes up in their dialogue. I see them deliberately soften it in execution so they won't come across as mean or unlikeable. (That may be the actor's concern, but it's definitely not the character's.)

This unnecessary caution is unfortunate because it highlights the degree to which the actor is underplaying the material. In fact, it's more accurate to say the actor is executing the material incorrectly, without awareness. *The writers didn't add sarcasm to their dialogue so the actor can effectively remove it.* When this happens, the actor appears to have no discernable sense of humor.

Also, if you read a sarcastic line without emphasizing the bite underneath the words, the dialogue comes across as sincere. Sarcasm is obviously *insincere* speech. When you don't lean into sarcasm when it's written, your character comes across as oblivious and simple. It shifts the entire character that exists on the page to another archetype altogether. In other words, your lack of sarcastic punch can make a Cynic on the page seem like an Innocent when performed; literally the opposite character that the writer created.

Sarcasm is constructed of sharp, spontaneous wit. It's often a direct insult to someone else's intelligence, taste, or character. It requires a bold, possibly caustic delivery. When actors consciously or unconsciously avoid the confrontational aspect of sarcasm, they are not working at a competitive level. They are likely not an appropriate actor to cast in a comedic role.

The writers aren't pulling any punches when they write sarcasm into their dialogue. Believe me, they don't want actors pulling any punches in delivery.

Meryl Streep understood this well when she crafted her characterization of Miranda Priestly in the feature film, *The Devil Wears Prada*. Miranda weaponized sarcasm, reducing her underlings to emotional rubble. "By all means, move at a glacial pace. You know how that thrills me," she sneers at a slow-moving Andy (Anne Hathaway). When a page editor lobs a weak pitch during a meeting, Miranda cuts her off with unbridled disdain, "Florals? For Spring? Groundbreaking."

I could provide endless examples of sarcasm from television and film comedy. I thought hard about which ones to include for reference in this book. I'd like to illustrate the range of emotion and intention that exists under sarcastic commentary.

With that in mind, here are some further examples:

The Golden Girls

SOFIA: Was that a plumber?

DOROTHY: No, Ma, no. It was a little girl selling Girl Scout toilets.

Just Shoot Me

NINA: Well, I did it! Twelve years in a row.

FINCH: What? Turn 40?

Veep

MINNA: I would like you to understand that in my country, politics is a lot more honest.

SELINA: In your country, people fuck snow. And I hope you understand that I say that with the utmost respect.

Nurse Jackie

JACKIE: By the way, your husband's testicles have migrated. I'll let you know if we find them.

Arrested Development

MICHAEL: You seem more villainous than usual, Mom. Are you sober?

LUCILLE: Michael, it's 8 AM!

MICHAEL: So, it's not that.

Will & Grace

WILL: Jack, she's just doing her job. (THEN) I think that's the first time I used the words "Jack" and "job" in the same sentence without "needs to get a" in between.

Everybody Loves Raymond

DEBRA: You know what? I'm tired! Could you just call yourself an idiot?

Frasier

FRASIER: Oh, I'm sorry. Was I snippy? I didn't realize it was too much to ask that there not be gunplay in my living room!

The Office

JIM: Call Froggy 101, say that we're the tour managers for Justin Bieber and we're giving away free tickets. We give them a number to call for the tickets and it's his number.

DWIGHT: Who is Justice Beaver?

JIM: He... is a crime-fighting beaver.

Sex and the City

CHARLOTTE: We are having Trey's sperm tested.

MIRANDA: Why? Is it not doing well in school?

Sarcasm can be silly and playful. It is not always pointed and meanspirited. I think the creators and writers of *Roseanne* understood this brilliantly.

Although Rosanne Barr is widely regarded as caustic, her character Roseanne Conner is far less so. Roseanne Conner is tough, but she serves up sarcasm like it's comfort food. It's her way of lightening day-to-day life and taking the edge off her family's financial difficulties.

Her sarcasm is clearly intended to make her husband, sister, daughters, son, and many friends laugh. Yes, Roseanne can lay into someone and give them a solid dressing down. However, she is usually not sarcastic when tearing into someone. She's strong, straightforward, and literal.

The writers' use of sarcasm throughout the series is consistent and more often than not, joyful. The words are sharp, but the intentions underneath are loving. Anyone who doesn't have a friendly relationship with sarcasm should watch some episodes. Roseanne provides an excellent example of sarcastic teasing and teaching in a family setting with solid laughs exactly where they should be. If anything, Roseanne's sarcasm often takes the edge off what might be an otherwise more tense conversation.

BECKY: It's none of your business!

ROSEANNE: It is my business when you start sneaking out of this house to meet some guy I'd consider leaving your father for.

DAN: Hey, we missing an offspring?

ROSEANNE: Yeah. Where do you think I got the bacon?

JACKIE: What kind of obscene material could D.J. have?

ROSEANNE: Oh, I don't know... probably one of Dan's Playboys or our credit report.

BECKY: When you first met Dad, did you want to kiss him all the time?

ROSEANNE: Well, somebody had to do it. And you know me... work, work, work.

DAN: Oh my God! I can't believe we forgot about him again.

ROSEANNE: Boy, he better learn how to bitch and moan like his sisters or he ain't gonna make it in this family.

CRYSTAL: Lonnie told me about Becky's unfortunate accident. I'm so sorry.

ROSEANNE: Yeah, we're thinking about putting her to sleep.

ROSEANNE:	You knew when you married me that I had a sister!
DAN:	But I didn't think she'd be here every weekend.
ROSEANNE:	I didn't think *I'd* be here every weekend!
BECKY:	Mom!!
ROSEANNE:	She's not here.
ROSEANNE:	We can't control everything our kids do. Sooner or later, they're just gonna do what they're gonna do. They're like people that way.
BECKY:	Mom, Darlene and D.J. are killing each other out there.
ROSEANNE:	What's the bad news?
DARLENE:	What happened to Aunt Jackie?
ROSEANNE:	Some say environment, but I think she was born that way.
ROSEANNE:	What's the worst that could happen? A tornado picks up our house and slams it down in a better neighborhood?
DARLENE:	I just couldn't go on being part of the Conner family money-making death machine.
ROSEANNE:	Oh, now you come up with a name for the restaurant?

All these lines are sarcastic and none of them are hurtful. Most aren't even aimed at any one person. The target is... being alive.

Roseanne's sarcasm is defined by warm, observational humor, which is part of what makes the series iconic.

Hopefully these collective examples illustrate what sarcasm is and isn't. Reviewing several examples from different shows and characters exposes a range of tone and intention. Sarcasm has a clear definition, but there is great latitude regarding the impact any individual sarcastic remark might have.

When we're deliberately and boldly sarcastic, we create chemistry with whom we're speaking. It's like daring someone to verbally spar with you. It's a little exciting. It's dancing with words. Delivering sarcasm on the fly takes intelligence, a certain amount of bravado and an overall enjoyment of communicating in an edgy way. It's worth asking yourself if that's you.

Actors and writers who want to level up their comedy would benefit greatly from a thorough review of their relationship with sarcasm.

31

Improv, Sketch and Stand Up

M any actors who invest in a comedy career incorporate improv, sketch and stand up training into their full range of performance skills. I did. I can proudly say that I'm a master improviser with thousands of hours of improvisational performance under my belt. In addition, I've performed thousands of more hours in plays and scripted sketch shows.

Improv and Sketch Are Different

Improv and sketch performances often occur within the same venue but they are not the same thing. Sketch shows require preparation, which means organization, communication and a greater commitment of time. Improv shows require training but pointedly little or no preparation. When I first started out, the distinction between improvising and performing sketch was much clearer. Now I find many people incorrectly use the terms interchangeably.

Here's a case in point; I asked a prominent casting director friend of mine to read the casting section of this book and offer feedback. One of his comments was that someone in his office had recently attended an improv show. (I wrote that it was no longer common for casting directors in Los Angeles to attend improv shows, although it certainly does happen). He added that they'd gone to see The Sunday Company at The Groundlings.

I didn't correct him, but The Groundling's Sunday Company *only* performs **written** *sketch shows.* They may do an improvised set during the show, but the whole point of the company is to showcase its actors in a *scripted* format. A sketch show is more comparable to a play than an improv show. So my *very* well-known casting director friend inadvertently made my point. Casting doesn't often venture out to see an *improv* show.

Even people within the industry mistakenly lump improv and sketch shows together, although there is an obvious major distinction. Written sketch shows have greater value to casting directors in terms of finding talent. Since they are scripted, directed and rehearsed, they more directly relate to television and film production, which is also scripted, directed and rehearsed.

So, we're clear that improv and sketch shows are entirely different beasts. Check. Both can be done well or poorly. Both can be executed by amateurs or expert craftspeople. All subjectivity or opinion aside, however, performing in a sketch show requires a personal investment of time and energy that performing in an improv show does not. The material must be written, the roles cast and time is scheduled for rehearsals with direction. More than likely, there are a guaranteed number of performances which the group endeavors to replicate. That's decidedly *not* like performing in an improv show!

I offer no value judgment on either. I've practiced, taught and directed both to a degree that I can confidently call myself an expert. I thought I would be negligent if, in a book called *The Comedy Code,* I didn't take a moment to untangle those words and bring clarity to this subject. Further, many of my students have questions about improv training, like whether or not it's necessary and if there are differences in the training. Let's explore!

Do I Need Improv Training to Work in Film and Television?

There is absolutely not a one-size fits all answer to the question, "should I take an improv class?" All performance training and performance experience will collectively support an actor's evolution. Is improv training *necessary* to work in film and television comedy? No.

Here is some context for you. There are currently more than 200 improv shows a week, every week of the year in Los Angeles. There are improv performances happening every single night of the week, not just weekends. You want to catch an improv show on a Monday night? No problem. You've got more than ten choices. Some bad, some brilliant, many in the middle. Either way, that's a lot of improv even for a city the size of Los Angeles.

Some of those folks are working actors, some are in pursuit of acting work but importantly many are not interested in a career as an actor or writer at all. The improv community has become so large, at least in Los Angeles, that many people study and even perform regularly as a creative outlet with no greater ambition in mind. I'm highlighting this evolution because when I was improvising in my twenties, we all wanted careers. We wanted to navigate off of the stage and into acting and writing careers. That's no longer true for all. A large percentage of students in any current improv class are there simply for fun, personal growth or other reasons. Perfectly fine. However, if I am someone who desires a career in television and film, I probably don't want to spend much time in classes with people who aren't like-minded. I do want to be in classes with others who have agents and managers even if I don't. I want to spend time with those who are forging their own way into the industry. I want to know other actors who have relationships with casting directors, great headshot photographers and up-and-coming directors and producers.

Not that long ago, improv shows were few and performed only by top notch experts. Now they're quite common. Many are free or only charge a few dollars for admission. Price of admission alone doesn't dictate the quality of the show, but it does tell you something about any show's overall value. In stark contrast, tickets for a mainstage sketch show run up to $25. That's a considerable difference.

Whatever your thoughts or opinions on improv, we can agree that it's no longer unique as a performance outlet. And while it can be valuable training *in addition to* foundational acting training, it is not a *substitute* for foundational acting training. I understood that clearly when I was performing sketch and improv on the stages of Los Angeles and I made a point of taking on-camera audition technique classes to round out my skill set. It's therefore worth considering, whatever market you live in, what *exactly* you want from improv training. Empower yourself by asking smart questions throughout.

What is my personal goal with improv training? What's the quality of the training I'm receiving? How much individual attention am I getting as I train? How experienced/knowledgeable is my teacher? Do I prefer choosing my performance instructor or am I happy with whatever teacher the program assigns me? How saturated with improv and sketch artists is the community around me? Are others in my immediate circle leveling up in their careers for their efforts? Am I clear or confused about what the program is teaching me?

I've helped a lot of students over many years navigate this topic by posing simple, direct questions like those. What you definitely *don't* want to do is wander into a program with a vague understanding of why you are there, how much money you're willing to spend or what you want from the investment.

I'm in full support of anyone expressing themselves creatively in any way they see fit. Further, I incorporate improv exercises into my on-camera acting classes as well as my writing classes. Viola Spolin is one of history's great acting instructors who pioneered improv training for actors and is one of my great inspirations. I know how important it is to alternate exercising actors with scripts and without them. However, I also see agents, managers and casting directors tell actors to enroll in improv training like it's mandatory, a magic path to comedic success or both. I don't think that's fair and I know it's not universally true. Jim Parsons, for example, is one of the highest paid actors in television history (in any genre) for portraying Sheldon Cooper on the sitcom, *The Big Bang Theory*.

He's not an improviser or associated with any of the known improv training franchises, just to make the point. He earned a Master of Fine Arts degree from the Old Globe and University of San Diego Shiley Graduate Theatre Program. In other words, he studied classical theater and that served his comedic ambitions just fine. I'm well aware of the long list of improv and sketch artists who transitioned successfully from the stage to television and film. I'm merely debunking the myth that improv training is the discerning factor to a successful **on-camera** career.

Further, a lot of people become invested in a performance group that lacks strong direction. They stay because it's fun and they like the people they work with. Perfectly fine, but keep an eye on the calendar. How much time is passing? Is the time you're investing providing equivalent value? Is someone knowledge-able confidently leading the group? If you want a career, it's wise to have an exit strategy. There is always value in practicing, performing and collaborating within a troupe. Just remember, careers rarely blossom as a group effort. They manifest individually with focus and direction.

It's also quite relevant to consider that some people are not comfortable improvising. How will it help someone who dislikes it? Improvisation asks you to write *as* you're acting. That's not for everyone. I'm a writer, so I love improv. However, I've had countless actors ask me why they'd need to train in improv after they've earned a theater degree, graduated from an acting conservatory or *simply don't want to spend the time and money on that type of training*. The simple answer is that you don't have to.

Don't They Improvise on TV?

Not as much as people seem to think. Most scripted television series, even comedies, do not call on actors to improvise. If they do, it's minimal. Going beyond the lines of a written scene for a bit of exploration is something most trained actors can accomplish well without years of additional improv training. Improv schools teach you how to start and execute *complete* scenes from beginning to end, based on a suggestion *spontaneously* given to the actors in the moment.

On-camera acting jobs are nearly all scripted and would never ask that of an actor. *Saturday Night Live* is a scripted television show. When the actors drop their lines on *SNL*, they read them from the teleprompter next to the camera. They generally do not start improvising. They do stay on script. *Curb Your Enthusiasm* is the rare exception of a television series that's mostly all improvised. It's worth noting, however, that top-level, highly regarded improvisers are cast on that show. A moderate amount of improv experience probably won't help the typical actor land a guest spot there anyway.

So do improv skills help actors book work? Yes! Of course. Again, *all* performance, breath, body and vocal training collectively make an actor better. More specifically, knowing how to improvise well will likely help you most on commercial auditions.

Across the board, most film and television auditions ask you specifically to **not** change any words. I know there are exceptions but for the most part, writers want to hear the words they wrote.

Lastly, if you are unsure of your sense of humor, need to develop your comedic voice or you're just plain shy, improv classes will *definitely* help you. Confidence is key to any successful performance. Training in improv should ideally make anyone braver and more playful in their work.

What's Your Advice?

When it comes to this topic, I just want people to assess their aspirations and ultimately make the best choice for themselves. Improv training can be hugely beneficial if it is an arena that excites you and you thrive within it. It can be extremely detrimental if you think it's something you *have* to do to work in comedy but makes you feel uncomfortable or unsuccessful.

Many of Shakespeare's plays are comedies. It's very easy for me to support the notion that the in-depth study of Shakespeare will make you a stronger comedic performer. Studying iambic pentameter will undoubtedly help you land a joke that lies within the rhythmic dialogue of a current scripted comedy. Theoretically that statement is true for *everyone* and you should therefore *all* study Shakespeare to become better comic actors!

If you happen to love Shakespeare and linguistics, I've just given you the best advice in the world. If studying old plays and poring over language bores you, then not so much. Two to four years of studying Shakespeare would be a dreadful chore. It would make you feel inferior in comparison to those around you who excel in their studies and application. The same is true for improv, method acting, voice acting, commercial acting or any other type of specific performance training. Just because something *could* help you in theory, doesn't necessarily mean it *will* in practice. What will always work in your favor is a course of study that aligns with your particular goals and enables your strongest assets. If you want to work in television and film, what you'll need most is the skillset to break down scripts accurately, audition well and work knowledgably with a camera.

Is All Improv Training the Same?

Hardly. Different schools have different goals, philosophies and focus on different formats. The core tenets are similar but there are various styles of improv like short form (game based), long form, the Harold, etc. Some schools focus strongly on character work, others don't focus on character development at all. Some mainstage performance companies are famous for their **written sketch shows** while others are known primarily for their **improv troupes.**

All of them teach their curriculum as it applies to their main companies, however. Improv schools don't teach improvisational technique broadly. They teach inward toward their stage, not outward to a broader understanding of the industry. Remember the goal of *any* improv/sketch program is to teach students how to improvise, write and perform in the specific style *of that particular venue*. They're teaching you to improvise *their way*.

There's absolutely nothing wrong with that. It's just that most people don't consider the narrow scope of each school's curriculum. The information, experience and training you receive can of course be helpful and applied elsewhere. You should, however, view your improv training through this lens. Whether you become a master improviser or not, there's a lot more to know about the entertainment industry than how a single improv or sketch company functions.

If you decide to take improv classes, I recommend that you simply do your homework. Decide clearly what you want.

Research the differences in the various training programs and see if the curriculum they offer enables your desires.

What About Stand Up?

On any given year, Forbes' list of the highest paid stage comedians who also work in television and film are known for stand up. Jerry Seinfeld, Jim Gaffigan, Kevin Hart, John Mulaney, Aziz Ansari, Sarah Silverman, Wanda Sykes, Kathy Griffith and Amy Schumer may be able to improvise, but they're primarily known for stand up. If you review actor success stories, it makes every bit as much sense to invest in studying and performing stand up as it does to invest in improv classes.

That said, countless actors working in comedy right now, today, invested in *neither*.

Plenty of actors work simply because they're well-trained and they're disciplined in cultivating their careers. Maybe they can also sing, dance, write and produce their own video content. Whatever skills you happen to possess, the real question is, are you applying them with discipline toward a career? Are you training in a place that teaches you how to do that?

Final Thoughts

I wrote *The Comedy Code* so you can thrive in the entertainment industry regardless of the sum total of the training you've had. We all have our personal collection of education and knowledge. What we each possess is perfect for each of us. If we need more, all we need to do is seek more. There isn't one combination that will unlock the gates to success. If you happen to find a key, use it. If not, you may have to climb those gates or burrow a tunnel underneath.

I hope these thoughts empower all actors, especially those who might be confused on the subject, to make a personal decision that feels right for them. Some people move to Los Angeles *just* so they can train at a world famous improv school. I had the time of my life learning to improvise in several of them. I hope you have the time of your life, too!

On the other end of the spectrum, some actors move to Los Angeles with significant acting training and are disheartened to hear that they now need improv training from an LA based school listed on their resume. Especially when completing a program can mean several years of classes that cost thousands of dollars.

If that's you, take a breath. You don't have to do anything, regardless of what anyone says. Lucille Ball didn't study improv and *I Love Lucy* has been on television since 1951. So let's all keep perspective. There were iconic comedic actors working success-fully in film and television long before there were improv schools.

Improv training intersects with acting training. One is not the other. One cannot replace the other in its entirety. Simple.

Wherever you land in this conversation, I see you, I hear you and I understand you. I've had countless discussions about improv as it's evolved in my city over decades. I've heard every point of view, every kind of success story and every complaint there is to lodge. I've thought about it. Improv won my heart when I was very young and has influenced many of the decisions I've made throughout my life.

I also trained in a market that was far more intimate than it is today. I received a lot of individual attention and mentorship as I studied and practiced. Auditions weren't demanded immediately via email. We'd actually get a phone call from our agent and a day or two to prepare. We were not required to self-tape and submit those auditions ourselves if we wanted a shot at booking work. I met important people in person often because every job had a callback session. That's no longer the case. Technological advances hadn't put so much of the day-to-day operations on us, the creatives.

I think about how improv training addresses these new demands or doesn't. World renowned Emerson College in Boston now offers a BFA in Comedic Arts, the first of its kind degree in comedy! The curriculum, which was initially offered in 2015, includes some improv training but also writing, production, voice and movement classes, studies in Shakespearean Comedy and more. The Second City improv and sketch company created the Harold Ramis Film School, the only film school in the world focused entirely on comedy. They opened their doors in Chicago in 2016. Their curriculum includes comedic theory, writing and obviously filmmaking courses. In Los Angeles, Actors Comedy Studio is singularly devoted to acting, writing and auditioning comedy for film and television.

Show business continually evolves. Training and education for a much faster-moving entertainment industry have evolved along with it. We've innovated for the benefit of our students. All over the country, this evolution has produced high-caliber training centers that offer a clearer path to a career because they teach more than just one, specific skill. What a great thing. The future of acting and writing in Hollywood is digital and there is no question, it is already here.

Summary

Over the years, a lot of my students have said they wish they could have me around on auditions or when they needed to break down a script. Well... here you go. I've done my best to unload my brain into *The Comedy Code*.

I thought I would write this book quickly. I did not. It took me six years. I can't even estimate how many hours of television I have watched.

When I began, streaming anything and everything online was just getting started. As it became easier to find and watch shows, I did just that. It helped to revisit moments from past series, but it also added a lot of time as I checked, double-checked and triple-checked what I thought I knew. I'd go looking for a specific moment in a specific episode of a show and end up watching an entire season.

All things happen as they should. I'm glad I got to live through the emergence of streaming services before releasing *The Comedy Code*. The entertainment industry has changed tremendously since I began this journey. Those changes are reflected within these pages. This book is current. I like to think this is the information that's needed for this moment.

The Comedy Code is designed to help you grow as an artist by discovering who you are. Once we know ourselves, we can express our thoughts and feelings honestly. When we are wholly authentic, we come to rest in our own power. We're funniest when we tell our own, naked truth. I'm glad if you came to this party to learn more about comedy. I hope you found undiscovered parts of yourself along the way.

About the Author

Gunnar Todd Rohrbacher is one of Hollywood's best-known acting coaches. He is also a highly regarded writer, director, producer and actor within Hollywood's comedy scene, earning rave reviews for more than 25 years. Simply put, Gunnar's credentials for teaching comedy are unmatched.

He is the Founder of Actors Comedy Studio in Los Angeles, California. Much of his early training was at The Groundlings where he was mentored by some of the industry's most respected comedy authorities, including Lisa Kudrow, Gary Austin, Cynthia Szigeti, Phyllis Katz, Karen Maruyama, Mindy Sterling, Tim Bagley and many other illustrious comedians.

A published author, Gunnar is extremely proud of his comedic scene books for actors, *The Funniest Scenes in the World, Volume 1, Volume 2 and Volume 3*. The books contain comedic, two person scenes for actors that Gunnar has given permission for actors to use to shoot reel footage; an amazing tool for actors living in a digital world. He's also a Contributing Expert to *Backstage*, one of the industry's leading trade magazines.

Before launching ACS, Gunnar spent a decade teaching on-camera audition technique classes in multiple venues throughout Los Angeles. Prior to teaching TV & film acting, Gunnar taught all levels of improvisation and sketch writing for an additional 10 years at one of LA's top improv schools. With every aspect of comedic instruction under his belt, Gunnar carved a niche for himself in Hollywood's vast teaching landscape as the "go-to" Comedy Coach.

Gunnar has appeared on virtually every comedy mainstage in Los Angeles, including The Groundlings, Upright Citizens Brigade, ACME, Second City, iO West, Comedy Central Stage at the Hudson, HBO Workspace, The Comedy Store and The Improv. Gunnar further broadened his horizons when he co-directed the multimedia rock opera, *The Hunchback of Notre Dame* with Vox Lumiere to sold-out crowds at the John Anson Ford Amphitheater.

In addition, Gunnar designed and exclusively taught the Acting for Animators program for Disney's Animation Studio. He was a Character Consultant on two of Disney's feature films; *Bolt* and *Meet the Robinsons*.

He created the current Acting for Sitcoms programs at The American Academy of Dramatic Arts and The New York Film Academy.

Gunnar teaches performance and writing workshops at various comedy festivals and private acting studios around the country. Of note, he's been a guest instructor at The Groundlings, CalArts, SAG•AFTRA, The SAG•AFTRA Conservatory, The American Film Institute, LA Comedy Fest and Filmbase in Dublin, Ireland.

Over decades, he's produced and directed dozens of live shows of all kinds, including improv, sketch, actor showcases and one-person shows.

As an actor, Gunnar starred in two pilots for NBC; *Prime Time Comedy*, produced by the famed George Schlatter of *Laugh-In* and the semi-improvised sitcom *The Weekend*. He's a proud union actor (SAG•AFTRA) as well as a member of the Television Academy.

Rounding out his knowledge of the entertainment industry, Gunnar has worked in both theatrical and commercial casting. He spent two seasons as a network acting coach for a prime time NBC sitcom, where he gained essential insight that helps his students become working actors.

Lastly, Gunnar is a graduate of the renowned Warner Bros. Comedy Writer's Program and is a featured Comedy Expert in Judy Kerr's Hollywood survival guide, *Acting is Everything*. He's appeared as a hilarious, thought-provoking guest on dozens of podcasts.

www.gunnarrohrbacher.com

Actors Comedy Studio

Gunnar opened Actors Comedy Studio in 2011 along with his partner Lauren Bertoni. ACS, as it's come to be known, is the only school in the world dedicated to comedy acting, writing and auditioning.

The curriculum is innovative, current and creates working actors. It includes world-class script analysis, character development for the screen and pro-level audition skills. All students get personal attention at Actors Comedy Studio. You'll never get lost in an impersonal program with a vague outcome.

Centrally located in Los Angeles, California, ACS is training actors for the new age of television comedy. The path Gunnar and Lauren created helps actors transition to Los Angeles and integrate into the industry quickly and efficiently.

New actors and working actors alike benefit from their real-world experience coaching actors at every level in class and on sets.

Improv and stage work are fun but most actors want to be paid to work in television and film. ACS teaches career-building skills that other comedy schools simply do not.

www.actorscomedystudio.com

The Self Tape Place

As the entertainment industry changes, Gunnar and Lauren change with it. Actors are often asked to self-tape their auditions now. To keep pace, they could have simply added an audition taping service for their students at Actors Comedy Studio.

Instead, they opened The Self Tape Place. A companion to ACS, The Self Tape Place is its own enterprise. As audition technique experts, they felt they had a lot to say about what goes into an audition taping.

Growing busier by the day, The Self Tape Place produces some of the best looking and sounding auditions you'll find anywhere. Our readers are trained faculty members who give care and guidance to every actor.

New actors and recognizable faces stop by daily to record auditions that casting directors love. Just one more way the creative team behind Actors Comedy Studio gives personal care and attention to their creative clients.

www.theselftapeplace.com

CPSIA information can be obtained
at www.ICGtesting.com
Printed in the USA
BVHW061052260321
603416BV00012BA/1269